FIRST PUBLISHED 1977
© J. A. CROSS 1977

JONATHAN CAPE LTD, 30 BEDFORD SQUARE
LONDON WCI

British Library Cataloguing in Publication Data

Cross, John Arthur
Sir Samuel Hoare, a Political Biography.
Bibl. – Index.
ISBN 0–224–01350–5
941.083'092'4   DA566.9.H/
Hoare, Samuel John Gurney, Viscount Templewood

PRINTED IN GREAT BRITAIN
BY W & J MACKAY LIMITED, CHATHAM

Sir Samuel Hoare,
a Political Biography

with a foreword by
The Rt Hon. Lord Butler, K.G., C.H.

J. A. Cross

JONATHAN CAPE
THIRTY BEDFORD SQUARE LONDON

Sir Samuel Hoare,
a Political Biography

Contents

Illustrations

between pages 336 and 337

Foreword

THE RT HON. LORD BUTLER, K.G., C.H.

Sam Hoare gave me my start in political life making me first Parliamentary Private Secretary and then, on the retirement of Lord Lothian, Under-Secretary for India for nearly five years. I succeeded as Parliamentary Private Secretary my uncle, Sir Geoffrey Butler, Senior Burgess for the University of Cambridge. He was a great admirer and friend of Hoare's and advised him from an early age to press for the Foreign Office. Sam's wife Maud was even more ambitious and advised him to press for the Prime Ministership. When I got to know Sam I was not in favour of either of these pieces of advice for the reason that we had had such a gruelling time together during the India Bill that I knew his physique could not stand an immediate transference to the Foreign Office and this proved alas too true, ending in the trauma of the Hoare-Laval Pact. Sam Hoare's health, although maintained by skating, was never very robust and he ought certainly to have taken three months' holiday after working from sixteen to eighteen hours a day on the India Bill and being opposed by the cunning and ruthlessness of Winston Churchill.

To show how high Sam Hoare should rank in a series of British ministers of his generation, I refer to a phrase in this book which says, 'The weary months and years of trial and tribulation before the Government of India Bill could be presented to the Commons in 1935 were a triumph for Hoare's courage, persistence and sheer ability to master complex issues and constitute a personal ministerial achievement without previous parallel in modern British history.' This is tribute enough for any man and in my opinion was more than justified in the event. I have had a lifetime experience of politics and political offices and do not know any man in my long experience, including Churchill, who was more efficient at handling papers and dispatches. He was exceedingly quick and returned his overnight boxes ready for his faithful officials, including Sir Findlater Stewart, early next morning.

Another feature of Sam Hoare's character was what I wrote in May 1959, 'In my experience of serving many chiefs over all these years, Sam Hoare was distinguished for his anxiety to help his subordinates.'

Perhaps Hoare's greatest achievement during the passage of the India Bill was his answering of questions on the Joint Select Committee. Lord Salisbury, one of his great opponents, wrote to him to admire 'his intellectual achievement in sitting for hours in that chair and answering questions on every conceivable subject.'

The author of this book is very perceptive in pointing out that the team at the India Office suited Hoare better than the team at the Foreign Office. Hoare himself describes the difference between the two rooms, the small one, now a part of the Foreign Office, with Mogul paintings, in the India building, and the huge draughty chamber in which I have sat myself in the Foreign Office.

It would be interesting to compare Sam Hoare to George Canning. They were both obliged to take an Iberian Embassy due to discomfort in home political life. Of course, Canning was an infinitely greater orator than Hoare ever claimed himself to be and Canning had infinitely more time and more scope at the Foreign Office. The Madrid Embassy was the only way out for Hoare when his great enemy, Churchill, became the national Prime Minister in wartime. There was a difference between the tenancy of Canning and Hoare since the former held it for a very short time and the latter for the majority of the war. Sam Hoare was two or three times tempted to seek and accept the viceroyalty of India but on the second occasion Churchill was in no mood to give it to him and on the first occasion his application was really too late. His services in Madrid are well recognised by the author in this book and the importance of keeping Spain out of the war could not then and cannot now be exaggerated.

I now come to the central disaster or turning point in Sam

Hoare's career, namely the Hoare-Laval Pact. The chapter in this book on the Foreign Office does build up the Abyssinian picture in a very particular way and shows that the action of Sam Hoare, aided by Vansittart, in signing an agreement with Laval was not all that a departure from developed policy. What was really wrong about the affair was that only a few weeks before Sam Hoare had made a magnificent speech in support of the League of Nations and the Covenant. Hence the great upset when the British public read of the Hoare-Laval Pact which seemed *Realpolitik* rather than collective security. I remember as an M.P. having more letters about the Hoare-Laval Pact than on any other subject when I was in Parliament. Here we come up against one of the most interesting features of Hoare's character and life. He was of Quaker descent and as Home Secretary he embraced both liberal and radical reforms. He had what may be described as a Quaker conscience and he had a high sense of morality in public affairs. Nevertheless he did not seem able to distinguish between the speech on the Covenant and the occasion in Paris and this I put down to his inveterate habit of working exceedingly quickly and being able not only to move from one subject to another but from one job to another. He was in fact, like George Canning, invested with vaulting ambition. However, I think a human view must be taken of the Hoare-Laval Pact. He wrote to Clive Wigram to ask for royal permission to take his Permanent Secretary with him to Paris. He writes, 'As you know I have had no proper holiday for several years. My doctor has been insistent upon my getting off as soon as possible, particularly as I have recently had a series of fainting fits, one of which took place last night.'

This all goes back to what I said at the opening of this introduction, that Hoare should have had a proper holiday after the terrible strains of the India Bill. It is rather extraordinary that Vansittart, who played an important part in the Hoare-Laval discussions, should have remained even in my time 1938–41, as principal adviser at the Foreign Office, while Sam Hoare's career should have had such a forced interruption. Of course he made good again at the Admiralty and the Home Office and has left a name as a first-class diplomat.

The biographer does not miss any of the more curious acts of Sam's life, such as the peculiar letter from Maud to Beaver-

brook asking for money or his own ill-chosen explanation to his
Chelsea constituents of the Hoare-Laval proceedings, or his
unwise declaration just before March 1939, when Hitler invaded
Czechoslovakia, about a prospect of peace ahead. These lapses
make all the more remarkable the tributes which I have already
paid and the solid achievements of a life's work. His achievements
fell short of the hopes he had himself entertained by the high
point of his career in June 1935, but not below his own statement
on leaving the House of Commons after a speech as Secretary of
State for Air, following upon the Norwegian fiasco and prior to
the big change of government which led him into the overseas
post at Madrid. He told his wife on leaving the House that that
might be his last speech as Minister, and this shows a sense of
reality which redeems many of the rather cold impressions
which he left on his colleagues. Perhaps his own statement that
he was a Liberal amongst Conservatives and a Conservative
amongst Liberals is a true one. He was certainly a Liberal as
Home Secretary and later when working on the Abolition of the
Death Penalty in the House of Lords. He states about himself
that he preferred committee discussion in Parliament to heated
scenes of partisan fury.

It is very timely that a book dedicated to his career should be
written so fairly. Considering the vital part he played in many
crises of our national life, tributes paid to his tenacity and
forward-looking policy are long overdue. There has in fact been
too much ignorant criticism of Sam Hoare and too little
admiration for his oustanding qualities.

Preface

The political career of Samuel Hoare, first and only Viscount Templewood, spanned most of the first half of the twentieth century and took in some of the highest ministerial offices. As Secretary of State for Air in the 1920s he successfully defended the R.A.F. from take-over bids by the older services. As Secretary of State for India in the early 1930s he presided over the enactment of the greatest measure of Indian constitutional reform before the post-war granting of independence. His short tenure of the Foreign Office, during the international crisis provoked by the Italian invasion of Abyssinia in 1935, ended in the failure of a diplomatic initiative (the so-called 'Hoare-Laval Pact') which continues to arouse controversy over forty years later. Restored to office after a brief period in the political wilderness Hoare became a member of the inner group of four in the Chamberlain Cabinet most closely associated with the policy of 'appeasement', in addition to being that still fairly rare ministerial phenomenon, a reforming Home Secretary. Discarded from the War Cabinet by Churchill in 1940 he emerged in a new guise as an unorthodox but highly effective wartime Ambassador to Spain.

There has as yet been no comprehensive study of Hoare's career. The present work is an attempt to fill this gap. The need to keep it to a length which is publishable in present economic conditions has compelled the use of a broad brush to delineate most of what was a long and eventful record of public service. The central episode — Hoare's six months as Foreign Secretary — was, however, so crucial to his career and to our understanding of it that it has deliberately been treated here at more than proportionate length. The aim throughout has been to reveal Hoare as what he undoubtedly was — one of the most important figures in pre-war British politics.

I am grateful to the staffs of the libraries and repositories which house the sources used for this book; to several former political and official colleagues of Hoare who gave me their impressions of the man and his work; to the Leverhulme Trust for financially assisting my research; and to the staff of Jonathan Cape, above all David Machin and Belinda Foster-Melliar. I am honoured that Lord Butler so readily agreed to contribute a foreword which he is uniquely qualified to write. My particular thanks are due to my Cardiff colleague, Paul Wilkinson, who first drew my attention to the need for a study of Hoare and who throughout its compilation has been an unfailing source of stimulation and informed criticism.

My chief debt is to Lord Templewood's nephew and heir, Paul Paget, who allowed me complete freedom to use as I saw fit the extensive collection of Templewood papers of which he holds the copyright. He also gave me the benefit of his special knowledge of his uncle's life and career: a knowledge derived not only from the close family bond (in some ways he took the place of the son Templewood never had) but from acting on occasion as one of his uncle's private secretaries (as at the Air Ministry in the early 1920s) and as designer, with his architectural partner John Seely, of the Norfolk house from which Hoare took his title on his elevation to the peerage and which Mr Paget eventually inherited.

The final work, including any undetected errors, is, of course, the entire responsibility of the author.

J. A. CROSS

Cardiff

Acknowledgements

I am grateful to the following for permission to quote from material of which they hold the copyright: Her Majesty the Queen, The Rt Hon. Julian Amery, M.P., The Beaverbrook Foundation, Lord Brabazon of Tara, Major-General Viscount Bridgeman, K.B.E., C.B., D.S.O., M.C., R. H. W. Bullock, Esq., C.B., The Rt Hon. Lord Butler of Saffron Walden, K.G., C.H., Mrs Stephen Lloyd, Sir John Lomax, K.B.E., C.M.G., M.C., The Marquess of Lothian, Sir Godfrey Nicholson, Bt, P. E. Paget, Esq., C.V.O., F.R.I.B.A., F.S.A., Sir Folliott Sandford, K.B.E., C.M.G., R. J. Stopford, Esq., C.M.G., Lord Trenchard, M.C., and Lady Vansittart.

I

Early Career

Although the Hoares are an old-established English family, tracing their lineage back at least to the fifteenth century, the branch from which the future Lord Templewood descended had its origins in Ireland, in Cork, where Edward Hoare had been given land as a reward for his services to the Cromwellian cause in the Civil War. When, towards the middle of the eighteenth century, the first of six generations of Hoares to bear the name Samuel (Lord Templewood being the last) moved from Cork to London, he took with him two firmly established family traditions: a vocational commitment to banking and a religious commitment to the Society of Friends. With the Quaker persuasion went an active interest in questions of social reform, and at various times Hoares played leading parts in the campaigns for the abolition of slavery in the British Empire and in the improvement of conditions in British prisons. The third Samuel Hoare (1783–1847), for example, was brother-in-law to both Elizabeth Fry and Sir Fowell Buxton and with them founded in 1816 the Society for the Reformation of Prison Discipline, the progenitor of the Howard League for Penal Reform. It was a family inheritance which was to have considerable influence on the subject of this biography, the sixth Samuel Hoare.

Quakerism (but not the interest in social reform which accompanied it) was abandoned well before the middle of the nineteenth century, to be succeeded by evangelical Anglicanism, and, later still, by the Anglo-Catholicism of which the sixth Samuel Hoare was a devoted adherent. The family fortunes prospered. A base in London was always retained but from the beginning of the nineteenth century substantial family property was being acquired in Norfolk, in Cromer and its vicinity, and, with it, a marked enthusiasm for the traditional field sports of East Anglia. The inheritance which the fifth Samuel Hoare (Lord Templewood's father) entered into in 1875, at the age of 34, represented something between £150,000 and £200,000, even after ample provision had been made for other members of the family.

Samuel Hoare, who married Katharin Hart Davis in 1866, was the first member of the family to forsake the primary vocation of banking for a parliamentary career. In 1884 the Birmingham banking firm of Lloyds offered to buy the Lombard Street firm of Barnetts, Hoare and Co., in which Samuel Hoare was a partner (and which until then had been acting as Lloyds' London agents). The offer was accepted and, thus released from his London business responsibilities, Hoare felt able to respond to the local Conservative association's invitation to stand as candidate for the newly formed constituency of North Norfolk in the election of November 1885. This first electoral foray was unsuccessful but there was not long to wait for a more favourable opportunity. In April 1886 the invalidation of the election of a Conservative member in the two-member Norwich constituency led to a by-election for the seat which Hoare won unopposed and held for the next twenty years, for much of the time in double harness with a Liberal colleague.

Samuel Hoare senior was in many ways an archetypal Conservative backbencher: solid, loyal, in touch with the feelings of the party's grass roots. He never sought office and never obtained it. He performed his constituency functions conscientiously and saw his majority increase in each election. In 1899 he received the recompense of the faithful Conservative backbencher, a baronetcy. His loyalty was, however, strained after 1903, when Joseph Chamberlain launched his Tariff Reform campaign and the party split on the issue. Hoare remained a convinced free trader and joined with 50 other Conservative M.P.s to inaugurate the Free Food League as an answer to Chamberlain's Tariff Reform League.[1] But the Norwich Conservative association, like so many others, was captured by the tariff reformers and Hoare lost the Conservative nomination and thus his seat in the 1906 election. He regained the nomination, but not the seat, in the January 1910 election, which returned his eldest son to Parliament for the first time. For that son he had long been maturing plans for the political advancement he had never himself pursued.

The eldest son was the fifth of seven children born to Samuel and Katharin Hoare in the nineteen-year period from 1867 to 1886. The first four — all girls — were Muriel (born in 1867), Annie (1868), Elma (1871) and Marjorie (1876). It was not until 24th February, 1880, that their first son, christened Samuel John Gurney, was born, at the Hoares' London home in Park Lane. Two years later came another son, Oliver Vaughan Gurney, and then in 1886 the Hoares' last child, another daughter, Christabel.

There seems no doubt that although Samuel and Katharin Hoare were exemplary parents to all their children, it was on their eldest son that their chief devotion was lavished. Nothing was denied him and in so far as a spoilt child was possible in a large family, young Samuel was such a child. He returned the affection with due respect but there is no evidence that he was attached to his parents with any great warmth. His father, a bluff, extrovert Norfolk squire with no pretensions to intellectual distinction (despite attendance at Harrow and Trinity College, Cambridge), was quite unlike the man his son was to become. To his mother, who survived her husband sixteen years and lived to see her son a minister and a leading figure in the Conservative party (she died in January 1931), Samuel John Gurney was a devoted but perhaps slightly distant son all her life.

Among his sisters, two of the eldest — Annie (later Mother General of the Anglican Community at Wantage) and Elma (who married Luke Paget, subsequently Bishop of Chester) — were closest to Samuel along with the youngest, Christabel, who was widowed at an early age and later became a Norfolk notable as local government councillor and local historian. He was close also to his brother Oliver, his partner and opponent in most of the sports in which both developed considerable skill, and who followed him, two years behind, at both school and university.

Samuel Hoare senior may have laid no claim to intellectual distinction or political advancement but this fact perhaps increased his determination to guarantee his eldest son's prospects. Success in politics, he knew, requires a highly developed competitive spirit. While he did not compete for political office himself he valued the element of competition in the various sports in which he had a passionate interest (especially cricket, but also tennis and golf), and sought to instil the same spirit in his son. By 1890 he had blooded young Samuel in the family enthusiasm for field sports, and the family game book (on which much of Lord Templewood's *The Unbroken Thread* is based) noted on 20th December of that year that 'S.J.G.H. shot a cock pheasant over his head'.[2] Thus began an activity which Hoare pursued with great skill — he was one of the finest shots in England — until just before his death. Then there were the ball games, which the elder Hoare insisted on playing to win, however unimportant the contest might be. He coached his sons at home and took a much closer interest in their athletic achievements than in their academic progress at school. After four years at a preparatory school, the Abbey School at Beckenham, the young Samuel gained an entrance scholarship for classics to Harrow and entered the school in the summer term of 1894, exactly forty years after his father. Athletically his Harrow career was distinguished but mixed. To his father's disappointment, he never gained a permanent place in the cricket eleven. But in the individual game of rackets he was much more successful, representing the school and later going on to win a university blue. A game like rackets, in which the player is alone responsible for his own play, appealed to Hoare more than a team game in which he was one of several players. It would be a mistake to read too much into this preference for individual over team effort, but it is noticeable that the principal active leisure pursuits of Hoare's subsequent busy career were predominantly those which maximised individual success and the will to win: shooting, tennis and ice skating.

Another element in Hoare's will to succeed, even in such relatively trivial activities, may have been the dynamism that many small men seem to generate as if to compensate for their lack of inches. Samuel Hoare was short (much shorter than his father) and while he developed a neat and trim figure his appearance was in no way impressive. Here he was quite unlike his brother Oliver, who was tall and stunningly good looking. Oliver was naturally good at games, but played them for the enjoyment; Samuel ensured that he was good at games by application and effort and played to win. Oliver Hoare's subsequent career in various kinds of business was only spasmodically successful. While there is no evidence for believing that his elder brother ever looked upon politics as a game for demonstrating individual prowess it is undoubtedly true that he wanted passionately to succeed in it and that his measure of success would be the attainment of the highest political prizes.

If Hoare's athletic achievements at Harrow fell a little short of family expectations his brilliant academic career provided some compensation. Of his five years there four were spent in the upper sixth. Characteristically he prevented himself from, as he termed it, 'going to seed' during four years in the same form by competing for school prizes. In 1897 and again in 1898 he won the coveted Arthur Macnamara Memorial Prize and in 1898 also the Charles Herman Prior Divinity Prize (hagiography was his favourite reading at Harrow, along with Borrow, Kinglake, and R. L. Stevenson). He later wrote:

> The occasional efforts had the excellent effect of concentrating my energies on a limited objective. In addition ... to the pleasure ... of winning a competition, they helped to teach me a lesson which since has been very useful in political life — how to master quickly a particular subject and a mass of detail.[3]

Harrow had been a valuable experience for Hoare, but mainly, he felt, because it had inculcated the habit of self-study rather than from contact with brilliant teachers. From the school the transition to university was inevitable: not, however, to his father's college, Trinity, Cambridge, but, by way of a classical exhibition gained in 1899, to New College, Oxford. There he more than confirmed the academic and athletic promise he had displayed at Harrow. He represented the university at both rackets and tennis and played cricket with rather more success than at Harrow, although without gaining a blue. After securing a first in classical moderations (in April 1901) he turned to history, in which he also (in July 1903) received the highest classification and developed an interest which was to remain with him throughout his life. His New College tutor was H. A. L. Fisher who, years later, as Warden of New College, was to invite Hoare to become an honorary fellow of his old college. One of his lecturers was the distinguished medieval historian Reginald Lane-Poole of Magdalen, whose academic eminence was unmatched by any skill in holding the attention of an undergraduate audience: on one embarrassing occasion, Hoare found himself the sole attender at one of Lane-Poole's lectures. Hoare later recalled that, according to the contemporary Oxford gossip, Lane-Poole was thought to have 'descended through a long line of maiden aunts'. Perhaps some of the scholar's passion for academic precision rubbed off on to Hoare for this was the very phrase which was applied to him by a ministerial colleague of the 1920s, Lord Birkenhead (F. E. Smith). As an Oxford man of a slightly earlier vintage Birkenhead would have been familiar with Lane-Poole's reputation but clearly did not allow any fear of an accusation of plagiarism to interfere with his own reputation as a devastating wit. Hoare, with becoming modesty, later admitted that he thought the maiden aunt gibe 'not inaptly applied to me'.[4]

Unlike many future politicians of distinction Hoare did not seek to shine in the Oxford Union in which, in fact, he played little part regarding it, as did all good New College men of his day, as a Balliol preserve. Much more of his time was spent in the less spectacular but more intimate Conservative political societies. With Philip Kerr (later Lord Lothian) and Edward Cadogan, he was a leading spirit in the Chatham and Canning Clubs, where toasts were drunk to 'Church and King' and tobacco consumed in churchwarden pipes.[5] He also participated fully in such exclusive social clubs as the Bullingdon and the Gridiron (of which he was president for a time).

After taking his degree in 1903 he was persuaded by Fisher and Spooner (the Warden of New College), like so many gifted men before him, to enter for an All Souls fellowship. He only narrowly missed the coveted prize, being beaten to it by Edward Wood (later Lord Halifax), the son of an old family friend of both Hoare and his father. Fisher then induced him to have another try in the following year but he was again unsuccessful. Hoare did not feel that the extra year had been wasted, however, since he was able to do a great deal of reading and learnt Italian in preparation for a three month stay in Rome when he eventually went down from Oxford.

Despite Hoare's failure to take full advantage of the opportunities for political training that Oxford offered, there was never any doubt that he was intended for a parliamentary career and his father made full use of his contacts to expedite his entry into it. As early as April 1901 he was approached to stand as candidate in a Liberal-held London seat and again the following year in a Conservative-held Essex constituency. Both offers were refused but when, with Oxford behind him, Hoare was offered Ipswich, he seized the opportunity and, in January 1905, was adopted as the Conservative running mate with Sir Charles Dalrymple, who had held one of the seats in the two-member Ipswich constituency since 1886 (the other currently having a Liberal incumbent); on 13th February, 1905, Hoare made his first speech as a parliamentary candidate.

There was now a constituency to nurse but still time, his father thought, for one of those minor patronage posts which give useful experience and helpful contacts to their holders. Sir Samuel secured for his son an unpaid assistant private secretaryship to Alfred Lyttelton, the Conservative Colonial Secretary, and for most of 1905 Hoare performed the relatively humble duties involved. These included arranging the seating for a royal birthday banquet at the Colonial Office and — at a slightly higher level of activity — preparing reports on such topics as the emigration of pauper children, sugar and the Colonial Marriages Act. The circumstances may have been lowly but at least Hoare got his first introduction to a great government department and some opportunity to observe the flow of work at ministerial level: experience which by no means always comes the way of an aspirant backbencher.

In January 1906 came a massive Liberal electoral victory in terms of parliamentary seats (if considerably more modest in terms of the popular vote). At Ipswich, Dalrymple and his young Conservative colleague (who came bottom of the poll) participated in the general Conservative rout. Ill-health had prevented Hoare from taking much part in the campaigning but this could have had only a marginal effect on the final result: the Liberals had a majority then unprecedented in Ipswich's electoral history.[6]

He had not, however, long to wait for an electoral success, although in a somewhat different arena. Through the good offices of one of his father's friends he was nominated for the

London County Council seat in Brixton as a candidate for the Municipal Reform League (as London Conservatives were then known). In March 1907 he participated in the Conservative capture from the Liberals of the largest local authority in the country and joined at County Hall a group which included established Conservative parliamentarians like Lord Midleton (the former St John Brodrick), Hayes Fisher and William Peel and younger M.P.s like Walter Guinness, an exact contemporary of Hoare. He was also introduced to prominent Labour politicians, including Sidney Webb (who, when Hoare left the L.C.C. in 1910, assured him 'It has been a great pleasure to work with you, and to find how – except in opinion – we nearly always agree'[7]) and the Reverend Stewart Headlam, who became a particular friend. Even at this early stage in his political career, Hoare demonstrated a freedom from partisan rigidity which inclined him very much more to the liberal wing of the Conservative party than to the traditionalist elements.

Hoare's main work during his three years on the L.C.C. were with the education and fire brigade committees. After only a year he became chairman of the fire brigade committee, and even more important, chairman of the higher education subcommittee of the main education committee. He was to use the experience gained in the latter office with marked effect as a young Commons backbencher.

For there was no question of the L.C.C. being anything more than a preparatory period to gaining entry to Parliament. In 1908 the Conservative nomination for the Chelsea constituency fell vacant with the death of C. A. Whitmore, who had in 1886 defeated Sir Charles Dilke (the member since 1868), following Dilke's involvement in the Crawford divorce case. Whitmore held the seat for the Conservatives for twenty years until, in the 1906 election, the Liberals were able to wrest it back from their opponents by the slim majority of 629 votes. The vacancy left by Whitmore's death was thus a most attractive one for a parliamentary hopeful, an eminently winnable seat. Chelsea was (as it still is) Cadogan country, for Lord Cadogan owned most of the property in the area. With proper deference to so powerful a magnate the local Conservative association unanimously adopted the Earl's sixth son Edward as their candidate in place of Whitmore. Many years later, in a letter to Lord

Templewood, Sir Edward Cadogan described what happened next:

> ... the matter had to be referred to my father. He told me that he would favour my getting any other seat to fight but that he had always been friends with all parties on his Chelsea property, and that he did not want to prejudice the good relations he had established with both political friends and political opponents.[8]

But Lord Cadogan's withdrawal from his position of influence was not absolute – he commissioned his son to find an alternative candidate. Edward's choice fell upon a friend of Oxford days, Sam Hoare. Lord Cadogan gave his approval (after Alfred Lyttelton had written in support of his former assistant private secretary) and the constituency obliged in December 1908 with another unanimous nomination. The local Conservative press welcomed the new candidate in fulsome terms, congratulating the association on 'selecting a young, supple, vigorous, bright and thoughtful man', especially in view of the contemporary political situation of 'socialistic and other dire perils ahead', when the country needed 'all the knowledge, the cool nerve, the steady resource and the patriotism it can obtain'. Hoare, it was predicted, would become 'the most pervasive politician in Chelsea since the days of Sir Charles Dilke'.[9]

Before Hoare's candidacy was put to the test of the polls another even more important event occurred in his life. An advantageous marriage was an obvious asset to a rising politician when politics were still dominated by an élite based upon social position. There is no doubt that such a marriage figured prominently in Sir Samuel Hoare's plans for his son's career. It seems that the young Samuel had formed an attachment of some warmth with a beautiful Norfolk girl but the match did not commend itself to his parents on grounds of the lady's lack of the required social connections. But then, through his L.C.C. work, Hoare came into contact with the Lygon family, the family of the ancient peerage of Beauchamp (a fifteenth century barony had preceded the earldom created in 1806). The sixth Earl Beauchamp, who had held minor office in Conservative governments in the 1870s and 1880s, had died in 1891, leaving five children by his first wife, Lady Mary Stanhope (who died in 1876), and four by his second wife, Lady Emily Pierrepoint, the eldest daughter of Earl Manvers (who survived Lord Beauchamp by over forty years). The children's marriage connections were impeccable: one daughter married Lord Ampthill, another a son of the twentieth Baron Clinton, yet another the second son of Viscount Peel, former Speaker of the House of Commons; two served in the household of the Queen. The eldest son who succeeded to the earldom rather surprisingly pursued a career in the opposite political camp from his father and family, becoming a member of the Liberal Cabinet in 1910. Hoare's link with the Lygons came through the younger branch. Henry Lygon served with him on the L.C.C. education and fire committees and in fact succeeded him as chairman of the latter. A senior L.C.C. associate of both Hoare and Lygon was William Peel, brother of a brother-in-law of Lygon. It was through Henry Lygon that Hoare met Lady Maud, the youngest and only unmarried daughter of the sixth Earl, who was two years younger than himself and, like him, a devoted Anglo-Catholic. The affair blossomed, and an engagement was announced on 11th August, 1909. Two months later, on 16th October, the couple were married at St Paul's Church, Knightsbridge, with Hoare's brother-in-law, Luke Paget, then Bishop of Stepney, officiating.[10]

Thus began a marriage which was to last until Lord Templewood's death, a few months short of fifty years later. It would probably be more appropriate to describe it, at any rate at the outset, as a *mariage de convenance* rather than a love match. It brought Hoare into touch with an ever wider circle of the social and political élite, and into partnership with a woman who was possibly even more ambitious for his political success than he was himself and who shared fully in the chores, particularly the constituency chores, that are inseparable from a politician's life (Lady Maud began, immediately after the wedding, to organise a strong women's group in the Chelsea constituency association). They became devoted to each other and indeed were rarely apart from one another. Nevertheless, outsiders considered it to be a relationship somewhat lacking in warmth or in a very developed sense of fun. Perhaps things would have been different had there been children of the marriage, as Hoare himself almost certainly would have wished. Why none came is

impossible to establish, but it could well have been the consequence of a very severe attack of typhoid fever which Hoare
suffered in 1910 and which may have affected his capacity to
beget children.

By the time of the Hoare wedding the political crisis provoked by Conservative opposition to Lloyd George's budget of
1909 was welling up, with the very distinct possibility that
the government would be defeated in the Conservative-dominated House of Lords. The wedding was, indeed, directly
affected by the crisis since Lord Beauchamp, who was to have
given his half-sister away, was unable to absent himself from
his governmental cares for the ceremony and his place had to be
taken by Lady Maud's eldest brother, Robert. And the subsequent honeymoon in Paris and San Remo had to be shortened
in expectation of an early election to resolve the crisis: the pair
returned on 25th October and took up residence in Chelsea.

The Lords rejected the budget on 28th November and Asquith secured the dissolution of Parliament on 3rd December.
The newly married couple threw themselves into the Chelsea
campaign. On 31st December Hoare made his official adoption
speech and while he was careful not to align himself too closely
with the Lords' precipitate action he attacked the budget itself roundly as a class assault on capital and land. He also emerged, unlike his father, as a staunch tariff reformer, standing
explicitly as a 'unionist and tariff reform candidate'. He himself felt that his subsequent campaign speeches were rather too
long and insufficiently popular in content. But any shortcomings there may have been were hardly revealed in the result
of the election on 19th January, 1910, which in Chelsea converted a Liberal majority into a Conservative majority of 1,562 in a
poll of 86 per cent (just about the average over the country as
a whole). Hoare's victory launched a 34-year continuous period
of representing Chelsea in the House of Commons.

The political complexion of the House Hoare entered in
February 1910 was quite different from the chamber he would
have joined had he been successful at Ipswich in 1906. The 1906
Liberal majority of 243 seats over the Conservatives had been
transformed into a mere two, and there were now 273 Conservatives confronting 275 Liberals. The Liberals remained in office
by permission of the Irish Nationalists, who had 82 seats, and,

to a lesser extent, of the Labour party, with 40 members.

Despite this comparative electoral success for the Conservative party all was not well with its morale and leadership: however narrowly it may have done so it had failed to secure the reins of government again and, although the party had virtually turned its back on free trade after the alarums and excursions of the Chamberlainite campaign, discontent about the nature of the alternative – whether pure or diluted protectionism – and of the somewhat equivocal attitude to it of the party leader, Arthur Balfour, still rumbled along on the backbenches (and eventually led to Balfour's supersession by Bonar Law in 1911). Although the second indecisive 1910 election in November only marginally affected the position in the Commons (where there were now 272 M.P.s for both main parties) the party was not in a position effectively to confront the major political crises, over the House of Lords and over Ireland, which were soon to descend on it and be exacerbated by the party's own actions.

On the main issues of party policy the new member for Chelsea was not likely to create any disciplinary problems for his party leadership. Although he had attacked the 1909 budget in his election campaign there was nothing to suggest that he in any way identified himself with those on the right of the party who looked to the House of Lords as a means of permanently baulking a non-Conservative government: indeed, he played no part in the Commons debates on the Parliament Bill. On the merits of tariff reform he was utterly convinced (he was later to be a leader of protectionist movements in the party in the 1920s and 1930s). The tariff issue at the time of Hoare's arrival in the House was mainly an internal party one, rarely obtruding in the debates on the floor. The measure which dominated those debates from 1912 to the outbreak of war – Irish home rule – did not excite Hoare in the way it did no many of his colleagues despite the loyalist southern Irish strain in his family history. He later recorded:

> In my innermost mind I felt a great measure of sympathy with John Redmond [the Irish Nationalist leader] and his followers ... The various attempts to reach a settlement between 1910 and the start of the war had my fullest support.[11]

On some issues Hoare stood out from the main ruck of Conservative backbenchers. He was, for example, a dedicated supporter of female suffrage, at a time when the overwhelming majority of his party and many of the Liberal party, including most of its leaders, were opposed to any extension of the parliamentary vote to women. And the subject in which Hoare to some extent specialised during his early days on the backbenches was also an unusual choice among grass-roots Conservatives at the time. Largely as a result of his service on the controlling committee of the largest education authority in the country (the L.C.C.) he had developed a genuine interest in public education. His intense religious faith led him to have a particular interest in denominational education which, with a Liberal government pledged to force church schools to lose most of their religious identity or cease to enjoy local authority financial support, was now in some danger. In his maiden speech, delivered on 10th March, 1910, Hoare vigorously defended denominational teacher training colleges and drew on his L.C.C. experience to demonstrate that a sensible *modus vivendi* was possible between secular and denominational education without destroying the latter.[12] On the more general question, as he told the House in a debate on 20th April, he was in favour of educational expansion and increased governmental expenditure to assist local education authorities to achieve it; he also advocated — thirty-four years before it was finally accomplished — the raising of the school-leaving age to 15.[13]

Hoare's maiden speech had gone well. Balfour, the party leader, was apparently pleased with it but, perhaps even more important for an ambitious backbencher looking for opportunities for advancement, it led Lord Balcarres (later the Earl of Crawford), one of the Conservative whips, to take a personal interest in the new member for Chelsea.

It was Balcarres who first alerted Hoare to the political significance of what seemed merely a local Chelsea issue and encouraged him, and a group of more senior backbenchers, to play it for all it was worth to embarrass the government. In 1909 the War Office had moved the Duke of York's School, a famous military academy, from its eleven-acre site in the King's Road, Chelsea, to a fine new site in Dover. It had obtained Treasury approval to do so only on the understanding that the Treasury's estimate of the cost of the removal would not be exceeded. The actual cost incurred by the Office of Works (the responsible department) was, however, twice the Treasury's estimate. It seemed that the best way to meet the shortfall was to sell the King's Road site for development as flats and shops. But an unexpected difficulty presented itself. There was a consecrated chapel on the site and the only way to secularise it and free the land for development was by Act of Parliament. The government thus prepared a short bill which it thought would pass unnoticed and unopposed on second reading at the end of a day's session. But ministers reckoned without the new member for Chelsea, eager to please the whips' office and his Chelsea constituents (who were concerned about the threat the site development proposals posed to an historic local amenity) at one and the same time. When the brief bill came up on 17th March, 1910, Hoare moved delaying amendments and, with sterling assistance from other London M.P.s, the measure was talked out. After this success, which Hoare knew might only be temporary, the attack was widened to cover the whole development scheme of which the chapel site was only a small part, and it became a typical example of what in contemporary terms would be called a confrontation between environmentalists and commercial developers.

Prompted by a letter from Hoare on 8th April *The Times* gave prominence to the affair and it became clear that the opposition was seeking to save the main building of the former Duke of York's School and as much as possible of the site for an alternative use: Hoare suggested that it be used as the headquarters of the Territorial Army. A large meeting in Chelsea town hall on 22nd April voted by an ample majority in favour of Hoare's proposal (with, however, the local traders' association dissenting). The Prime Minister was then approached. He was asked to meet a deputation and on 27th April a group including the vice-chairman of the London Territorial Forces Association, Hoare and other London M.P.s, was cordially received by Asquith in his room in the House of Commons, where he was flanked by two Cabinet colleagues: Lewis Harcourt, the First Commissioner of Works, and John Burns, President of the Local Government Board. Hoare acted as chief spokesman for the group and the Prime Minister listened attentively to his statement of the situation. Asquith's response was all that could have been desired: he promised, according to the report issued to the press (almost certainly the work of Hoare himself),

> to give sympathetic consideration to the suggestion that the site should be used as the Territorials' Headquarters, and that, whilst unable to say anything of a more definite nature for the moment, he strongly deprecated the possibility of the site being built over, and of the amenities of the neighbourhood being injured, and would do what he could to preserve a building and open space so much associated with historic and military tradition for a public purpose.

If this were indeed to be the case, Hoare delicately indicated, he would withdraw his opposition to the chapel bill, the loss of which had been so embarrassing to the government in general and to the First Commissioner of Works in particular.[14]

In the weeks that followed the issue became not whether the Territorial headquarters would be established on the site but how much of the site it would be allowed to occupy. At first it seemed that it would be just the four acres left after the main part of the site had been sold to meet the cost of the Dover transfer. But in the end a remarkable victory was achieved. In June, Harcourt told the House of Commons that the whole of the site, all eleven acres, was being made available to the Territorials and no part of it would be sold for other development. So the campaign in which Hoare had played so leading a part had achieved even more than it had originally set out to achieve. His first backbench foray had proved a triumphant success. He was not, however, present in the Commons to witness the government surrender. In May he was laid low by a severe attack of typhoid fever and was out of action for the rest of the parliamentary session. But he was associated *in absentia* with the final rites since Balcarres had ensured that his name appeared beside the parliamentary question which elicited the confirmation of the government's change of plan. 'I am anxious you should be connected with this last stage in the episode', Balcarres wrote, 'as it is owing to your activity that Harcourt's proposal has been killed.'[15]

A few days later Hoare left on a convalescent Baltic cruise with Lady Maud, from which they returned in the middle of

August. In September the local Chelsea press reported that he was looking well but walking with a slight limp as a result of his illness. The physical effects may, however, have been considerably more serious and long-lasting if, as apparently sometimes does happen in such cases, the disease had induced sterility.

By the time Hoare was back in political circulation the second 1910 election was approaching. Parliament was dissolved on 28th November and Hoare found himself opposed in Chelsea by a Liberal rival of the same name, Hugh Hoare, a former M.P. for West Cambridgeshire. Hoare decided that use of his Christian name (rather than just his initials) was essential to avoid the risk of confusion in the voters' minds and, since his father, so recently an election candidate, had the same name as himself, Hoare appeared in his election literature and on the ballot paper as 'Sam Hoare'. While he himself disliked the truncated form of his name outside the family circle and intimate friends and usually signed his private letters 'Samuel Hoare', it was as 'Sam Hoare' he was more usually to be known by political friends and foes alike for the rest of his Commons' career.

In the event confusion between the two Hoare candidates was lessened by Hugh Hoare's enforced absence through illness from the whole of the election campaign, in which Hoare received sterling help from Lady Maud. When the Chelsea result was announced 'Sam Hoare' was in with an increased majority (1,719, compared with 1,562 in January) in a much reduced poll (73 per cent, as opposed to 86 per cent).

At the swearing-in ceremony of the new House in January 1911 Hoare made the acquaintance of the man whose friendship was to be the most important and long-lasting of his political career. But he could little have realised this when he exchanged a few friendly words with the new Conservative member for Ashton-under-Lyne, a Canadian called Max Aitken. Lord Beaverbrook recalled the incident many years later in a letter to Hoare:

On the morning when I went to the House of Commons to be sworn for the first time I was in a state of intense anxiety and nervous to a degree. I expected to find a full Chamber. Instead there was not a soul in the place except you. We carried on a brief conversation.[16]

The conversations were to become longer and more frequent as the years went on, and from 1922 Beaverbrook was an essential adviser in most of the important steps in Hoare's career in politics. The future Lord Beaverbrook played no part, however, in the step which Hoare took within two months of the opening of the 1911 Parliament and which was to give him perhaps his greatest backbench triumph. This was the so-called Holmes Circular affair, which for the first time projected Hoare on the stage of national politics and, after grave embarrassment for the Liberal government, led to the replacement of both the education minister, Walter Runciman, and his chief permanent official, Sir Robert Morant.

The 'Holmes' of the Circular (or, more properly, memorandum) was Edmond Holmes, an inspector of elementary schools at the Board of Education (as the education ministry was then known) from 1875 and chief inspector from 1905. Until the Conservative government's Education Act of 1902 elementary schools alone were supported from public funds and thus were the only schools with which the Board of Education and its locally based officials, the inspectorate, were officially concerned.[17] Yet both Board officials and inspectors were by their own educational backgrounds and élitist perceptions singularly ill-equipped to understand or sympathise with the problems of elementary education. They had not gone to such schools themselves and did not send their own children to them nor had they ever taught in them. Elementary education at the time was essentially education for the 'labouring poor' and was rigidly mechanical, inculcating obedience rather than spontaneity. It was in the hands of teachers who were themselves mainly of working-class background, graduating to teaching by way of apprenticeship as pupil-teachers to existing teachers, with only a small minority able to scrape together the financial resources necessary to undertake a professional training course.

The attitude to the products and practitioners of elementary education displayed by the Board's inspectorate and even more by the London officials remote from the problems of the classroom was one of infinite superiority — an attitude reinforced for the inspectorate by the system of 'payment by results', under which the bulk of the central government grant, constituting roughly half a school's income, depended upon each child's

performance in annual examinations in the three 'Rs' conduc-
ted by the inspectors and, to a lesser extent, on regular attendance. Edmond Holmes, looking back on his inspectorial experiences in the 1870s and 1880s, confessed that for him then,
elementary school children were merely examinees belonging
to 'the lower orders' in whom he took little interest either as
individuals or as human beings.[18] Although payment by results
was officially abolished in 1895 its effects on educational out-
looks persisted for much longer since its products remained in
the system.

To supplement the periodic inspections by the Board's
inspectorate several local education authorities employed their
own inspectors who, unlike the central inspectors, were often
recruited from the ranks of elementary school teachers. But the
practice raised problems, to which Edmond Holmes addressed
himself as soon as he became the Board of Education's chief
inspector in 1905. After much internal office discussion and
investigation by the Board's inspectorate Holmes prepared a
memorandum dated 6th January, 1910, for the consideration
of his official superiors, L. A. Selby-Bigge, the principal assistant secretary at the Board, and Morant, the permanent
secretary. This document was the so-called 'Holmes Circular'.[19]

Holmes's memorandum began by recording that of the 123
local authority inspectors (75 of them employed in the 12
largest towns outside London such as Liverpool, Leeds, Manchester and Birmingham), no fewer than 104 were ex-elementary
teachers, and of the remaining 19 only two or three had the
educational qualifications normally looked for in the Board's
own inspectorate, namely a public school education followed
by Oxford or Cambridge. It then drew an obviously controversial distinction between the two types of local inspector:

> The differences in respect to efficiency between ex-elementary
> teacher Inspectors and those who have had a more liberal
> education is very great. Very few of our Inspectors have a
> good word to say for local Inspectors of the former type,
> whereas those of the latter type are, with three exceptions,
> well spoken of ...

In the same vein the memorandum went on to castigate the
majority of elementary teachers as 'uncultured and imperfectly

educated and ... creatures of tradition and routine'. It was thus not to be wondered at that local inspectors recruited from such teachers were 'on the whole a hindrance rather than an aid to educational progress' and needed to be replaced by 'men of real culture and enlightenment'. These would be provided by men of the 'Varsity type' who, by contrast with ex-elementary teachers ('usually engaged in a hopeless task of surveying or trying to survey a wide field of action from a well-worn groove'), had the advantage 'of being able to look at elementary education from a point of view of complete detachment, and therefore of being able to handle its problems with freshness and originality'.

Although Holmes's memorandum had originally been intended only for the eyes of Selby-Bigge and Morant it seems that the permanent secretary thought it of such importance that it should be given a 'strictly confidential' circulation to the hundred or so members of the Board's inspectorate, and this was done early in May 1910. In November 1910 Holmes retired from the Civil Service, but his memorandum lived on. At the beginning of 1911 various references to the rather brutal phraseology it used about elementary school teachers began to appear in the press, presumably as a result of a leak by one of the circulated inspectors, and protests by teachers and their professional association, already ill-disposed to what was considered to be the élitist and authoritarian attitude of the Board, began to build up; local education authorities, too, resented this new evidence of central interference in their undoubted area of competence. The matter came to the attention of Runciman, the President of the Board (he later told the Commons), early in February (1911), and Morant then gave him to understand that the circulation of the memorandum had been a mere formality which had slipped through his fingers at a time when he was busy with other things. But apparently neither Runciman nor Morant — despite the obviously explosive nature of the issue — took any steps to ward off the parliamentary storm that was just about to break over their heads.

It fell to Hoare to provoke that storm. He was approached, it does not seem possible to establish exactly by whom, to put down a Commons question on the affair. He was still in close touch with his former L.C.C. colleagues but it seems likely that it was the National Union of Teachers which sought his help, and it would not have taken him long to perceive the political implications of the issue. Although the N.U.T.'s general secretary, James Yoxall, was an M.P. himself there were clear advantages in the opening attack being made by a young opposition backbencher who had already demonstrated his interest in educational matters and, above all, his ability – as in the Duke of York's School affair – to draw the government's blood. Hoare's question appeared on the order paper on 10th March and asked the President of the Board of Education

> whether a circular was issued from the Board of Education, on or about 6th January, 1910, in which the Board's inspectors were advised to use their influence with local education authorities to persuade them to restrict their important administrative appointments to candidates educated at Oxford and Cambridge.

It was quite obvious from press comments in the interval between the question's appearance on the order paper and the ministerial answer four days later, on 14th March, that the essential contents of Holmes's memorandum were well known.[20] Yet with an astonishing mixture of effrontery and naivety Runciman attempted to brazen it out. He simply replied: 'No, Sir. The Board have given no such advice and intend to give no such advice.'[21] This answer, as Runciman was soon to have to demonstrate at exhaustive length, may have been technically correct since the Holmes memorandum was a personal document and not official Board policy, but it was obviously equivocal in the light of the evidence of widespread knowledge of the content of the document. He could hardly have expected that the matter would be allowed to rest there. Nor was it. Hoare was shown typewritten extracts from the memorandum by a Conservative colleague in the L.C.C. (possibly his brother-in-law, Henry Lygon) and armed with this fresh material – and encouraged by Balcarres – he intervened in the general debate on the Vote on Account the following week (21st March). For some time past, Hoare said, there had been friction between the Board of Education and local education authorities, arising from the local authorities' feeling that the Board was increasingly interfering in their administration and, above all, in their appointment of officials. Rumours which had been rife about a Board circular on local inspectors had created considerable anxiety among local authorities and teachers and had prompted him (Hoare) to ask his question last week. In view of the nature of the minister's reply he now proposed to read extracts from the circular and enable the House to judge whether that reply was adequate. The document, Hoare explained, had been prepared by the chief inspector of elementary schools (he did not name him) and distributed, on Board of Education headed notepaper, to all divisional inspectors.

> I think the House will say the document is well worthy of the attention of every Member of the House. It is headed, I acknowledge, 'strictly confidential', but at the same time it has been brought to my attention from a variety of sources, and as it is already being circulated, or at any rate extracts from it, in the public press, it seems to me that this House has a perfect right to hear what I am going to read.

Hoare then read the extracts which have already been quoted. Having done so he began to draw on the rich reserves of political capital that the memorandum obviously presented to opponents of the Liberal government and the widely unpopular Board of Education. While they might all have their own opinions about the superiority of Oxford and Cambridge education, Hoare said, it did seem to him curious that a circular of this kind should be issued under a Liberal government which, on another but recent occasion, the junior minister at the Board of Education, C. P. Trevelyan, had lauded as institutionalising 'a revolt of the common man against the privileged man'.[22] But the circular raised a serious situation since it seemed to lay down Board conditions for the appointment of local officials, to restrict the entry of elementary school teachers to posts which they considered 'plums' and, by its manner of distribution, to keep those teachers in official ignorance of the Board's policy in the matter. If, as Runciman had indicated in his cryptic reply of the previous week, the document's contents did not represent Board policy why had it not been withdrawn? Hoare ended by asking the President

> what guarantee he is going to give this House and the great

teaching profession outside that this policy has been abandoned and that in future the Board of Education do not intend to bring to bear the great weight of their authority and
to confine these important appointments to candidates from
Oxford and Cambridge universities and the great public
schools?[23]

There was nothing apologetic about Runciman's response.
He insisted that his earlier reply had been completely accurate
and that if Hoare had paid careful attention to it he would have
realised that what he had been describing in his speech was 'not
the policy of the Board of Education, never has been the policy
of the Board of Education, and so long as I am connected with it
never will be the policy of the Board of Education'. He then
launched a bitter attack on the young backbencher who had
dared to raise the issue:

> ... the hon. Gentleman has taken upon himself to produce in
> this House a document which is the property of the Board of
> Education and is a private communication passing between
> officers of the Board ... It was marked in the most prominent
> way 'Strictly Confidential', and the hon. Gentleman ad-
> mitted that ... I do not understand the hon. Gentleman's
> code of conduct ... I am surprised that he thought he was
> serving any useful purpose in raking about the musty waste
> paper baskets from which he must have extracted this docu-
> ment. Indeed, the hon. Gentleman, if I understand the nature
> of the document, is a receiver of stolen property.

Runciman then went on to identify, for the first time, the writer
of the memorandum and briefly traced its genesis as being exclusively within the chief inspector's own department. Holmes
had made inquiries about local authority inspectors and embodied the resulting information in a minute which he had then
had printed – 'as hundreds of departmental documents are
printed' – and circulated to inspectors on his staff (Runciman
did not then know of Morant's authorisation of the circulation).
Throughout it expressed his own individual views and never
once claimed to be expressing the view of the Board as a whole.
Circulation had been confined to the Board's own officials until
– and here Runciman chose to ignore the circumstantial

accounts which had already appeared in the press — Hoare 'gave it the publicity he thought necessary in fulfilment of his public duty'.

The memorandum, Runciman maintained, had nothing to do with the relations between the Board and the local authorities. He did not believe that the local authorities would have known anything about Holmes's views or paid any attention to them had Hoare not given them publicity (again Runciman ignored recent press comment). Hoare's actions could only be explained as emanating from a desire to make as much mischief as he could between the Board and elementary school teachers. It was neither desirable nor practicable to withdraw the memorandum since it had gone out to its recipients months ago. The important thing was the policy of the Board and that was as he, the minister, had stated it.[24]

Runciman's phraseology, particularly the accusations of 'raking about' in 'musty waste paper baskets' and 'receiver of stolen property', was not calculated to lower the temperature of debate. And clearly even his own side was unhappy. Josiah Wedgwood expressed relief that the memorandum did not represent Board policy and congratulated Hoare on bringing the matter forward and thus affording the Liberal benches 'an opportunity to dissociate themselves from what has been done'. The Conservative benches were, of course, quick to take advantage of the minister's intemperate words — 'language of indecent violence', as Arthur Balfour described them. Lord Hugh Cecil and others expressed complete disbelief that a document reflecting purely private opinions could have been circulated in this way and voiced the strong suspicion that if Hoare had not initiated the debate the policy contained in the Holmes memorandum would never have been repudiated. Alfred Lyttelton, from the Conservative front bench, accused the minister of substituting verbal abuse for relevant fact. When, he asked, did Runciman first hear of the document? Lyttelton guessed that it must have been some time before questions began to be put, in which case why had Runciman not repudiated it then?[25]

In the days following the debate attention began to switch to the question of the real responsibility for the memorandum. Curiously, everyone seemed anxious to exculpate Holmes (including Hoare and Yoxall, the N.U.T. secretary, in letters to the press).[26] Holmes himself was abroad while the controversy was raging but a letter he sent from Venice was published in a number of papers, the *Morning Post* and *Daily Telegraph* included, on 25th April. He explained that the roughness of the language of the memorandum arose from its being addressed to officials already familiar with the situation and with whom it was not always necessary to weigh one's words. Had he had any suspicion that what he wrote was likely to see the full light of day he would not only have expressed himself much more guardedly, and with much less emphasis, but he could have added explanations unnecessary in the case of 'the high officials' for whom he intended the memorandum and 'which would at any rate have toned down the crudeness of certain passages which have given dire offence'.

The emphasis Holmes's letter placed on the fact that his memorandum had been written for 'high officials', and his complete confidence that it would not see 'the full light of day', seemed to suggest that Morant had taken the lead in suggesting its distribution to the inspectorate and thereby running the risk, by reason of sheer numbers, that it might come into 'the full light of day'. Morant was the man for whom many, not least the teachers' union, were gunning. His dominating personality, his élitist view of education, seen in the apparent exalting of secondary education, restricted to the few, over the elementary education which was the only schooling the mass of the population could expect, created many enemies. There was undoubtedly sufficient opposition to him within the Board itself to account for a 'leaking' of the memorandum by one of the inspectors to whom it was circulated in order to embarrass Morant rather than the universally liked Holmes. Sir George Kekewich, who had been eased out of the permanent secretaryship of the Board eight years before to make way for the forceful but relatively junior Morant, took the occasion of the parliamentary storm not only to attack the sentiments expressed in the memorandum but to indicate that departmental matters had been better arranged in his day.[27] Several of his former colleagues may well have agreed with him.

Not the least worrying aspect of the affair for the Liberal government was the apparent contrast it presented with the Liberal commitment to social reform. Hoare had, of course, realised the potentialities of such a contrast for the purposes of partisan politics. But inside the Liberal ranks there was anxious questioning about the Morant regime at the Board of Education. The Liberal weekly, *Nation*, edited by H. W. Massingham, spoke of the degradation suffered by a Liberal government which had under its rule 'seen the education of the country restricted, the teachers depressed and insulted, and the public service paralysed by a personal tyranny [i.e., Morant at the Board of Education] which is as inept and wayward as it is cruel'. Massingham told Runciman privately that he was impenitent on 'the Morant business' since Morant had done things 'which are against all my educational views and tendencies'.[28]

In the preliminary parliamentary exchanges on the affair, however, no mention was made of Morant's role: neither in the debate which Hoare initiated on 21st March nor on 23rd March when there was further discussion on the second reading of the Consolidated Fund Bill. On that day Morant penned a long and rambling letter to his ministerial chief, from which Runciman learnt for the first time that Morant's part in the circulation of the memorandum had not been quite as perfunctory as the permanent secretary had earlier indicated. Morant now explained that he had approved the circulation and directed the inclusion of an appendix listing the local authorities which employed inspectors. He maintained that the purpose of the memorandum, apart from some of its phraseology, was absolutely proper, pointing out as it did one of the hindrances to educational reform, and that it was suitable for wider distribution (although he acknowledged that Holmes might have meant it for himself and Selby-Bigge only). He now frankly admitted that it had been sent to the inspectors with his approval 'and for all I know upon my suggestion' but asserted the propriety of doing so without first securing ministerial sanction. But then Morant's tone changed. He felt compelled to apologise for what he now saw to be an error of judgement and for which he was anxious that he, rather than Holmes, should publicly accept responsibility by Runciman's revealing his part in the affair in the House of Commons:

I do not seek, I could not possibly in the circumstances desire to seek, to plead no responsibility for the mistake of sending to a hundred Inspectors a document containing some of the phrases used in this one. I certainly ought to have read it more carefully at the moment of sanctioning the distribution ... so far as I know it is the first time in eight years of strenuous hard work as Head of this Office that I have made a mistake of this kind, and the first time (so far as I know) on which I have, by a mistake of judgement ... landed this Office or my Minister in any real difficulty. I realise to the full that unfortunately this present instance, though the first one ... has led to a situation of the most deplorable and regrettable nature ... May I say how deeply I regret the lamentable results ... [29]

This, coming from one of the great civil servants of the period, was an extraordinary confession, but it did not mollify Runciman, who was clearly furious at being placed in such an exposed position by his officials. Among other things, he directed the permanent secretary to issue an office instruction that no circular, memorandum or other document was to be printed or circulated except with the express sanction of the parliamentary secretary, acting for the President of the Board; and that printed documents containing individual views only should be headed by some such statement as that 'the views expressed in this Memorandum are not to be taken to be an expression of the Board's policy'.[30] The door of the stable from which the horse had already bolted was in future to be securely locked.

Meanwhile Runciman was being continuously pressed on the affair at question time in the Commons, and Morant's role began to emerge: that, for example, he had authorised circulation and had admitted lack of judgement in so doing. The actual memorandum and relevant papers – but not Morant's letter to Runciman of 23rd March – were made available to interested M.P.s. From the Labour benches on 5th April Philip Snowden asked whether Morant was still to be kept 'in the service of the Department'. Morant's resignation, after this almost unprecedented exposure of his conduct on the floor of the House of Commons, was clearly becoming a real possibility.

After these exchanges at the beginning of April the Commons temporarily ceased to give concentrated attention to the Holmes–Morant affair. But outside, the campaign against the Board – and against Morant and to a lesser extent Runciman in particular – was steadily mounting, with the National Union of Teachers in the van. Bitter attacks on Morant and the Board appeared week by week in the N.U.T. journal, the *Schoolmaster*. The N.U.T. Easter conference at Aberystwyth gave the opportunity for a full-scale denunciation of the Board and all its works, and the passage of a unanimous resolution of thanks to Hoare for having uncovered this latest instance of the Board's 'anti-democratic policy and practice'.[31] The scope of the attack was soon widened to include the method of recruitment to the Civil Service as a whole, which was considered to exhibit the same élitist preconceptions that underlay the Holmes memorandum. A vast protest meeting at the Albert Hall on 13th May (to which Hoare was invited but perhaps conveniently found himself unable to attend) was addressed not only by N.U.T. leaders but by speakers from the Civil Service unions; a similar meeting was held in Manchester on 26th May. On 4th July there were press reports that the N.U.T. intended to put up a candidate in Runciman's constituency, Dewsbury, at the next election. By 3rd August, 140 resolutions of protest had been received by the Board.

On 13th July the affair erupted again in the Commons, in the debate on the education estimates, and it was widely felt that if a vote had been taken the government might well have been defeated, so great was the dissatisfaction on the Liberal back-benches.[32] Runciman vigorously denied the suggestion that the Board's inspectors (the original point of the imbroglio – the qualifications of the *local authority* inspectorate – had long been left far behind) were recruited from one social class, although the figures he gave showed an overwhelming Oxbridge predominance among the present incumbents and he was unable to say how many had had elementary school experience. Yoxall, in a bitter attack, demanded an inquiry into the affair but Hoare, who followed him, declared himself in favour of Snowden's memorial (which Hoare had signed) calling for a royal commission on the general question of Civil Service recruitment. Hoare returned to his earlier point, made in the 21st March debate, about the rough treatment local authorities had received at the hands of the Board but also expressed concern lest the Board's officials, and public schools and universities, should be depreciated. Trevelyan, for the Board, expressed profound regrets (in a way which Runciman had not felt able to do) at the effect the Holmes memorandum had had on the feelings of teachers but felt that the Board had done everything that could be done in the circumstances: the document had been withdrawn (despite Runciman's earlier statement that it was not possible to do so) and it had been stated unequivocally that the sentiments it expressed did not represent the policy of the Board.

But something further was done, by forces outside the Board itself. Although Runciman had refused to take ministerial responsibility for the affair his government colleagues clearly felt that his usefulness at the Board of Education had come to an end and on 23rd October he was transferred to the Board of Agriculture as part of a ministerial reshuffle which also included the advent of Winston Churchill at the Admiralty. Ministerial reshuffles are, however, fairly common features of political life. The resignation of the permanent head of a government department at the height of his powers is quite a different matter. Morant's enemies had that satisfaction in the following month when, on 28th November, his resignation was announced in the House of Commons. The blow was softened by Lloyd George's invitation to him to become secretary of the new National Insurance Commission, a post which eventually led to his major role in the creation of the Ministry of Health, of which he became the first permanent secretary. But there was no doubt that the incident of the Holmes 'circular' represented a permanent setback in a public career which otherwise might well have taken Morant to the very highest Civil Service post.

The Holmes affair was later described by Morant's successor at the Board of Education (Sir Amherst Selby-Bigge) as 'a matter of no intrinsic importance'.[33] This may be true, but it is difficult not to feel that both Morant and Runciman showed a remarkable lack of foresight in not realising the explosive nature of the memorandum's phrasing and in not taking corrective action as soon as the leak became known, well before Hoare asked his question on 14th March. Such perception is a *sine qua non* for the top leadership of a government department and Runciman and Morant showed themselves deficient in it. Hoare had performed the classic backbench investigatorial function in exploiting the situation. Runciman's difficulties would have been less had Hoare chosen to raise the matter with him privately beforehand but it is hardly incumbent upon backbenchers to consider ministerial susceptibilities too sympathetically, especially when they are in opposition at a time of acrimonious political controversy. There is no reason to believe that Hoare himself wished the affair to go any further than embarrassing a minister and the Liberal government as a whole, and he certainly had no animus against Morant nor envisaged at the outset that the permanent secretary's resignation would result from his probing. But as a staunch supporter of church schools Hoare had no brief to defend the administration of a Board of Education which had looked with little favour on such schools. The post-Morant Board of Education was a more tractable department for all the interests which had campaigned over the Holmes affair.

Hoare had secured an undoubted parliamentary triumph and firmly established his reputation as an alert and penetrating backbencher. He had, too, his first taste of national fame, as press coverage of the affair was extensive. Indeed, on the day after the debate on 21st March a class in one of the schools in Hoare's Chelsea constituency, asked by their teacher for the name of the Prime Minister, with one accord returned the reply 'Sam Hoare'![34] On a more immediately practical level one by-product of his activity was an invitation from the Prime Minister, Asquith, to serve on the royal commission on the Civil Service set up in March 1912 largely as a result of the widening of the original Holmes debate to include recruitment to the inspectorate and to the Civil Service as a whole. The Mac-Donnell Commission met fairly frequently for a period of over three years – March 1912 to July 1915 – and while Hoare was by no means its most assiduous attender (for much of the time he was engaged in the most intense activity of his pre-war parliamentary career) he did not look upon his membership as a sinecure and in fact attended his last meeting in February 1915, several months after he had been commissioned in the army. The MacDonnell inquiry was probably the most extensive of the many such investigations the British Civil Service has had to endure and Hoare must have gained a unique insight into the administrative machine in which in a few years he was to hold ministerial office.

Another by-product was the first of his many assignments to

assist in the formulation of Conservative party policy. In July 1913 F. E. Smith asked Hoare to be chairman of the education sub-committee of the Unionist Social Reform Committee, an organisation which Smith, a Conservative frontbencher, had just started with the object of interesting Conservative M.P.s in social questions (other inquiries covered housing, poor law and agriculture). In a matter of months the report of Hoare's committee, almost wholly written by himself, was published and attracted favourable notice in the press as a sign of a new wind blowing in Conservative policy-making.[35]

But the experience which Hoare himself in retrospect considered truly launched his parliamentary career was his leading role in the Conservative team led by Alfred Lyttelton (until his death in July 1913) which from 1912 to 1914 fought tooth and nail the Liberal government's measure to disestablish and disendow the Anglican Church in Wales. This was a cause dear to Hoare's heart, one in which he could leap to the defence of the church to which he was passionately devoted and which demonstrated his sense of history, his power of logical argument and mastery of complex detail – all to be hallmarks of Hoare's parliamentary style. The battle for the integrity of the Church in Wales was waged virtually contemporaneously with that against the Liberal home rule legislation for Ireland and for many, including Hoare, it was the more important battle.[36]

Like the question of home rule for Ireland (towards which, indeed, the disestablishment of the Irish church in 1869 had seemed to point) Welsh church disestablishment aroused fierce passions in both Liberal and Conservative parties. The four Welsh dioceses were integral parts of the Province of Canterbury, their bishops were members of Convocation and eligible, if of sufficient seniority, for membership of the House of Lords. To disestablish and disendow the Welsh dioceses threatened, so many Conservatives believed, the whole established church, not just its Welsh portion. But in the Liberal party in the Commons there was an important Welsh contingent: after the 1906 election all but one of the 34 M.P.s from Wales were Liberals, the solitary exception being, not a Conservative, but Keir Hardie, the Labour M.P. for Merthyr Tydfil. For these the established church represented a facet of an alien domination in a land of fierce cultural pride, belief in national consciousness and — most important of all — an overwhelming commitment to nonconformity in religion.

The Established Church (Wales) Bill, which had its second reading in May 1912, was the fifth such bill Liberal governments had introduced and was somewhat more liberal to the Welsh church than its predecessors had been. Under it the four Welsh dioceses ceased to be dioceses of the Province of Canterbury and their ecclesiastical jurisdiction was abolished. But the church's organisation was kept in being and power was given to hold synods for its future government. All the cathedrals and parish churches, ecclesiastical residences and closed burial grounds, together with that part of the church's endowment income which it was allowed to retain, were to be vested in three Welsh Commissioners with instructions to transfer the whole property to a Representative Body to be instituted by the church itself. The income of the Church in Wales was estimated at the time of the Bill's introduction to be some £260,000. Of this the Bill originally allowed it to retain £87,000, representing the income which it had accumulated from endowments subsequent to 1662, which was the date selected on somewhat dubious grounds — questioned by Hoare during the debates — as the establishment of nonconformity and the ending of the church's exclusive position as the recognised religion of the populace. Endowments received before 1662, it was argued, might properly be regarded as national property, and the Bill provided for the sum so arrived at (originally £173,000) to be alienated, for charitable purposes only, to the Welsh county councils and, to a much lesser extent, to such national institutions as the University of Wales, the National Library of Wales and the National Museum.

Every stage of the Bill was contested by the Conservatives, among whom the two Cecils (Lord Hugh and Lord Robert), Sir Arthur Griffith-Boscawen, William Ormsby-Gore, Viscount Wolmer and William Bridgeman were, with Hoare, the most prominent. They were faced with a massive government majority since they could naturally expect no support on this issue from the Liberals' parliamentary allies, the Irish Nationalists and the Labour party. The long-term effects of their campaign were obviously circumscribed, even if the short-term effects were damaging to a government which already had a full

legislative programme and could ill afford time devoted to so
relatively marginal a bill.

After four days spent on the second reading debate in May
1912 the question remained dormant until November, when the
government announced a time-table to restrict debate on the
remaining stages. The committee stage occupied from early
December to the end of January 1913 and the report and third
reading stages were completed early in February. In the same
month the House of Lords — where the Conservative majority
were even more adamant in defence of the established Welsh
church than the party in the Commons — delivered the first of
its rejections, voting against the second reading after a three day
debate by 252 to 51. In June and July 1913 the Bill passed a
second time through the Commons, only to be defeated again on
second reading in the Lords on 22nd July by 243 to 48. This
time there was a nine month gap before the Bill was again introduced in the Commons, where it passed all its stages for the
third time between 20th April and 19th May, 1914. Under the
recent Parliament Act of 1911 it could then have gone for the
royal assent without resubmission to the Lords, having been
passed three times by the Commons, with two years between the
first second reading and the final third reading. But in fact it did
return to the Lords where the government agreed, in June 1914,
to the delaying tactic of submitting certain questions to a select
committee, which had not completed its deliberations when war
came in August 1914. It was not until 18th September, 1914,
that the Bill, along with the Government of Ireland Bill, at last
received the royal assent but, under a separate Suspensory Act,
the actual date of disestablishment was postponed until after the
war had ended.

The campaign against the Bill in the Commons did achieve
some practical successes. But, as so often in British parliamentary
politics, these came only when a significant number of the
government's own backbenchers had given evidence of willingness to sponsor or support amendments, with the consequent
possibility that governmental intransigence might bring an
embarrassing defeat. Thus during the first committee stage the
government agreed to amendments to increase the annual income left to the church by £15,000, and to the commutation of
life interests. It did not, however, yield on two other matters

which worried some of its own backbenchers: it refused amendments to allow for compensation to curates (as opposed to their ecclesiastical superiors); and to leave glebe, or the land which went with a church living, to the Church in Wales.

In debates which were often acrimonious Hoare's frequent contributions, although coming from one deeply committed to the maintenance of the church's status and property, stood out as moderate in tone and careful and informed in argument. His speech on 13th May, 1912, during the original second reading debate, dealt mainly with the historical arguments that the proponents of disestablishment had been advancing, including the knotty point as to whether or not Welsh tithes could be traced back to Giraldus Cambrensis in the twelfth century. With considerable force and logic he questioned the argument that since Welsh members so passionately desired it, disestablishment should be granted them. Hoare called it the 'local option' argument and maintained that what was sauce for the Welsh goose should equally be sauce for the English gander: what, he asked, about granting the sort of religious education in schools that many English members desired?[37] As with other Conservative critics of the Bill it was disendowment and expropriation rather than disestablishment of itself which most perturbed Hoare and which indeed created the government's greatest problems with its backbenchers, apart from the inflexibly dogmatic Welsh M.P.s. On disestablishment Hoare was even prepared to contemplate 'concurrent establishment', or the establishment of all Welsh churches rather than the disestablishment of one.[38] He urged the Welsh members not to destroy a national institution which had existed unbroken in Wales for centuries. It had its faults, as had every institution. But in spite of its faults it might, in the hands of Welshmen (and in 1912 all four bishops were Welsh), prove in the future a great instrument for national regeneration.[39] With disestablishment so closely interwoven with the Welsh national movement this was a shrewd argument, but passions were too aroused for it to have any effect.

On disendowment Hoare was adamant and it was his inward anger at what he felt to be the injustice of the disendowment provisions which fired his opposition to the Bill and kept him alert during the long and often tedious debates. Realising that this was the weakest point in the government's case he was in the van of the Conservative effort at the end of November 1912 to get disestablishment and disendowment in separate bills. There would then, it was hoped, be a reasonable prospect that Liberal backbench pressure would compel the government to amend drastically, or even withdraw, the disendowment provisions. But the move inevitably failed (as it did again, the second time round, in July 1913), and the long committee stage was devoted to an undivided bill. This stage, together with the third reading, occupied from 5th December, 1912, to 5th February, 1913, and saw perhaps the period of greatest activity by Hoare, no doubt refreshed from a visit he paid to Canada during the preceding summer recess in connection with the affairs of the Employers' Liability Assurance Company (of which he had become a director in 1909). He moved or seconded something like twenty amendments, including ones to continue the jurisdiction of the ecclesiastical courts in Wales, to delay the property apportion-ment provisions (where Hoare displayed what even McKenna, the minister in charge of the Bill, praised as a 'thorough under-standing of what everybody has recognised as a most complicated clause'),[40] and to retain certain of the existing rights of the Welsh bishops (for example, their membership of the Convocation of Canterbury). None of these amendments met with any success in the division lobbies, but the value of Hoare's work was fully recognised by his party leaders. Immediately after the con-clusion of the (first) third reading debate the leader of the Opposition team on the Bill, Alfred Lyttelton (who died, at a relatively early age, only five months later), wrote to Hoare to thank him for his 'first-rate work ... You have spoken often but never without a scholarly precision and knowledge most refresh-ing in the House of Commons'.[41] At that time — February 1913 — many weary months of Commons' debate lay ahead, in which Hoare continued to play a full part, before the House finally dis-charged its functions in relation to the Bill with the final third reading on 19th May, 1914.

Unlike the Holmes circular affair, Hoare's involvement in the Welsh church debates did not make much public impact. The general public was, indeed, little exercised by the complexities — historical, doctrinal or other — of Welsh disestablishment whether the arena was the House of Commons or Hyde Park, where a massive series of protests (in which Hoare participated) were held on a Saturday in June 1913. But on the *cognoscenti* of Westminster politics the still youthful backbencher made a definite impression. Lobby correspondents in February 1913 noted that Hoare had 'become a man to be reckoned with', a backbencher whom ministers had to treat with respect for his 'ability to speak well' and his 'persistence in pursuing an argument that compels attention'.[42]

It was not all praise, however, although the criticism was largely directed at the manner rather than the matter of Hoare's parliamentary interventions. His careful, precise way of speaking could often sound rather precious and affected: there were press comments, for example, on his 'drawing room style' and 'the sugary crust' which lay over his speeches.[43] A manner of delivery not entirely removed from the clerical, especially when combined with Hoare's deep interests in church affairs, on at least one occasion led to some fairly gentle banter at Hoare's expense. The episode is discreetly blanketed by the *Hansard* reporters at the time as an 'interruption', and so the detail has to be gathered from an anonymous contributor to *London Opinion* for 2nd November, 1912. Hoare had raised, in a midnight debate on the Expiring Laws Continuance Bill, a brief but rather obscure point about the inadvisability of including the Ecclesiastical Jurisdiction Act of 1847 among those to be renewed by the general legislation under consideration, on the grounds that a still unredeemed pledge had been given at the time of its passage in 1847 that it would be replaced by more comprehensive permanent legislation. In reply the Solicitor-General, Sir John Simon, explained that if the 1847 Act were not renewed there would in certain dioceses be no authority who could grant a licence for a church marriage. Hoare observed, with some reason, that this hardly met his point about the need for permanent legislation.[44]

Describing Hoare as 'a pale, ascetic and fragile-looking young man, with a simpering voice that suggests a newly ordained and nervous curate', the *London Opinion* account of this exchange went on to record that

The monotone of the first five minutes of his speech was amusing the House, but the enjoyment reached a climax when little

Mr. Jowett, the mildest-mannered Socialist that ever scuttled a ship of State, interjected in a weak, piping voice: 'Dearly beloved brethren'. Members on both sides had to hold their sides with laughter, and the fun was further increased when one of the Hibernian contingent, in a voice that was an equally faultless imitation of Mr. Hoare's, ejaculated 'I don't like London'. Memories of the distressed curate in 'The Private Secretary' [a well-known play translated from the German by Charles Hawtrey] flashed through all our minds and it was some time before Mr. Hoare was able to resume his speech. The polite attentions were continued from that moment to the end of his remarks, one member piously exclaiming at one point 'Amen' and another 'The collection will now be taken up' ...

Elsewhere in the press this description of Hoare's discomfiture was dismissed as 'pure caricature'.[45] A better test of Hoare's standing, it was claimed, was the tribute paid to him by the Prime Minister himself only a few days after this incident, in the committee stage of the Government of Ireland Bill. Hoare had moved an amendment to increase the membership of the proposed nominated Irish Senate from forty to eighty, on the grounds that since the Irish Lower House was to have 164 members the Senate would be easily out-voted in any joint session convened to resolve differences between the Houses. Asquith, while rejecting the amendment on the familiar argument of the popular sovereignty enshrined in the elected Lower House, prefaced his remarks by congratulating Hoare on 'the great ability and moderation' with which he had presented his case and expressing the general pleasure at hearing 'a comparatively junior member develop a proposition of great importance like this with so much skill and parliamentary ability': a commendation which, according to *The Times*, evoked cheers of approval (which, however, went unrecorded in *Hansard*).[46]

By August 1914 Hoare had established a reputation as (to use his own retrospective words many years later) 'an industrious apprentice to the trade of politics'.[47] To informed observers the next step in his career was seen to be office in a Conservative administration, the formation of which – in view of the Liberal government's by-election record – might well come sooner rather than later. The post most frequently mentioned for him by unofficial Cabinet-makers was that of President of the Board of Education; and the widespread welcome given to the progressive proposals in the report he wrote on 'Education and Social Reform' did nothing to lessen the appropriateness of the selection.[48]

With the coming of war predictions of an early Conservative administration had to be revised. In May 1915 what would have been inconceivable a brief year before took place and Conservatives entered a coalition government with the Liberals. By that time, however, Hoare — now the second baronet on the death of his father in January 1915 — had begun a new, if temporary, career as a soldier. In the scramble for posts which the coalition entailed no one seems to have thought of recalling Hoare from his military duties. The beginning of his ministerial career, the *terminus ad quem* of his industrious political apprenticeship, had in fact to wait until the end of coalition government in 1922.

2

Wartime Missions
and Post-war Politics

With the declaration of war against Germany Hoare had no
hesitation in deciding that his political career must take second
place to military service. But not having been a territorial he did
not find it easy to secure an army commission. Approaches to
the Brigade of Guards proved unproductive, as did his attempt
to get a place in the regiment of Norfolk Yeomanry being
formed for overseas service. In some desperation he even got
himself empanelled as a special constable at Fulham town hall
so that he could feel he was making some contribution to the
national war effort. Eventually, in October 1914, he obtained,
through the good offices of his Norfolk friend Lord Hastings, a
commission as a temporary lieutenant in a second regiment of
Norfolk Yeomanry and there followed weeks of training and
cavalry exercises at Melton Constable in Norfolk, preparatory
to posting to a front. The training had not been completed,
however, when just before Christmas 1914 Hoare contracted a
serious illness the nature of which his papers do not reveal, although it could conceivably have been a recurrence of the
typhoid fever that had struck him down four years before.
Whatever the illness, the medical opinion was that on recovery
he would not be fit for active service overseas. Thus when Hoare
returned to military duties in the spring of 1915 he was placed
in charge of the Norfolk Yeomanry recruiting office, based in
the cattle market at Norwich. This was to be the rather in-
congruous milieu of Hoare's war service for the next nine
months or so, made more tolerable by the fact that as Lady
Maud was able to join him in a house in Norwich they could
resume something akin to normal domestic life.

The duties afforded in Norwich cattle market were unlikely for long to satisfy Hoare's constant urge to be productively employed. He searched about for some kind of absorbing mental activity: and, as at another period of relative marking time – during his final year at Oxford waiting for a second try at an All Souls fellowship – he turned to the study of a language. At Oxford it had been Italian but now, with some prescience, he selected a language which was hardly known in England at the time although spoken by one of its two principal allies in the war against the Central Powers – Russian. Its mastery would clearly present an intellectual challenge and once acquired would provide, Hoare calculated, the possibility of an interesting wartime assignment, perhaps as an interpreter on one of the missions that from time to time were sent to Russia. Fortunately a large library of Russian books was at his disposal at the house, ten miles north of Norwich, of his friend and distant cousin, William John Birkbeck, much of whose life had been devoted to fostering relations between the Anglican and Russian Orthodox churches and who knew Russia well. And Hoare was even able to obtain the services of a Russian tutor through the agency of the Russian ambassador in London. By the end of 1915 he felt he was sufficiently competent in the language to put it to use and jumped at Birkbeck's suggestion that he accompany him on an unofficial goodwill mission to Russia as his secretary. But the proposal was turned down by the War Office and the Foreign Office on the grounds that Hoare's position as army officer and M.P. would detract from the private nature of the mission. At almost the same time two separate military missions were departing for Russia; Hoare tried to join the staff of both but again his efforts were in vain. Then, on a short visit to London at the end of January 1916, he chanced to meet John Baird, a parliamentary friend who had just returned from military service in Belgium and was now in the department of the Director of Military Intelligence at the War Office. Baird promised to explore the possibilities of a job in the D.M.I.'s department and to let Hoare know if anything came of it. In a week or two's time Hoare was delighted to get from Baird a letter whose depreciatory tone could not conceal the fact that here at last was something that could really absorb his energies. 'There is a billet in Petrograd', Baird wrote, 'but not a very good one. It may suit you however. Come and talk about it when you come to London.'[1] Hoare needed no further bidding. He hurried to London, where he had a brief interview with the head of the secret intelligence service, Captain Mansfield Cumming, and somewhat more extensive discussions with the Director of Military Intelligence and his staff, particularly with a friend from cricket and tennis, Colonel Freddy Browning, the head of the War Trade Intelligence Department which co-ordinated economic intelligence work in close co-operation with the Admiralty. Baird's 'billet' turned out to be an assignment with the British intelligence mission attached to the Russian imperial general staff at Petrograd (as St Petersburg had been retitled in 1914).

All the Allied Powers had secret service missions in each other's countries — directed against the enemy and not (at least, ostensibly) against the host country. The missions were engaged, on the one hand, in espionage and secret service work and, on the other, counter-espionage to protect the Allies from the multifarious enemy attempts to obtain information about them (in Britain the first activity came under M.I.5, the latter — counter-intelligence activities — under M.I.6). They were duly accredited to the various governments, working in closest liaison with them and usually installed with the allied army or in the offices of its general staff. A British intelligence mission had been sent to Russia in the early days of the war and had worked in Petrograd alongside the Russian general staff with varying success ever since.

Being new organisations and working in a delicate and some-what indeterminate field demarcation problems sometimes arose between secret service activities and those of the established institutions of inter-allied relations, the embassies and legations, and particularly the military and naval attachés on the embassy staffs. There were some, indeed, who argued that military intelligence or secret service work should be handled by embassy service attachés along with their other duties. But the British tradition of functional separation between diplomacy and secret service was a strong one, while the complexity and novelty of secret service work in wartime was not necessarily to be easily mastered by officials trained in the more conventional methods of diplomacy. The organisational problems, however, were considerable and inter-departmental wrangling about the exact place that secret service should hold in the official hierarchy echoed in both Whitehall and missions overseas. One such controversy had been rumbling away for some time in connection with the British special intelligence mission in Petrograd and Hoare's 'billet' was to go out as an additional member with the particular function of smoothing out the differences which had arisen; he was initially to go for two or three months in order to study the situation and then return to London to make a report.

Before leaving for Russia Hoare had to undergo several weeks of specialist training in espionage and counter-espionage, coding and ciphering, war trade and contraband, postal and telegraph censorship and other tools of the intelligence trade. On 18th March, 1916, he sailed from Newcastle and eight days later, after a circuitous passage of the North Sea to avoid German submarines and a tedious series of train journeys through Norway, Sweden and Finland, arrived in Petrograd. He lost no time in getting down to work, for on 28th March he was writing to Lady Maud (who had not been able to accompany her husband):

> It takes a day or two getting one's feel especially as my commission is a somewhat vague one. However, I am now started ... Things are much smoother although there are still various points to be improved and reformed ... As a result of various conversations I am going through all the papers in the office. This will certainly take me several weeks ...[2]

He found time, however, to make the contacts which were so essential for intelligence work. On the very day of his arrival in Petrograd he found himself lunching in his hotel at the next table to Professor Bernard Pares, a leading authority on Russia who was then working with the Russian Red Cross. The two men had a long talk about the current situation and from their conversation soon came contacts of even greater importance to Hoare: with Harold Williams, correspondent of the *Daily Chronicle* (and later to be foreign editor of *The Times*), probably the best-informed Englishman on Russian affairs; and with the distinguished Russian economist and politician, Peter Struve. At the British Embassy Hoare renewed an acquaintance, made during the investigations of the Royal Commission on the Civil Service, with Frank Lindley, who was now counsellor and thus second in command to the ambassador, Sir George Buchanan. Lindley and his wife were invaluable in showing the new arrival the sights of Petrograd and introducing him to a whole range of diplomatic and Russian contacts. On 28th March Hoare lunched with the ambassador and on the following day — only three days after his arrival in Petrograd — with a senior member of the Russian government, Sazonoff, the Foreign Minister (who three months later was to be unceremoniously dismissed from office by the Tsar). In May he lunched in even more august company when he was invited, along with numerous other guests, to visit the Tsar's military headquarters at Moghilieff. The Tsar, who spoke to Hoare on two occasions during the visit, struck him as being 'very lively', while he thought the Tsarina 'very beautiful' and the young Tsarevitch 'a delightful and very good-looking boy tearing about all over the place and in riotous spirits'.[3]

By the middle of May Hoare considered that he was in a position to return to London in order to report on his investigation of the workings of the intelligence mission. But before he could do so he was amazed to receive from London instructions to take over command of the mission himself from its current chief, Major C. J. M. Thornhill. Hoare was by no means pleased by this turn of events. He wrote to his wife on 25th May that Thornhill was much the best man for the job and the sudden change would 'make hay of the whole mission', just when he (Hoare) was 'on the point of getting everybody smoothed down'. He persuaded London to agree to keep the whole thing quiet until he could give a personal report on the difficulties.[4] On 9th June he arrived back in England. His first tour of duty in Russia had come to an end.

Hoare seems to have spent about a fortnight in London. On 12th June he was received by the King and Queen at Buckingham Palace. He spent much time in discussion with, among others, the Foreign Secretary, Sir Edward Grey (whom Hoare thought evinced 'hopeless fatalism' about war prospects), Lord Robert Cecil, the Minister of Blockade, Freddy Browning and senior members of the D.M.I.'s department in the War Office. Despite his reservations about it in Petrograd he now definitely accepted appointment as head of the intelligence mission. But he was troubled about the military status of the post. It was important, he felt, in view of the rather equivocal nature of the mission *vis-à-vis* other British military organisations in Russia, that its head should have a rank which would put him on more or less level terms with more orthodox British officers in the Russian capital. Thornhill, three years his junior in age, had been a major; he himself was only a captain. Hoare began what he described as an 'agitation' to get himself promoted lieutenant-colonel.[5] The desired promotion seems, however, to have presented difficulties for the authorities and in the end Hoare had to be content with only partial success: he was promoted lieutenant-colonel but only on a temporary and unpaid basis. The question of status was still rankling with him when his Russian service came to an end.

Towards the end of June 1916 Hoare left Britain for Russia again, this time in company with Lady Maud, and officially assumed control of the intelligence mission in Petrograd on 1st July. He had initially been somewhat nervous of his reception there since while he was away efforts had been made to retain his predecessor, Thornhill, and the ambassador, Buchanan, had telegraphed to London with this request. But the problem seems to have been solved by appointing Thornhill to a vacancy as assistant military attaché at the embassy.[6] Hoare was now head of his own show which, although a relatively modest one, gave him unique insights into war operations, the domestic politics of allied countries and international relations.

The British intelligence mission had grown considerably since Hoare first joined it in March. Then it was wholly accommodated in the office of the Russian general staff in Dvortzovaya Square, facing the Winter Palace. Now its staff, under Hoare, of five army officers, three naval reserve officers and nine civilians was rather inconveniently dispersed over this and two other buildings. In addition to its secret service work the mission provided interpreters for visiting British military personnel; organised the exchange with the Russians of military intelligence, particularly about troop dispositions (called 'identifications') on both Germany's military fronts; maintained control over all travellers proceeding to the West from Russia and Romania; and — a function which was much expanded under Hoare's regime — the collection and transmission of war trade intelligence, especially as concerned the blockade of the Central Powers. The mission was not officially concerned with intelligence about Russia itself nor with purely political or diplomatic activities which were within the province of the British embassy. But Hoare himself was not disposed to interpret this restriction too literally.

Much of the 'straight' secret service work was of a routine character: 'the signalling of suspected persons, the holding up of contraband, the transmission of agents' reports, and the exchange of departmental memoranda.'[7] It also, of course, involved the esoteric business of codes and ciphers — both using one's own and cracking the enemy's. Hoare was expected to work closely with the Russian secret service but this was no easy task. The Tsarist administration in Petrograd was no Whitehall, and Hoare felt his superiors in London did not sufficiently realise this. As he wrote later:

> When I received urgent wires from London demanding at a moment's notice this or that confirmation about a suspect or contraband trade or troop movements, there was no one man or single department that could give it to me. For hours, perhaps even for days and weeks, I must have recourse to official after official and it was probable that by the time I received any answer the information was useless.[8]

One of the principal tasks picked out in Hoare's terms of appointment was that 'to inquire into all matters connected with Enemy Trading ... [including] questions affecting the improvement of our own trade, which would otherwise be taken by the enemy.'[9] And it was in this field that Hoare made perhaps his most significant contribution to the allied war effort while in Russia. Rather belatedly the Russians had set up a blockade organisation following the Inter-Allied Blockade Conference in Paris early in 1915. The organisation, within the Ministry of Trade and Industry, consisted of a Russian Committee for the Restriction of Enemy Supplies under the chairmanship of Peter Struve, to whom Hoare had been introduced by Harold Williams. Struve invited Hoare to join his committee, and although this was one of those matters which involved demarcation problems with the embassy — since strictly speaking the British representative should have been an embassy official —

Hoare was helped by the fact that no appropriate embassy official could speak Russian. Thus, *faute de mieux,* he participated in Struve's committee, putting his hard-won knowledge of Russian to excellent account.

The work of the committee led to the tightening of the blockade in the Baltic and better control of certain important exports from Russia to Germany, while the information Hoare gained from his attendance, including memoranda on contraband between Germany and Russia and secret intelligence about the internal state of Germany, was invaluable for the blockade authorities, particularly the War Trade Intelligence Department. It does not seem that Hoare was overstating his case when, in a report on the work of his mission he prepared at the end of January 1917, he wrote:

> When I took charge of the Mission last July I found that the various Russian Departments dealing with War Trade and Blockade were practically without any information whatever as to the policy and statistics of the Blockade. A similar ignorance of the statistics and policy of the Russian Government existed in London. The result was not only mutual ignorance but the existence of friction which threatened to become serious to the continuation of the Blockade. I accordingly did what I could to remedy this state of affairs. The result has been that, with the knowledge and approval of the Embassy in Petrograd and the Foreign Office in London, I have arranged for an extensive interchange of the numerous War Trade returns and Reports that are circulated in London and Petrograd, and I am now regarded as the Representative of the Ministry of Blockade in Russia ... The Russians would have been unable to produce the Black List [of firms trading with the Central Powers in goods which helped their war operations] without my assistance.[10]

Hoare sent to the War Trade Intelligence Department four series of weekly returns of (1) export licences granted by Struve's committee; (2) goods exported from Russia; (3) goods passing the Finnish frontier in transit from Russia to Scandinavia and (4) direct exports from Finland (then still under Russian control) to Scandinavia. An official of the department in effect confirmed the value of the information Hoare had sent when, in May 1917

— after Hoare had left Russia — he wrote to the Foreign Office to bemoan the fact that in Hoare's absence and with the disorganisation of administrative machinery under the Russian Provisional Government his department was no longer getting reliable statistics from Russia.[11]

Although the terms of Hoare's appointment formally excluded him from concern with the political and diplomatic matters which passed through the British embassy, this interdict was difficult to observe for someone with Hoare's political experience and interests and he does not seem to have made any superhuman efforts to deny himself. Indeed, it was hardly necessary to do so since the ambassador himself made use of Hoare's services for various purposes, including occasional visits to see the Tsar at his headquarters or at his palace at Tsarkoe Selo, some miles from Petrograd (which the Tsar rarely visited after assuming command of the army in September 1915). But Hoare's contacts with Russian political life ranged much more widely and deeply than those afforded at the increasingly isolated imperial court. He made discreet but effective use of his intelligence 'cover' as a British M.P. to associate with Russian politicians. He had particularly good contacts, largely through Harold Williams and Peter Struve, with the constitutional democratic party, or Kadets, which was one of the largest of the numerous party groupings in the fourth Duma (1912–16), whose proceedings Hoare frequently attended. The Kadet party was the most attached to western forms of parliamentary government and was determinedly pro-Ally and pro-war. With their commitment to the war and their liberal reformist programme they represented for Hoare the left in Russian politics, and the main opposition to reactionary and pro-German elements on the right. He did not take into account those with more radical solutions, either democratic socialists like Kerensky or — more understandably, since it was largely underground and its leadership either in prison or in exile — the Bolshevik movement.

Hoare's rationalisation of his attempts to feel the political pulse of Russia while being ostensibly a military intelligence officer was that the state of administration and public morale had serious reactions on Russia's fighting capacity. He was convinced that 'the rear in Russia mattered more than the front, and that politics were often more important than strategy'.[12]

His evaluations of the rapidly changing situation were incorporated in long periodic letters to the Directorate of Military Intelligence at the War Office (although he was careful to keep Sir George Buchanan informed of their contents). Several of these reports were published in his book *The Fourth Seal*. They record his contempt for an administrative machinery which could not alleviate crucial food shortages, in a country which normally grew large quantities of wheat and had recently enjoyed a good harvest; his belief — shared by his Kadet friends — in the malign policy influence at the imperial court of Rasputin and others, the so-called 'Dark Forces', although Hoare later came to realise that the charges of pro-German and anti-war sympathies of the court circle were almost entirely unfounded. He reported the Duma debates in some detail, including those in November and December 1916 (just before the Duma's adjournment) in which liberals and right-wing conservatives joined in condemning the Dark Forces and submitted a 'Grand Remonstrance' to the Tsar calling for administrative reform. On 28th December, the very day the Duma was adjourned, Rasputin was murdered and Hoare sent to London one of the first accounts of that sensational event. Indeed, so close was he to the twists and turns of Russian affairs that he and his staff came under suspicion at the imperial court of being implicated in the deed in some way and Buchanan had to have an interview with the Tsar to deny the ludicrous charge.[13]

Robert Bruce Lockhart, who was acting consul-general in Moscow while Hoare was in Petrograd, and frequently met him, has testified to the 'unflagging and unobtrusive enthusiasm' with which Hoare, having mastered sufficient Russian, set about the task of gathering political intelligence. Hoare, he wrote, 'made it his business to meet every class of Russian. He gathered in his information from many fields, and, unlike most intelligence officers, he showed a fine discrimination in sifting the truth from the chaff of rumour.'[14] It would, however, have needed quite remarkable insight and unique sources of information for even a highly intelligent observer like Hoare to have anticipated, at the end of 1916, the world-shaking events of the year about to open. He exaggerated, as he later admitted, the likely beneficial effects of Rasputin's murder, from having earlier subscribed to the general over-estimate of Rasputin's influence while he was alive.[15] In one of his last reports, dated 20th January, 1917 (which owed much to a long conversation he had had with Prince Lvov, chairman of the influential union of Russian local authorities and a leading member of the Kadet party) he did speculate on the possibility of the declaration of a provisional government but on the whole thought it would not happen in the immediate future 'though it is much nearer than might be supposed'. Of the two other possibilities he discussed in the same report — that 'the Emperor may give way as he gave way in 1906, when the Duma was established' and that 'things may continue to drift from bad to worse as they are drifting now' — he thought that mere drift was the more likely. 'In any case the situation is most unsatisfactory.'[16]

But if at this time Hoare, along with every other observer, did not foresee the Russian revolution at least he had no illusions about Russia's war-weariness and longing for peace. In his report on 26th December, 1916, he wrote:

> The conditions of life have become so intolerable, the Russian casualties have been so heavy, the ages and classes subject to military service have been so widely extended, the disorganisation of the administration and the untrustworthiness of the Government have become so notorious that it is not a matter of surprise if the majority of ordinary people reach at any peace straw. *Personally I am convinced that Russia will never fight through another winter.* The danger of an immediate peace has been for the moment removed by the fact that the peace proposals are identified in the public mind with the intrigues of the reactionary clique that has lately made itself so unpopular. People in England should not, however, be blind to the fact that amongst the civilian population of Russia there is little enthusiasm for the war.[17]

It was in an attempt to bolster the waning Russian war effort that a joint British-French-Italian delegation under the leadership of Lord Milner, a member of Lloyd George's new War Cabinet, was sent to Russia at the end of January 1917. Hoare was sceptical of the mission's chances of alleviating the situation short of an undertaking (which the French would never give) to divert troops and material from the western to the eastern fronts. He made it his business, however, to brief Milner on the depressing facts of the current position and arranged for him to meet Struve for dinner at the Hoares' flat. The meeting was not a great success — there was a language difficulty and the two men seemed unimpressed with each other — but there is some indication that the report Milner gave to the Tsar at the end of his mission discreetly reflected the bitter criticisms of administrative failings that had been made to him by Struve.[18]

The Milner mission in fact represented the effective end of Hoare's work in Petrograd. He had become increasingly dissatisfied with his role there. There were the long-standing difficulties inherent in the complexities of the Russian bureaucracy with which he had to deal, coupled with the simpler but nonetheless aggravating problems of maintaining supervision of a mission staff dispersed over three separate buildings. And then there was his health. He had not been fully fit when he came to Russia and the climatic extremes of Petrograd weather — which Hoare loathed — had exacerbated his disposition to heavy colds and influenza.

But the decisive blow seems to have been a redefinition of his terms of reference, made without his prior knowledge or concurrence. The secret and thus inevitably rather vague nature of Hoare's duties had from the first raised the possibility of demarcation disputes with the more conventional military representatives, particularly the military attaché, Colonel Alfred Knox, and his staff. Hoare's relations with Knox were strained, especially after he had replaced Thornhill in charge of the intelligence mission: Knox's two volumes of Russian memoirs (published in 1921) significantly make no mention of Hoare but give the impression that Thornhill was 'Chief of the Intelligence Section' throughout Hoare's time in Russia.[19] The decision to alter Hoare's responsibilities, which was notified to him in January 1917, undoubtedly reflected this conflict with the military attaché. Henceforward the attaché and his staff were to take over identifications (of enemy units on the fighting fronts) and the distribution of military intelligence reports, leaving only war trade information, military control of travellers and secret service work with the intelligence mission.[20]

Hoare did not take this demotion lying down. General Sir Henry Wilson had accompanied the Milner delegation to Russia and Hoare seized the opportunity of enlisting his influential help on his side. In a letter to Wilson dated 7th February, some two weeks before the delegation left Russia, Hoare gave voice to his complaints:

> I cannot continue in Russia if the question of the mutual rela-
> tions between the various organisations is continuously re-
> opened. As it is, I have been working for a year ... with the
> temporary rank of Lieutenant-Colonel and the pay of a Yeo-
> manry Captain. I do not, however, mind so much about the
> pay as the fact that so long as I am not a General Staff
> Officer, I appear not to be fully recognised by the War Office.
> Thirdly, my health has been so bad during the last year that
> from every personal consideration I would welcome the
> opportunity of giving up my present work ...[21]

Hoare's outburst does not seem to have led to any reconsidera-
tion of the new division of functions but it may well have precipitated the decision that, in view of his health, he and Lady
Maud should accompany the Milner mission on its journey back
to Britain so that he could take some convalescent leave.

The Hoares arrived back in Britain at the beginning of
March. After some two weeks of much needed convalescence
Hoare set about composing a series of reports about his work in
Russia for his superiors in the War Office and the Foreign
Office. By this time the dramatic events subsumed under the
title of the February Revolution[22] had taken place: the Petro-
grad riots of 10th March, the formation of the Provisional
Government under Prince Lvov on 12th March, the Guards'
mutiny in Petrograd on 13th March and the abdication of the
Tsar on 15th March. In general Hoare was optimistic about the
effects of the revolution on the Russian war effort, largely because he believed that the politicians he knew best — people like
Prince Lvov and Mikyukov of the Kadet party — were now in
command of the situation. He concluded a report dated 17th
March with the confident assertion, all too soon to be falsified
by events:

> ... the Allies may now rest assured that Russia will not make
> a separate peace. For months past I was convinced that in-
> ternal demoralisation made it impossible for Russia to con-
> tinue the War over the winter of 1917. I now believe that the

unity of national action which has been made possible by the Revolution will enable Russia to continue fighting until Germany is definitely defeated.[23]

The original intention seems to have been for Hoare to return to Petrograd, either to resume control of the intelligence mission (a subsequent idea no doubt prompted by his difficulties with the military attaché) as war trade adviser to the embassy.[24] In the event he did not return to Russia. Instead he was appointed to command the special intelligence section of the British military mission to the Italian general staff and by May 1917 Hoare and Lady Maud were installed in Rome. His status there was to be more assured than that which had troubled him in his similar post in Russia. Although still a temporary lieutenant-colonel he was now paid as such and before long he was to gain the rank of general staff officer, first grade, which had been denied him in Petrograd. Moreover, his Russian services were recognised by the award in the 1917 Birthday Honours List of a companionship of the order of St Michael and St George (C.M.G.), to add to the Russian order of St Stanislas that he had received from the Tsar. He had reason for some satisfaction with his achievements to date as he took up his new duties in Rome.

Hoare's instructions for his Italian mission required him to transmit to London information on the dispositions ('identifications') of enemy forces on all fronts other than the Italian front itself (the sphere of the British military attaché), the Russian and the Romanian; on neutral countries; on internal conditions in enemy countries; on espionage and counter-espionage; on war trade and economic matters; and on naval questions.[25] But while Hoare discharged these functions with his usual competence his politician's eye discerned the key importance of another task, outside his formal terms of appointment: that of fostering those forces in Italian life which favoured whole-hearted commitment to the war against the Central Powers. For the Italians were reluctant combatants only. Until 1915, indeed, Italy had formally been a partner of Germany and Austria-Hungary in the so-called Triple Alliance of 1882. It had joined the rival combination in April 1915 only on the guarantee in the secret Treaty of London that the eventual peace settlement would give Italy very substantial territorial gains at the expense of its neighbours, in addition to colonial expansion in Africa. From the first the leaders who had brought Italy into the war, like the Foreign Minister, Sonnino, wanted the commitment to be limited. The original declaration of war was confined to Italy's territorial neighbour and rival, Austria-Hungary; with Germany it was at first merely a severance of diplomatic relations, with a declaration of war not coming until August 1916. The fact that Britain and France looked upon Germany, not Austria-Hungary, as the main enemy, together with Italian reluctance to become more deeply involved, gave Italy an insecure and equivocal position among the Allied Powers.

The year of Hoare's arrival in Rome — 1917 — was to be the moment of truth for Italy. Lack of support from its allies, the material losses inflicted on its seaborne supplies by the new German campaign of unrestricted submarine warfare, the difficulties of the terrain on the battlefront in northern Italy, and the concentration of Austro-Hungarian troops in Italy following the final military collapse of Russia, led to the disastrous defeat at Caporetto on 24th October. But the task of the Italian armed forces was made no easier by the strong social and political currents running against Italian involvement in the war. The orthodox Socialists, among whom the former Prime Minister, Giolitti, was a leading influence, were pacifist and, at the other end of the political spectrum, the hierarchy of the Roman Catholic Church in the Vatican had divided allegiances in a war in which Italy was ranged as an ally with Orthodox Russia against enemies which included Catholic Austria: a papal encyclical calling for immediate peace was published soon after Hoare's arrival in Rome. For many Italians the war in any case must have seemed a very distant affair, even if they acknowledged the merits of Italian participation. Indeed, the profitable financial and commercial traffic between Germany and industrial northern Italy through Switzerland went on virtually uninterrupted, both before and after the Italian declaration of war against Germany.

Hoare early formed the impression that, as in the case of Russia, insufficient account was being taken of the danger signs in Italy. He made it his business to collect the necessary information and relay it to London in the form of regular reports to Colonel Browning at the War Office.[26] He was well placed for making contacts with various official and unofficial levels of Italian society. The special intelligence mission of which he was head had its headquarters in Rome, where it co-operated with the Italian directorate of military information; but it also had offices in Milan and Turin that were in touch not only with front line intelligence but with public opinion generally in northern Italy. Hoare at once developed this contact with industrial and commercial Italy, first by opening an office in Genoa and then by attaching intelligence officers to the British consulates in Leghorn and Naples. This chain of information posts enabled him, as he later described it, 'to penetrate into some of the inner recesses of Italian life'.[27]

In Rome Hoare, with the knowledge and approval of the British ambassador, Sir Rennell Rodd, sought out contacts who could give him first-hand information about political developments. As with Harold Williams in Petrograd, it was a newspaperman — this time William Miller, Rome correspondent of the *Morning Post* — who was able to introduce Hoare to some of the leading political figures: men like Giolitti and Luigi Luzzatti outside the government and, among ministers, Bissolati (whom he found to be a 'very attractive Socialist' ready to keep him 'regularly informed of the swaying battle in the Cabinet and the Chamber between the war party and the neutralists'),[28] Sonnino and Nitti. With non-official political life Hoare's chief link was Professor Matteo Pantaleoni, an extreme nationalist but ardent anglophile whom Hoare frequently visited at his house in the Via Giulia, which was a centre of the pro-war or interventionist circle; Ricciotti Garibaldi, son of the great Italian patriot, also became a firm friend among the same circle.

As the summer of 1917 advanced Hoare became increasingly disturbed about the state of Italian morale, particularly in the industrial north. In several towns, notably Turin, there had been serious food riots. In the key city of Milan, in which much of Hoare's efforts were concentrated, the daily paper *Avanti* was the main vehicle of the neutralist propaganda of the pacifist wing of Milan's Socialists, the strongest party in the city. But the Milan Socialists also had an interventionist wing, of which the leading voice was the daily *Popolo d'Italia*, edited by Benito Mussolini, to whose name and career as 'a dashing and brilliant journalist' Hoare was one of the first to draw the attention of the authorities in London. It was Mussolini's influence, Hoare told Browning, that had prevented the kind of unrest in Milan which had afflicted other northern cities in the late summer.[29]

Hoare was in England for leave and consultations when news of the Austro-Hungarian offensive leading to the Italian rout at Caporetto on 24th October began to reach London. He hurried back to Italy, to witness at first hand the universal signs of overwhelming military defeat in the masses of dishevelled soldiery and displaced civilians thronging the roads in frightened disorder. The Italian army, having lost its main positions and hundreds of thousands of men, was in desperate need of Allied reinforcements. The time was past for Allied dismissal of the Italian front as a sideshow or Italian reluctance to accept significant aid for fear of becoming committed to a wider involvement in the war. Five divisions of British troops were sent to Italy from France in November, and Hoare's intelligence mission was closely involved with this British expeditionary force. It was now that he became a general staff officer, represented at the front by two of his staff while he himself concentrated his main work behind the lines in Rome, Milan, Naples and Genoa.

From the point of view of continued Italian participation in the war the most important domestic political event was the formation in December 1917 of a new interventionist group in the Italian Parliament under the title of *Fascio di Defensa Nationale* (Association for National Defence). The leaders were Hoare's friend Pantaleoni and the fiercely anti-German republican deputy Pirolini, and it was at Pantaleoni's house that Hoare got early information of the group's founding. It was soon able to claim a membership of 158 deputies and 92 senators, all pledged to combat defeatism and keep the coalition government which Orlando had formed after Caporetto from flirting with the neutralist Giolittian Parliamentary Union.

The *Fascio* set about organising a network of pro-war 'cells' in the country to support its parliamentary efforts. Hoare immediately saw an opening for channelling some discreet British assistance for activities so obviously expedient for the Allied cause. At the beginning of the new year (1918) he wrote to Sir

George Macdonogh, the Director of Military Intelligence at the War Office:

> I have seen Pirolini and am in touch indirectly with most of the active members of the pro-war party. I am absolutely convinced that if we are to keep Italy in the war we must play up to these people. Accordingly I have taken the step of giving them £100 towards the big pro-war demonstration that they are organising on the day of the opening of Parliament in a few weeks' time. Workmen will be brought from all the industrial cities of Italy and it is intended that the demonstration will be so representative and impressive that it will be impossible for Orlando to shilly-shally over the war. I hope that you will approve of this action ... I shall not be connected directly with the transaction at all ... I understand the French are also supporting the demonstration.

At the same time as seeking the D.M.I.'s retrospective approval of his initiative over the Milan demonstration, Hoare had a proposal to make to assist Mussolini's journalistic activities in the same city:

> The French are also prepared to support the pro-war labour paper in Milan, the *Popolo d'Italia*. Would you let me use my discretion in supporting it as well? ... If you agree I will take every precaution to avoid having any direct connection with the transaction whatever.

It was essential, Hoare impressed upon Macdonogh, to seize opportunities of this kind when they offered themselves if Italy were not to collapse as he had seen Russia collapsing. All that was needed now was a little judicious financial help. For the moment the intelligence mission was without funds and Hoare had advanced the £100 for the demonstration from his own account.[30] In a few days £250 was telegraphed to him and Macdonogh, in informing him that his proposals had been agreed in principle, asked him to estimate the cost of assisting Mussolini's newspaper. Hoare replied that his approximate estimate was £50 a month but that he proposed to pay by results only. Macdonogh was clearly well content to leave matters in Hoare's hands.[31] Thus it was that a British wartime military intelligence officer and future Foreign Secretary was able to assist a socialist agitator and journalist in Milan and future Italian dictator in the common cause of defeating Germany and its allies; it seems virtually certain, however, that the two men never met at the time — Hoare's discretion saw to that.[32]

Hoare clearly felt that the investment in Mussolini was worthwhile. He increasingly feared that Italy might succumb to the forces that had engulfed Russia. In a report in February 1918 he described Italy as providing particularly favourable soil 'for the spread of Bolshevism'. The two chief danger points were Florence and Naples. In industrial Milan, however, the working classes, earning high wages in the munitions factories were, on the whole 'adopting a patriotic attitude'. Mussolini's *Popolo d'Italia* was 'not only carrying on a most vigorous pro-war propaganda, but had increased its circulation from 30,000 to 60,000 copies a day'.[33] By June, when Hoare returned to Italy after two months' home leave, he found the internal situation slightly more encouraging than when he had left for England in April. Morale had improved with the removal of the fear of famine, and the position in northern Italy, always Hoare's main centre of interest, was encouraging: in the problem cities of Turin and Genoa as well as in Milan which (as he reported to London on 28th June) 'thanks not a little to the action of the Socialist Mussolini has always had its heart in the war'. But he was still worried about the potentialities of a Bolshevik revolution, expecially in Turin where food prices were higher than in any other city in Italy and still rising. Hoare came increasingly to look upon the Catholic Church, despite its lukewarm attitude to the war, as the main bulwark against the spread of communism. As Cardinal Gaspari, the Papal Secretary of State told him (in a conversation Hoare recorded in his report of 16th November, 1918), 'We do not like Revolution. The Vatican has too many windows on the street.'

Hoare's horizons while in Italy were by no means limited to the Italian domestic situation. He continued, for example, to take a close interest in Russian affairs and he was able in Rome to help advance a cause which he had much at heart: the struggle of the exiled leaders of the Czechoslovak minorities of the Austro-Hungarian empire to win recognition for Czechoslovak nationality from the Allied Powers in the eventual post-war settlement. The most distinguished British advocate of the cause, R. W. Seton-Watson, Hoare knew from his Oxford days and Seton-Watson had introduced him to Thomas Masaryk in 1915 before Hoare went to Russia; in the following year Hoare met both Beneš and Stefanik, the other principal members of the Czechoslovak leadership. In August 1917 Beneš, now secretary-general of the Czechoslovak National Committee in Paris, visited Rome and Hoare was able materially to assist him in making contacts with the Italian authorities which led to an agreement to allow Czechoslovaks among the Austro-Hungarian prisoners of war in Italy to be formed into military units. And while on leave in London in October 1917 Hoare again effected contacts for the Czechoslovak leaders with, among others, Milner, Balfour (the Foreign Secretary) and Lord Robert Cecil (Balfour's deputy). Beneš later recorded his appreciation of Hoare's efforts:

> Sir Samuel Hoare rendered valuable services to our cause in Rome, and later also in London. I kept him informed about everything I was doing in Rome, and he passed this information to his Ambassador there, from whom details reached the Government circles in London. Through him, too, I made an attempt from Rome to secure the consent of the British Government to our military enterprise, and he it was who suggested that I should visit London for the purpose of taking the same measures there with regard to the recognition of the National Council as I had done in Rome. He promised to prepare the ground in London to this end, and he kept his promise. Later on, when I actually visited London, he introduced me to Government circles, and notably to Lord Robert Cecil, who was then acting as deputy Foreign Secretary. When I sent telegraphic reports to Masaryk on the subject of my negotiations in Rome it was Sir Samuel Hoare who forwarded them through English official channels.[34]

Hoare undoubtedly played a part in securing British recognition of the Czechoslovaks under Masaryk and Beneš as an Allied nation and of the Czechoslovak National Council as trustee for a future Czechoslovak government which was enshrined in the declaration signed by Balfour as Foreign Secretary in August 1918. The new nation marked its appreciation of his services with the award of the Czechoslovak *Croix de Guerre* in March

1919. Even ten years after the war had ended Beneš could still recall with gratitude Hoare's role as 'one of the first and most helpful advisers in our struggle for ... Czechoslovak independence'.[35]

In October 1918 Hoare was once again back in London on leave from his Italian mission, and it was there that he heard of the decisive Italian victory at Vittorio Veneto just as, exactly a year before, he had heard of the devastating defeat at Caporetto. This time there was no need for him to rush back to Italy. Indeed, with a general election clearly imminent, he would have liked to have been shot of the Italian post there and then and to resume his place in British politics. When the Armistice came he naturally felt that his work had come to an end but, after over eighteen months in Italy, he had created so many contacts and initiated so many activities that the actual task of winding up his organisation proved a complicated one. Adopted as the official 'coupon' Coalition Unionist candidate at Chelsea on 19th November, he had to return to Italy before the election on 14th December. He was still there when the result was announced a fortnight later (the delay being caused by the collection of the scattered forces' votes): Hoare had captured nearly 80 per cent of the votes in a low poll, with a majority of 6,740 over his only rival, an independent candidate.

It was not until the middle of January 1919 that, with the closing of the Rome office, Hoare was able to return home again and not until the spring that he was entirely free from his Italian commitments. But if Hoare was glad to have ended his mission, others were not. The *Morning Post* (whose Rome correspondent, William Miller, knew Hoare's activities there well) in its issue of 7th January regretted the closing of the mission which, as a result of making contacts with all classes in the country, had, 'done excellent work in supplying the British Government with sound and accurate information about the real conditions in Italy, such as was not always available before its time'. Hoare's skills in unorthodox but effective diplomacy were to be called on again over twenty years later in Spain. But now it was time to renew — indeed to re-establish — his political career.

The House of Commons which assembled in February 1919 after the election of December 1918 was almost unrecognisable from that in which Hoare had last served full-time over four years before. Among other things, it contained 260 new members, more than any subsequent inter-war Parliament. There had, of course, been the winnowing caused by wartime casualties but even more significant had been the political winnowing, not least in the Liberal party, dichotomised as it was between Lloyd George coalitionists and independent Asquithites. For the Conservative party the chief difference from the last peacetime Parliament was that it was now part of the government ot the day, although it did not exclusively control it.

For Hoare, the reputation he had been building for himself as a diligent backbencher and workmanlike if not exciting parliamentary performer, clearly destined for office, counted for little in the entirely different post-war parliamentary situation. On the other hand, his wartime virtual abstinence from domestic political activity gave him at least two advantages. He was in no way beholden to the coalition government and was thus able to strike out for himself as an independent Conservative, which proved an asset when the time came to form an exclusively Conservative government. Moreover, although he had to construct a second reputation for himself on the backbenches he was immeasurably better equipped as a politician in 1919 than he had been in 1910, or even in 1914. His wartime overseas intelligence service had given him an insight into foreign affairs and defence questions which had previously been outside his scope.

As in the pre-war Parliament Hoare was once again essentially a full-time politician. True, he held directorships in several companies, including the Employers' Liability Assurance, of which he became deputy chairman in 1921, and the Belize Estate and Produce Company (which gave him the opportunity to visit British Honduras early in 1921), but these, while obviously welcome sources of income, did not divert him from his political goals. At this stage those goals, at least the immediate ones, did not include the holding of office in the coalition government: intensely ambitious though he was, there is no evidence that he sought office under Lloyd George. Nevertheless his services were from time to time requested for various other forms of public service and he rarely refused. He was thus able to gain an insight into governmental administration without the constraints that ministerial office would have brought. In 1919, for example, he presided over the Imports Restriction Council of the Board of Trade, which under his chairmanship made recommendations on over 2,000 restrictions on the importation of a wide range of manufactured goods.[36] From May to September 1922 he was chairman of a committee of civil servants (who included the redoubtable Sir John Anderson, then permanent head of the Home Office) which was set up to supervise relief and compensation for Irish loyalists who had fled to England in the wake of the post-war troubles in Ireland.[37] For several weeks at the end of 1921 and early in 1922 Hoare had been concerned, as League of Nations deputy high commissioner for Russian refugees, with another group of civil war victims, much more numerous and in far direr plight: those remnants of the White Russian forces and their supporters who, after final devastating defeat by the Soviet Red Army, had fled to Constantinople. Hoare's report on his mission to Asia Minor led to increased League of Nations assistance and to a speeding up of the permanent resettlement of the refugees in countries like Greece and Czechoslovakia (both of which Hoare also visited).[38]

These last two appointments — as League of Nations deputy high commissioner for Russian refugees and as chairman of the Irish distress committee — in fact serve to symbolise the two main areas of Hoare's political activity in the 1919–22 Parliament. Right at the beginning of that Parliament, in February 1919, he formed with Walter Guinness what came to be known as the Coalition Government Foreign Affairs Committee, although its membership of about twenty backbenchers (with Hoare as chairman and Guinness as secretary) was almost exclusively Conservative. The committee's chief preoccupation initially was with stimulating British governmental support for the various anti-Bolshevik White Russian groups campaigning in Russia. It had close links with the Russian *emigré* organisation in Paris, in which the former Foreign Minister, Sazonoff, and Hoare's Russian colleague Peter Struve were prominent; and with Harold Williams, the foreign editor of *The Times* and the most intimate friend from Hoare's Petrograd days. But the most important link was inside the coalition government — with Winston Churchill, the vehemently anti-Communist Secretary of State for War and Air, whom Hoare kept constantly posted with the views of his committee and the information he gleaned from visits to Paris, Czechoslovakia and Austria.[39] In the spring of 1919 it looked for a brief moment as if the anti-Bolshevik forces might triumph in Russia and on 31st May Hoare wrote to Churchill in euphoric mood to send his 'most sincere congratulations and gratitude' for all that he had done 'in the matter of Russia':

> For the last six months I have been convinced that the whole future of Europe, and indeed of the world, depends upon the Russian settlement and the destruction of Bolshevism. If I may say so you alone of the Allied Ministers have consistently held and expressed the same view. Whilst there was little that I or the group of members with whom I work could accomplish, you fortunately were in a position to carry your convictions into effect. The result is not only a great personal triumph for yourself but also a long step towards a permanent peace.[40]

For his part, Churchill privately acknowledged Hoare's committee to be an 'invaluable aid in the House of Commons' in furthering his campaign for continued British military and other support for the White Russians.[41] But the success was short-lived, and the White Russians lurched from defeat to defeat. All British troops had been withdrawn by the end of October 1919 and all other aid was finally cut off by the end of March 1920. By November 1920 the last White Russian leader, Wrangel, had been driven out of the Crimea and all Russian soil was under the control of the Communists. Hoare bitterly regretted this failure and wished, with Churchill, that the British effort had been more effective. But he did not blame Churchill who, he considered, had done all that it was humanly possible to do as a member of a Cabinet deeply divided over the issue of British intervention in Russia.

When, some fourteen years after its dissolution, Hoare came to write a retrospective (and unpublished) account of his activities in the 1919–22 Parliament he singled out his involvement in the sad and tumultuous affairs of Ireland.[42] Despite his own ancestral connections with southern Ireland he had not, as we have seen, played much part in the pre-war debates on Irish home rule. But this was due not so much to disinterest on his

part as to his even more passionate concern with the con-
temporaneous Welsh church bill. After the war his close connection with Walter Guinness, from one of the most prominent
southern unionist families, brought him into much more immediate touch with Irish affairs. Ireland was in fact the main cement
of a small informal 'Group' of Conservative backbenchers which
numbered Hoare, Guinness, the Irish peer Lord Winterton and
(until he joined the government as a junior minister in April
1921) Edward Wood among its leading members. Among Conservatives Hoare played a mediatorial role in this bitterly contested question. At one extreme, southern unionists like
Guinness were prepared to go a long way in meeting the
demands of Sinn Fein for an independent Irish republic, in
order to ensure reasonable prospects for the 300,000 loyalists in
the south; but they were obstructed at every point by the
vociferous Ulster faction in the Conservative party led, until
February 1921, by the almost insanely uncompromising Carson.
Hoare tried to steer a middle course between the factions, as he
did in other disputes in the party: he was opposed both to the
establishment of an Irish republic and to the coercion of Ulster,
but unlike the diehards in his party he supported conciliation
and concessions to legitimate Irish national feeling. He was, for
example, in favour of the Government of Ireland Bill, the
debates on which occupied much of the time of the House of
Commons in 1920, since it provided immediate practical partition in the shape of separate Dublin and Belfast parliaments,
coupled with an institutional framework for eventual reunion by
agreement. But he thought concessions needed to be made in
the Bill to enlist Irish support and was disappointed when
amendments proposed by his Group to remove the provision for
Irish contributions to the Imperial exchequer and to entrust
the Irish parliaments with full fiscal autonomy were rejected by
the government.[43]

The Government of Ireland Act, when eventually passed at
the end of 1920, proved almost completely irrelevant (except,
later, that part which related to the Belfast parliament). Violence
now completely dominated the situation not only on both sides
of the Irish divide but also, to the permanent detriment of
Britain's good name, among elements of the 'Black and Tans'
and Auxiliaries — of the supposed forces of law and order. Hoare

and his Group were concerned at the failure of the government, in their view, either to prosecute the anti-terrorist campaign effectively or to begin the inevitable negotiations with Irish leaders. After a visit to Ireland in the spring of 1921 Hoare and Guinness submitted a memorandum on the position as they saw it to the Prime Minister and soon afterwards had a meeting with Lloyd George, Austen Chamberlain and Sir Hamar Greenwood, the Chief Secretary for Ireland (whom Hoare considered a 'blusterer ... the worst type of Minister for so delicate a state of affairs').[44] This seemed to have little effect on the government's attitude and the Group was led to step up its campaign to secure an Irish settlement. From June 1921 its members worked in the closest concert with Beaverbrook, whose liberal standpoint on Ireland was in marked contrast to that of his hero Bonar Law (who had resigned from the government on health grounds in March 1921). Hoare, Guinness and other members of the Group were frequent visitors to Beaverbrook's Fulham house, the Vineyard, where serious discussion could always be lightened, weather permitting, by repairing to the tennis court for which Hoare and Beaverbrook (and Bonar Law) shared a passion.

Hoare's collaboration with Beaverbrook over Ireland from the early summer of 1921 seems to have been the real beginning of what for Hoare was his most important political friendship. The Templewood Papers, and even more the Templewood files in the Beaverbrook Papers, contain a frequent and detailed correspondence between the two men which clearly demonstrates that at all major stages of Hoare's political career — except, perhaps, over India in the 1930s, on which their views fundamentally differed — Beaverbrook was his first and principal recourse for advice. It was in many ways a curious relationship, very much a friendship of opposites: between the precise and rather prim although deeply ambitious Conservative politician and the sybaritic, extrovert newspaper owner and political manipulator; between the devoted high churchman and the lapsed presbyterian. For Beaverbrook Hoare represented the best element in the only party through which he could hope to achieve any influence on policy: a progressive and pragmatic element, perhaps open to the sort of radical ideas Beaverbrook wished to purvey. And when Hoare became a minister he was clearly even more influential in the party, besides being an excellent source of intelligence on government thinking. For Hoare there was the benefit of a loyal if erratic friend to encourage and stimulate his political ambitions, and a helpful press medium for the projection of his ideas and career. Until 1940 Beaverbrook never ceased to look upon Hoare as a potential Prime Minister and the references to Hoare in his newspapers were often made in this context.

In the early summer of 1921 any pressure Hoare's group and Beaverbrook might exercise was in practice against a rapidly opening government door. Despite Cabinet agreement on tougher measures against the I.R.A. in May and June,[45] Lloyd George was moving towards some form of settlement, as were Austen Chamberlain and two former ministerial firebrands, Birkenhead, the Lord Chancellor, and Churchill, since February 1921 Colonial Secretary and as such soon to have responsibility for relations with southern Ireland. In July a truce was declared and then began the often tortuous negotiations which led to the signing of the 'Articles of Agreement for a Treaty between Great Britain and Ireland' on 6th November. It was Hoare whom Lloyd George invited to move the Address in reply to the King's Speech opening the special session of Parliament to approve the treaty on 14th December, 1921; a suitable recognition of his prominence in the effort to secure Conservative party backing for a settlement.[46]

The Hoare Group-Beaverbrook alliance was concerned with more than the specific if vital question of Ireland. Ireland was a reflection of a wider factional tension in the Conservative party between the diehards, led by Colonel John Gretton in the Commons and Lord Salisbury in the Lords, and with Lord Hugh Cecil, Sir William Joynson-Hicks and Ronald McNeill prominent in its membership, and the Tory-democratic or progressive wing, in which Hoare and the rest of the Group were recognised to be a central core.[47] The fear of Hoare and his friends, and of Beaverbrook, was that an issue so traumatic for the party as Ireland might lead to a diehard takeover: so pessimistic did Hoare feel about the prospects for his party in November 1921 that he estimated to Beaverbrook, with some obvious exaggeration, that '90 per cent of the Conservative party is drifting Die Hard'.[48] For Ireland was not the only divisive issue. An 'anti-waste' movement against government expenditure was spreading among the Conservative rank and file, fanned by the Rothermere press and Horatio Bottomley. In January 1921 an anti-waste candidate defeated an official Conservative at a by-election at Dover and in June two more official Conservative candidates were defeated in the normally safe Conservative seats of Hertford and St George's, Westminster. In the eight months after the Dover by-election anti-waste candidates were adopted in over twenty constituencies, most of them in London.[49] Hoare had such a candidate in his own constituency of Chelsea and was forced to take counter-action. This he did negatively by demonstrating that he was on the side of the angels as regards economy in public expenditure (for example, by criticising the over-manning of certain government departments) and, more positively, by developing in public speeches what he described to Beaverbrook (who saw that the speeches were covered in his papers) as 'the principles of Tory Democracy against a negative policy of Anti-Waste'.[50]

Hoare was never an enthusiastic supporter of the coalition government and looked with disfavour on the various ineffectual moves, most notably early in 1920, to secure a merger between the Conservative party and Lloyd George's coalition Liberals (in February 1920 he told his friend Frank Lindley, then British representative in Vienna, that he was against a permanent fusion since he did not want 'political cleavage to take the line of Capital v. Labour').[51] On the other hand he believed until well into 1922 that Lloyd George's continuance as Prime Minister was in the best interests of the Conservative party, not least to save it from being dominated by its diehard elements. In a memorandum which Hoare sent to Churchill (with a copy to Beaverbrook) in November 1921 he urged that the Prime Minister should fight the diehards to get an Irish settlement:

If the Prime Minister wants the support of the new generation of Conservatives, he must fight ... If there are any Die-hard Ministers, they must be allowed to resign and their places at once filled by live men of undoubted Tory principles. The Prime Minister should then face Parliament with his newly constituted Government and demand immediately a vote of confidence. If he obtains it, he must go boldly and swiftly on with a definite Irish programme and use every effort to have a *fait accompli*. If he is beaten he must not retire unless he wishes to see his [Conservative anti-diehard] followers destroyed. He must rather make an arresting election appeal to the moderate men of all parties.[52]

Early in the summer of 1922 Hoare's attitude to Lloyd George as Prime Minister underwent a revolutionary change. As late as February of that year he was quite happily forecasting to Frank Lindley that 'there will be an election in June and ... the Coalition in a slightly altered form will get in with a large majority.'[53] But Lloyd George missed the opportunity of an election then and subsequently nothing seemed to go right for him. The European economic conference at Genoa in April and May, hailed by Lloyd George at its opening as the greatest gathering of European nations ever assembled, produced negligible results and damaged Lloyd George's reputation as an international statesman. Moreover, the fact that the Soviet Union was represented aroused the fears of Conservatives (including Hoare) that the Communist regime might be officially recognised. But the event which Hoare and many other contemporary observers felt was most instrumental in bringing to a head Conservative backbench discontent with the coalition government and especially its Prime Minister, was the so-called 'Honours scandal' which, after simmering for several months, erupted into open political conflict in July 1922. In this conflict Hoare played a major critical role and the fact that he did so was symbolic of his new view of Lloyd George. Three months later Lloyd George was out of office, never to return to it – and for that consummation Hoare's responsibility was as great as that of any other political figure.

The question of the award of honours for political services of a financial nature had frequently been aired in Parliament, particularly the House of Lords, since 1914.[54] It was peculiarly one that disturbed the backbenches since it was clear that both coalition parties benefited from such financial contributions, the respective Chief Whips and central offices splitting the proceeds 50–50. It seems unlikely that either of the party leaders (Lloyd George and, until March 1921, Bonar Law) had any direct involvement in the honours traffic although it would be difficult to acquit them of all knowledge of a dubious practice. In the case of the coalition Liberal share of the proceeds it was rather more personal to Lloyd George than was the Conservative share to the Conservative leader since it went to Lloyd George's 'political fund', to which the Asquithite non-coalition Liberals were denied access. And it was Lloyd George who as Prime Minister actually made the recommendations to the King for most of the controversial honours. Any mud from the scandal was likely to adhere to Lloyd George more than to any other political leader. In the summer of 1922 the army of Lloyd George mud-slingers was numerous, with Hoare now a discreet but effective assailant.

In the eighteen months from January 1921 to June 1922 Lloyd George's recommended honours included 26 peerages, 74 baronetcies and 294 knighthoods. Many of them were eminently respectable if not uniformly distinguished; but the sheer volume was daunting. The final straw for the tenderer backbench consciences of an anti-Lloyd George persuasion was the Birthday Honours List of 1922, published in June. It contained the award of baronies to three men of somewhat suspect commercial integrity for whom further honours (they were already baronets) seemed so obviously inappropriate as to give ample grounds for the suspicion that they had bought their peerages; in the case of Sir Joseph Robinson, who was later induced to refuse the proffered honour, the payment was said to have been £70,000. The activities of the so-called 'honours touts' like Maundy Gregory and Shaw were freely commented upon. There were angry debates in the Lords in June while in the Commons the running was made at question time by two sympathisers of the anti-waste movement, Godfrey Locker-Lampson and Lord Henry Cavendish-Bentinck. Locker-Lampson, who was a friend of Hoare, asked him – perhaps to achieve an appeal beyond the normal anti-waste, diehard and permanently anti-Lloyd George elements – to second an early day motion calling for the appointment of a joint select committee of both Houses to investigate the procedure for recommendation for honours. Hoare agreed to do so. By the time the government had reluctantly consented to a debate on the Locker-Lampson/Hoare motion it had attracted 78 signatures and was clearly a dangerous thrust at the coalition.

Hoare, with a greater sense of political realities than the more extreme members, like Ronald McNeill, who wanted to rake up as much scandal as possible, was concerned to focus the attack on future procedure rather than past sins (especially as not all these had been committed by Lloyd George). Even before the motion was debated on 17th July there were moves to transfer the proposed inquiry from the partisan atmosphere of a select committee to the more judicial one of a royal commission. Hoare and Locker-Lampson saw Bonar Law, now returned to active politics after his illness, to suggest a royal commission and Law wrote to Lloyd George to commend the proposal.[55] There were also pressures inside the government for some positive response to the anxieties being expressed about the honours system, some five junior ministers threatening to vote against the government on the issue if there were not.[56] The result was that in the course of an often acrimonious debate (which, however, had been opened by Locker-Lampson and Hoare in studiously moderate terms) Lloyd George, whose speech was a rather rambling and unimpressively defensive effort, announced the government's intention to establish a royal commission.[57] Appropriately, when its membership was announced early in August, the list included Hoare's name: its deliberations led to the creation of the Political Honours Scrutiny Committee to vet the names of political candidates for honours.

The honours affair was only one of several occasions when Lloyd George betrayed a marked falling off in his old parliamentary skill. Another was his failure to see the implications for his pro-Greek policy in the Near East of the rapidly disintegrating position of the Greek army in Anatolia in face of the Turkish advance under Kemal Ataturk (Hoare had seen the Graeco-Turkish struggle at first hand when in Constantinople at the beginning of the year). At the end of the parliamentary session in August Lloyd George was still expressing his confidence in the ability of the Greeks to hold up the Turks. But in the middle of September came an even more serious development: the potential confrontation between British troops and triumphant Turkish nationalists at Chanak. Britain's involvement in a possibly disastrous armed conflict with the Turks was avoided, not so much by a government whose leading members like Lloyd George and Churchill continued to breathe bellicosity to the last, but by the level-headedness of the British generals on the spot. Lloyd George could claim little responsibility for the sensible resolution of the Chanak crisis and it left his Near Eastern policy in ruins.

A combination of such factors led numerous Conservative constituency organisations and backbenchers to crystallise their opposition to fighting the general election, due within the next few months, in close association with Lloyd George's political machine. Hoare was now very definitely of their number. Recent developments had shown that the Prime Minister was a liability to moderates in the Conservative party rather than, as he had once seemed to Hoare, their potential saviour from the party diehards; and that Conservative membership of a coalition government headed by Lloyd George was positively inimical to the party's interests. And he saw an even greater threat being posed by the moves by some of the Conservative leaders in the coalition, including Austen Chamberlain and Birkenhead, to effect with Lloyd George, Churchill and other coalition Liberals a merger between the two party groups: for anyone who, like Hoare, believed passionately in the virtues of an independent Conservative party such a development appeared as rank treachery. This issue was one on which he could ally himself with the diehards, with whose attitude on so much else he found himself unsympathetic.

With characteristic efficiency Hoare set about organising the Conservative backbench campaign to bring down the coalition. His indispensable ally outside Parliament was Beaverbrook. The closeness of the links between the two men at this period may be gauged from the fact that there is a gap in their normally full correspondence between the last week of September 1922 and May 1923: they clearly saw each other so constantly that letters became superfluous. And it was through Beaverbrook that Hoare had his main direct and personal contact with Bonar Law, the only Conservative possessing sufficient prestige to lead a separate Conservative party. In the summer of 1922 the three were playing tennis together almost weekly at the Vineyard and while as the autumn approached these social occasions became less frequent there was no lack of opportunity for Hoare to see both of them as the political crisis developed.

The story of the downfall of the Lloyd George coalition, one of the most crucial events in modern British political history, has often been told and will not be rehearsed in detail here.[58] But it cannot be omitted from Hoare's biography since his role was a decisive one. He was not only a leader of one of the main power elements in the situation — the Conservative back-benches — he was also an intermediary between the other elements: between Bonar Law; the ministerial dissidents (especially Baldwin in the Cabinet and Wood and Amery out-side); and the party organisation, represented most notably by the party chairman, Sir George Younger, himself a backbench M.P. In many ways Hoare's position was unique, as a back-bencher of obvious ministerial calibre and one who, although as consistently devoted to what he saw as his party's interests as any diehard, had yet been prepared to support, even to prod, the government when he felt it to be on the right general lines (for example, over Ireland, the issue on which the mass of Con-servative backbenchers found it most difficult to forgive Lloyd George). Here was no atavistic Tory but a clear-sighted political realist. The final backbench revolt against the Lloyd George connection was immensely more potent for being led by Hoare rather than by Gretton or any other convinced diehard.

A good deal of the parliamentary recess was occupied for Hoare by the business of the Irish distress committee over which he presided. He returned to London from ten days of discussions with the Irish provisional government on 19th September, and on 28th September he lunched with Churchill, now the minister responsible for relations with southern Ireland; the only other luncheon guest was Philip Sassoon, Lloyd George's parliament-ary private secretary. It was not long before the conversation turned to the Chanak crisis, then reaching its climax, and to the current political situation. Hoare learnt for the first time that, if the Near Eastern crisis allowed, Lloyd George, Churchill and Birkenhead were planning for a general election on 28th October, before the annual conference of the Conservative party National Union due in November and widely expected to come out strongly against continued Conservative participation in the coalition. Sassoon argued that it was much better to get the election out of the way before the conference since 'there was no particular point in giving the Prime Minister an unnecessary kick'. Hoare said that he did not believe that the conference would make much difference one way or the other 'as the majority of Conservatives were anyhow going to stand and be returned as independents at the election'. Churchill, for his part, deplored any Conservative break with the coalition before the election because it would 'let down' coalition Liberals like himself who had many natural affinities with the Conservative party.[59]

On the following day Hoare, now alerted to the necessity of speedy action, had the first of a series of meetings with Bonar Law which intensified after 8th October when he finally returned to London from Norfolk for the new session due on 14th November. From 9th October until the Carlton Club meeting ten days later they met for often extended discussions on at least nine occasions: on 9th, 11th, 13th, 14th, 16th (twice) and 18th (three times). Of the rather depressing milieu of these talks Hoare wrote:

> When I came back after the recess I found Bonar Law installed in his drab and untidy house in Onslow Gardens. He evidently foresaw an immediate crisis, equally evident, however, he had refused to make up his mind as to what he should do. Beaverbrook was determined to make him act and I did my best by constant visits to persuade him that the party was sick of the Coalition. I usually found him sitting sad and solitary in a stuffy and untidy room and smoking incessantly and ruminating over the position.[60]

Hoare and Beaverbrook — together with J. C. C. Davidson, a close friend of both Law and Baldwin (the only Conservative Cabinet member indubitably hostile to the coalition) — knew how essential it was to secure Bonar Law's adherence. They persevered in their efforts to do so, despite the many discouragements of Law's almost manic-depressive alternations of mood, at one time contemplating the formation of a Conservative government under his leadership, at another drafting a letter of resignation from his parliamentary seat to the chairman of his local constituency association. It has been suggested that Bonar Law's role in the 1922 crisis has been exaggerated and that he did not turn any Conservative backbencher against coalition who was not already an anti-coalitionist. Whether or not this was in fact the case it remains unquestionable that had Law come out *in favour* of the coalition the anti-coalitionist elements would not — at any rate at that time — have been able to bring the coalition down.[61] No one was more active than Hoare in keeping Law up to the mark.

The need for immediate action became even more urgent after a group of pro-coalition ministers had decided, at a dinner at Churchill's house in Sussex Square on 15th October, that the ground-swell of opposition to the coalition might be headed off by a hurriedly convened meeting of Conservative M.P.s. A party meeting at the Carlton Club on 19th October — in a mere four days' time — seemed to hold much more favourable prospects for the continuance of the coalition than the less easily managed mass party conference in the following month, when local party activists as well as M.P.s would be making their corporate wishes felt. But unfortunately for the coalitionists it was Hoare and his colleagues, not they, who stage-managed the Carlton Club meeting: Austen Chamberlain, with a fatal lack of organisational skill which would have made his leadership of the Conservative party short-lived even had there been no Carlton Club meeting, made no attempt to ensure support for the leadership. On the contrary, the summoning of the Carlton Club meeting was an act of confident defiance, providing the opportunity for Chamberlain to tell the party bluntly, as he himself put it, 'that they must either follow our advice or do without us, in which case they must find their own Chief, and form a Government *at once*. They would be in a d——d fix.'[62] And both he and Lloyd George fully expected that the coalition would be given a boost on the very day of the meeting by the announcement of the result of the Newport by-election, in which an independent Conservative candidate was opposing a nominally coalition Liberal as well as a Labour candidate.

Following a defence of the coalition by Chamberlain in a speech in Birmingham on 13th October — among other things, on the grounds of its being the best defence against the 'common foe' of Labour — and a truculent one by Lloyd George in Manchester the following day, full of fire and fury against the Turks and dissident Conservatives alike, Hoare resolved to attempt to set the record straight and to encourage Bonar Law by writing to *The Times*. He used the good offices of his friend Harold Williams, who showed the letter Hoare drafted on 15th October to the editor, Wickham Steed. Steed decided that it should have the greatest prominence in *The Times* of the 16th and be accompanied by a warmly supporting leader written by himself. Meanwhile Hoare sent a copy of the letter to Davidson, who showed it to Baldwin: both were strongly in favour of its immediate publication.[63]

Hoare's letter was an able exposition of the anti-coalitionist case and attracted widespread attention among those most involved in the developing crisis. It is, of course, impossible to determine its actual influence, but appearing as it did only three days before the Carlton Club meeting it would be surprising if it had no effect on the attitudes of the participants, if only to strengthen rather than change their resolve. The letter, as it appeared in *The Times* on the 16th, had a few textual differences from Hoare's original draft, reflecting the comments of Davidson and Wickham Steed — they in no way affected its clear message. The version as published ran as follows:

Conservative Members who were returned to Parliament upon the Coalition programme are naturally reluctant to criticise leaders who have faced with no little success the almost insuperable difficulties of the last four years. Particularly are they reluctant to attack them when public support seems to turn against them [the original draft here had 'is abandoning them']. The Prime Minister and Mr. Chamberlain, however, have forced an issue upon which it is the inevitable duty of every one of us to express his opinion. Are we to accept some vague arrangement that may lead to a new centre party and will certainly lead to the break up of the old parties, or are we to return to the old party system modified by the fact that there are now three parties instead of two?

Mr. Chamberlain made the speech at Birmingham that many of us expected, brave [in the original: 'honest'] of purpose, loyal to his leader, lucid in the expression of his views. No one can say that he was not fully entitled to make his appeal [this sentence was not in the original]. But just as he has every right to his opinions upon the need of an Anti-Labour Coalition, so also have the rank and file of the party the right to hold the view that the time has come for a return to the system of independent parties. When Mr. Chamberlain says that the Conservative Party cannot hope for a clear majority after the General Election, he may be right or he may be wrong. No one has ever been able to foretell correctly the result of any General Election, least of all a General Election with an electorate that has been hugely increased. But Conservatives who, like myself, believe that the vital need is not so much to form a Government as to keep the party united are not convinced by this argument *ad terrorem*. The Coalition of 1918 was a temporary expedient based upon the general acceptance of the Conservatives and Lloyd Georgian Liberals. As long as the Conservative Party continued to accept the expedient, the majority of the Conservative Members of the House of Commons were prepared to support it. It is now certain [in the original: 'appears obvious'] that the rank and file of the Conservative Party have withdrawn this general acceptance. It is useless, therefore, for Mr. Chamberlain or any other Conservative leader to attempt to impose from above the continuance of an arrangement which nine out of ten of the party desire to see ended.

What Conservatives are demanding is a means to close the divisions in their own ranks. Mr. Chamberlain's policy would only dig them deeper. Fortunately, as there seems to be general agreement amongst the rank and file, it is to be hoped that a bridge for restoring unity will soon [in the original: 'the means for closing up the divisions would speedily'] be found.[64]

Hoare undoubtedly exaggerated the extent of anti-coalition feeling among the Conservative backbenches but he could be confident that he was voicing majority opinion. Not the least important of the letters of support he received was one from the former party chieftain and Chamberlain's rival for the leadership in 1911, Walter Long, who had retired from the coalition government on health grounds twenty months before. Long congratulated him on giving clear expression to the views of 'an immense majority in the Conservative Party'. He hoped Hoare and his friends would be able

in the course of the next few days [Long was writing on the 16th], to bring about a recognition by the Leaders of the facts of the case and thereby pave the way for a re-union of the

Conservative Party, without which it seems to me that nothing but disaster is in store for us.[65]

Hoare's next, and even more important, initiative was directly related to the question of establishing the exact degree of anti-coalition feeling on the backbenches. It arose from a meeting on the following day (the 17th) with Baldwin, engineered by Davidson. Hitherto Hoare had kept himself somewhat aloof from the ministerial anti-coalitionists in order that his movement could be seen as a genuine backbench, rank and file one. However, as Davidson told him that Baldwin was anxious to see him the three men lunched together at Hoare's house, 18 Cadogan Gardens, for a discussion which continued long into the afternoon (Baldwin was due to attend a Port of London ceremony at 2.30 p.m. but rang to excuse himself). Baldwin gave Hoare his first detailed insight into the attitudes of members of the government revealed at a meeting of Conservative ministers the previous day. According to Davidson's account Baldwin was depressed because some of the junior ministers who as a group had been the most consistently anti-coalition element in the government seemed to be wavering. With Parliament still in recess it was difficult to gauge backbench opinion and the three therefore decided that a representative group of backbenchers should be asked to attend a meeting at Hoare's house on the following afternoon. With uncharacteristic modesty Hoare wrote in his published account that the idea arose 'I think at my suggestion', but Davidson's account is quite firm that 'Sam proposed that we should canvass backbench opinion'. The three pored over the list of M.P.s in Vacher's *Parliamentary Companion*, selected over seventy names and then Hoare went off with the list to the House of Commons to send off telegrams inviting the selected members to a meeting in Cadogan Gardens at 5 p.m. the next day – the day before the Carlton Club meeting.[66]

Nearly sixty backbench M.P.s seem actually to have attended at Hoare's house in the late afternoon of 18th October, constituting a reasonable sample of the 264 or so backbenchers who attended at the Carlton Club at 11 o'clock the next morning.[67] Hoare now began a period of almost uninterrupted activity which continued through much of the night and on to the very start of the Carlton Club meeting. He began his own meeting in Cadogan Gardens in some despair for that morning Bonar Law had told him that he had definitely decided not to come out against the coalition and, far from leading the party, he intended to resign his seat. Nothing that Hoare said could shake his resolution, which was based on his natural pessimistic caution, his doctor's prognosis (he had passed Law for two years only), and his disinclination to do battle with former Cabinet colleagues. And when Edward Wood had come to lunch with Hoare he had little better news to convey on the more general front: despite the resentment which many of the junior ministers felt against their pro-coalition leaders, particularly Birkenhead, who had lectured them as if they were errant schoolboys, Wood was convinced that any compromise involving the continuation of coalition which Chamberlain might propose with Balfour's backing would carry the day, either at the Carlton Club or at the party conference in November.[68]

But if he started with doubts the meeting itself did much to lift Hoare's spirits. Over twenty members spoke and the general drift was clearly anti-coalition, or at least in favour of independent Conservative action at the election. The upshot, under Hoare's skilful direction, was that Hoare and two very senior and respected backbenchers, E. G. Pretyman (a former junior minister) and George Lane-Fox, were unanimously deputed to convey to both Chamberlain and Law the strength of feeling of the meeting in favour of independent Conservative action, an independent programme and an independent leader in the forthcoming election. They could not see Chamberlain immediately and first went to Law, who was obviously impressed with the calibre of those present at the meeting. Although he still professed reluctance to take any positive action himself this was something of an advance on the flat refusal he had given Hoare that morning. There was no change, however, to be observed in Chamberlain's attitude when the three delegates were at last admitted to their leader's presence. This was how Hoare described the ensuing discussion in one of his unpublished accounts of the political crisis:

I told him [Chamberlain] the position in as friendly a way as possible, gave him ample opportunity to agree to all that was really demanded, namely that the Conservative Party should fight the election as a party and on no account should it be fused into some new organisation of the centre. I further told him that the meeting from which we had come seemed very representative of the party in the House of Commons and I hinted that unless he could meet us I felt sure that there would be very strong opposition to the Government at the Carlton Club meeting next morning. Austen was completely wooden. He did not attempt to discuss the position. He gave us no suggestion that he would meet us in any way and finally told us that he knew more about the party than we did and that the great majority of the Members in the House were with him. We, therefore, left him in as polite and friendly an atmosphere as we could maintain.[69]

Before returning home from this unsatisfactory meeting with Chamberlain Hoare called in again at Onslow Gardens to give Bonar Law a report. He was immediately heartened to find that Law's resolution now seemed to be firm, the result (he later heard from Beaverbrook) of the combined efforts of Beaverbrook and Law's formidable sister, who presided over the Law household. Law listened attentively to Hoare and then, with a smile (the first Hoare had seen on his face during the whole crisis), told him: 'I have decided to go to the meeting, and I intend to make a speech at it.' With the meeting only hours away the chances of yet another change of mind seemed small, and Hoare went home more confident than he had been at any earlier point in the crisis.

His day's work was far from finished, however. After dinner he had a long telephone conversation with Beaverbrook and then telephoned Baldwin. After hearing Hoare's account of his various meetings of the day Baldwin asked him to come round to his house in Eaton Square for what turned out to be yet another meeting. All the chief dissident Conservative elements seemed to have gathered at Baldwin's house that evening. In the hall Hoare had a few words with the party chairman, Sir George Younger, who told him that the executive of the National Union had just rejected a proposed compromise by which there would be an immediate coalition-fought election, to be followed by a party meeting to decide on whether the Conservatives should continue to participate. In the drawing-room were Leslie Wilson, the Conservative joint Chief Whip, and Davidson, to whom Hoare expressed his growing confidence in an anti-coalition victory at the Carlton Club. But then Baldwin ushered him into the dining-room where, around the table, sat virtually the complete group of Conservative junior ministers and whips. Hoare was invited to report on his day's work, particularly the backbench meeting at his house, and was then cross-examined by the group. By no means all were friendly. Gilmour and Mitchell-Thomson, in particular, struck Hoare as being 'rather offensive', implying that he was being intransigent in refusing to accept the suggested compromise. Hoare retorted that it would not avoid a party split and in any case had been repudiated by the mass party organisation. Nor was he impressed with their argument that the coalition government needed to be kept in being to cope with the Graeco-Turkish crisis. Edward Wood and Leo Amery both seemed to favour a compromise but both nevertheless intended to resign whatever happened. The most resolutely anti-coalition were Bridgeman, Sanders and Tryon, and these fully backed Hoare's stand. The discussion then turned to the individual positions of particular ministers and Hoare felt it was time for him to go and seek a night's rest before the further excitements of the morrow.[70]

But Hoare had a disturbed night, with his mind continually revolving around the question of the best tactics for the crucial meeting in the morning. If that meeting were not to end in un-certainty and confusion, he reasoned, there must be a clear resolution on which members could vote. The resolution needed to be strong enough to put strict limits on any future Conserva-tive party arrangement with the coalition Liberals but — follow-ing a point made to him by Younger in their brief conversation at Baldwin's — it should be couched in unaggressive terms so as to attract the widest possible support. The division of view that the junior ministers had revealed only reinforced the wisdom of this course. Before breakfast Hoare had hammered out a formula which he thought would meet the situation:

That this meeting of Conservative Members of the House of Commons declares its opinion that the Conservative Party, whilst willing to co-operate with the Coalition Liberals, should fight the election as an independent party with its own leader and its own programme.

The breakfast papers contained the heartening news for anti-coalitionists that the independent Conservative at Newport, Reginald Clarry, far from having been overwhelmingly defeated as the Chamberlainites had expected, had won the by-election comfortably, with the Liberal, not he, in third place after Labour (Clarry polled 2,000 votes more than the Labour candidate and nearly 5,000 more than the Liberal). But while this was obviously a helpful augury of the electoral appeal of undiluted Conservatism Hoare did not want to take any chances. He was convinced a definite resolution was still needed at the meeting. Pretyman and Lane-Fox were the obvious men to move and second it and he rang them and secured their assent — in Pretyman's case very readily but in Lane-Fox's rather more reluctantly, Hoare having to argue him out of his belief that a general agreement might be arrived at without an actual resolution.

The time had come to leave for the Carlton. He called in for Pretyman on the way and once there began distributing copies of his resolution to members assembling for the meeting at 11. Some felt it was too mild and would have preferred the reference to co-operation with the coalition Liberals omitted, but Hoare was able to convince them that the resolution should stand, with the possibility of its being strengthened in the course of the discussion.

The speeches at the Carlton Club on 19th October, 1922 — the most famous private party meeting in modern British political history — have often been summarised, on the basis of the almost verbatim account issued by Conservative party headquarters that evening and which appeared in full in *The Times* on 20th October.[71] In addition to reproducing the official report *The Times* had a summary with comment contributed by 'a correspondent'. That correspondent was none other than Hoare himself, who had given his account to S. K. Ratcliffe, *The Times* lobby correspondent, in the afternoon, almost as soon as the meeting was over.[72] There was no mistaking the triumphant mood in which he must have written it:

Even as the members assembled the feeling of the party was

made manifest. When Mr. Chamberlain and Lord Birkenhead arrived they were coldly received by those who had already taken their seats in the room. When, however, Mr. Bonar Law arrived about two minutes to the hour, he was the object of a demonstration of enthusiasm which left no doubt as to the mind of the meeting. The issue was, indeed, already decided ...

Chamberlain's speech Hoare obviously thought much too long at thirty minutes and was merely a restatement of his oft-repeated argument that the maintenance of the coalition was essential to ward off the challenge of Labour: it provoked, according to Hoare, 'protesting cries' which 'showed that the speaker had not the assent of the meeting'. Much of Hoare's contemporary account was devoted to the eight-minute speech by Baldwin which followed Chamberlain's, with its description of Lloyd George as the 'dynamic force' who had already split the Liberal party and would, if given the opportunity, split the Conservative party as well. Baldwin spoke, said Hoare, 'very simply, clearly and logically. He is not an eloquent speaker, but the manner of his delivery was good.' Of the speech by Bonar Law Hoare's account was surprisingly terse, drawing attention chiefly to Law's obvious feeling of constraint at having to criticise former Cabinet colleagues. Of Balfour's attempt to appeal to members' loyalty to the leader Hoare was dismissive: he was 'felt to be an ineffective advocate'.

When Hoare came to write retrospectively of the Carlton Club many years later one of his chief impressions was surprise at this failure by Balfour who, distinguished party figure though he was, gave the impression of being totally remote from feeling in his party. But the big mistake, Hoare felt, was made by Austen Chamberlain who, instead of accepting the resolution as a not unfriendly motion, treated it as a root and branch vote of censure: Hoare believed that this was sufficient to turn quite a number against him who had come to the meeting undecided. Baldwin's speech was 'almost crude in its directness. In so many words he said he did not believe anything that Lloyd George said'. Hoare wryly observed that no one at the meeting made the obvious comment that, believing this, it was surprising that he could have remained a member of Lloyd George's government for so long. Bonar Law 'made exactly the speech that was required', insisting that party unity came before any personal considerations: 'There was nothing personal or bitter in it and when it ended there was no doubt whatever about the majority behind him.'[73] Curiously, in none of his accounts does Hoare refer to the contribution against the coalition made by Leslie Wilson, the Chief Whip and party manager in the Commons, which may well have had as much influence as any: Chamberlain was in the incredible position for a party leader of having been repudiated both by the chairman of the party organisation and by his chief whip. The speeches by the backbenchers — five, in addition to the two movers of the resolution Hoare had framed — were less important than the negative or positive influence of the speeches of their leaders. Hoare himself remained silent during the meeting — his contribution had been made before it started.

Hoare had calculated in advance that the majority for his motion would be about 80. In the event, according to the official figures issued after the meeting, it was exactly 100: 187 to 87.[74] With a possible 15 or so abstentions in addition it would seem that the surprisingly large number of around 290 M.P.s (including ministers as well as backbenchers) of the total Conservative strength of some 380 had managed to attend a meeting called in the recess with such indecent haste by the pro-coalition leaders of the party. But of this number almost two-thirds rejected their leadership's advice. The device had exploded in the leaders' faces. The coalition was not vindicated, it was dead.

There was, however, an undoubted element of uncertainty about the Carlton Club meeting and matters could have gone differently, especially if Chamberlain had made any attempt at conciliatoriness or, above all, if Bonar Law, almost at the eleventh hour, had not been spurred into action. There could have been no successful revolt without a credible alternative leader. Things turned out as Hoare predicted but this was not so much because the result was inevitable as because Hoare and his allies had worked diligently to produce the desired result. Baldwin and Davidson were in no doubt of the extent of Hoare's share in the final triumph. Immediately the Carlton Club meeting ended they looked round eagerly for Hoare to express their thanks to him, but he had already left. They went round twice to Cadogan Gardens only to find Hoare out and it was not until Hoare himself called in later at Eaton Square that Baldwin was able to tell him how grateful he and Bonar Law were for all that he had done.[75]

The destruction of the Lloyd George government meant that the Conservative party once again resumed its separate existence freed from a dominating political personality who had become an embarrassing encumbrance. With Lloyd George's resignation immediately after the Carlton Club meeting a Conservative government was formed, under Bonar Law, for the first time for seventeen years, and for the first time since Hoare had become a Member of Parliament. For Hoare the stage was set for the beginning of a ministerial career which continued for most of the next eighteen years.

3

Air Ministry and Shadow Cabinet

Hoare had every reason to hope for important office in the new Conservative administration. His crucial role in the dramatic events which had made the administration possible; the temporary severance from the party of leading members like Austen Chamberlain, Balfour, Birkenhead, Horne and Worthington-Evans, who for the moment retained their loyalty to the coalition which had been so unceremoniously destroyed; the energetic advocacy of Beaverbrook, for so long Bonar Law's confidant and adviser – these were among the factors that nourished his hope and expectation.[1] The press, too, was strongly tipping him for Cabinet office, perhaps as Home Secretary or, with his exploits in the Holmes-Morant affair and his general pre-war interest in educational matters in mind, as President of the Board of Education. But when the list of Cabinet appointments was published on 24th October his name was not among them. It was not until 30th October that he received the long-awaited summons to Downing Street, where Law invited him to become Secretary of State for Air, outside the Cabinet. In making the offer, however, Law implied that the post might soon be abolished since he had been advised that the independent air force and separate Air Ministry were too costly and that there was much to be said in peacetime for reverting to naval and army control of the air arm.[2] Discouraging though this must have been to Hoare he had no hesitation in accepting his first ministerial appointment, which was announced on 31st October; on 2nd November he was sworn of the Privy Council and received his seals as a Secretary of State.

Despite the depreciatory way in which he was initially

invited to assume the office Hoare was to remain Secretary of State for Air — with a nine-month gap for the first Labour government in 1924 — until the fall of the second Baldwin government in June 1929 (he was to hold the office again, briefly, in 1940). It was a measure of his accomplishment that none of his successors, at least until the absorption of the three service departments into the Ministry of Defence in 1964, was presented with the suspended sentence of death that Bonar Law held over him in October 1922. His incumbency had three chronological phases. The first began officially on 2nd November but in practice not until after the election on 15th November, in which the Conservatives, despite having cut adrift from Lloyd George, secured a comfortable overall parliamentary majority (in Chelsea Hoare gained nearly three quarters of the votes cast in a straight contest with Labour, represented by none other than the distinguished philosopher, Bertrand Russell[3]). From then until Bonar Law's resignation on health grounds six months later he was Air Minister without a seat in the Cabinet, although he frequently attended its meetings. When Baldwin became Prime Minister on 22nd May, 1923, he asked Hoare to continue at the Air Ministry but now as a full member of the Cabinet. This second phase continued until January 1924 and the defeat of the government following the surprising election called by Baldwin (with Hoare's full support)[4] to test the issue of a protective tariff. With the triumphant Conservative electoral victory of October 1924 and the formation of the second Baldwin government began the third and longest phase of Hoare's peacetime incumbency of the Air Ministry.

Writing years after — in a moment of profound despair with political life — Hoare referred to the *damnosa hereditas* which confronted him in all his first three ministerial posts, at the Air Ministry, the India Office and the Foreign Office (from which he had just resigned).[5] The Air Ministry *hereditas* was implicit in the discouraging terms in which Bonar Law had couched his invitation to office. One of the newest of government departments (created in January 1918), supervising the newest armed service (formed by the merger of the naval and army air services in April 1918), the Air Ministry was apparently awaiting abolition and the air force was about to lose its recently acquired status and become an adjunct of the senior services. The contrast with the situation at the end of the war was striking. At the armistice the Royal Air Force, with over 3,000 front line aircraft and over 20,000 more in reserve, and over 291,000 officers and men, was one of the two largest air forces in the world (the other being the French).[6] Nor did it lack powerful political leadership. While the first holders of the office of Secretary of State for Air (Lords Rothermere and Weir) were not politicians in the ordinary sense in February 1919 the post was entrusted to one of the major political figures of the day, Winston Churchill. Churchill combined the office, however, with that of Secretary of State for War, a conjunction which reflected official uncertainty about future administrative arrangements. It was an immense ministerial burden and even Churchill's fire and energy were hardly sufficient to ensure that the difficult transition from war footing to peacetime role was effected without damage to the long-term interests of the army and air force.[7] In April 1921 Churchill was succeeded at the Air Ministry by a much lesser figure (his cousin, F. E. Guest) who, while having the advantage of exclusive responsibility for the air force and civil aviation, was weakened by being the only service minister outside the Cabinet. When the coalition fell there were only some 100 front line aircraft to provide for Britain's air defence (although in August 1922 Lloyd George had announced an expansion programme): the few squadrons in service were mainly committed to naval co-operation or to air control work in Palestine, Iraq and the North-West Frontier of India where it was thought they could maintain order more cheaply than the army.

The most damned element in Hoare's 1922 ministerial inheritance was undoubtedly the long-standing and bitter inter-service and inter-departmental war over the status of the Royal Air Force and the Air Ministry *vis-à-vis* the two senior services and their departments. Was the air force a service in its own right with exclusive control of warlike operations in the air, or was it a kind of 'common service' at the behest of the army and navy and supportive to their operations on land and sea? Was there a need for a third service, in fact, rather than naval and army air co-operation units? Should not the R.A.F. become a kind of aerial Royal Marines and the Air Ministry, freed from its military responsibilities, become a ministry of civil aviation or, perhaps more realistically, a section of the Ministry of Transport or the Board of Trade?

In this long and exhausting conflict the most bloodthirsty campaign, covering the two decades from the end of the war, was that waged by the navy and the Admiralty for the restoration of their erstwhile control of naval aircraft, both those borne afloat and those based on land. R.A.F. resistance was the more dogged from being founded on the belief that the removal of the naval air squadrons would spell virtually the end of its independent existence. The army's dispute with the R.A.F. over the army co-operation units was only slightly less virulent and initially, at any rate, the army was even more opposed to air force autonomy than was the navy, believing that aircraft should simply be absorbed by the army as artillery had been in an earlier day. Sir Henry Wilson, Chief of the Imperial General Staff from 1919 to 1922, was implacably opposed to the R.A.F. but his successors, much less intellectually agile than he, proved less resolute and by 1925 were prepared to accept and, what was more important, abide by, a reasonable compromise. The navy carried more guns, both inside and outside the government, and had in Beatty, Chief of the Naval Staff from 1919 to 1927, a skilled and prestigious protagonist, whose encounters with the doughty R.A.F. champion, Sir Hugh Trenchard, Chief of the Air Staff for the whole of Beatty's period at the Admiralty, were often of almost epic proportions. The development of this inter-service conflict was marked by successive reformulations of that independence of the R.A.F. that was implicit in its original establishment as a separate service in 1918. It was only to be during Hoare's tenure of the Air Ministry that the older services came to accept, however reluctantly, the fact of an autonomous air force and Air Ministry; an acceptance which, in the navy's case, was coupled with a determination to miss no chance of winning back control of the naval air arm.[8]

The civil aviation responsibilities of the Air Ministry were also in an unsatisfactory state when Hoare took over. The various commercial companies which had sprung up mainly to provide services to the continent found it impossible to run them profitably. A committee under Lord Weir had in 1920 recommended state subsidies for them but Churchill, the responsible minister, was cool to the idea and the Treasury

definitely hostile. Subsidies were refused, and by the end of
February 1921 all regular services had ceased. But before they
had done so the government at last decided on a temporary
grant of £60,000 for 1921–2 and air services were revived a few
weeks after their withdrawal. A further stage came in April 1922
when the subsidy was renewed, on the basis of 25 per cent of
gross earnings. The situation that Hoare inherited was thus one
in which several air transport companies competed against each
other and all were subsidised. Moreover, what at one time had
seemed one of the most promising technical developments in
air transport was in abeyance. In March 1922 all work had
been stopped on airship development: a decision about the long-
term future was clearly overdue.[9]

Hoare was determined to make a success of his first portfolio,
however intractable the problems it might pose. Trenchard,
never spendthrift with his praise, was obviously impressed by
the way his new minister shaped at the very outset. Writing to
Sir John Salmond, the air commander in Iraq, on 9th November, less than a fortnight after Hoare had been appointed and
when he was in the middle of the election campaign, Trenchard
described Hoare as

> a young man of 42, with a good and quick brain, and ap-
> parently very nice to deal with as far as one can judge after
> two or three interviews. He is keen on maintaining the Air
> Service and its prestige, and keen on being put in the Cabinet
> in order to maintain our side of all questions raised; and I
> have put in a paper saying that I consider that the office
> demands a minister with a seat in the Cabinet ... He is very
> keen to know all about the Naval controversy, and I think
> will be a tower of strength when he understands all the
> difficulties of the subject ... He is more determined, though,
> to run the policy and his own show than was our previous
> Secretary of State.[10]

But a determination to run 'his own show' did not blind Hoare
to the need to seek advice and, where necessary, to appoint
subordinates who could provide it. There was no doubt at all
about who was the dominating official figure in the Air Ministry
at that time. Trenchard had become Chief of the Air Staff for
the second time in March 1919, and he was still there when

Hoare left the Air Ministry seven years later. Whatever controversy may surround his enormous impact on the development of the R.A.F. — and the influence of his emphasis on the
war-winning potential of strategic bombing by an independent
air force is still energetically and voluminously debated — all
those who encountered him seem united in believing that they
had brushed with greatness. Thus for Hoare, recalling his first
meeting with Trenchard many years after, it was one with 'the
first really great man I had ever met in my life'. But the great
and dedicated man was neither notably articulate nor adept at
those skills so necessary for success in Whitehall in-fighting.
Hoare was well-equipped to supply those deficiencies. Trenchard for him was the Prophet of Pushkin's poem, whose soul
strained and struggled to give an inspired message to the world.
Hoare's mission, he later wrote,

> was to be the prophet's interpreter to a world that did not
> always understand his dark sayings. Thenceforth, for nearly
> seven continuous years, I was destined to play the interpre-
> ter's part. Whether it was in Cabinet, in the Committee of
> Imperial Defence, or in the country, my task was to explain
> the doctrine of the independence of the air in its many ramifi-
> cations.[11]

It was certainly a formidable combination, Trenchard launching 'his broad attack' and Hoare following it up with 'precision
bombing on the special targets', and grew even more formidable
the longer their official association continued. Hoare was well
aware of its value and stepped in every time Trenchard's retirement from office became due to persuade him to continue;
on one such occasion, at the end of 1926, Hoare expressed his
pleasure at having linked 'my political go-cart on to a motor
power of unexampled strength and reliability', and it was no
empty compliment.[12] Someone who knew both men well, the
aviation pioneer and politician Lord Brabazon, retrospectively
considered it to have been 'a national blessing that these two
men, so entirely different from every point of view, got on so
well together. Neither one nor the other alone could have done
anything. Together they were irresistible.'[13]

Among Hoare's other professional advisers, Air Marshal Sir
Geoffrey Salmond (the brother of the R.A.F. commander in

Iraq), who was in charge of research and development, and Sir Sefton Brancker, the Director of Civil Aviation, were outstanding. On the political side he was well-served by his parliamentary under-secretary of state, initially the Duke of Sutherland, a keen amateur aviator, and then, from 1924, Sir Philip Sassoon, the most opulent of political hosts at a range of magnificent residences; both were Hoare's own choice. Sassoon remained under-secretary for the whole period of Baldwin's second government and proved an enthusiastic and completely loyal colleague. His style of life was quite different from Hoare's but they apparently found each other congenial company (they were both keen tennis-players) and Sassoon's wealth and lavish hospitality introduced Hoare to a social and political world which even he had not hitherto fully comprehended.[14]

When Hoare arrived at the Air Ministry he found it lacked that indispensable adjunct of a minister's private office, a Civil Service secretary. Instead there was an Air Secretary, a Royal Air Force group captain who, although a most efficient officer, could hardly perform the manifold semi-political functions of a minister's private secretary. Hoare set about regularising the situation but surprisingly it took him until August 1923 to secure a civilian secretary, in the person of Christopher Bullock. Bullock was one of the ablest officials of his generation, a fact of which he himself seems not to have been entirely unaware. Still only in his thirties Bullock built up for himself a quite exceptional position for a civilian official in a service department. He had served as Trenchard's secretary before Hoare appointed him to his private office and worked throughout in the closest accord with that impressive if not notably articulate man. Bullock, a wartime pilot, had a degree of passionate commitment to the cause of the Air Ministry and the R.A.F. which completely belied the impartial tradition of the senior Civil Service.[15] He was, indeed, a propagandist and initiator rather than merely the instrument of policy. In the policy and strategic fields, as the chief official support to both Hoare and Trenchard, he eclipsed the modest and retiring permanent secretary, Sir Walter Nicholson, who seems to have willingly co-operated in his own effective demotion; Nicholson in fact retired early from his post at the end of 1930, when he was 54, enabling Bullock to succeed him as permanent secretary, over the heads of many of his seniors, at the unusually early age of 39. Many years afterwards Bullock, in a letter to Lord Templewood, summarised his own estimate of his efforts on behalf of the air force at this period:

> I drafted countless Parliamentary Questions for our supporters to put, wrote scores of speeches for them to deliver, organised Parliamentary Debates in both Houses, helped with the text of one book after another, kept people like Liddell Hart and Arnold Wilson in touch with developments, wrote countless official papers for the Cabinet and the C.I.D. stressing the weakness of the R.A.F. *vis-à-vis* other Powers, and actually initiated many measures to improve our position and fought endless battles with the Treasury for them.[16]

An egocentric catalogue, no doubt, but it is clear that Bullock went beyond both the call of duty and the normal conventions of the Civil Service in his defence of the Air Ministry. It might almost appear that with such a permanent official a minister was hardly necessary. But Bullock fully recognised Hoare's contribution and, in a private account he wrote in 1946 (not seen by Lord Templewood until nine years later), stressed that any contribution he (Bullock) had been able to make had been under the aegis of Hoare, whose 'great constructive work at the Air Ministry has never received the recognition it should'. A relatively small detail in the same account by Bullock illustrated Hoare's ministerial style: when Hoare was out of office (in 1924 and 1929–31) Bullock drafted the wide-ranging ministerial speeches which each year introduced the Air estimates in the Commons, but when Hoare was minister he wrote his own estimates speeches. Not for him the mere departmental brief, however ably prepared.[17]

Bullock's brilliant career in the public service ended under a cloud in August 1936 when he was dismissed from the service for having made what was considered to have been an improper approach to Sir Eric Geddes, chairman of Imperial Airways, concerning the possibility that if at some future date he retired prematurely from the civil service, he might succeed Geddes at Imperial Airways. In his subsequent search for jobs in commerce and industry Bullock had every reason to be grateful for Hoare's material assistance.[18] Hoare was an excellent man to have served: he was always ready to help those who had done so, whether officials or fellow politicians.[19]

For his parliamentary private secretary Hoare ('with his usual flair for picking the right man' as Bullock put it in his 1946 account) chose Sir Geoffrey Butler, M.P. for Cambridge University, Fellow of Corpus Christi College, historian, Conservative party intellectual and, not least, air enthusiast. Until his early death at the age of 41 in April 1929 Butler was in many ways more an additional junior minister for Hoare than merely the hewer of wood and drawer of water of P.P.S. tradition: Hoare later described him as his 'guide, philosopher and friend'.[20] His main policy contribution was in the creation of university air squadrons but not less important was the wide range of contacts he made for his minister. Through Butler, Hoare met Cambridge scientists and others whose work was highly relevant to the concerns of the Air Ministry — men like Dr John MacCurdy, university lecturer in psychology, whom Hoare engaged to undertake consultancy work for the R.A.F. medical branch on pilot reactions to flying.[21] Such academic contacts were made even more readily from July 1926 when Hoare received an honorary Cambridge degree and became an honorary fellow of Corpus Christi. It was Butler, too, who in 1925 introduced Hoare to the military commentator Basil Liddell Hart, who had been one of Butler's history students at Corpus. Hoare consulted Liddell Hart on many occasions thereafter, not only about air force affairs but also on wider problems of defence and disarmament; the association soon convinced Liddell Hart of Hoare's 'genuine enthusiasm for air progress, not merely as a means to aid his political ambition, but an ardent belief ... '.[22]

The primary aim of Hoare's term at the Air Ministry had necessarily to be the maintenance of the integrity of the R.A.F. and of the department itself. The battle was joined as early as February 1923 when Beatty and other sea lords demanded action to restore the naval air wing to the navy and threatened resignation if it were not.[23] Hoare lost no time in taking counteraction. On 18th February he saw the Prime Minister and on the following day wrote to him to summarise the points he (Hoare) had then made and which he was to continue to argue in various arenas thereafter. There were, he told Law, 'two opposite conceptions of Air administration, for either of which there is much to be said'. On the one hand, the army and navy could have their own air services and develop them on their own lines, with a small department, possibly within the Board of Trade, to assist the service departments with aircraft procurement and be responsible for civil aviation. Hoare was prepared to concede that such an arrangement might allow the two air services to develop 'more quickly and economically'. But, on the other hand, there was the conception that was implicit in all the decisions taken on the air force since 1918: that of a 'single air service with a Ministry with the rank of a Secretariat of State and naval and military wings as integral parts of the single force'. Such a force, as Trenchard had argued in numerous memoranda and committee meetings, provided both economy and efficiency in any role it might be called upon to play, not least the strategic role. Only by a centralised air force, Hoare declared, 'can we undertake the strategic operation that is likely to be the crisis in a continental war'. There were the two further considerations that the army and naval air services had not in fact 'developed quickly and harmoniously when they were separate' and that 'the present moment would be peculiarly inappropriate to abandon our strategic unity when we are admittedly defenceless in the face of France' (the country which, extraordinarily, was then looked on as the main potential danger and on whose formidable air strength Hoare had just prepared a Cabinet paper).[24]

The two conceptions of air force organisation could not be mixed without 'insuperable disadvantages', Hoare went on to argue. Either the air force was to be divided up between an army and a naval air service — thus bringing to an end the Air Ministry's 'programme of ambitious development' — or it must remain integrated, in which case 'the Navy cannot have its separate [air] service without removing one of the principal foundations of the structure'.

Hoare told the Prime Minister that he would prefer, in effect, to let sleeping dogs lie for the next few years. The air force was a mere four years old and the 'sudden wrench' which the lopping off of the naval air wing would represent 'might finally cripple it'; moreover, what Hoare regarded as 'the only real solution', the creation of a Ministry of Defence integrating all three services, might in a few years 'be brought into the field of practical politics'. But Hoare must have realised that general acceptance of the *status quo* was an impossible hope: Beatty had just shown that the sea dogs, far from sleeping, were barking obstreperously. His second preference was thus for the appointment of a Cabinet committee of 'impartial civilian members' to advise the Cabinet on the decision to be taken. He insisted, however, that the committee should not be concerned merely with the naval air problem in isolation but should consider the whole question of the relations between the air force and the other two services.[25]

On 9th March a committee was established under the chairmanship of Lord Salisbury, the Lord President of the Council, with terms of reference that conformed to a considerable extent with Hoare's desiderata. It was to inquire into inter-service co-operation in the context of national and imperial defence, and to examine army-R.A.F. relations as well as those between the R.A.F. and the navy. It was also to make recommendations on the expansion of air force strength to meet the needs of home defence. It was to be a civilian committee but by its nature could hardly be impartial since among its eight ministerial members were the three service ministers (Amery for the navy, Derby for the army, and Hoare). But the committee also had two members from outside the government, Balfour and Weir. As his papers reveal, Weir worked in the closest liaison with Hoare and Trenchard (who gave evidence to the committee, along with the other service chiefs) to foster the air force's interests; from the point of view of the Air Ministry he was the best kind of 'impartial civilian'.

The first fruit of the Salisbury committee came after Baldwin had succeeded Law as Prime Minister: a recommendation in June 1923, which the Cabinet accepted, that there should be a home defence force 'of sufficient strength adequately to protect against air attack by the strongest air force within striking distance of this country'. This was put at 600 front line machines, or 52 squadrons.[26] Hoare lost no time in pointing out the link between the needs of Britain's air defence and the continued independence of the air force. In a Cabinet paper early in July he wrote:

If the Air Force is broken up and Air Power is definitely re-

garded as a subsidiary weapon of the two older Services, the
enthusiasm of British Air Personnel will be choked and the
development of British Air Power crippled at the very
moment when the air menace is acute and the need for Air
Force expansion urgent.[27]

That view was increasingly coming to be accepted on the committee and in the government as a whole, despite the initial
traditional reservoir of sympathy for the navy's case as opposed
to that of the upstart junior service. The army's rather unsubtle
frontal assault on the R.A.F. and the Air Ministry — a demand
to the Salisbury committee that they should cease to exist as
separate entities — was rejected by the committee at the end of
June and on 9th July, after lengthy debate, the Cabinet confirmed 'the present arrangement under which the Royal Air
Force is administered by a separate Department of State'.[28]

That left the problem of the naval air wing (the name Fleet
Air Arm was officially adopted in April 1924). A special sub-
committee of the main Salisbury committee, consisting of Balfour as chairman, Weir and Peel (Secretary of State for India),
was set up to examine this in detail. It concluded, in essence,
that the Admiralty's claim to complete control of the naval air
units should be rejected: under its proposals the Air Ministry
retained administrative control on land of the ship-borne units,
while the Admiralty had operational control of them afloat.
The Balfour report was approved by the main committee,
although the First Lord of the Admiralty (Amery) and the
Secretary of State for War (Derby) insisted on recording their
dissent.[29]

The Sea Lords were furious at what they considered to be a
betrayal and informed Amery of their intention to resign *en
masse*.[30] For their part Hoare and Trenchard were equally
resolute in support of the Balfour report and its approval by the
Salisbury committee but purposely refrained from making any
counter-threat of resignation. When the matter came to the
Cabinet on 31st July, Baldwin was in an unenviable position.
On the one hand there could be no question of the Salisbury
committee being repudiated, but on the other the resignation of
the naval members of the Board of Admiralty (Amery made
clear that there was no possibility of any ministerial resigna-

tions) would be highly damaging to the government's reputation. Baldwin himself said little at the meeting, according to Hoare's later account.

> The protagonists first stated the case at considerable length. He [Baldwin] then asked each Minister in turn to give his view. The discussion lasted most of the day. When, however, he went round the table and questioned each Minister in turn, it was clear that the majority was on the side of the Report. The cleavage of view was deeply significant, the Conservatives on the right such as Cave [Lord Chancellor] and Willie Bridgeman [Home Secretary], taking the Admiralty side, the younger Conservatives, with the exception of Cunliffe-Lister [President of the Board of Trade], supporting the Report. When the Cabinet ended, the decision had been reached to abide by the Committee's recommendations.[31]

But still Beatty and his fellow Sea Lords did not give up the fight. They made a last ditch effort to get the Prime Minister to include in his Commons announcement, to be made on 2nd August, a statement to the effect that the agreement was provisional and that the Sea Lords' view of the necessity of naval responsibility for the Fleet Air Arm had not been accepted. The effort achieved some success. Baldwin's statement went a long way towards meeting the Sea Lords' demand, providing sufficient scope, it would seem, to allow them to withdraw their resignation threat without too much loss of dignity. The Prime Minister referred to the fact that 'The Admiralty were rightly concerned to maintain the absolute control over all the fighting equipment in the Fleet which is essential to its efficiency' and pointed out that while the Balfour inquiry had been 'unable to meet the views of the Admiralty to the extent of destroying the principle of a single Air Service' it considered that its recommendations secured for the Admiralty 'absolute control afloat'. However, the government did not hesitate to accept the necessity of a single air service, for three main reasons: (1) that aircraft 'are governed by the same principles whether flying above the sea or elsewhere'; (2) that the rapid development of air power required a concentration of effort; and (3) that unity of method was needed in those contingencies in which shore-based and fleet-based aircraft might be called upon to act together. Within this framework it was possible to meet the detailed objections the Admiralty might have to the way in which the Fleet Air Arm was currently being operated. Baldwin then gave a hostage to fortune by declaring: 'It is impossible without experience to pronounce a final judgement on these arrangements.' This hint that nothing was necessarily immutable was coupled with an expression of the Prime Minister's confidence that 'both Services will do their utmost' to make the proposed arrangements successful.[32]

The Salisbury-Balfour inquiry was by no means the end of the affair but it did constitute an authoritative point of reference for the Air Ministry in its continued efforts to defend the autonomy of the air force. The next major inter-service confrontation came in the second Baldwin government when Churchill, in his surprising role as a fiercely economising Chancellor of the Exchequer, engineered the establishment, in August 1925, of the Fighting Services Economy Committee, consisting of the industrialist Lord Colwyn as chairman and two former heads of the Treasury (Lords Chalmers and Bradbury). Both the army and navy suggested that economies could be made if they were to have their own air services. The Colwyn committee, which submitted its report to Baldwin in December 1925, did not agree, however. It foresaw greater savings accruing from the achievement of two of the Air Ministry's long-term ambitions — the substitution of air power for the older arms wherever possible(as had been done in Iraq, which Hoare had just visited by air) and the strengthening of air force control over the Fleet Air Arm — than from the setting up of separate air arms for the navy and army. The committee was not, in fact, impressed with the financial management exercised by the Admiralty, which it thought too sailor-dominated, out of touch with civilian experience. The Air Ministry was acquitted of the charge of ignoring civilian experience but was not considered as financially efficient as it might be, partly from inexperience and partly as a result of 'frequent changes of government policy and perpetual inter-departmental warfare with the older services'. The committee was satisfied, however, that the Secretary of State for Air and the Chief of the Air Staff 'were working energetically to remove these defects'.[33]

The Admiralty thus came away from Colwyn with a bloody nose (Roskill describes the committee's criticisms as 'one of the heaviest fusillades ever fired at a government department'[34]), while the Air Ministry had grounds for solid satisfaction. Once again the Admiralty had over-played its hand and the quieter tactics which Hoare found congenial had paid dividends. But the report was not mandatory and its Whitehall circulation merely led to another bout of inter-departmental jousting, in the course of which Baldwin felt it necessary to reaffirm in the House of Commons that the government had no intention of reopening the question of the independent status of the Air Ministry and the Royal Air Force.[35] On detailed matters relating to the operation, training and personnel of the Fleet Air Arm Baldwin had to give an arbitration in the inter-departmental conflict in July 1926, and was appealed to for yet another in July 1927. But by then the Prime Minister had had enough of the bickering and said he had no time to devote to the task. The mantle of arbitrator passed to Lord Salisbury, whose judgement was delivered in March 1928 and approved by the Prime Minister and the Committee of Imperial Defence. On the broad question, he envisaged in the long term that the Fleet Air Arm might eventually be separated from the R.A.F. but in the present years of freedom from a major war he felt the navy could only benefit from the existing arrangements.[36]

For no very obvious reason — unless it was the exhaustion of the combatants — the Salisbury arbitration of March 1928 marked a pause in the inter-service strife. Not for another eight years were relations between the Admiralty and the Air Ministry to be in such a state of deadlock that appeal had to be made to higher authority. For at least the last year of his incumbency at the Air Ministry Hoare could feel reasonably free of the Fleet Air Arm albatross. He was to meet it again, in rather different circumstances, at the Admiralty in 1936.

Hoare was not content as minister merely to preserve the *status quo*, however. He wanted to develop both the military and civil potentiality of air power and as an essential prerequisite for this, to create a sympathetic climate of public opinion towards this potent new force in everyone's life. But the positive objective of developing air power proved more difficult of achievement than the negative one of fighting off the various

assaults by the older services on the independence of the R.A.F.
The post-war combination of financial stringency and world
disarmament hopes was not conducive to any rapid progress and
indeed at times it became almost impossible to maintain the air
force at existing levels of efficiency. The Air estimates (military
and civil) totalled about £15½ million in 1925 and thereafter
either increased only marginally or even, on two occasions,
were actually reduced. The 1929 estimates were still only around
£16 million. The 52 squadron scheme for metropolitan defence,
announced in June 1923, made but slow progress. In view of the
improvement in Franco-British relations (it was French air
strength that had motivated the expansion in the first place)
and the new atmosphere engendered by the Locarno discussions between France, Britain and Germany, the Cabinet
decided at the end of 1925 to put back the completion of the
scheme, initially envisaged for 1928, to 1935–6. While Hoare
was clearly doubtful about the long-term implications of Locarno for really significant reductions in armaments he thought
that at the very least it made the risk of the war in the near
future less that it was before. To that extent, he told the House
of Commons in his Air estimates speech in February 1926, 'it
surely justifies us in taking a somewhat longer period than we
should otherwise have taken for the completion of our expansion programme.'[37] Thus when Hoare left the Air Ministry
in June 1929 not more than 60 per cent of the scheme he had
launched six years before had been completed. It is difficult,
however, to see how he could have done more in the circumstances.

Hoare took a close interest in that essential element in any
fighting service, the creation of mobilisable reserves. When he
came to the Air Ministry there was no R.A.F. equivalent of the
Territorial Army. Trenchard had long favoured what he called
an auxiliary air force but had met opposition from those who
were sceptical as to the value of a reserve of part-time fliers of
problematic efficiency. A bill to establish an auxiliary air force
was drafted during Hoare's first term at the Air Ministry and
was seen on the statute book by his Labour successor, Lord
Thomson, in 1924. Its implementation had to await Hoare's
return to office soon afterwards. The experiment was a success,
and the part-time fliers soon showed their value. Hoare made a

point of visiting every town where it was intended to start an auxiliary squadron and always presented the annual Esher Trophy to the squadron judged the most efficient. Trenchard's biographer, no doubt quoting from Trenchard himself, has testified to Hoare's personal role in getting the auxiliary squadrons established: 'Combining the roles of intermediary and travelling salesman, the Minister did much to break down the apathy of local authorities and local business interests and local citizens by his energy and sincerity.'[38] It was appropriate that when he left the Air Ministry in 1929 he should be appointed honorary air commodore of one of the London auxiliary squadrons.

Trenchard had also visualised another non-regular supportive service on army lines: the creation of university air officer training corps. But Hoare, and even more his P.P.S., Geoffrey Butler, insisted that if the experiment were to succeed it must be made upon new lines. As Hoare wrote later:

> He and I ... evolved the conception of the University Squadrons. They were [unlike the O.T.C.s] to be non-military, they were to be small and exclusive and they were to be kept in the closest possible touch with the scientific and engineering work of the Universities.[39]

On 1st October, 1925, Hoare inaugurated the first university air squadron at Cambridge; and ten days later, the squadron at Oxford. Over fifty years later the air squadrons of the universities which founded them remain among the most sought-after undergraduate activities, not least because of the insistence of Hoare and Butler that their basis must be primarily civilian.

If the air force needed its own version of the Territorial Army and O.T.C.s it also needed officer training facilities on the lines of R.M.A. Sandhurst and R.N.C. Dartmouth. The R.A.F. equivalent had been opened at Cranwell in February 1920 but was housed in dilapidated wartime huts. The efforts of Trenchard and Hoare to get a permanent officer cadet college met with fierce Treasury resistance, perhaps in the hope that the abolition of a separate R.A.F. — always a possibility in the 1920s — might render the project unnecessary. Hoare kept plugging away at the Treasury and eventually — in his last estimates, presented in March 1929 – was able to include a modest financial provision for permanent buildings at Cranwell. In part to tie the hands of his successors Hoare arranged for an early initiating ceremony and Lady Maud laid the foundation stone of the new buildings on 26th April, just six weeks before Hoare left office. He subsequently donated a double avenue of lime trees to mark the occasion.[40] The new college was not officially opened until 1934 but its successful completion had already been ensured by Hoare's persistence several years before.

The development of civil air transport was not immune from the financial constraints that dogged the development of the R.A.F. But nevertheless, significant advances in this field of aviation were made under Hoare's administration of the Air Ministry. One of his first actions on becoming minister was to appoint a Civil Air Transport Subsidies Committee consisting of two business friends from the banking and insurance worlds – Sir Herbert Hambling (as chairman) and Sir Joseph Broodbank – and his brother, Oliver, then at Barclays Bank, to examine the unsatisfactory system of subsidies to competing air lines. With commendable speed the Hambling committee produced its report in February 1923, coming out in favour of a single commercial company to run Britain's air routes, supported by a £1 million government grant over a ten-year period, provided a similar sum could be provided by public subscription.[41] Hoare strongly approved of this proposal and, despite the Treasury's serious objections to a long-term subsidy agreement, the protests of the companies being eliminated and the misgivings of aviation experts like Weir and Sir Frederick Sykes (Brancker's predecessor as Director of Civil Aviation), he pressed on with the implementation of the Hambling report. In December 1923, just at the end of his first term at the Air Ministry, the four principal air transport companies were merged into the Imperial Air Transport Company, renamed, in the following year, Imperial Airways.

Despite its £1 million government subsidy Imperial Airways' European services had great difficulty in paying their way in face of competition from other European companies, especially the much more heavily subsidised German and French airlines. Concerned though Hoare was with this situation (among other things, he secured an extension of the subsidy period), his attention was much more directed to the exciting possibilities of intra-imperial communications being opened up by aviation pioneers like Alan Cobham, who in 1926 made flights to both Australia and South Africa. It was on these prospects that Hoare dilated at the imperial conference in October 1926, introducing a wide-ranging memorandum on imperial air communications prepared under his direction by his able young assistant private secretary, Geoffrey Lloyd. The dominion delegates were profoundly impressed: it was clear that Hoare intended the title 'Imperial Airways' to be no empty one.[42]

The two key imperial air routes, in Hoare's view, were those to India and to South Africa. He negotiated with the Treasury a £93,600 annual subsidy over a five-year period to enable Imperial Airways to open up a service between Cairo and India in continuation of a service which had been carrying military mails between London and Cairo since 1921. Hoare's most spectacular flight as Secretary of State for Air – and he undertook many – was made to launch the new India route. With Lady Maud (who thus became the first woman to fly to India) he left Croydon in a 'Hercules' aircraft on Boxing Day 1926 and arrived in Delhi, via Cairo and Bagdad, on 8th January. After a month's stay in India as guests of the Viceroy – his old friend Edward Wood, now Lord Irwin – Hoare and his wife returned to England on 17th February to the accompaniment of something like a hero's welcome after their 12,000 miles of air travel (both Hoare and Lady Maud were included in the 1927 Birthday Honours List on Baldwin's recommendation, he as G.B.E., Lady Maud as D.B.E.).[43] The actual opening of the route, first to air mails and soon after to passenger traffic, did not, however, take place until two years after the Hoares' inaugural flight. Difficulties with Persia about over-flying rights delayed the introduction of the service until April 1929, just before Hoare left the Air Ministry.

With the Indian route settled, Hoare's next concern, occupying much of his last 18 months in office, was to establish the imperial air route across Africa to Cape Town.[44] This involved long negotiations with, among others, the Colonial Office, the various British African colonial governments concerned and the South African government to obtain both their agreement to the route itself and a contribution to the subsidy that Imperial Airways would need to operate it. Hoare was able to announce the final agreement necessary — that with South Africa — shortly before he left office.

Whatever the financial or geographical constraints the increase in British civil aviation in the 1920s was little short of phenomenal. Between 1924 and 1929 the number of miles flown by British civil aircraft on regular routes increased from 699,990 to 1,166,000, the number of passengers carried from 10,321 to 28,484, and the cargo from 350,700 to 994,300 ton miles.[45] The minister who initiated Imperial Airways and presided over the formulation of policy which made its expansion possible can claim a substantial share in this achievement.

Much to Hoare's disappointment, none of the increased passenger capacity of British civil aviation was accounted for by airships, in which he, like so many others, had placed high hopes. In his first term at the Air Ministry he almost completed negotiations with the Airship Guarantee Company, founded by the formidable aeronautical inventor and M.P., Commander C. D. Burney, for the production of six airships. But when the Labour government took over in January 1924 Hoare's plans were profoundly modified and instead of the whole development being undertaken by a commercial firm with a government subsidy there was a very much smaller scheme for two airships only, one (the R.101) to be constructed under the Air Ministry's direct supervision and the other (the R.100) by Burney's company. Hoare had to take over this compromise arrangement unchanged when he returned to the Air Ministry later in the year.[46] Things did not go smoothly with either project and Hoare was frequently pressed in the Commons for speedier results, especially in view of German progress with the 'Graf Zeppelin', which flew round the world in 21 days in August 1929 before going into regular transatlantic service. Neither British airship had been completed when Hoare left office in June 1929 although he had fully expected to participate in the maiden flight of the R.101 to India before then. He was naturally not involved in his successor's decision, taken against the advice of Sir Sefton Brancker and in the face of much uncertainty about the R.101's performance, to embark on 4th October, 1930, on the flight which ended so disastrously in

France a few hours later, killing 48 passengers, including Thomson and Brancker. But with that disaster the story of British airship development came to an abrupt end. Perhaps if Hoare's tenure of the Air Ministry had not been interrupted on two occasions in the 1920s the story might have been different. His original plan was for a wholly commercial development: and, in fact, the commercially produced R.100 always had the edge on its government-sponsored rival (it made a spectacular flight to Canada and back just two months before the R.101 set off for India). Moreover, Hoare's natural caution would never have allowed him to ignore expert advice as Thomson had done in pushing ahead with the Indian flight.[47]

The third strand in Hoare's administration of the Air Ministry — along with the maintenance of air force integrity and the development of both military and civil aviation — was the creation of a public opinion sympathetic to air power: the stimulation, as he once put it in the Commons, of the air sense of the nation.[48] That he was successful in this objective is indicated in the valedictory comment in a leading aviation journal on Hoare's departure from the Air Ministry in June 1929:

> He has raised the prestige of British Aviation. Air stock has, metaphorically, gone up hundreds per cent since he became a believer in and an advocate of aviation ... Sir Samuel Hoare has done more than any one man to make the British People, at home and in the Dominions overseas, airminded.[49]

Public projection of aviation was not a role for which Hoare was particularly well-equipped, lacking as he did any kind of personal flamboyance (apart for a fondness for ceremonial uniforms[50]) or skill in popular communication. But he realised that it was a task which needed to be performed and which he alone in the Air Ministry could undertake with sufficient authority. Trenchard was primarily concerned with the R.A.F., and disposed to look askance at civil aviation as derogating from military air development. In any case he was less equipped than Hoare in both personality and position to be an expositor to the public, either for the R.A.F. or aviation in general. If the job were to be done at all Hoare must do it.

Hoare's approach was two-pronged: to emphasise the excitement, even glamour, of the air but yet at the same time to establish its ordinariness, to get the public to treat air travel in the same way as they looked on the well-established methods of transport. Thus his 1926–7 flight to India was both an attempt to inject drama – a Minister of the Crown and his wife (the daughter of an earl) flying to India at a time when long distance flights were the preserve of the air pioneers like Cobham and Lindbergh – and a demonstration that such an immense journey was quite feasible. And not only feasible, but safe. The relative safety of flying was a point essential to establish if the development of air communications was to receive public backing. In point of fact the regular civil routes had a very good safety record but there was a considerable problem about R.A.F. air accidents. Indeed Hoare discussed it with Baldwin just before setting off on his India flight and they agreed that the Prime Minister should make a personal investigation. Hoare had been pressed in the Commons for inquiries into each accident and for statistics of the percentage of fatal accidents to total flying hours but Trenchard was convinced that publication of such details would be bad for service morale. In an intervention in typically simple and direct style during the 1927 Air estimates debate, Baldwin was able to do much to quieten the agitation down and restore public confidence.[51]

One of the more glamorous of Hoare's efforts to project the air and the air force was to win back for Britain what had become the blue ribbon of international aviation, the Schneider Trophy for seaplanes, originally founded in 1913 and revived in 1919. A British civilian pilot (H. C. Biard) had won it in 1922 but in three subsequent races (1923, 1925 and 1926) the trophy had gone to foreign competitors. Hoare was determined that at the next contest, to be held in Venice in September 1927, an R.A.F. plane should be entered for the first time. Trenchard was not enthusiastic about the project since, as Hoare later wrote, he 'was naturally reluctant to concentrate upon a contest of this kind so much of the energies of the Air Force', but nevertheless gave Hoare his full support. Even more important, the romantic nature of Churchill, so long submerged under his iron Chancellor role, seems to have been stirred and he made no objection to an expenditure of two or three hundred thousand pounds. The subsequent news that the British entry at Venice – a 'Supermarine' S5 seaplane piloted by Squadron Leader Webster – was the outright winner at an average speed of 281·66 m.p.h. made one of the happiest days of Hoare's time at the Air Ministry. He instructed preparations to be put in hand for the 1929 race, which, three months after he had left office, was again won by the British entry, as was the 1931 contest. The Schneider Trophy races, as Hoare realised, were much more than opportunities for prestige publicity for national aviation achievements. They had important developmental implications, enabling engines and airframes to be tested in something like operational conditions and at speeds which would not in fact become operational for several years. Second World War fighters owed much to the aircraft designed for Schneider Trophy racing.[52]

Less glamorous but more widespread in its effects was Hoare's encouragement of the light aeroplane club movement as a stimulus to amateur civilian flying. There had been a certain amount of private activity in this field before 1923 but there was no general organised movement and the very few light aeroplanes available were all of unproven safety and reliability. Sir Geoffrey Salmond, in charge of Air Ministry research and development, and Hoare were determined to start such a movement. The trouble was to find a safe machine and an effective organisational framework. Salmond eventually evolved the plan of a number of subsidised clubs. But the only possible light aeroplane – the de Havilland 'Moth', eventually launched in 1925 at the incredibly low selling price of £500 – was almost unanimously condemned in advance by Air Ministry experts, apart from Salmond, as unairworthy. Salmond and Hoare took their courage in both hands and authorised production of the 'Moth' for use by light aeroplane clubs. There was then the problem of how to extract a few thousands a year from the Treasury to cover the subsidy to an initial ten clubs. The task had not been completed when the first Baldwin government fell and it was left to Hoare's successor Thomson to announce in August 1924 that ten clubs were to be assisted financially for an initial period of two years, with the possibility of further extension. On his return to the Air Ministry Hoare spent a good deal of time visiting the clubs in order to attract public attention to their activities. This was an important method, he felt, of establishing flying as a normal part of the physical environment

rather than merely an esoteric whim of the foolhardy. By the
end of 1929 there were 23 clubs, 13 of them (with a total membership of 3,648) financially assisted by the Air Ministry. As for the
'Moth', the faith of Salmond and Hoare was abundantly justified
as it was to remain in universal use for private flying and service
training for over thirty years.[53]

If air transport were to be expanded there had to be aerodromes, both those for the international routes and the many
more needed for internal routes. It took a great deal of effort —
in which Hoare fully participated — to interest even large cities
in the provision of a municipal airport.[54] By the end of 1929,
however, some twenty-five municipal aerodromes were either
established or in course of construction. London's main airport
had by then only just become firmly based on Croydon. There
had been much controversy as to whether the site was suitable
for a civil aerodrome owing to the unsatisfactory weather conditions and the limited size of the existing property. Hoare
instituted an inquiry into possible sites and this came down in
favour of Croydon by a process of eliminating the other available sites as even less suitable. The site was bought on Hoare's
instructions and subsequent purchase of surrounding land substantially enlarged the capacity of the aerodrome. Lady Maud
opened the new airport buildings at Croydon on 2nd May,
1928.

Hoare also arranged for the purchase of Hendon aerodrome,
which had been in the hands of receivers. It was here that the
first annual R.A.F. Pageant had been held in July 1920. In 1925
Hoare had them renamed R.A.F. Displays. But more significant
from the point of view of the public projection of the R.A.F. and
air powers, he persuaded King George V and Queen Mary to
grace the occasion with their — at first — very reluctant presence
from 1923 onwards. The royal couple hated the noise and were
always afraid that there would be a serious accident. The King,
moreover, had the strongest of prejudices against the air force
and the Air Ministry (as an old sailor he always took the navy's
side in the Fleet Air Arm controversy) and it called for all
Hoare's efforts, helped by his being a Norfolk neighbour of the
King and a fellow-country sportsman, to moderate this prejudice. Decisions about such matters as R.A.F. uniforms and
ranks (the King thought 'Air Marshal' an outlandish designa-

tion) all required careful preparation of the royal mind.[55]
Younger members of the Royal Family who attended the Displays were, however, more enthusiastic, particularly the future
George VI. By great good fortune the long series of Hendon
Displays during Hoare's incumbency were free from accidents
and uniformly enjoyed some special dispensation from the usual
climatic hazards of open air occasions.

This involvement of the Royal Family in the projection of
aviation was not the least influential of the methods Hoare chose
to achieve his aim of popular acceptance of the fact and potentialities of air power. Britain in the 1920s was still conspicuously a
class-oriented and deferential society. The dynamic of orderly
change was provided more often than not by the upper class and
from there dispersed through the social system. As Professor
Michael Howard commented, in a perceptive review of Lord
Templewood's *The Empire of the Air* when it appeared early in
1957: 'it is easier to secure major reforms if one works with the
social grain of the country rather than against it.' The same
reviewer compared what he termed the 'adventurous antics' of
the Hoares — the newsworthy flights and so on — with the
aristocratic agrarian and industrial innovators of the eighteenth
century, with their independent means and assured position:
'original and inquiring people with deep roots outside the
political system for which they were working but on which they
were in no way dependent'.[56] It was probably not a model that
Hoare himself had in mind, despite his historical bent — there is
no evidence that he regarded himself as a kind of aerial Coke of
Holkham. But the parallel is not inapposite. Hoare was indeed
a propagandist for technological innovation in his years at the
Air Ministry between 1922 and 1929 and did not hesitate to use
his social and political position to disseminate change.

Few among the tributes Hoare received on the conclusion of
his tenure of the Air Ministry could have given him greater
pleasure than that from the King, conveyed through his private
secretary, Lord Stamfordham. There was no trace of anti-air
prejudice in the royal description of Hoare's departure as 'a
great loss to the Air Service, where you have displayed your
powers of administration and given splendid examples of
exceptional flights'.[57] The dragging of a reluctant monarch to
the Hendon Air Display year after year had paid dividends: the

social grain had not after all been rubbed the wrong way.

Other tributes Hoare must have particularly valued came from people with intimate knowledge of his work. The distinguished aviation pioneer, Lieutenant-Colonel J. T. C. Moore-Brabazon (who had been with Hoare at Harrow and served in a junior ministerial post until 1927) wrote after the 1929 election, in which he lost his own seat, to record his sorrow at Hoare's departure from the Air Ministry where '... you have been a great Minister and have faced the difficulties that I know more than anybody else, and have come out triumphant. The country owes you a great debt of gratitude.' Hoare's private secretary, Christopher Bullock, wrote from the Air Ministry on the day Hoare had officially left it to express his thanks to his chief and his feeling of 'melancholy at the passing of your regime. It really is dragging the Office up by the roots, for it will seem all wrong that someone else should be occupying your chair.'[58]

Trenchard's tribute made up in absolute sincerity for what it may have lacked in eloquence. In the six years they worked together they had developed a close relationship. Hoare appreciated Trenchard's utter dependability and single-minded dedication to the welfare of the R.A.F. and Trenchard recognised Hoare's political skills and administrative grasp. As Trenchard told Hoare in December 1929, when his own turn came to leave the Air Ministry, it was a pleasure 'to work with a man who not only went to an immense amount of trouble, but also had the determination to understand the whole question with which he was dealing'.[59]

Hoare's record at the Air Ministry has since been criticised for the very closeness of his relationship with his chief professional adviser. It was this, some have maintained, which led to a weak acceptance by Hoare of Trenchard's refusal to let the navy secure control of the Fleet Air Arm which so soured inter-service relations then and for long afterwards. Perhaps even more serious, critics suggest, was Hoare's failure to subject to more searching examination Trenchard's views on the strategic role of the R.A.F., his emphasis on the bomber deterrent at the expense, so the critics urge, of fighter development and scientific research.[60]

There is no evidence that Hoare had any initial reluctance

about accepting Trenchard's views on the Fleet Air Arm. Hoare early realised the implications of a naval take-over at that time for the service and department he headed: it was, in fact, just the sort of challenge to fire an ambitious politician anxious to prove his political and administrative ability in his first ministerial post. Far from being a mere puppet of Trenchard in the wearisome confrontation with the older services Hoare may well have been more royalist than the king for he later wrote (without, however, producing any evidence) that more than once Trenchard had been 'ready to go too far on the road to concessions' to the navy over the Fleet Air Arm.[61]

Trenchard's views on the strategic role of the bomber and its effectiveness as a deterrent have been hotly debated.[62] It is one of those many controversies for which it is difficult to see any objective resolution. But as far as Hoare as the responsible minister was concerned it does not seem unreasonable — to put it at its lowest estimate — that he should have backed the judgement of his immensely experienced professional adviser. In the circumstances of the 1920s the bomber was clearly the military aircraft on which the main emphasis had to be placed: not only for its widely accepted deterrent value against would-be aggressors[63] but because it represented, by 'substituting' for some of the more expensive operations of the older arms (as in Iraq), economy rather than extravagance. Money was tight for the R.A.F in the 1920s and within the rigid constraints Hoare and Trenchard left an air force capable of subsequent expansion when it was needed. Without them there might not have been an R.A.F. at all.

As Air Minister Hoare certainly did not have one of the least onerous portfolios in the Conservative governments between 1922 and 1929. But he was naturally concerned in governmental decision-making on a much wider range of issues than the purely departmental, including foreign policy (he was, with Churchill and Amery, one of the leading members of the Cabinet group which frustrated Austen Chamberlain's efforts to secure an Anglo-French alliance in 1924–5),[64] disarmament and various domestic questions. In the most notable domestic event during Baldwin's second government — the General Strike of May 1926 — Hoare had both departmental and extra-departmental functions to perform. Baldwin asked him to attempt to persuade the newspaper proprietors that, in view of the exiguous supplies of newsprint and manpower, they should run a joint newspaper. But when he met the principal proprietors with the proposition he found them adamantly opposed to it — Fleet Street rivalries prevented co-operation even in a unique period of crisis. The idea of a press-managed paper had to be set aside and that of a government gazette took its place. It was Hoare who suggested that it should have 'British' in its title and thus the 'British Gazette' was born. Gwynne, the owner of the *Morning Post*, offered to print the paper if the government supplied him with the newsprint and staff. Hoare went with Churchill to take over the *Morning Post* office for the *British Gazette* but from that moment Churchill, in what Hoare later described as 'a state of great exaltation', took charge and Hoare faded out of the picture. He came back into it after the strike was over to help to induce Churchill, with the greatest difficulty, to bring his journalistic venture to an end.[65] As a member of the Supply and Transport Committee during the strike Hoare's immediate concern was with the maintenance of communications, for which the air force had been made responsible. It was clearly a key role since, 'If the country could be convinced that communications were being maintained, there would be no panic, the strike would appear incomplete and there would be an outward and visible sign that the Government was in control of the situation.'[66] The R.A.F. air services went into operation immediately, distributing, among other things, Churchill's *British Gazette* all over the country. But they obviously could not cope with any bulk transportation: their main function was to keep areas in touch. One of the more sinister cargoes carried by the aircraft to the main industrial centres was at the suggestion of Liddell Hart, conveyed to Hoare by Geoffrey Butler. They were canisters of tear gas which Liddell Hart recommended as preferable to bullets for controlling the angry mobs it was feared the General Strike might engender.[67] While the strike was not quite the friendly affair painted by subsequent legend fortunately neither technique of crowd control had to be invoked.

Although Hoare retained the same office throughout the Conservative governments of the 1920s his status within it sensibly increased as the years went on. It was, for example, no idle suggestion by Neville Chamberlain when, consulted by Baldwin on Cabinet appointments after the Conservative electoral victory in October 1924, he mentioned Hoare as a possible Chancellor of the Exchequer.[68] That post went, however, to Winston Churchill, whose inclusion in the government (although not necessarily as Chancellor) had been urged by Hoare himself, among others, in order to bring in new blood and to complement the new unity of the Conservatives secured by the adherence of former coalitionists like Austen Chamberlain, Birkenhead and (later) Balfour.[69]

Neville Chamberlain, Minister of Health for most of the time Hoare was at the Air Ministry, was the colleague with whom Hoare probably had his closest personal and official relations. They had a high regard for each other's abilities. According to Hoare, Chamberlain — whose ambitious programme for the reform of local government structure, finance and services, embodied in twenty-five bills over the life of the 1924-9 Parliament, was the chief legislative achievement of the second Baldwin government — 'knew his case better than anyone else in the country — and possessed great talent for Cabinet discussion and for drafting formulas and resolutions that reconciled differences of opinion.'[70] Many of Chamberlain's own differences of opinion were with Churchill who, as Chancellor, was intimately concerned, for example, in the de-rating provisions of what was to become the Local Government Act of 1929. 'Chamberlain was as persistent as Churchill was mercurial', Hoare later wrote, 'and it was Chamberlain who invariably had his way.'[71] Chamberlain, for his part, admired Hoare's political insight, telling him on one occasion that 'I look on you as one of the acutest observers of Parliamentary practice and current political opinion';[72] while his view of Hoare's administrative abilities may be gauged from the fact that he thought him worth suggesting as Chancellor of the Exchequer. The two men shared an interest in country life and country sport which took them both to several country houses during the shooting season where, as Hoare wrote, 'we came to know each other better than was ever possible in Whitehall and Westminster.' They had similar habits of work, both finding the interest of politics lay in hard work to achieve definite objectives. Moreover, as Chamberlain remarked some years later, they usually found themselves in agreement on policy questions.[73]

There is no evidence to suggest that Hoare was particularly close to Baldwin, and a good deal (in his unpublished record of the 1924-9 government) to indicate that Hoare felt his leadership to be often casual and indecisive. But, on the other hand, there is no reason to believe that Baldwin thought of Hoare as other than a very efficient member of his governmental team. Indeed, when discussing possible Cabinet changes with his crony Thomas Jones in March 1929, almost at the end of his government, Baldwin spoke of Hoare as Minister of Health — an office considerably more prestigious than formerly as a result of Neville Chamberlain's tenure of it — or as a Foreign Office minister with particular responsibility for League of Nations affairs.[74]

Perhaps the most significant testimony to Hoare's contribution to the second Baldwin government came from Bridgeman, the First Lord of the Admiralty. When, with the circulation of the Colwyn report at the end of 1925, the running battle between the navy and the air force over the Fleet Air Arm broke out again with fresh violence one of its features was a lengthy departmental correspondence between Bridgeman and Hoare of sometimes notable frigidity.[75] Some of the navy's champions found it difficult to forgive the small but persistent figure of Hoare standing in the way of the consummation they so devoutly wished. Beatty, never conspicuous for the restraint of his language, dismissed Hoare as an 'intriguing little brute'; while even J. C. C. Davidson, who owed a good deal politically to Hoare's friendship but who was at this time a junior minister at the Admiralty, later recalled Hoare in the 1924-9 government as 'small-minded and tremendously ambitious'.[76] Bridgeman, on the other hand, did not allow the inter-departmental strife to cloud his recognition of Hoare's ability and contribution to the Conservative Cabinet. Writing of his Cabinet colleagues in his diary immediately after the 1929 electoral defeat Bridgeman said of Hoare that although his manner was 'very stiff and cold' he 'had plenty of courage and was quick and skilful in discussion'. And he was by no means blinkered by his departmental responsibilities, Bridgeman thought, but displayed general political judgement — for example, 'His opinion on electioneering problems is usually good.' Bridgeman believed that Hoare 'could undertake most Cabinet posts with a very

1 Hoare's parents: Samuel and Katharin Hoare

2 Hoare as a boy

3 The young Hoare in levée dress

4 The aeroplane which flew the Hoares to India in December 1926

5 At the 1927 R.A.F. Display at Hendon with King George V and Queen Mary. Hoare is on the King's right, Trenchard on his left

good chance of success, though he is never likely to be a popular figure in the House or on the platform'.[77] A grudging compliment from an adversary is often better than the adulation of friends, and Bridgeman was a shrewd judge of character, a quality which, as Hoare himself noted, made Baldwin value his counsel more than that of anyone else in the Cabinet.

The electioneering insights which Bridgeman remarked in Hoare were not notable in the confidence in victory with which he and most of his colleagues entered the electoral contest of May 1929, after a string of by-election reverses over the preceding months. Hoare had just undertaken a long flight to and from the Sudan to inspect sections of the proposed Cape to Cairo air route. On his return after Easter he found all his friends (he wrote in June, immediately after the election),

> confident of a Conservative victory. At Philip Sassoon's weekly luncheons we found everyone, except perhaps Winston, in a happy mood. Davidson was sure of a clear majority and according to such impartial advisers as Tom Jones [deputy secretary to the Cabinet and Baldwin's confidant] ... the socialists had no real hope of becoming the largest party in the House of Commons. The Lobby correspondents ... were equally certain we should do well.[78]

But the result was even worse than in December 1923, with the Labour party indeed becoming the largest single party, although lacking an overall majority.

In Chelsea, Hoare's personal victory was, however, a comfortable one. He secured 58 per cent of the vote against Labour and Liberal challengers, an excellent result at a time of general Conservative electoral decline. Despite quite a strong Liberal showing Hoare's majority of nearly 9,000 over Labour was greater than it had been in 1924. Chelsea with Hoare was a safe Conservative seat and the rest of his incumbency only served to make it safer. He had a simple way with the various forlorn candidatures against him. He rarely mentioned their names during the contest and never appeared on the same platform with them: when one is firmly established and the opposing candidates have not the remotest chance, he once told Beaverbrook, 'it is always policy never to advertise them in any way'.[79] From the 1929 election Hoare may well have gained an advantage through the 1928 franchise Act, which (very much with Hoare's approval) had extended the vote to women between 21 and 30. Not only had the total Chelsea electorate increased from 29,582 in 1924 to 41,945 in 1929, but women voters, who had formerly constituted just over half, now accounted for over 60 per cent. Lady Maud Hoare, who had been conspicuous in organising the women's section of the Chelsea Conservative association, became even more important as an influence in the dimensions of her husband's electoral successes.

In June 1929 began the second period of Conservative opposition to a Labour government, and one which was to endure nearly three times longer than the first experience in 1924. It was an unhappy time for the Conservatives, quintessentially the party of government and relatively unused to seeing the leaders of a still new and unproven party, of doubtful doctrinal tendencies, in the seats of power which they considered were rightfully theirs. After the 1923 election the Conservatives, although in opposition, were still the largest party in the House of Commons; now even that consolation was removed – they were the junior party. The effect was traumatic and it was perhaps inevitable that party frustrations should be vented on the leadership and on the person of the apparently slow-thinking and indecisive leader of the party in particular. The period 1929–31 was one of the most internally strife-torn in Conservative party history. The strife centred in two major fields of policy: the old albatross of protection (under various aliases, including industrial 'safeguarding' and, most importantly, Beaverbrook's 'Empire Free Trade' campaign, which posed such a threat to party unity); and the newer issue of Indian self-government, on which Baldwin took a more liberal and far-sighted position than was acceptable to a large part of his followers. On India Hoare was to play an increasingly important role, first as his party's principal delegate to the first Indian round table conference at the end of 1930 and then, after August 1931, as the minister responsible for Indian affairs: it will be discussed as a whole in the following chapter. On protection, he had a personal commitment, favourable to protective measures provided that they could be presented in terms that were electorally viable (as he was convinced *post facto* had not been done in the surprise election of December 1923); but his chief function here was as intermediary between the party leadership and a progressively disgruntled Beaverbrook.

Before he immersed himself in the affairs of his party in opposition Hoare had to secure his financial position. He was relieved to be reappointed to the boards of two companies in which he had held directorships in his last period of opposition but which he had naturally surrendered on returning to office in November 1924. These were the Employers' Liability Assurance (whose directors he had first joined in 1909)[80] and the Clerical, Medical and General Life Assurance. He soon added two more: the newly formed Anglo-Portuguese Bank and the General Reversionary and Investment Company.

Hoare's financial and commercial links led Baldwin to ask him to undertake what seemed a rather thankless assignment for the party. Hoare was invited in December 1929 to succeed Lord Younger (the former Sir George Younger) as treasurer of the party organisation. Younger, although a distinguished ex-party chairman, had never held ministerial office while his only predecessor as treasurer, Lord Farquhar, had held no post higher than Lord Steward. Thus the treasurership was hardly an appointment to attract the politically ambitious, and it involved the wearisome business of soliciting party contributions from industrial and commercial firms. Not surprisingly, Hoare accepted the task with reluctance and it says a good deal for his devotion to his party that he accepted it at all. He told Baldwin:

> It is not a job that attracts me. It is outside my beat, and I am bad at getting money. I am, however, most anxious to make myself as useful as possible to you and the Party, and as you wish me to try my hand at it, I certainly will. I do so with the less reluctance after the kind assurance that the post will not prejudice my political future.[81]

The party chairman, Davidson, added further assurance by telling Hoare that his assumption of the post would signal a change from the treasurership as a home for 'some distinguished but completely worn out political figure' to a job which, while by no means full-time, was filled by someone who, in talking to 'captains of industry and others of that ilk', was fully in touch with current political trends. Hoare intended to take over towards the end of January 1930 but an accident to Lady Maud while the Hoares were on a skating holiday in Switzerland (a regular feature of his life since Hoare learnt to skate well in 1927) prevented his starting at Conservative central office until March.[82]

In all his voluminous published and unpublished writings on various phases of his career there is no record of his eighteen-month tenure of the treasurership. But at least one of Hoare's *ex-officio* activities had long-term effects. He was a member of a committee under Davidson which in March 1931 submitted to Davidson's successor as party chairman, Neville Chamberlain, a report on the reorganisation of the Conservative central office: from it, a subsequent party chairman was to write in 1961, 'the present structure of the Central Office derives in almost every particular'.[83] Among its recommendations were the replacement of the principal agent by a general director in overall charge of the office, and the appointment of the party chairman from the ranks of the Cabinet or Shadow Cabinet rather than from more junior party members; the chairman was to be empowered to appoint a deputy on a regular basis, especially when the party was in the office and the chairman consequently burdened with Cabinet duties.

It was thus as both a senior member of the Shadow Cabinet and an official of the mass party organisation that Hoare witnessed and participated in the intra-party controversies of 1929–31. The debate on the merits of industrial protection versus free trade was never far below the surface in the Conservative party and the 1929 election defeat provided ammunition for those who could represent that it was caused by the absence of the clear and indubitably Conservative stance that a commitment to protection would have produced. Beaverbrook gained a response in many a Conservative breast when in July 1929 (two months after the election) he launched in his *Daily Express* the 'Empire Crusade' to secure what he shrewdly if nonsensically called 'Empire Free Trade' as a means to overcome the country's economic ills. Essentially he was advocating free trade within an empire insulated from the rest of the world by insurmountable tariff barriers; its obvious disadvantages were that the dominions were hardly likely to cast away their own tariff protection from the competition of British manufactured goods and that the only British tariffs which would interest the dominions would be those against non-dominion food imports — which would raise once again the old bogy of 'food taxes'. In a pivotal position as an intimate friend of Beaverbrook and a leading member (with Amery, Neville Chamberlain and Cunliffe-Lister) of the tariff reformers in the Shadow Cabinet Hoare did what he could to prevent an open breach between the crusading zeal of Beaverbrook and the more circumspect attitude of the party leadership. At his invitation, for example, Beaverbrook and Neville Chamberlain met for the first time at dinner with Hoare in Cadogan Gardens on 4th November, 1929, to try to hammer out some common policy. The two men seem to have got on rather well, despite their contrasting personalities, but even at this early stage it was clear that the issue of food taxes — which Beaverbrook was prepared to face but which was too much for a leadership conscious of electoral considerations — would be the eventual breaking point. At the same meeting, too, Beaverbrook gave notice of his intention to run Empire Free Trade candidates at by-elections.[84]

Hoare's dinner was the prelude to a meeting between Beaverbrook, Baldwin and Chamberlain a week later. This was similarly inconclusive but in his speech to the party annual conference ten days later Baldwin included a friendly word for Beaverbrook and his concept of a united empire which Beaverbrook for a brief moment thought might indicate a conversion to his policy. But it was not to be. At a Shadow Cabinet meeting on 30th January (1930) the party leadership, Amery apparently alone dissenting, set its face against food taxes while committing itself to an extension of industrial safeguarding. Baldwin made this decision public in a speech in London on 5th February.[85] A week later Rothermere and Beaverbrook formed the United Empire party with a programme which, in Beaverbrook's eyes, was confined to Empire Free Trade, but which in Rothermere's was soon to include a whole range of other fields, including India and government economy, on which he was at odds with the Conservative leadership and Baldwin in particular, and which he hoped to use to ensure Baldwin's removal. When, on 4th March, Baldwin announced that he would submit the question of taxes on food to the people in a referendum Beaverbrook temporarily made his peace with the party. He was soon disillusioned, however, when he realised how profoundly conservative a device a referendum was: Baldwin, he complained to Hoare on 15th May, was using it 'as a shield instead of a sword'.[86] He thereupon renewed his alliance with Rothermere to wage an all-out electoral attack on the Conservative party.

The complex story of the Empire Free Trade campaign until what was considered to be its *coup de grâce* — the victory of the pro-Baldwin candidate over Beaverbrook's nominee in the St George's, Westminster by-election on 19th March, 1931 — has been recounted elsewhere and will not be recapitulated here.[87] Hoare's role in it is difficult to assess since although he appears quite frequently in the record — for example, at several important meetings — his own views, particularly on the crucial issue of food taxes, do not emerge clearly and he does not refer to the crisis in any of his retrospective memoirs, published or unpublished. He was always a tariff reformer at heart and the Beaverbrook programme clearly attracted him, conscious though he was of the electoral disadvantages of any explicit commitment to food taxes; but much of what the Empire Free Trade campaign was seeking could, he felt, become part of a convincing Conservative programme if properly projected. He saw much of Beaverbrook at this time and undoubtedly used his friendship with him to try to prevent a final breach between Beaverbrook and Baldwin.

In his contacts with Beaverbrook Hoare was scrupulous not to appear to condone his friend's criticisms of what he saw as Baldwin's backslidings.[88] But to a confidant rather less dangerous than Beaverbrook — Irwin, in India — he wrote on 17th May:

> Politics here are in a most unsatisfactory state. Stanley [Baldwin] gives no lead to the party, either in the House or in the country. The modus vivendi that we fixed up with Beaverbrook looks like breaking down, each side accusing the other of having destroyed it. If only Stanley had taken the lead and made it appear that we were embarked upon a new chapter of Conservative policy, he could perfectly well have kept Beaverbrook and everyone else happy ... I have tried to do what I could with Stanley and Beaverbrook and at present I am disheartened with the result of my efforts.[89]

And when the movement against Baldwin's leadership really

gathered strength early in 1931 Hoare was numbered among those who thought he should resign. Even before Neville Chamberlain, as party chairman, had received from the party's chief official, H. R. Topping, a memorandum dated 25th February expressing the view that 'it would be in the interests of the Party that the Leader should reconsider his position', Hoare had reported that 'feeling in the House could not be worse'. Hoare was naturally among the party leaders Chamberlain consulted separately about the Topping memorandum and, along with Austen Chamberlain, Cunliffe-Lister, Hailsham, Bridgeman and Eyres-Monsell (the Chief Whip), agreed that it should be shown to Baldwin; all but the faithful Bridgeman also felt that its contents made Baldwin's resignation virtually inevitable. They were clearly surprised by the speed with which Baldwin on 1st March seemed to accept their suggestion to resign but perhaps less so by his change of mind within a few hours, after seeking Bridgeman's advice. His resignation was put off at least until after the crucial St George's by-election, due on 19th March. Duff Cooper's victory in that by-election was generally thought to have both confirmed Baldwin in the leadership and effectively killed the Empire Free Trade campaign. On 25th March Baldwin had a very frank discussion with his dissident colleagues, including Hoare, about their criticisms of his leadership of which the upshot was 'a request that he would show as much vigour in attacking the Socialists as he did in attacking recalcitrant Conservatives and the Press'.[90] The drawing of Beaverbrook's electoral claws was effected within a few days of the St George's by-election. At Hoare's suggestion Neville Chamberlain, in one of his last acts as party chairman, got in touch with Beaverbrook and found him ready to come to terms. On 30th March an agreed correspondence was released to the press in which Beaverbrook promised to assist the Conservative party at the next election if he were assured, as Chamberlain was prepared to assure him, that the party's policy would be directed towards increasing agricultural as well as industrial production by the most efficient and practicable method.[91] The Empire Free Trade candidates Beaverbrook had been recruiting for the coming general election were presumably dispersed. Beaverbrook hardly became henceforth a model supporter of the Conservative party but at least his future challenges did not take the form of direct electoral confrontation. The warm personal relations between Hoare and Beaverbrook seem also to have been fully resumed, following a slight cooling at the height of Beaverbrook's anti-Baldwin campaign. When Hoare wrote to Beaverbrook to sympathise with him on the death of his friends Tim Healy and Arnold Bennett, Beaverbrook replied on 30th March that 'The loss of old friends makes it necessary for me to do what I can to hold on to those who live'.[92]

Much of Hoare's time in his second bout of frontbench opposition was taken up with representing his party on several inter-party conferences. In addition to the Indian round table conference from November 1930 to January 1931, there was, in the first half of 1930, the inconclusive conference on electoral reform presided over by a former Speaker, Lord Ullswater, at which Hoare led the Conservative delegation. He regarded it as his main task to prevent a combination between the Liberals under Herbert Samuel and the Labour party. Hoare was convinced that the Liberals were prepared to pledge their support to the Labour government in exchange for the alternative vote in the counties and proportional representation in towns. He felt that the alternative vote was likely to harm the Conservative electoral position and that to prevent this it was worth conceding the Liberals P.R. in a selected number of large towns; but he was unable to persuade his Shadow Cabinet colleagues to make this concession. In July 1930 Ullswater had to inform the Prime Minister that it had been impossible to obtain that inter-party agreement on which measures of electoral reform had always in the past been thought to depend. The Labour government, after some indications of secret discussions with the Liberals, eventually introduced an electoral reform bill which, among other things, would have introduced the alternative vote and abolished plural voting (the business and university votes). Hoare moved the Opposition's rejection of the bill on second reading and was active in leading the Conservative attack at all stages of its Commons' consideration. It passed the House, nevertheless, only to be mangled by the Lords and disappear without trace with the fall of the Labour government.[93]

From March to July 1931 Hoare also took part in an all-party sub-committee of the Committee of Imperial Defence which, under the chairmanship of the Prime Minister, Ramsay

MacDonald, met to prepare the ground for the world disarmament conference which was due to meet in Geneva under
League of Nations auspices early in 1932. There was here a considerable degree of consensus, with the committee explicitly
repudiating unilateral disarmament and declaring that any
further reduction of British armaments could be undertaken
only as part of 'an international agreement containing comparable reductions by other Powers, and after taking into account
the particular obligations and dangers of each country'. But by
the time the world disarmament conference actually convened
(and Hoare was present at its opening session) the replacement
of the Labour government by a Conservative-dominated
National Government, faced by a small but understandably
bitter Labour opposition, had brought the question of British
disarmament back into the realm of partisan politics.[94]

The most important inter-party conference that Hoare
attended differed markedly from these formally constituted
gatherings. From 22nd to 24th August, 1931, he was closeted
with Neville Chamberlain (acting for Baldwin, who was on his
usual mandatory holiday at Aix-les-Bains), and Sir Herbert
Samuel (on behalf of a sick Lloyd George) and Sir Donald
Maclean for the Liberals, in a series of discussions, amid the
rapidly mounting financial crisis, with Ramsay MacDonald and
the Labour Chancellor, Snowden, which immediately preceded
MacDonald's resignation and his emergence as leader of a
National Government of Conservatives, Liberals and a handful
of his supporters from the Labour party. Hoare's published and
unpublished accounts of this intense episode are brief and add
little to the main lines of the narrative as established, for example, in Reginald Bassett's now classic account.[95] They make
clear, however, the dominant role played by Chamberlain who
alone among the party leaders seemed to know where he was
going. For him the central objective was the immediate establishment of the country's credit which had been imperilled by the
conviction of overseas countries that excessive public expenditure and lax administration were hastening Britain's bank-
ruptcy. Their confidence could be restored only by balancing
the Budget by means of drastic expenditure economies and
heavier taxation. Any hesitation or partial measures would
plunge the country into the worst of all worlds: they would

provoke domestic discontent without stopping the flight from the pound abroad. Chamberlain kept to this diagnosis and prescription throughout the talks, remaining impervious to the difficulties MacDonald and Snowden were obviously having with the Cabinet over the size of the proposed expenditure cuts and, even more, over the propitiation demanded by all the proponents of 'sound finance', above all, the Bank of England — a substantial reduction in the unemployment benefit.

It was not surprising that MacDonald, when confronted by Conservative insistence on a level of cuts which he knew he could not get through his Cabinet, let alone the parliamentary party and the trade unions, should have concluded that his resignation as Labour Prime Minister was inevitable. But Hoare's published account is also clear that MacDonald revealed no preconceived intention of seeking a coalition government.

> Through all the discussions, I never saw the least sign of any desire on MacDonald's part to become Prime Minister of a Three-Party Government. His talk to Chamberlain and me was of resignation, and it needed considerable persuasion to dissuade him from throwing in his hand.[96]

Rather was it Chamberlain and Hoare who saw that party interest could be conveniently combined with meeting the national need for a co-operative approach to the problems facing the country; that the Conservative party could only gain from the formation of a coalition government under Mac-Donald. This was their firm recommendation when, on the evening of 22nd August, they gave an account of their discussions to Baldwin (just returned from France at Chamberlain's urgent summons) and other colleagues. The reaction to the idea of a National Government was, however, mixed. Baldwin was clearly unhappy at the prospect: having destroyed one coalition he did not wish to join another, he constantly repeated (perhaps forgetting Hoare's own part in that destruction). But on the insistence of Chamberlain and Hoare that there was no other way out of the crisis he was prepared to concede that if such a government really were inevitable he would be ready to take part in it; otherwise he saw no reason to help the Labour government out of a mess of its own creation. Baldwin was not alone in his reluctance for although Cunliffe-Lister readily agreed Hailsham was definitely hostile and others, like Gilmour and Eyres-Monsell, needed a good deal of convincing.[97]

Events moved rapidly after that to resolve the doubts and uncertainties of Baldwin and the others. After various comings and goings of party leaders between Buckingham Palace and Downing Street on 23rd August the issue of a National Government still seemed in the balance with MacDonald apparently intent on the resignation of both himself and his government. But on the following day all had changed. Under the enthusiastic sponsorship of the Palace the party leaders hammered out their agreement on a 'co-operation of individuals' rather than a coalition in the ordinary sense (although the semantics of this distinction were a trifle obscure) for the specific and temporary purpose of dealing with the emergency. Hoare played no part in these discussions but was naturally among the group of senior colleagues whom Baldwin consulted before confirming the arrangement and who unanimously supported his action.[98] No such unanimity met MacDonald as he gave his report to the Labour Cabinet. When on the afternoon of that day (24th August) he resigned and was immediately commissioned to form a National Government he and the handful who followed him from the Labour party must have known that they were going into probably permanent party exile. Meanwhile Hoare and Chamberlain were exchanging congratulations on the way their tactical judgement had been vindicated. Chamberlain expressed warm appreciation of Hoare's supporting role:

> It has been a constant source of comfort and pleasure to have you at my side. Your cool judgement, your fertility of ideas and the fact that you never are jealous make you an ideal colleague in such a crisis and when looking back I feel we have no mistake in tactics to reproach ourselves with, I know that I have to thank you for more than your share of our common task.[99]

In the ten-man Cabinet announced on 25th August Hoare joined Baldwin, Chamberlain and Cunliffe-Lister as one of the four Conservative representatives. Chamberlain, who had clearly played a part in the allocation of posts (like Hoare, Cunliffe-Lister was one of his closest colleagues) told Hoare that his name had been mentioned as a possible Foreign Secretary or as Lord Privy Seal without department. The post finally offered to him, and immediately accepted, was that of Secretary of State for India. India, to which Hoare had devoted considerable attention while in opposition, was now fully to absorb his energies in the next — and most outstanding — phase of his ministerial career.

4

India

The problem of what to do to meet the rising tide of Indian nationalism had become progressively more insistent for British governments with the war and its immediate aftermath. There were two components of Britain's Indian empire: British India ruled, under overall British control, by the Viceroy and Government of India at the centre with governors in charge of the various provinces; and, in a quite different constitutional position, the 560 or so Indian states ruled in semi-feudal conditions by princes in treaty relationship with Britain. It was developments in British India which were of the more direct concern but it was clear that any attempted solution there would eventually have to take account of the India of the princely states. More immediate account, however, had to be taken of the complex conflicts inherent in the heterogeneous religious, racial and communal groupings of India and, above all, that between 230 million Hindus and 70 million Muslims (in part institutionalised in the main indigenous political organisations of British India, the predominantly Hindu Indian National Congress and the Muslim League).

Constitutional development had taken the form of increasing the autonomy of the Government of India and of widening its representative character. Thus in 1919 India, despite its dependent status, became a founder member of the League of Nations and in the same year was conceded fiscal autonomy (which it used, among other things, to impose import duties both for revenue purposes and to protect Indian industry, particularly — to the concern of Lancashire — its developing cotton textile industry). In August 1917 Edward Montagu, Secretary of

State for India and as such the British Cabinet minister responsible for supervising the Government of India, announced that the goal of British policy in India was 'the progressive realisation of responsible government as an integral part of the British Empire'. The Government of India Act of 1919 was the first legislative earnest of this resolve. It introduced a division of responsibility in the provinces, known as dyarchy, under which certain matters such as local government, vernacular education, medical relief, sanitation and agriculture were transferred to Indian ministers responsible to elected legislative councils, while powers over justice, police, and, in effect, finance were reserved to the governors and their officials. At the centre a bicameral legislature was created, largely elective in composition, but with final authority remaining with the Viceroy and his Executive Council, in which Indian members were in a minority. A small breakaway group from the Indian Congress, later constituted as the Liberal party, was prepared to work these reforms but for the Congress majority, led by M. K. Gandhi, they fell far short of their demand for *Swaraj*, complete self-government, for India. Moreover, certain actions which the government or its officials had felt compelled to take to deal with endemic violence had inflamed Indian feeling, notably the so-called Rowlatt Acts, which gave the government increased powers of arrest and summary trial, and the Amritsar massacre of March 1919 where the British military commander, following riots in which four Europeans had been murdered, instructed his men to fire on an unarmed crowd which had refused to disperse, with horrifying results (379 killed and 1,208 wounded). Against this background Gandhi and Congress with, initially, the support of many Muslims, launched an ostensibly non-violent campaign of civil disobedience and boycott, only called off by Gandhi after 21 police officers had been killed in an attack on a police station in February 1922. But violence continued, and now it was the ugliest kind of all, that between Hindus and Muslims: from 1923 to 1927 inter-communal strife accounted for 450 deaths and injuries to thousands more.

The 1919 Government of India Act had made provision for a parliamentary commission to be established to examine its working after ten years. But the second Baldwin government, conscious of the need for some further move on the political front, anticipated this provision by two years and in November 1927 set up a commission with Sir John Simon as chairman. But unfortunately the decision had at that time been taken, surprisingly on the urgent advice of Lord Irwin, the liberal and reforming Viceroy appointed by Baldwin in 1925, to make the Simon commission an exclusively British body, with no Indian members.[1] The result was disastrous, for it destroyed any hope that the commission would be accepted by political India as an impartial instrument of constitutional advance; indeed, the commission had a most uncomfortable experience when it visited India in the course of its deliberations.

Even before the Simon commission had reported, the Baldwin government's Labour successor decided, on Irwin's prompting, that an initiative had to be taken. It was to centre around a new declaration of the aim of British policy, to be made by the Viceroy. Montagu's 1917 declaration, later embodied in the preamble to the 1919 Act, had spoken of 'responsible government'. The term 'dominion status' had not then been invented but was to gain official currency with the Balfour report definition, adopted by the imperial conference of 1926, of the equality of status of the then dominions (Canada, Australia, New Zealand and South Africa) with the United Kingdom and their free association in the British Commonwealth. This seemed more precise than responsible government since it explicitly excluded central imperial control and might even be interpreted to imply, by the term 'free association', the possibility of secession from any form of imperial link. In the eyes of Indian politicians dominion status understandably represented something in advance of responsible government. There had thus been considerable fluttering in Indian political dovecotes when, in a speech in February 1924 to the Indian central legislative assembly, Sir Malcolm Hailey (later an Indian governor of great distinction) differentiated between 'full Dominion self-government' and a more restricted 'responsible government'; it was the latter which alone was implied in the 1919 Act.[2] But by 1929 even this more modest target was largely unattained. It was only in the Indian provinces that there was anything approaching responsible government and there it was in conjunction with a degree of British control over the 'reserved areas' of governmental activity far in excess of that in Canada 90

years before. Dominion status implied for political Indians both
the removal of external constraints and the political unity of the
country. The Indian Congress party had resolved in December
1928 that if dominion status were not conceded within a year it
would demand complete independence and back its demand
with a campaign of civil disobedience. The proposed new
declaration of British policy was clearly in part designed to head
off this demand, although in the event it signally failed in its
objective (since full-scale civil disobedience and non-co-operation began early in 1930).

The Viceroy's announcement was made on 31st October,
1929. Its key passage read:

> ... in view of the doubts which have been expressed both in
> Great Britain and India regarding the interpretation to be
> placed on the intentions of the British government in enacting
> the Statute of 1919, I am authorised on behalf of His Majesty's
> Government to state clearly that in their judgement it is
> implicit in the declaration of 1917 that the natural issue of
> India's constitutional progress, as there contemplated, is the
> attainment of Dominion Status.[3]

It then went on to visualise some kind of union of British India
and the India of the princely states, and ended with the announcement of a British and Indian representative conference
to be convened to consider the forthcoming report of the Simon
commission and any other evidence on both British Indian and
All-Indian problems.

Nearly five decades later, with scarcely a trace of Britain's
former imperial responsibilities remaining, it is difficult to credit
the vehemence of the reaction within the Conservative party to
the seemingly anodyne words of the Irwin declaration. Irwin
and the Labour government – and Baldwin (who was shown
the statement before it was delivered) – believed that, while
there might be a risk of raising Indian hopes that the proposed
conference would lead directly to dominion status when, in
British eyes, this was dependent on the solution of such apparently intractable problems as Indian communal rivalries
and the future of the princely states under British protection,
it was still worthwhile to proclaim the aim, however difficult
and long-term its eventual attainment might be. But what par-

ticularly exercised most of Baldwin's Shadow Cabinet colleagues (as well as many backbenchers) was that the declaration
anticipated, indeed almost certainly exceeded, the recommendations of the still uncompleted report of the Simon commission and had not, apparently, received Simon's approval.
Beyond this, some members – above all, Churchill (who was to
resign from the Shadow Cabinet in January 1931 in order the
more effectively to lead a diehard rearguard action against
any Indian constitutional reform) – were quite unable to
accept dominion status as even a tacit policy goal. Churchill
told Irwin privately at this time that he did not consider
dominion status for British India as a whole 'as in any way
attainable or even approachable in any period which it is now
profitable to consider'. Far from welcoming the prospect of an
Indian constitutional conference he argued that if Indians were
not prepared to take advantage of the 'already enormous possibilities' for provincial autonomy (the only responsible government he would tolerate in India) which the 1919 Act provided,
the British government 'need not hesitate to resume in form as
well as in fact the direct administration of every branch of the
Indian services'. And the reactions to that situation of 'the evil
elements' – Churchill's phrase for the widely representative
Indian Congress party – would be met by 'the will power of
Britain', by which he presumably meant stern repression.[4] In
an acrimonious debate in the Commons a week after Irwin's
announcement Baldwin felt compelled by his colleagues' concern to dissociate himself technically from the statement but at
the same time he skilfully contrived to express complete confidence in the Viceroy and unequivocally pledged himself to the
goal of a self-governing India.

Hoare's own interest in India had first been stimulated by his
backbench participation, briefed by officials of the India Office,
in a debate on the Indian civilian services in August 1922. He
had even toyed at that time with the idea of seeking an Indian
governorship, but this rather surprising ambition was overtaken
by his accession to ministerial office soon afterwards.[5] The interest (but not the gubernatorial ambition) was revived by his
month-long visit to India as Air Minister in January 1927.
In the Conservative storm which greeted the Irwin declaration
he played a consciously emollient role in support of his leader.

He did not have an opportunity of speaking in the debate on 7th November but made a contribution in a briefer and much less acrimonious debate on 18th December. Hoare's speech was sympathetic to Indian advance but avoided reference to any specific proposals and, above all, to the dominion status phrase which had so offended the bulk of his Shadow Cabinet colleagues and party backbenchers. His own belief was that the phrase was unobjectionable and contained nothing either new or revolutionary, but he saw no reason for needlessly arousing opposition by employing it.[6] Not for the last time in the long saga of the Conservative party and India in which he was to play so conspicuous a part Hoare showed a keen concern for the maintenance of basic party unity along with a commitment to reform. At times, indeed, his emphasis on the need for party unity was to make him appear less of a reformer than he in fact was. On the available evidence, however, there seems no reason to doubt that among the Shadow Cabinet he and Amery were the only members to give consistent support to Baldwin's liberal position on India.

Throughout the first few months of 1930 India continued to agitate the Conservative ranks, particularly when news came of some act of terror committed in the course of the Congress campaign of non-cooperation. Then, in June, the massive report of the Simon commission was published. This came down unambiguously in favour of the abolition of dyarchy in the provinces, each of which should, according to the report, become 'as far as possible mistress in her own house', with the governor retaining only essential reserve and emergency powers. But on responsibility at the Indian centre it was much less positive and, to Irwin's great disappointment, there was no mention of the aim of dominion status.[7] But now that the commission's work was finished the Labour government was anxious to proceed with the arrangements for the Indian constitutional conference, or round table conference as it was coming to be called. The process was not free from a good deal of inter-party wrangling. There was, for example, the problem of what the conference would be allowed to discuss: the Conservatives (and the Liberals, for whom Lord Reading, Irwin's predecessor as Viceroy, played a leading part) wanted it confined within the framework of the Simon report; Irwin and the government, believing that the

Simon report by itself was quite unacceptable to Indian opinion, were prepared to announce publicly that the conference would be free to discuss anything, including steps to be taken in the direction of dominion status. In the end, despite Conservative protests, the government held fast to the freedom of discussion, but all reference to dominion status was dropped from the public announcement. There was conflict, too, about the composition of the British conference delegation, Conservatives and Liberals insisting that it should be an all-party one, with Simon included, so to speak, *ex officio*. Once again the government, stiffened by Irwin, did not fully concede the position and it was eventually decided that all three parties — Labour government, Conservatives and Liberals — would send separate delegations which together would theoretically form the British delegation; Simon's membership therefore depended on his being included in the Liberal delegation (and in the end he was not).

In the various inter-party discussions on these questions Baldwin, either from inertia or indecisiveness, allowed the Conservative running to be made by Austen Chamberlain, a former Secretary of State for India, whose views on Indian constitutional reform were notably less enlightened than his own.[8] But, amazingly, when it came to choosing the Conservative delegation of four for the conference another senior member of the Shadow Cabinet of even more rigid views — Lord Salisbury — strenuously opposed Baldwin's suggestion of Chamberlain on the grounds that his share in the Irish settlement might mean that he would lend himself to a similar surrender on India.[9] The choice fell on Lord Peel, the last Conservative Secretary of State for India, Lord Zetland, an ex-Indian governor, Hoare and, at Hoare's suggestion, a representative of the younger element in the party in the person of the 34-year-old Oliver Stanley.[10] Peel was officially the leader of the delegation but from the beginning Hoare, rather than his respected but somewhat indolent colleague, emerged as the real leader.

The first Indian round table conference, with 57 delegates from British India (but none from Congress, which had boycotted the conference), 16 from the Indian states and 16 British parliamentary representatives, was formally opened on 12th November, 1930, in an atmosphere of some tension and uncertainty as to what was to be expected from it. True to its undertaking that the discussions would be free-ranging the government produced no brief to direct the conference and there was no sign of any particular Cabinet effort to settle policy in advance. The main dynamism was in fact to be supplied by the Indians themselves, in the form of a movement among the Indian states representatives (apparently initiated while on the ship bound for England) in favour of what everyone, including the Simon commission, had until then visualised as a distant ideal: an all-India federation which would embrace both British India and the princely states. Hoare, for one, immediately recognised the significance of this surprising new development. At a meeting of the opposition delegations with the government on 16th November, on the eve of the first plenary session of the conference (which had been adjourned for five days after its formal opening), he pressed Ramsay MacDonald 'to weigh the scales in favour of federalism'. At first 'rather sticky', the Prime Minister eventually agreed to present the facts to the conference 'in such a way as to make federalism the most favourable line of advance'. But Hoare was astonished to find how little preparatory work the government had done on the federal question.[11]

When the conference met in plenary session on 17th November the backroom influences for federation were seen to have done their work. Princes like the Maharaja of Bikaner and, not less significantly, respected British Indian representatives like Sir Tej Bahadur Sapru, publicly testified to their commitment to an all-Indian federation. At a stroke, federation was transformed from a distant prospect into the fundamental working premiss of the conference's discussions: indeed the main forum of the conference henceforward was its federal structure committee, on which sat the principal delegates, including Hoare. Dominion status as such withdrew for the moment into the background, its place taken – on Indian initiative – by the even more challenging concept of a federal India.

The motivations of the various delegates in their approach to the federal idea were mixed and complex. The princes saw federation as a barrier against both British interference in their affairs and against the force of nationalism in British India which could not fail to have an impact on their own authoritarian regimes. The more realistic representatives of British India like Sapru (whose role at the conference was crucial) saw it as the most favourable framework for immediate constitutional advance.[12] For Hoare it seemed the best way to make real Indian reform acceptable to the Conservative party. But if the preservation of party unity provided the initial impulse for Hoare it has to be acknowledged that he was in the forefront of those on the British side who grasped the federal concept and were prepared to work out its implications. While most British politicians (even Churchill) were prepared for something approaching autonomy in the provinces of British India, few could contemplate a responsible central government for a vast country of such conflicting communal and religious elements and in which the most powerful political organisation, Congress, was overwhelmingly Hindu (however much it might claim to speak for the whole of India, Muslims and the Indian states included). In the prevailing circumstances of British politics federation provided the only viable way of getting a reformed centre and any possibility of dominion status for India as a whole. It could convincingly be argued that Hoare, as conference delegate and even more as responsible minister, showed considerable tactical skill in emphasising federation and thereby de-emphasising dominion status.[13]

It has, however, been suggested that the chief motivation among Conservatives who came to favour federation for India was a desire to hold up political reform and head off the demand for dominion status by introducing a princes' veto on future developments. Federation could come into existence only with actual princely accession and until then central government remained unreformed. Provincial responsible government was only a means, so the criticism goes, of 'dividing and ruling' by creating Muslim blocs (that is, the provinces in which Muslims could be in a majority) in what might have been a unitary state of British India. Even more serious, it has been argued, the future partition of the Indian sub-continent was implicit in the insistence of Hoare and others on federation with princely India before responsible central government could be achieved.[14] But this argument seems to under-estimate the inherent centrifugal force of Indian communalism, which led not only to the 1947 partition but to a Congress-dominated India which began and has continued as a federal state. Pakistan, too, began as a federation but not even federalism could abate the fissiparous

tendencies within the Muslim state or avoid the violent secession of Bangladesh. Perhaps nothing could have prevented the
bloody division of the sub-continent in 1947 but at least Hoare's
preference for a federal structure made more constitutional and
political sense than a unitary structure which ignored both the
existence of princely India and, even more fundamentally, the
realities of Indian communalism.

In the context of the first round table conference and as a
leader of a divided opposition party Hoare tended to appear less
flexible than he would have liked. His real constructive achievement came with his period of office which began a year later;
but many of the ideas he developed with patient skill in the
gestation of the Government of India Act of 1935 were formed
in 1930–31. During the conference, however, at the sessions of
the full conference and the federal structure committee, at the
joint discussions held between the Liberal and Conservative
delegations outside the conference and between both delegations and the government, Hoare had constantly to look over his
shoulder at likely reactions in the party. To him more than to
any other member of the Conservative delegation fell this task
of intra-party liaison. At one end of the delegation spectrum
Peel could express the more traditional Conservative views on
British imperial responsibilities, while at the other Hoare's
young nominee Oliver Stanley could show his more radical
paces. Hoare contrived to hold the balance. As one of the
government's expert advisers at the conference told Irwin,
Hoare was

> becoming recognised now as a more prominent representa-
> tive of Conservative opinion than his previous career would
> suggest ... If the Conservatives get rid of some of their old
> diehard elements, such as Lord Brentford [the former Sir
> William Joynson-Hicks], Mr. Winston Churchill and the like,
> he [Hoare] would occupy a somewhat important position as
> being in some senses much more advanced than they but in
> others not so idealistic as Mr. Baldwin himself and some of
> the younger men like Oliver Stanley.[15]

A major party test for Hoare came with the meeting of the
Shadow Cabinet on 15th December to consider the delegation's
approach to the situation unfolding at the conference. Only

three days before, Winston Churchill, still a member of the Shadow Cabinet, had delivered an impassioned diatribe against any concessions to Indian nationalism. On the same day as Churchill's speech Hoare completed an important policy brief for his colleagues. The balance he had to keep between what he himself felt was called for and what he thought he could persuade the Shadow Cabinet to accept is painfully clear throughout this document. Hoare was emphatic about the magnitude of the change that Indian acceptance of the federal principle had wrought and the necessity of coming to an immediate decision about the question of responsibility at the centre which the Simon report had virtually ignored. For obvious tactical reasons he painted federalism as a restraint on popular government:

> In the nature of things a federal government is inclined to be more conservative and stable than a unitary government. Almost necessarily, it operates under a written constitution and a Supreme Court. Its representation is based upon a less popular foundation, whilst the constituent governments, each regarding itself as much more sovereign than a Parliamentary constituency, exercise a steadying influence upon the legislature and the executive.

On the subject of how much responsibility an Indian federal government might be given Hoare outlined the scheme that had been put forward by the leader of the Hyderabad state delegation for a Viceroy with over-riding powers for law and order, minorities and financial stability, and exclusive powers, subject to the United Kingdom Parliament, in defence, foreign affairs and relations with the Indian states; and an elected Indian federal ministry, responsible to the federal legislature, with portfolios of finance, home affairs, commerce, development, communications, labour and justice. The delicate balancing act Hoare was attempting became explicit in his comment on this scheme: 'Upon the face of it such a system of government would appear to be an almost complete abdication of British control. I do not underrate the magnitude of the change that it would involve.' But he asked his colleagues

to consider without prejudice the question as to whether or

not it is possible to give a semblance of responsible government and yet retain in our hands the realities and verities
of British control ... to hand over these portfolios to Indians
and yet keep to ourselves the threads that really direct the
system of government.

It was here that the question of safeguards arose — the question that dominated discussions on Indian constitutional development in the 1930s. Hoare assured his colleagues (no doubt
with Churchill particularly in mind) that it would be possible
to devise 'safeguards so effective as to confine Indian responsibility within very narrow and clearly defined limits'. They could
include continued control of the army and of perhaps 80 per
cent of federal revenues through the agency of a statutory
currency board, a reserve bank and a system of permanent
prior charges (e.g., for loans, salaries and pensions). A trade
agreement could be written into the new Indian constitution
and a statutory railway commission could control communications.

Was it or was it not wise, Hoare asked, to create a measure of
good will in India by (and here the careful balancing proposition appeared again) 'giving the semblance of responsible
government, though at the same time retaining the essential
safeguards in our hands'? He himself favoured an extension of
responsible government at the centre on the lines he had indicated, although he thought that the Conservative delegation
should make it clear that approval of such a step was entirely
dependent upon an effective federation being in actual existence in India. There was also the consideration that both the
government and, now, the Liberals seemed ready for a considerable advance and if the Conservative delegation were to
remain rigid it would find itself isolated and the possibility of a
united British position would have been destroyed. Hoare's
Shadow Cabinet memorandum ended with a reaffirmation of
his faith in federation which, he said, was 'the only effective
system for ensuring strong and stable government in India. The
atmosphere is at present surprisingly favourable for a federal
development. We may not have again so good a chance of laying
the federal foundation.'[16]

No official record appears to exist of the Conservative Shadow

Cabinet meeting of 15th December but it is clear from the subsequent actions of the Conservative delegation that Hoare did not get the clear mandate he was seeking. With such die-hards as Churchill and Salisbury still members and with a no doubt anxious Austen Chamberlain even Hoare's carefully hedged expression of sympathy with Indian aspirations had to be watered down and the line he was required to follow was the much tougher one that Conservatives would not express any views on the idea of a responsible federal centre until they had examined and approved in advance the detailed scheme. To formulate so rigid a policy not much more than a month before the conference was due to end – and with the Christmas fes-tivities supervening – was to impose a condition impossible of achievement. The result was that the conference was concluded on 19th January, 1931, with a much more general statement about India's constitutional future than certainly Irwin and the Labour government had hoped.

The Conservative attitude was not sufficiently rigid, how-ever, to retain Churchill in the party leadership. In a debate on 26th January (in which Hoare also participated) Churchill attacked the whole round table conference principle lock, stock and barrel and expressed horror that provision had been made for further discussions to be held on Indian constitutional advance. On the following day he wrote to Baldwin to resign from the Shadow Cabinet in order to have complete freedom to attack the policy. He was not, however, unmindful of the efforts of the Conservative delegation to moderate what he saw as the incontinent rush to make concessions to Indian nationalists. He paid tribute in his speech on 26th January to the 'skill, patience and tact' with which the Conservative delegates had 'extrica-ted themselves from an exceedingly difficult situation, and for the manner in which they have preserved our party free to use its judgement upon future events ... for the care they have taken to safeguard our liberty of action.' It was one of the last such compliments Hoare was to receive from that source for several years.[17]

The preparations for the next round of discussions on India provided cause for concern for many Conservatives besides Churchill. At one time it looked as if the government intended to reconvene a version of the round table conference in India itself and the vehemence with which Conservative backbenchers reacted to this suggestion threw doubt on the party's willingness to take part in any further discussions until Hoare made it clear, in a statement on Baldwin's behalf issued from Conservative central office, that it was India as a venue rather than any further conference to which exception was being taken.[18] Conservatives were no happier with Irwin's decision to release Gandhi from prison and engage in negotiations with him, still less with the resultant 'Irwin-Gandhi pact' of 5th March under which the civil disobedience campaign was discontinued and Congress participation in future discussions on Indian constitutional reform was pledged. But despite all this the government went ahead with its plans to reconvene the round table conference although it now conceded that it had to be in London. Hoare and Peel were nominated to represent the Conservatives and so, at Hoare's insistence, was Hailsham whose presence, Hoare told Baldwin, was necessary both as a constitutional lawyer and as someone without whose backing 'it will be most difficult to carry the right of the party with us in the event of constitutional changes appearing to be practicable'.[19] By the time the conference actually opened on 7th September Hoare had been transformed from an opposition delegate into the minister responsible for India's constitutional future.

In marked contrast with the rapid ministerial turnover of present-day governments Hoare's first ten years were spent in just two departments. His six-and-a-half years at the Air Ministry between 1922 and 1929 were followed by three-and-a-half years as Secretary of State for India from 1931 to 1935. Each ministerial incumbency significantly increased his reputation. From being a tyro minister heading a junior department with an uncertain future in 1922 he had emerged by 1929 as a senior member of the Cabinet with a record as a shrewd and resourceful departmental administrator second to none. The India Office in the 1930s posed new problems: those of devising a policy for the future government of the vast Indian subcontinent, of ensuring its political acceptability, above all by his own party, and then of piloting through Parliament the resultant, immensely detailed, legislation. The weary months and years of trial and tribulation before the Government of India Bill could be presented in the Commons in 1935 were a triumph for Hoare's courage, persistence and sheer ability to master complex issues and constitute a personal ministerial achievement without obvious parallel in modern British political history. They also provide a case study of Hoare's approach to politics. We see, for example, his complete espousal of a policy which was progressive without being in any sense revolutionary; and his acute awareness of internal party pressures, coupled with his strength in resisting those he considered too extreme.

But before we turn to Hoare's onerous task at the India Office something needs to be said about his role as a member of the ten-man Cabinet of the government of national unity formed, so it was thought, purely to cope with the financial emergency in which Britain found itself in August 1931. In so senior a position Hoare had clearly a central part in the whole range of governmental decision-making, and at least until after the election at the end of October and the consequent reconstruction of the National Government on more orthodox lines (with a Cabinet of normal size) there is evidence that he performed it fully. But as time went on his inevitable absorption in Indian problems made it increasingly difficult for him to make a substantial impact on general policy.

The train of events in the early days of the National Government is too well-known to require more than brief recapitulation here: the balancing of the budget by dint of cuts in public service pay, the raising of large loans in the United States and France and, despite all this, the continuing weakness of sterling and drain on the gold reserves which on 19th September precipitated the decision to go off the gold standard. To the ordinary public — and to the foreign investor whose 'confidence' was all-important — the most sensational event of this hectic period was the so-called naval mutiny at Invergordon, sparked off by the cuts in naval pay. Modern economic historians have shown that the financial crisis of the late summer and early autumn of 1931 was in reality nothing like as serious as was thought at the time.[20] But with a naval mutiny, the collapse of the gold standard and ever-increasing unemployment (which did not reach its peak of just under three million until early in 1933,) contemporaries could be forgiven for believing that they were passing through a crisis of unique dimensions. 'I do not think that anyone outside England can realise the abnormality of the conditions in which we are living', Hoare wrote to the Viceroy, Willingdon, on 17th September, even before the country went off the gold standard.[21]

Hoare was convinced that the next step after balancing the budget was to balance British trade and that the only way to do this was by introducing tariffs. But in the small Cabinet such a step was strenuously resisted by Snowden and Samuel, both adamantine in the free trade faith. In Hoare's view (shared by Neville Chamberlain but by no one else in the Cabinet very strongly) this made an early election inevitable. Samuel was naturally against an election which he knew could only be to the detriment of the Liberals while MacDonald, according to Hoare's retrospective account, was vacillatory on this issue as on so many others. Baldwin on the whole was in favour of an election but did not seem to regard it as vital. Conservative central office had no strong opinion. The decision to have an election on 27th October was, according to Hoare, exclusively the work of Neville Chamberlain and himself.[22]

If this claim was true there could be no doubt that the election result triumphantly vindicated their tactical judgement. A swing of some 12 per cent from Labour to the Conservatives represented an electoral landslide of quite extraordinary proportions. The Labour party in the Commons was decimated while the Liberals, although fighting the election as part of the national coalition, were now formally divided between Samuelite Liberals who, with Lloyd George outside the government, adhered to free trade, and the National Liberals under Simon, who were prepared to accept tariffs. The election had, moreover, provided an opportunity for sealing the rapprochement with Beaverbrook who, no doubt sensing the time to be more propitious than ever before for the implementation of something akin to 'Empire Free Trade', threw himself into the campaign on the Conservative side.

Hoare's own constituency contributed handsomely to the general electoral triumph. In a turn-out as usual considerably below that of the nation as a whole (65 per cent compared with over 76 per cent nationally) Hoare polled 83 per cent of the Chelsea vote against a single opponent, from the Labour party, and had the largest majority (18,289) he secured during his 34-year tenure.

In the government reshuffle which followed the election
Hoare continued at the India Office. The preceding six weeks
had, however, been so arduous that he would have been more
than prepared, had it not been for the urgings of MacDonald
and Baldwin, to exchange it for another post.[23] At one point he
was bemoaning to the Viceroy the fact that:

> I have been working night and day. What with the Round
> Table Conference, the constant emergency Cabinets and the
> many grave problems at the India Office, I am really begin-
> ning to wonder whether any human being can struggle with
> it all.

And two months later, that

> I knew that I should have a nasty job when I took on the India
> Office, but I had no idea it would be as bad as it is. If things
> go on much longer as they are now, it will be physically im-
> possible for any Secretary of State to stand the strain.[24]

It was indeed fortunate for Hoare that his service on the Conservative delegation to the first round table conference had made
him *au courant* with Indian questions for otherwise even a politician of his intellectual and administrative ability might not
have been able to cope with the rush of problems that immediately assailed him on taking over the India Office on 25th
August. There was, for example, less than a fortnight to prepare for the second round table conference, the prospects for
which — despite the promised representation of Congress by
Gandhi — were hardly promising. Gandhi had tried to secure
some sort of Hindu-Muslim accommodation in advance of the
meeting but little had been achieved in face of the continued
Congress claim to represent all political India, whether Hindu
or Muslim, and Muslim suspicion of Hindu predominance,
exhibited in renewed Muslim insistence on separate communal
electorates, a fixed number of seats in the legislature and a maxi-
misation of provincial powers in a federal India to counter-
balance an inevitable Hindu majority at the centre.

There was clear evidence, too, that the federal euphoria of the
opening stages of the first conference was rapidly being dissi-
pated. The princes were divided, among other things, on the
nature of their representation in the proposed federal legisla-

ture, small and medium-sized states which might lose their separate identities having quite different views from large states like Hyderabad; while many of them were having second thoughts about the desirability of hitching their waggons to an all-India federation in which the influence over them of a Viceroy 'advised' by a responsible Indian government at the centre would be a very different matter from that currently being exercised by a Viceroy responsible to the British government. One of the problems in eliciting princely opinion was the lack of a credible institutional voice. Each of the 560 or so states, great or small, had an individual treaty relationship with the imperial power and each considered itself an autonomous sovereignty. The sole inter-state organisation was the strictly consultative Chamber of Princes set up in 1921, membership of which was spurned by well over half the states, including some of the largest and most important. Effective consultation with the states was in the end to prove impossible of achievement.

The Government of India, which had not until the first round table conference envisaged all-India federation as anything more than a very distant goal but which had officially espoused it when it seemed to have become, with princely approval, a practical proposition, now also showed signs of losing its new-found enthusiasm. At the same time many of its officials appeared to be proceeding on the assumption that British rule would be ended in the fairly near future and certainly long before any estimate which might be attempted by the National Government or even Lord Irwin, whose recently completed viceroyalty had played so important a part in initiating the official reform movement. Less than a week after Hoare had taken over at the India Office an informed observer in India was expressing his disgust 'with the spirit of defeatism ... rampant in the various Departments of Government and ... the ill-concealed hostility ... to the Federal idea'.[25]

This was not the best atmosphere for an incoming Secretary of State who had to cope not only with the problems of constitutional advance but also with the application to India of economic crisis measures agreed on by the National Government. Nor was he helped initially by any intimate relationship with the man who headed the Indian administration, the Viceroy, Lord Willingdon. Willingdon, who had taken up his appointment in April 1931 under the Labour government, was by no means the ideal man for the post. Although he had Indian experience — he had been a successful Governor of Madras — he had just completed a five-year term as Governor-General of Canada and at the age of 65 should have been able to look forward to retirement rather than an even more strenuous assignment. Moreover, he did not possess that insight into current British politics often thought to be a desirable attribute in a Viceroy (his last governmental office, a minor one, had been held over twenty years before) and, while a man of great charm and presence, he had neither the force nor the intellect to provide leadership in India at a crucial time. The result was that more than most Viceroys Willingdon was in the hands of his officials who, although able, lacked the political antennae a more suitable Viceroy might have provided. It is safe to say that Willingdon would not have become Viceroy had Hoare been Secretary of State at the time of his appointment.

Hoare knew little of Willingdon — they met for the first time when the Viceroy came home for summer leave in 1934 — and their relations were never very close (it was not, for example, until after Willingdon's 1934 leave that they corresponded privately on Christian name terms). But willy-nilly a Secretary of State and a Viceroy had to be in continuous touch and some kind of rapport established. For the whole of his period at the India Office Hoare corresponded almost weekly with Willingdon. Recalling this correspondence twenty years later Lord Templewood wrote that 'although we never concealed our occasional differences, [we] came to understand each other in a way only possible between real friends'.[26] Coming to the Hoare–Willingdon letters now an outside observer might hesitate to describe them as the correspondence of 'real friends' but they are certainly detailed and frank and provide a remarkable insight into the developing relationship of the two men and of their contemporary reactions to events in and affecting India. The correspondence will be used extensively in what follows.

The 'occasional differences' began right at the outset. The first economic and political objective of the new National Government was a balanced budget, introduced by Snowden on 10th September. But what was sauce (or rather lack of it) for the imperial gander had to be sauce for the overseas imperial geese. The Government of India was peremptorily instructed to produce a balanced budget. It replied with a threat of resignation from six members of the Viceroy's Executive Council and two economy measures which caused more embarrassment for the British government than any lack of budgetary balance could have done. Indirect taxation was raised by 25 per cent all round, and this included the duties on Lancashire cotton goods — an increase which Hoare, with some exaggeration, described to Willingdon as 'the final nail into the Lancashire coffin'.[27] Inimical to Lancashire cotton interests though the impost undoubtedly was, it had perforce to be accepted. But the other proposal was resisted more strongly if in the end no more successfully. This was for a cut in the salaries of members of the Indian Civil Service and other officials working in India. The problem here was that some 2,500 older members of the I.C.S. had statutory protection for their salaries and salary cuts for them consequently required legislation at Westminster. Hoare's anxiety was that such legislation would inevitably cast doubt on the efficacy of the statutory safeguards which were seen, above all by Conservatives, as the essential concomitant of any Indian constitutional advance; the necessary bill was later passed without much difficulty, however, after Hoare had had a private word of reassurance to several Conservatives who might have raised troublesome objections.[28]

The Indian public service salary cuts and the increased cotton goods duties led to much excited telegraphing between London and Delhi. In a letter of 17th September Hoare remarked to the Viceroy, 'Our respective telegrams have given each other disastrous shocks. I will say nothing about them in this letter, but I do most earnestly hope that by the time this reaches you we shall not be exchanging ultimatums with each other.'[29] But by the time Willingdon received the letter an even bigger crisis in Indo-British official relations had erupted. For on 19th September the decision was taken to go off the gold standard, in effect to devalue the pound sterling. Hoare was told of the intended move the same (Saturday) morning and had only the weekend to ponder, with his advisers, on its implications for the Indian rupee, which was tied to sterling and thus indirectly to gold; everything had to be decided in time for the official announcement to be made in the Commons on Monday the 21st.

6 Hoare with Lady Maud and a young friend at Cromer, c. 1929

7 Hoare, as Secretary of State for Air, presenting the Esher trophy, 1929

8 Hoare and Lady Maud with the R101 construction team at Cardington, c. 1928

9 Under skating instruction at St Moritz, c. 1928

10 Hoare and Neville Chamberlain soon after the formation of the National Government

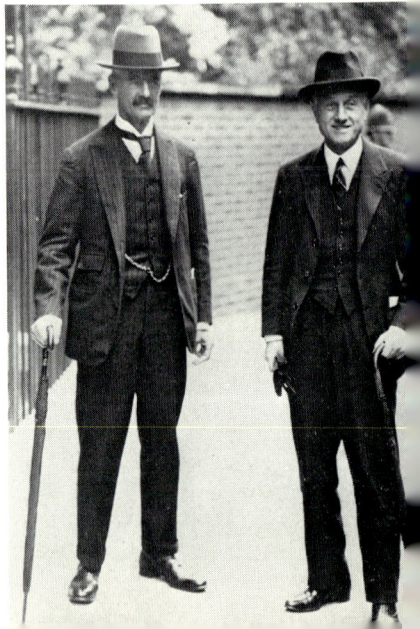

Hoare confessed afterwards that, having no pretensions to financial expertise, he found some difficulty in following the subtleties of the discussion. But he denied that this had affected the decision, which was taken on the basis of unanimous expert opinion and confirmed by the Cabinet. It was that the rupee must continue to be tied to sterling to avoid the possibly disastrous consequences for India of letting the rupee look after itself in the new and forbidding financial climate. Seized of the necessity for speed Hoare omitted the usual prior consultations with the Government of India and the consequential instructions were sent simultaneously to the Viceroy and to the Controllers of Indian Currency, a Government of India department. But Sir George Schuster, the Finance Member of the Viceroy's Executive Council, had already taken his own steps, which included issuing an ordinance cutting the rupee adrift from sterling. When news of this reached the India Office urgent instructions were cabled from London to Delhi to rescind Schuster's ordinance and substitute another implementing the original instructions. At this the wrath of the Government of India boiled over at what was seen as unwarranted Whitehall interference and London was told that if the Executive Council were overruled it would resign *en masse* since it would be 'impossible for us to carry on as a Government'.[30] The India Office then sent Delhi a further telegram which made no reference to the threat of resignation and simply told the Government of India to carry out instructions. At the same time Hoare got MacDonald and Baldwin, on behalf of the Cabinet, to send a personal telegram to Willingdon abjuring him and his council not to commit the criminal folly of resigning. These extraordinary measures produced the desired effect for on 24th September the India Office received a telegram confirming that the Government of India would conform with Cabinet policy and was issuing a statement to that effect. So ended what Hoare at the time described as 'one of the most serious crises in the relations between Britain and India'.[31] The Viceroy's feathers continued in a ruffled state for a little while longer and Hoare did his best to smooth them down, now that the immediate crisis was past. He apologised, for example, about the despatch of telegrams direct to the Controllers of Indian Currency, excusing it on grounds of the exceptional financial emergency and assuring the Viceroy

that there was no intention whatever of undermining his authority. A few months later Hoare had the satisfaction of hearing
that the Government of India now felt that his actions over the
rupee had been right.[32]

All this was going on while Hoare had to bear the burden of
the second round table conference. After the enthusiasm generated by the first conference, the second, following eight months
after, was a sad disappointment. The chief stumbling block, as
expected, was the definition and securing of communal rights
under the proposed new constitutional arrangements, on which
the competing arguments increasingly began to appear as quite
irreconcilable. Ten days after the conference had begun and
a full ten weeks before it was to end, Hoare reported to Willingdon that it

> has been dragging on most wearily. Everyone has been
> making the same speeches as he made last year at twice the
> length, and with nothing new in them. It does, however,
> appear that the differences upon matters of detail have be-
> come greater and that the Princes are more reluctant than ever
> to show their hand. I imagine that what is happening is that
> everyone is keeping back to see what is going to happen with
> the communal question.[33]

If they were, the deliberations of the sub-committee set up to
consider the question of minorities provided no comfort since
they broke down early in October, leaving the onus of making
inevitably unpalatable decisions at some later stage firmly on
the British government.

The presence of Congress in the person of Gandhi did nothing
to bring agreement any nearer. Congress commitment to outright independence and its refusal to recognise the legitimacy
of the fears of minorities ('untouchable' Hindus as well as
Muslims and other non-Hindu communities) of caste Hindu
predominance made real negotiations virtually impossible. But
rather unexpectedly Gandhi and the Secretary of State got on
rather well with each other and this was at least one item on the
credit side to emerge from the needlessly prolonged and in the
end almost completely fruitless discussions at the second round
table conference. After their first long meeting together, soon
after the conference had opened, Gandhi reported to a friend

that the Secretary of State was a man with whom he could talk, however great the differences between them. He felt Hoare was a genuine man who spoke his mind openly, unlike Ramsay MacDonald, whom Gandhi thoroughly disliked for his evasions and pious platitudes.[34] Gandhi told Hoare himself some months later that the opinion he had formed of him was as of a 'knight sans peur et sans reproche'.[35] They had many discussions during the course of the long conference, on Hoare's part in a deliberate effort to maintain their good relations. The impression Hoare gained from these conversations, as he reported to the Viceroy, was that

> He and I have got on very well together, and I think for the reason that I have told him from start to finish that there was not a dog's earthly of satisfying his demand and that there was an unbridgeable gap between us. He appears to prefer this method of approach to the method of approach that implies there are no differences between Congress and British policy.[36]

Unhappily the accord between Gandhi and the responsible minister in London was not matched by a similar relationship between the Congress leader and the Viceroy. Willingdon's refusal to meet Gandhi on his return to India before certain conditions had been met did nothing to abate the renewed civil disobedience campaign which itself led to Gandhi's speedy reincarceration and the intensification of the campaign. It is noticeable that, while Hoare in his correspondence with Willingdon was anxious not to be accused of interfering in the Viceroy's indubitable responsibility for the maintenance of law and order, he was constantly on the watch for opportunities to induce Willingdon to modify his implacable opposition to Gandhi and all his works.

Hoare's disillusion with intransigent and conflicting Indian attitudes at the round table conference caused him for once to flag in his devotion to the concept of an all-India federation, at any rate in the immediate future. He began seriously to think that, amid princely doubts and communal deadlock, a programme for provincial responsibility to precede federation might be the only viable one, despite the ease with which critics would be able to represent it as a reversion to the much more deliberate approach of the Simon report. After canvassing the opinions of many of the Indian delegates and discussing the matter in Cabinet Hoare felt that it was generally agreed that the only practical course was for the government

> to declare their intention to push on with the centre as soon as they can, secondly, to start provincial autonomy at once, and thirdly, to create the machinery for the consultation of various Indian opinions at the important stages of the future.[37]

However, news of the plan leaked in the press — notably to the Labour-oriented *Daily Herald* — and the subsequent hostile publicity caused a reaction among the conference delegates. 'In the course of a few hours', Hoare told Willingdon, 'all the Indians who had been in favour of the suggested course ... terrified by the outside propaganda ... repudiated in public every word that they had said to us in private.'[38] In his statement closing the conference on 1st December the Prime Minister disclaimed any intention of 'urging a responsibility which, for whatever reasons, is considered at the moment premature or ill-advised'. No constitutional change would be made except as part of one all-embracing statute. In the meantime the government would have to make a provisional decision about minority representation and there would be continuing discussions with representative Indians through the agency of a consultative committee which the Viceroy would constitute from among the returning Indian conference delegates.[39]

The Prime Minister's statement had been discussed in Cabinet and Hoare had a large part in its drafting. In view of the doubts about the advisability of responsible central government for India that he and Peel had felt constrained to express at the first round table conference it was of symbolic significance for Hoare's own developing attitude to the Indian question that the Prime Minister categorically reaffirmed the aim of British policy as being responsible government for the all-India federation as well as for the provinces. Hoare's commitment to responsible government at a federal Indian centre was now unequivocal, although it was one which consistently rested on a conviction of the need for adequate institutional safeguards and a confidence that the princely states — whose accession to the federation in sufficient numbers was absolutely essential – would bring a stabilising, conservative and pro-British element to a self-governing India.[40] Henceforward one of the main tasks was to bring the bulk of the Conservative party in and outside Parliament into line, and this required an infinite capacity for taking pains: a constant refrain in Hoare's letters to an often impatient Viceroy was that 'we must go very carefully and constantly keep in mind not only the great strength but also the deep anxiety of Conservative opinion here'.[41] On occasion, indeed, it seemed that the very existence of the National Government might be at stake and Hoare had to stand firm against pressure to drop Indian reform in the interests of party unity. At the other extreme there was the Labour party, freed from the responsibilities of the office and thus able to chide the government for not going fast enough and for retaining the financial, defence and other safeguards which the first round table conference, convened by a Labour government, had agreed to be essential. But reduced to a mere 52 seats by the general election the party had little influence on the situation, apart, perhaps, from hastening the physical and mental decline of its erstwhile leader, Ramsay MacDonald, by constant bear-baiting.

The Commons began a two-day debate on India the day after the conference ended. MacDonald, frequently interrupted from the Labour benches and by Churchill, opened the first day's debate and Hoare closed it. Hoare was pleased with his reception, writing to Willingdon:

> The Prime Minister was very tired when he spoke and I was not at all happy as to the effect that his speech might have. I had imagined that he would make a speech on the side of the left, whereas he did make a rather ambiguous statement that looked as if he was gravitating towards the right. This being so, I somewhat altered the emphasis of my own speech for I had originally imagined that I should have to reassure a lot of discontented Conservatives, and I made it so far as I could more sympathetic to Indian aspirations. The House took it very well and at the end I had quite an ovation, a new experience for one who like myself is a very dull speaker.[42]

Hoare's speech was a skilful one. It had perforce to spell out the necessary conditions for Indian constitutional reform but this was done succinctly and not unsympathetically. There must be provision, Hoare said, for the retention of British control over the Indian Army ('until India is in a position to defend herself') and foreign affairs; the continuance of the relationship of the princely states with the Crown; the safeguarding of financial stability and, ultimately, of internal security; the protection of the position of minorities and British-recruited officials; and the prevention of unfair economic and commercial discrimination against British traders. But at the same time Hoare emphasised that for an India moving rapidly towards responsible government these safeguards were as much in India's interests as in Britain's. Even Churchill, who divided the House against the government motion (and was rewarded with just 43 votes), described Hoare's speech as admirable; while another auditor at the opposite end of the Conservative party spectrum on India – John Davidson – wrote to Hoare that night to say: 'You were superb ... It was just what was wanted and had had a great effect in steadying our people. Congratulations.'[43]

With the end of the second round table conference Hoare had completed just over three months at the India Office and was clearly well in the departmental saddle. The team which served him there was perhaps even more impressive than that at the Air Ministry, although there was naturally no one in the role of a Trenchard. At the head of the permanent staff was Sir Findlater Stewart, with whom Hoare developed a closer working relationship than with any of his other permanent secretaries and which continued after Hoare had left the India Office. Stewart, an immensely able and friendly Scot, had come to the post after two years as secretary to the Simon commission. Hoare later recalled that:

There was no side of Indian life that he did not understand, and no crisis in Whitehall that ever ruffled his equable mind or disturbed his balanced judgement. Amongst all the many Civil Servants who have helped me in my various departments, Stewart stands out as a dependable counsellor and friendly colleague.[44]

One of Stewart's particular skills was as chairman of committees, a device endemic in Whitehall and much in service during the prolonged inter-departmental discussions which accompanied the massive Indian legislation. The other permanent official with whom a ministerial head of department is in closest contact — his principal private secretary — was, during the whole of Hoare's term at the India Office, the invaluable William Croft. Other leading officials advising Hoare were Sir Maurice Gwyer (the Parliamentary Counsel) and Archibald Carter, who later followed Hoare to the Admiralty as permanent secretary. But in addition Hoare had the benefit of advice from distinguished administrators seconded by the Government of India, above all Sir Malcom Hailey, whose contribution to Indian constitutional progress was probably as significant as that of any India Office staff member.

Apart from his young parliamentary private secretary (R. A. Butler, the nephew of Sir Geoffrey Butler, Hoare's P.P.S. at the Air Ministry) Hoare had no political associate in the department until after the election. It was not until 10th November that a leading member of the Liberal party, Lord Lothian, joined Hoare as parliamentary under-secretary. Lothian (formerly Philip Kerr), an Oxford friend of Hoare and his brother Oliver, had previously occupied the post of Chancellor of the Duchy of Lancaster in the National Government. The India Office thus seemed to represent something of a demotion, but Lothian was deeply interested in Indian reform and clearly preferred a definite task to the less specific duties of a non-departmental minister. His biographer has stated that Lothian was able to impose conditions on his acceptance of the India Office post and that Hoare agreed to them: namely, that he would resign if the broad policy of developing Indian responsible government at the centre and in the provinces were to be postponed; and that he should have a more responsible status than that of an ordinary under-secretary, including direct access to the Prime Minister on Indian constitutional matters.[45] But when the existence of such stipulations was reported in the press Lothian hastened to reassure Hoare that he was not the source of the leak and that, 'I should think any imposition of "conditions" as quite improper, though I was anxious that there should be no misunderstanding about the fundamental views I take about the Indian problem before the appointment was made.'[46] It thus seems unlikely that there was ever a stipulation about a special status, although Lothian's role as a leading member of one of the coalition parties clearly gave him a position rather different from that of a junior minister in a politically homogeneous government. He was in fact to spend only some five months in the department. In December Hoare appointed him chairman of the Indian franchise committee, one of the three investigating committees sent out to India in January 1932 to examine specific aspects of constitutional reform (a committee under Davidson reported on federal-state financial relations while the third committee, under Lord Eustace Percy, dealt generally with federal finance). Three months after his return to England in May 1932 Lothian, with obvious reluctance, had to resign from the government with his Liberal colleagues over the abandonment of free trade represented by the imperial preferential trade agreements concluded at the Ottawa conference. But although his tenure was short it was nevertheless valuable to Hoare: there was the occasional tension between Lothian, an enthusiastic Indian reformer, and the more cautious approach of Hoare, always conscious of party pressures, but it was a fruitful partnership, which continued unofficially after Lothian's resignation.

Lothian's successor was Butler, who had accompanied Lothian to India as a member of his franchise committee (leaving Hoare, entirely voluntarily on his part, without either of his political assistants). Having entered the House of Commons as recently as the 1929 election and still not 30 years of age, Butler was by no means at the head of the party managers' list for promotion to junior office but Hoare had the highest regard for his abilities and fought hard, in the end successfully, for Butler's appointment. It was at the India Office under Hoare's patronage that Butler won his ministerial spurs and began one of the longest and most distinguished ministerial careers of this century.

As at the Air Ministry Hoare continued to demonstrate his skill in discovering and encouraging talent. Butler was an obvious example, but so was the man who succeeded Butler as Hoare's P.P.S., Michael (Micky) Knatchbull. In 1933 Knatchbull became Lord Brabourne on the death of his father and thus had to leave both the Commons and his P.P.S. post. Young though Brabourne was then (only 38), Hoare was able to overcome the considerable reluctance of both the King and the Viceroy to secure his appointment as Governor of Bombay and to launch a brilliant Indian gubernatorial career tragically cut short by Brabourne's death early in 1939 while Governor of the most important Indian province, Bengal. Brabourne had taken over in Bengal from another of Hoare's inspired appointments, though hardly this time of a young and relatively inexperienced talent: Sir John Anderson, whom Hoare had persuaded to leave the permanent headship of the Home Office to become Governor of Bengal at the beginning of 1932, when a campaign of anti-British terrorism was at its height in the province, and whose arrival soon transformed the security situation.

Hoare not only picked good staff, he treated them well. He may not have had a very warm personality and he was certainly sometimes rather distant but he was nevertheless considerate and loyal to his subordinates, fully prepared to defend their interests. It was one of the qualities Lord Butler most remembered about him when he came to write his obituary over a quarter of a century later. 'In my experience of serving many chiefs over all these years (Butler wrote in May 1959), Sam Hoare was distinguished for his anxiety to help his subordinates.'[47] Hoare also ensured that, where appropriate, those who served him received their due reward in the way of honours, to which he attached what today would seem a disproportionate importance. He liked honours for himself, of course, and was delighted when, at Baldwin's suggestion, he was awarded the G.C.S.I. – the highest Indian honour – in the 1934 New Year Honours List.[48]

The making of Indian policy was by no means the exclusive preserve of the India Office. At the detailed level there was an inter-departmental committee of officials presided over, at Hoare's request, by the Lord Chancellor, Sankey, who had played a prominent part in the first round table conference and was to be connected with Indian policy, although to a diminishing extent, down to his retirement in 1935. On matters of broader policy Hoare had the assistance of a Cabinet committee on India, established in January 1932 as a continuation and strengthening of a committee which met during the second round table conference. Its membership underwent some changes in its three years of existence but the central core consisted of Hoare, Sankey, Simon (now Foreign Secretary), Hailsham and, after he had joined the government in June 1932, Irwin (who succeeded his father as Lord Halifax in January 1934). MacDonald took the chair on the relatively few occasions he attended the committee, while Baldwin attended quite frequently and sometimes took the chair. But the usual chairman was Hoare himself, even when Baldwin was present. It was, Hoare told Willingdon, 'the best India Committee there has ever been in Whitehall'.[49]

It was unusual for a departmental minister to have so many colleagues with a direct and detailed concern in the field of his responsibilities. In Hoare's case, they included the Viceroy who had provided the main initial stimulus to the Indian reform movement; the author of a massive report on India whose recommendations and caveats Simon himself was disposed to feel had been too little heeded; and the two most senior members of the National Government — MacDonald, whose Labour government had initiated the first round table conference, and Baldwin, Lord President of the Council and leader of the main party in the government, whose views on India had frequently created trouble for himself with his party's right wing.

The Prime Minister continued to take a close interest in Indian affairs, despite the changed political complexion of his government since the first round table conference. Although it is possible to detect some occasional annoyance on Hoare's part at the extent of MacDonald's detailed interest, it was obvious that, as the departmental minister primarily concerned, he generally welcomed the support of his Prime Minister. Even during MacDonald's frequent illnesses and his trips abroad, Hoare kept in close touch with him on Indian affairs, as a voluminous correspondence between them, particularly during 1932, reveals.[50] The attempt was sometimes made, for example by Churchill, to demonstrate a difference of approach to Indian policy between an erstwhile Labour Prime Minister and a Conservative minister but there was never any real substance in the suspicion.[51] On a more general level Hoare fully shared his fellow senior colleagues' view that MacDonald's continuance as Prime Minister was an asset to the National Government. Reporting to Willingdon on the state of MacDonald's health in April 1932 Hoare added:

I do not gather that there is at present any risk of his having to resign, but it does look as if he would have to take things a good deal easier if he is to carry on indefinitely. We Conservatives in the Government are most anxious that he should go on, and we shall make it as easy as we can for him to continue as long as he can.[52]

Baldwin's dedication to a liberal policy towards India was undoubted. His 1969 biographers claim that in the period from 1931 to 1935 Indian affairs alternated with his work for rearmament in absorbing Baldwin's attention and that, in constant consultation with Hoare, Irwin and Findlater Stewart, he spent more time at the India Office than any other department. It is difficult to find any evidence to support this: indeed Baldwin's name appears relatively infrequently in the major source material for Indian policy in the period, including the Templewood collections in London and Cambridge. He certainly does not seem to have concerned himself with the details which were so vital in the complicated negotiations Hoare had to conduct in Cabinet, party, Parliament and innumerable committees, and with the Government of India. But Baldwin was always capable of intervening effectively in common sense and liberal ways. He did so, for example, in a long discussion on financial safeguards in the Cabinet India committee, under Hoare's chairmanship in November 1932. Hoare had been emphasising the political impossibility of denying financial powers to the proposed Indian federal government. Neville Chamberlain, attending in his departmental capacity as Chancellor of the Exchequer, expressed the grave anxieties of the Treasury at the prospect of a responsible Indian government exercising such powers. Indians, the Chancellor told his colleagues, were like 'spoiled, wilful, naughty' children who had to be prevented from injuring themselves. Baldwin's quiet comment on this was:

If you do not trust the Indians at all, if you say they are all going to be crooks, you may as well drop the Bill, but I would just as soon trust people in India to run the finances of India as I would a good many Englishmen.[53]

The awkward customers on the India committee seem to have

been Hailsham and Simon, particularly the latter. Both were lawyers, and it was the third lawyer on the committee, Sankey, who left the clearest contemporary account of their limitations. According to Sankey, Hailsham did not give trouble, 'as long as we say we will do our best to do a thing, instead of saying we will do it. He has rather a lawyer's mind, which is apt to say "wind, weather and circumstances permitting"'. The really tiresome member was Simon:

> If he approves of a thing he says, with a little laugh, 'I think that it is a good idea and it will be found in a certain report about India which was issued a couple of years ago'. If he does not approve of it he says it was not in the report. He is quite intransigent. He wants every problem reduced to a mathematical certainty.[54]

But although they needed careful handling their presence on the committee was valuable to Hoare since they both represented important strands of parliamentary opinion, Hailsham especially having considerable influence with the centre and moderate right of the Conservative party.

The major problem which Hoare and the government had to confront after the second round table conference was the determination of a timetable for Indian advance. There were several imponderables, all inter-related. For example, no progress could be made until the government, in default of Indian inter-communal agreement, had worked out its own communal award on the question of minority and other representation in the new provincial legislatures and this was not possible until Lothian's franchise committee had reported. And then there was the lengthy process of the legislative enactment of the whole complex constitutional scheme. Willingdon and the Government of India were constantly pressing for some immediate measure to show the constructive side of an imperial policy which was currently demonstrating more success in suppressing Indian political activity than in widening it. Hoare was, of course, just as alive as Willingdon to the need to improve the political climate in India and to replace the distasteful method of governing by ordinance which the violence generated by the Congress campaign of non-co-operation had necessitated.[55] But whereas the Viceroy and his advisers were more concerned with

the British India for which they were administratively responsible and hankered after some immediate move towards
further responsibility in its central government, Hoare kept his
eye steadily on the goal of all-India federation and on the steps
which could be taken within that essential framework. A much
more constructive channel for the impatience of the Government of India to show positive constitutional results was, Hoare
felt, a real effort to secure the definite adherence of major
princely states to the federal scheme. As early as the beginning
of March 1932 Hoare was urging the Viceroy to make 'a very
vigorous effort to bring the Princes in. If we don't get them in
now I believe they will either drift away or gradually crum-
ble.'[56] This was to be a constant refrain in the next three years
and at no time was Hoare satisfied with the rather half-hearted
efforts of the Viceroy and his officials to enlist the essential co-
operation of the princes in the creation of the federal structure.

Between April and June 1932 Hoare was heavily occupied in
communicating with the Viceroy and in the Cabinet committee
in an effort to hammer out a provisional time-table. He was
anxious to avoid another full-scale conference, having already
endured two of these marathon, time-consuming and rather inconclusive public debates on highly contentious matters. But
the Viceroy needed a good deal of convincing. In May Hoare
reminded Willingdon that:

> you have often told me with great truth in your letters that
> the time has now come for a decision by His Majesty's
> Government. Is it not better that we should now take the
> bull by the horn and say that we cannot go on forever with
> committees and discussions, but that we are anxious to have
> a few Indians to advise us upon specific points ... ?[57]

Eventually the Viceroy was brought round and on 27th June
simultaneous announcements on future steps were made by
Hoare in the House of Commons and by Willingdon in
India.[58] The government pledged itself 'to endeavour to give
effect to their policy by means of a single Bill which will provide
alike for autonomous Constitutions in the Provinces and for the
Federation of the Provinces and States'. On further consultation the statement was clear that 'the settlement of urgent and
important questions that still remain to be decided' would only

be delayed by formal sessions of 'large bodies such as the Round Table Conference'. The programme now proposed was to include, in turn, the announcement of the government's communal decision during the summer; discussions by the Viceroy's consultative council (constituted from Indian round table conference delegates); consideration of definite proposals by a joint select committee of Parliament, which would 'confer with representatives of Indian opinion'; and the introduction of legislation in Parliament.

A further meeting of the round table conference seemed thus pretty firmly ruled out. But Hoare was soon compelled to change his mind on this. With Congress now back to outright and violent opposition to British policy the only Hindu group in dialogue with the authorities was the Liberal party, whose most prominent and distinguished member was Sir Tej Sapru. The Liberals were aghast at what they considered to be the authoritarian tone of Hoare's statement and the absence of any reference to the reconvening of the round table conference in the autumn. Sapru and a colleague thereupon resigned from the Viceroy's consultative council, demanding a further conference session in London as a condition of their renewing co-operation. Although he put on a brave face in his letters to Willingdon — telling the Viceroy on 22nd July not to be worried by the break away of the Liberals, which would not in any way alter the government's policy or programme — Hoare was clearly shaken by the erosion of the only significant organised Hindu support for the projected constitutional proposals. He got the Cabinet committee to agree to an autumn conference after all. It was, however, to be much smaller than the previous conferences and would certainly not follow Sapru's definition of the conference method by which the government and the Indian representatives would conclude something in the nature of a treaty whose ratification by Parliament the government would then be obliged to secure. Willingdon made the conference offer at the beginning of September and, to everyone's relief, the Hindu Liberals accepted it and resumed their co-operation with the government.

Much of the summer was spent in settling the inevitably controversial details of the communal award, which was announced on 16th August. In general the award gave separate electorates in all eleven provinces of British India to the Muslims and, in those provinces where their numbers warranted it, to other minority groups (including Sikhs, Indian Christians, Anglo-Indians, Europeans and Hindu depressed classes or untouchables); and allocated seats on a communal basis in the various provincial legislatures. It was made clear that, although the British government would not enter into any negotiations, it was prepared to accept any modifications to the award which had been generally agreed among the communities concerned.[59] Indian reactions to the award were on predictable lines. The Muslims, having been given an overall majority of seats in two provinces and the largest block in two more, were, on the whole, satisfied. The Hindu Liberals reluctantly recognised the necessity of the British government cutting the gordian knot which had proved intractable to Indians themselves. Congress, which many of its leaders, including Gandhi, in jail and had had always claimed to represent all Indian communities, could not be expected to welcome or accept the award. But what aroused its particular ire were the separate electorates for the depressed classes and intense pressure – including a fast unto death by Gandhi in his prison cell – was put on the depressed class leaders to agree to their withdrawal. By the so-called Poona Pact of 25th September the separate electorates were replaced by reserved seats for the depressed classes, each with a general electorate. Since this came within the terms of the communal award the government had perforce to agree to make the necessary provision in the forthcoming legislation. Hoare felt the depressed classes, inherently weak and ill-organised, had been steam-rollered into accepting a much less favourable provision for their special needs; he was pleased, however, to detect some slight shift in Gandhi's posture of absolute opposition to British involvement in Indian affairs since the very conclusion of the pact implied tacit acceptance of the machinery for varying the government's original communal decision.[60]

The third (and last) round table conference was both the smallest and shortest of the series. Even before it opened on 17th November (1932) Hoare was conferring with all the principal delegates and found them anxious, as he was, to conclude the proceedings before Christmas. None of the princes had come over but most of the significant ones were represented by their chief ministers, of whom Hoare had already formed a most favourable opinion; the absence of their royal masters cut down the attendant junketing which again did not displease Hoare. MacDonald, the formal chairman of the conference, was unable to attend any of its sessions owing to illness and Sankey, who had been deputy chairman on the previous occasions, collapsed ten days before the conference ended.[61] Even more than the second round table conference the third was Hoare's conference (he was officially its vice-chairman), and it was appropriate that it should have been the most efficient and streamlined.

Although some matters had to be left for later decision a considerable number of useful agreements were made, and the general atmosphere of the conference was reasonably friendly — partly, no doubt, through the absence of Congress, but also through the non-attendance of sometimes rather prickly princely rulers. The states' representatives had explicit instructions not to commit their rulers too far, and thus no firm decisions could be taken on federal finance or states' representation; but nevertheless there was agreement on the proportion of total states' seats in both houses of the federal legislature. The Muslims were determined from the start of the conference to get a third of the representation in the federal legislature and they won their point. In his closing speech on 24th December Hoare announced — in what later became known as the supplement to the communal award — that Muslims would have a third of the seats from British India in each federal house and that the British government would use its best endeavours to secure a fair representation for Muslims among the members nominated from the princely states (which were predominantly Hindu). Agreement was also reached on direct elections by all-India constituencies to the federal legislature and on the right of the Viceroy to decide cases where doubt arose as to whether a subject was a central or provincial matter. Lothian who, as a Liberal delegate, had been present throughout the conference, was in no doubt as to who was responsible for its success. Writing to Willingdon immediately after the conference had ended he reported:

The really remarkable feature of the Conference was the way Sam Hoare handled it and gradually won the confidence of even the most suspicious of the Indian delegates. He has clearly made up his mind, and I presume the Government has also made up its mind, that the only policy is to drive ahead with the Round Table [conference] scheme of federation, responsibility and safeguards as quickly as possible and that they can carry it against the Diehards in their own party. Sapru and Co., as you know, arrived full of doubts and suspicions. They have got a good deal more than I think they expected because the Government has stood absolutely by the reports of the first Round Table Conference.[62]

Two of Hoare's colleagues on the Cabinet India committee and the British delegation wrote to congratulate him on the success of the conference, but the warmest tribute came from one of the states' representatives, Liaqat Hyat Khan, chief minister of Patiala, who wrote to Hoare:

I cannot leave the shores of England before submitting to you my personal and most sincere expression of congratulation and gratitude for the success of the Conference and for your sympathetic attitude towards the States and indulgence to me personally ... this Conference, and thereby Federation, owes more to your constructive statesmanship, sweet reasonableness, and far-sighted imagination than to any single person.

Hoare could be forgiven for basking in a glow of satisfaction at the plaudits and it hardly needed Simon to remind him that 'The real difficulties now begin': the drafting of precise proposals as a white paper and their passage through the parliamentary hurdles of the joint committee and the floor of the House of Commons.[63]

While Hoare, the India Office and the Cabinet India committee were working on the contents of the white paper, Churchill and the Conservative parliamentary diehards, with the backing of an outside pressure group — the Indian Empire Society (founded in July 1930 to seek to preserve unimpeded British rule in India) — were mustering their forces for battle. They instigated a critical Commons debate on 22nd February (1933), but the attack was beaten off comfortably, the diehard vote (at 42) being almost identical to that achieved in December 1931, after the second round table conference. They had more success with the organs of the mass party, a battlefield which, if it did not affect parliamentary votes, had the potential to create embarrassment for the party's parliamentary leadership. Churchill put down a critical resolution for the half-yearly meeting, on 28th February, of the central council of the National Union of the party, membership of which was open to Conservative M.P.s and peers, prospective candidates and four representatives from each constituency association; the voting was 189 to 165 but with a total attendance estimated at about 500 there may have been something like 150 abstentions. Early in March the Women's Unionist Conference for the Eastern Counties area voted with what Henry Page Croft, a leading diehard M.P., termed 'a great majority against the Indian surrender', despite an address by a local M.P., with particular knowledge of government policy, R. A. Butler.[64] The grand council of the Primrose League did likewise. Hoare was shaken. ' I have had a very worrying time the last few days', he told Willingdon. 'The Conservatives are deeply stirred and I do not know what is going to emerge out of the agitation.' And perhaps the most worrying feature was that the turmoil in the party was not just over understandable traditional Conservative anxiety about the future of British rule in India but was clearly being manipulated by Churchill (if not by all his associates) in an attempt to destroy the National Government. Hoare told Willingdon that Churchill 'is determined to smash the National Government and believes that India is a good battering ram as he has a large section of the Conservative party behind him'. But there was one consolation, he would not succeed. Hoare wrote on 17th March:

> ... however effective Winston's attack may be, there is a great body of opinion in the country that will never trust him and even the extreme right of the Conservative party, while they will use him for their own ends, would never take him as their leader.[65]

As well as elaborating on his suspicions of Churchill's motives Hoare's weekly letter to Willingdon on 17th March indulged in a moment of retrospection, for on that day the long-awaited government white paper on the Indian constitutional proposals was published.

Looking back over these difficult times I do not honestly believe that you or I could have produced a better scheme in
face of the difficulties with which we have been faced in India
and Great Britain, and I am deeply grateful to you and your
advisers for having met us upon so many points in which, it
may be, you have not entirely agreed with our views. Has it
been an attempt to square the circle? Only the future will
give the answer to this question. The future will, however,
give the verdict that it is an honest attempt to deal with almost
insuperable difficulties and to reconcile the British and Indian point of view in a field where reconciliation is almost
impossible.[66]

On the day before, in a letter to the Warden of New College,
H. A. L. Fisher, accepting an invitation to become an honorary
fellow of his old college, Hoare permitted himself a little more
optimism about the viability of the scheme and, in particular,
the willingness of moderate Indian opinion to work it. He was
inclined to think, he told Fisher, 'that Indians will admit an
accepted fact and that few of them will be able to keep out of the
elections and governments of the future'.[67]

It would not be appropriate to detail here the white paper
scheme which Hoare was to pilot through Parliament over the
next two years. Very broadly, its essential features were as
follows. The provinces of British India were to be granted
autonomy. Dyarchy was to be abolished and replaced by
provincial governments appointed by the governors but responsible to popularly elected assemblies (for provincial elections the combined electorates, as recommended by the Lothian
committee, constituted 14 per cent of the total population or 27
per cent of the adult population). Chief ministers or premiers
would become the effective heads of provincial administration
and governors were to be instructed to act on their advice so
long as their reserve powers (concerned primarily with the prevention of commercial discrimination, the protection of the
legitimate interests of minorities and the continuance of the
administration in the event of a breakdown of the machinery of
self-government) were not invaded. Another restriction on the
complete formal autonomy of provincial administration was that
provincial officials who were members of British-controlled

services like the Indian Civil Service and the police could be directed but not dismissed; although subordinate they were still to retain some degree of independence in relation to the provincial executive.

The unique feature of the scheme and the one that was not simply a development from past practice (as provincial autonomy in essence was) related to the centre, which was to be in the form of a federation of British India and the Indian states. It was a condition of the establishment of the federation that the rulers of states representing not less than half the aggregate population of the states (over 81 million at the 1931 census) and entitled to not less than half the states' seats in the upper house of the federal legislature had executed the necessary instrument of accession. The two federal chambers were to be the Council of State (the upper house or chamber) with 260 members, up to 10 of them nominated by the Governor-General, 100 appointed by the princes and the remainder elected by the provincial legislatures; and a Federal Assembly with 375 members, 125 appointed by the princes and the remainder elected by all-India constituencies arranged territorially, communally and by special interests (the total federal electorate was initially to be substantially smaller than the total provincial electorate, constituting about 6 per cent of the adult population).

The Governor-General had a dual capacity, being Governor-General as head of the federation and Viceroy as conducting relations with the Indian states in matters falling outside the federal sphere. There were three detailed lists of legislative powers, one federal, one provincial and one concurrent; the allocation of any additional powers was to be at the discretion of the Governor-General. The federal Council of Ministers, appointed by the Governor-General, was to be responsible to the federal legislature in all matters save those concerned with the three departments under the personal administration of the Governor-General, namely those for defence, external affairs and ecclesiastical affairs. The Governor-General was also to have special powers to be exercised only when circumstances demanded, for such purposes as the prevention of grave menace to peace and tranquillity, the safeguarding of financial credit, the rights of minorities and the interests of members of the public services, and the prevention of commercial discrimination. In addition he was to have a limited and temporary power to legislate at his own discretion. The Governor-General and the provincial governors were responsible to the Secretary of State for the exercise of their special powers or when acting in their discretion. Additional federal institutions to be created were a federal court for constitutional interpretation and the resolution of disputes; a federal reserve bank and a federal railway authority, over both of which the Governor-General was to have appointing and other powers.[68]

Federation, responsible government and safeguards – these were the triple pillars of the white paper structure. There was to be an all-India federation with responsible government at provincial and federal levels subject to safeguards for continuing British oversight of India's defence, external relations and good government. It was naturally the safeguards which sparked off the main controversy, both from those on the British political left and in India who felt that their existence was an insult to Indians and those who looked upon them as totally inadequate to prevent the collapse of British rule. This was the Scylla and Charybdis through which Hoare had to steer the 'monstrous boat' of the Government of India Bill.[69]

For the next eighteen months – from April 1933 to October 1934 – the process of Indian constitutional reform was dominated by the proceedings of the joint select committee of 32 members of Parliament, 16 from the Commons and 16 from the Lords (under the chairmanship of Lord Linlithgow). Although he had no idea at the outset that it would be quite so protracted Hoare had been instrumental in ensuring that the joint committee came at this stage rather than, as with the 1919 Government of India Bill, as part of the parliamentary consideration of the actual legislation. A pre-legislative committee made it possible for Indians to participate as 'assessors' and it was essential, Hoare knew, for moderate Indian political opinion to feel that it was being taken into account in the crucial decisions. He also hoped that a thorough examination by a respected and representative group of parliamentarians would expedite the subsequent bill's passage through Parliament.

On the whole these objectives were achieved, but only after an enormous physical effort by Hoare, made all the more onerous by the utter unscrupulousness of Churchill's attack on the government's policy and Hoare as its chief protagonist. It began with the very appointment of the committee. Hoare invited three of the principal diehards – Churchill, Page Croft and Lord Lloyd – to become members but they refused, obviously wishing to keep themselves entirely free to continue their parliamentary and public campaign of outright opposition to the proposals the committee would be examining. Their refusal did not, however, prevent diehard accusations that Hoare had packed the committee with steadfast supporters of the white paper policy. The accusations were without foundation for although – rightly and inevitably – there were indeed those who favoured Indian constitutional reform on the committee (some, like the four Labour representatives, in favour of more radical measures than those contained in the white paper), there were also at least five diehards, including the most respected of all, Lord Salisbury (whom Hoare consulted constantly about the committee's composition) and, above all, a substantial group of those specifically invited by Hoare as 'key men of the Conservative party who, whilst uncommitted and standing somewhat on the right, would be inclined to consider the question impartially and who would carry great weight in the House when it comes to the Bill'.[70] Of this group none were more important than Austen Chamberlain, who warned Hoare when accepting his invitation that 'you must not count upon me as an unqualified supporter ... though you may be sure that it will be my wish to be helpful';[71] and Lord Derby, a vital link with the Lancashire cotton interests which viewed Indian self-government with considerable anxiety.

The joint select committee was the high water mark of Hoare's involvement in the affairs of India, revealing to the full his complete mastery of his subject and his firm commitment to constitutional reform within a federal framework. Sir William Hailey, who in Hoare had prevailed on the Viceroy to release from his gubernatorial duties to assist him on the committee, reported to Willingdon soon after its sessions had begun that the Secretary of State had

completely identified himself with the White Paper proposals. Indeed, he has changed greatly from the very cautious and conservative attitude which I saw him taking in 1930 [at the

first round table conference] and ... he has attracted to his
own head the brickbats which a short time ago used to be
directed at Lord Irwin. It is indeed curious that we should
now find a small band of Conservative politicians who are
pleading the Indian cause with all the fervour (though, no
doubt, with far more discretion and with far more statesmanship) which was once displayed by Mr. Montagu [the Liberal
author of the Government of India Act of 1919] and who seem
willing to run the dangers which fell to his lot.[72]

Most of the running of the committee was made by Salisbury
and his fellow-diehards, who insisted on reopening all aspects of
the Indian question in minute detail and subjected witnesses,
Indian assessors and their colleagues to aggressive and wearisome questioning. Hoare's response was the decision to leave off
temporarily his status as committee member and go himself into
the witness box. From July to October (1933) he spent 19 committee sessions as a witness and dealt with over 10,000 questions.
It was a remarkable personal *tour de force*, but an incredibly
time-consuming one, devastating all his other work. On
technical questions he relied much on the advice of Findlater
Stewart and Hailey, who flanked him at the witness table, and
his private secretary, W. D. Croft, but Hoare was very much the
dominant figure of the India Office team. Hailey himself
testified at the time to the Secretary of State's pre-eminence;
he told the Viceroy:

> It is a severe strain on Sir Samuel, but he stands up to it
> admirably. We have, of course, behind the scenes, worked
> up a series of questions that we knew would be asked, and
> suggested answers: but he does not depend on these. He has
> Findlater Stewart on his left hand and I sit on his right; but
> save in more technical matters he does not ask for help;
> occasionally he turns some question to me to answer, but he
> nearly always takes them himself; he is very prompt and
> clear.

A government colleague on the committee, Lord Sankey,
avowed that he had 'never heard anyone so completely domi-
nate and convince his audience' while another, Irwin, recalled
many years later that Hoare displayed 'a grasp of his subject

that in comparable circumstances can never have been sur-
passed and seldom equalled by any previous minister of the
Crown'. There were even cheers from the Tuscan ranks, Salisbury writing a note to Hoare to express, 'my thanks to you for
your courtesy and my admiration at the intellectual achievement you have displayed in sitting for hours in that chair and
answering questions on every conceivably intricate subject.'
Hoare himself felt that all the effort had been worth while. 'I
think that I may claim', he wrote to Willingdon, 'that the result of my evidence has been to make the White Paper scheme
appear for the first time in concrete form, both to the British
public and the Indian delegates.'[73]

The diehards might lengthen the committee's proceedings
but they exercised little real influence on the shaping of the final
committee report. Far and away the most influential group in
the committee was that headed by Austen Chamberlain and
Derby, with Zetland, Lord Hardinge (an ex-Viceroy) and Lord
Eustace Percy, among others. Hoare looked upon Chamberlain
and his associates as the core element in the committee, whose
support was essential to secure the eventual passage of the bill
through Parliament. It was through them, Hoare reasoned, that
he could capitalise on general Conservative doubts about
Churchill. Churchill's leadership of the Indian diehards in the
Commons was an advantage to the government since suspicion
of Churchill among Conservatives was greater than their suspicion of the white paper policy. If men of the respect and eminence of Chamberlain and Derby were to endorse the policy
Conservatives would be content to follow their lead, however
unenthusiastically, rather than play into the hands of Churchill. In this context the white paper became something akin to
an initial bargaining position which admitted of, even implied,
concessions on detail if not principle. There was also the closely
allied tactical point that the Conservative backbenches would
be much more likely to accept the joint select committee's report as something more than just an underwriting of the white
paper if it were clear that it contained significant differences.[74]
Thus Hoare was prepared to bow a little to the Chamberlain
group's anxieties over the proposed transfer of law and order
to the newly responsible provincial governments by giving additional powers to the governors in connection with terrorism.

The only amendment of any real substance which he felt he had to concede (after consulting the indispensable Hailey, now back in India) was the substitution of indirect election by provincial legislatures for direct election to the lower house of the federal legislature, which the Chamberlain group thought would bring greater stability to the federal legislative system. Although he had some difficulty in persuading the Viceroy to agree, Hoare did not consider that direct election at the federal level (it was retained in the provinces) constituted a basic principle of the white paper; its sacrifice was, he felt, more than compensated for by securing the commitment of the Chamberlain group to responsible government at the Indian federal centre, the feature of the scheme which had aroused the greatest opposition in Conservative ranks.[75]

That opposition, particularly in the party's extra-parliamentary 'grass roots', was being sedulously fostered by Churchill and his diehard friends while the joint select committee sat. Several area and constituency organisations had shown their disapproval of government policy and in May 1933 the national Conservative women's organisation and the youth organisation (the Junior Imperial League) both voted decisively against responsible government at the Indian centre and the transfer of law and order to the provincial governments. The problem, as Hoare saw it, was that the government's case 'is a complicated case of detail, whilst the attack is an attack of headlines and platform slogans'.[76] Membership of the joint select committee constrained him, he felt, from full participation in public debate on the white paper policy. But there was nothing to stop an unofficial organisation from taking on the task and Hoare was certainly privy to the formation, announced in May 1933, of a body called the Union of Britain and India, whose members were mostly ex-Indian officials and others with Indian experience.[77] Churchill's group, which was already backed by the Indian Empire Society and a backbench committee calling itself the India Defence Committee, professed to being shocked by this attempt by supporters of Indian constitutional reform to beat the diehards at their own game. It responded with the formation of the India Defence League, which seems to have represented something like a merger between the India Defence Committee and the Indian Empire Society, although the latter body remained in separate existence for several years more.[78] The League's financial sponsors included the enormously wealthy and eccentric Lady Houston, Lord Rothermere and several dissident Indian princes (a primary objective of Churchill's campaign was to wean sufficient princes from a commitment to federation to make it impossible for the government to institute the federal scheme).

The diehard campaign against the government's Indian policy was able to demonstrate the impact it was having on the party's grass roots by the size of the vote its hostile resolutions attracted at the periodic meetings of the central council and the October party annual conference. Although the official platform was never actually defeated 316 diehard votes were mustered at the special central council meeting on 28th June, 1933 (compared with 165 in the same forum three months before), while at the 1934 annual conference at Bristol they missed victory by a mere 23 votes (543 to 520).

But Churchill's most wounding thrust was aimed at Hoare personally. On the morning of 16th April, 1934, quite out of the blue, he received from Churchill a letter announcing his intention to raise with the Speaker as a matter of privilege that same afternoon the role of Hoare (and Derby) in the decision of the Manchester Chamber of Commerce, the chief organised pressure group for the Lancashire textile industry, to alter the evidence it was submitting to the joint select committee.[79] The Speaker ruled that there was indeed a prima facie case of breach of privilege and two days later the matter was remitted to the Committee of Privileges. For the next month and more Hoare, already heavily engaged with the joint select committee, had to spare precious time to deal with Churchill's charges before the Committee of Privileges. It was true that Hoare, with the invaluable assistance of Derby, who wielded immense influence in Lancashire, had devoted a great deal of effort in attempting to persuade members and officials of the Manchester Chamber of Commerce to accept the facts of life about India instead of demanding, as some were, the abolition of the fiscal autonomy that India had been exercising since 1919 or, only marginally more realistically, constitutional guarantees for Lancashire cotton exports to India. It was also true that when, despite these efforts, the Chamber deposited with the clerk to the joint select committee on 28th June, 1933, a memorandum of evidence calling for a limitation of the Indian government's right to impose tariffs, Hoare saw that it was not circulated to the committee and did indeed seek to persuade the committee to amend the evidence. In the meantime Chamber officials were having discussions, first in London and then in India, with a leading Indian cotton manufacturer and it began to sink in that more was to be gained by conciliating Indian opinion than by gratuitously offending it, especially in face of fierce Japanese competition in the Indian market. Eventually, on 27th October, 1933, a fresh memorandum, in much less demanding terms, was sent to the committee and when, a week later, members of the Chamber appeared before the committee they accepted 'the legitimacy of the Indian desire to make considerable and rapid progress towards responsible self-government' but requested some form of safeguard against unfair discrimination. The result was the proposal in the subsequent committee report that the Governor-General be given a special responsibility to prevent the imposition of discriminatory tariffs against British goods (that is, those not applied to the same goods from other overseas sources). This, from Lancashire's point of view, was an advance upon the white paper's reference to the Governor-General's power to veto commercial discrimination, which covered internal trade only. Hoare thought it was a reasonable provision and was able to persuade the Indian assessors that it did not mean an infringement of fiscal autonomy.[80]

It was difficult to see how there could be a breach of parliamentary privilege in all this, and so the Committee of Privileges found in its report published on 8th June (1934). It concluded that the Manchester Chamber of Commerce had modified its evidence in the light of reports from its own mission to India and that at no point did the advice given by Hoare or Derby take the form of pressure or interference to restrict the absolute freedom of the Chamber to submit what evidence it saw fit. Hoare and Derby were completely exonerated: there was, the Privileges Committee declared, nothing dishonest or corrupt in a witness before a parliamentary committee being advised as the evidence he was to give on matters of opinion, particularly when, as in this case, the witness had invited the advice.[81]

Hoare was naturally relieved to have his reputation so clearly vindicated. The whole affair, in addition to absorbing so much valuable time, had given him many anxious moments. 'I do not think (he wrote to Willingdon soon after Churchill had dropped his bombshell) I ever felt so sick with politics, public life and everything to do with both of them.'[82] But the most important long-term aspect of the episode for Hoare's career was the exacerbation of feeling between Churchill and himself which continued long after the Government of India Bill was a *fait accompli*. While they had never been close colleagues they had worked together quite amicably in the past, from their co-operation over the immediate post-war intervention in Russia through to the five years of the second Baldwin government. Even in the early days of Hoare's involvement in Indian policy – for example, at the first round table conference – Churchill had seemed to recognise that Hoare was genuinely trying to prevent the Indian 'sell-out' that Churchill professed to fear. But by 1934 Churchill had suffered (and was to continue to suffer during the India Bill debates) from Hoare's quiet, well-informed and sometimes slightly and understandably waspish responses to his own often hectoring and always ill-informed rhetoric on India. As one keenly interested participant in the India debates later recalled of their confrontation:

> To watch Churchill's headlong attack and emotional rhetoric again and again disposed of by some simple rejoinder pitched in a minor key, or by a gentle reminder of the actual facts, was a real pleasure for the connoisseur of debate.[83]

The dislike was mutual. If Churchill could proclaim in the Commons smoking room at the time of the privilege affair, 'I will break this bloody rat Hoare's neck if I risk my own', Hoare could write to Sir George Stanley (Derby's brother) in India:

> I hope that Eddie [Derby] and the family will never forgive Winston. I certainly shall not. Winston and his friends are completely unscrupulous. They stick at nothing. They misrepresent everything that is said and spread about all kinds of groundless charges and baseless rumours.

These were not just incidents in the rough and tumble of politics, they represented real animosity, which Churchill's subsequent refusal to accept the impartiality of the Privileges Committee's report did nothing to mitigate.[84] They illustrated, too, the depths of emotion that the Indian issue aroused in Conservative ranks.

With the publication in November 1934 of the report of the joint select committee – in which all but the diehards and the Labour representatives backed the essential structure of the white paper policy – the stage was almost set for the introduction of the massive piece of legislation (478 clauses and 16 schedules) which would constitute the Government of India Bill.[85] There were indications that the Churchill campaign was losing its impetus in the extra-parliamentary organisation of the party and at a special meeting of the central council on 4th December the official policy on India received a massive majority of 712 votes (although the opposition vote of 390 was the highest it ever recorded at central council). The dimensions of dissidence within the parliamentary party were also becoming clearer and while greater than Hoare would have liked it was not by any stretch of the imagination sufficient to endanger the legislation. In a Commons debate on the joint select committee report on 12th December there were 77 rebel Conservatives in a vote of 410 to 127 in favour of the report (the Labour party voted against the government with the Conservative dissidents, as it was often to do in divisions on the Bill). This was to be almost identical with the highest rebel votes recorded during Commons consideration of the Government of India Bill: 79 on second reading in February 1935 and 78 on third reading in June.[86]

One of the main problems for the government before the introduction of the Bill, and one which occupied the Cabinet India committee under Hoare's chairmanship for many hours, concerned not the main substance of the legislation but its formal preamble. The preamble of the 1919 Act had incorporated Montagu's 1917 pledge about the aim of British policy being the progressive realisation of responsible government in India. What, if anything, was to be its 1935 counterpart? A mere reiteration of the pledge in the entirely changed circumstances might be seen in India as a retrogressive step, when in 1929 'dominion status' had been officially declared to be implicit in the 1917 statement. For Congress, of course, the goal was now not merely dominion status but complete independence, but the 1935 Bill had been drafted in the knowledge that it would not secure the approval of Congress even if Congress politicians might eventually be persuaded to work the new institutions it offered. But what of 'moderate' Indian opinion, at which the Bill was specifically aimed? Would it be satisfied by a pledge to anything that seemed less than dominion status? And if dominion status – a phrase which, as the 1929 rumpus indicated, was a red rag to the Conservative right, and not just to the diehards only – were included in the Bill what effect might it have on the size of the rebel vote? The compromise eventually arrived at (and agreed to by both Halifax, the author of the 1929 dominion status declaration, and Simon, whose report had studiously avoided the phrase) was that the question would be dealt with, not in the preamble, which would be brief, but in a statement by Hoare in the course of his speech on the second reading of the Bill.[87]

Hoare approached his second reading speech, due on 6th February, with some trepidation since, as he told Willingdon, 'I have made so many Indian speeches that I feel almost incapable of making another.'[88] Nevertheless it was a masterpiece of clear and logical exposition. Inevitably public attention was concentrated on the references to dominion status and here the contrast between Hoare's position as responsible minister with that as opposition delegate to the first round table conference just over four years before was striking.

> Let us face realities. The real danger in India is not Congress, or Communism, or misgovernment; it is irresponsibility. As long as Indian assemblies have no responsibility to govern, so must we expect negative criticism, and even mischievous obstruction. Has it not been the history of the British Empire that irresponsibility is the real danger to good relations between the Mother Country and its Overseas dependencies ...
> I do not take the view that, while irresponsibility is bad for men and women of British stock, it is good for men and women of Asiatic stock. I believe that unless we introduce this element of real responsibility, both into the Central Government and into the Provincial Governments, we shall see the state

of affairs going from bad to worse, we shall see these assemblies not becoming easier to deal with in the future than they have been in the past, but immensely more hostile, with a growing body of hostility from one end of the country to the other ... The fact is that irresponsibility is to most people the outward sign of inequality of status. We in Great Britain pay very little attention to questions of status ... not so our Indian fellow-subjects who, looking back over centuries of civilisation, feel as sensitive as any of the great peoples of the world to any charge of inequality of status. A move forward, therefore, on the road to responsible government is something much more to them than a mere political reform. It is the outward and visible sign of the recognition of their status.

Hoare then dealt with the reasons for not spelling all this out in a preamble. There was, he said, no need for this since 'no new pronouncement of policy or intention is required'. The government stood by the preamble to the 1919 Act (which would not be repealed) and the 1929 declaration that this implied that the 'natural issue of India's progress' was 'the attainment of Dominion Status'. There were difficulties to be surmounted before the conditions on which self-government rested could be fully established, notably those created by 'cleavages of race, caste and religion' and the requirements for the effective defence of India. Britain would do all it could 'to enable India to overcome these difficulties and ultimately to take [its] place among the fully self-governing members of the British Commonwealth of Nations'.

Hoare's speech concluded:

If there are still those who impugn our motives, if there are still those who doubt our word, we are ready to be judged by our actions. And of our actions this Bill is the outward and visible sign — a Bill that has been hammered out in the face of almost overwhelming difficulties, a Bill that is the result of years of incessant inquiry, a Bill that offers India a vast and fruitful field of self-government, a Bill that holds the balance fairly and honourably between conflicting interests and competing parties, a Bill that comes in the direct line of succession to the great Imperial measures of the past. Let Indians, though they may wish for a longer and swifter advance, mark the spirit in which we make these proposals. Let Parliament, realising the difficulties in any course of action, remembering the complexities of any scheme of Indian reform, admitting the many imperfections of any proposals, show by the majority for the Second Reading and its attitude in the subsequent stages of our discussions, that it intends to act, as it has acted upon great issues of the kind in the past, with resolution and expedition, no less than with caution and wisdom.[89]

Parliament heeded the request at the end of Hoare's speech. After all the years of discussions and negotiations the final stage of placing the Indian policy on the statute book was relatively short, considering the bulk and importance of the legislation. The four days of the second reading debate were followed by 30 days of exhaustive examination of the Bill in Committee of the Whole House between 19th February and 15th May. By 5th June the report and third reading stages had been completed and the Bill went to the Lords, from whence it returned for consideration of the Lords' amendments on 30th July. The royal assent was signified on 2nd August. This expedition was partly the result of an uncharacteristic show of co-operation by the diehards and, not so unexpectedly, by the Labour party, both of whom agreed to a voluntary time-table for the Bill, without the government having to resort to the threat of closure.[90] The government was helped, too, by the decision of one of the most redoubtable of its critics — Lloyd George — not to take part in the debates, despite earlier attacks on the government for not dealing with the real political leaders in India, Gandhi and the other Congress notables. He told Edward Grigg that his decision was prompted by a wish not to increase the difficulties of the Conservative leadership with the party diehards and by an admiration for Hoare's 'determination and courage'. Since he wanted the government as a whole to show more of these qualities 'he was not going to criticise a Minister who had displayed them so conspicuously'.[91]

The Indian marathon had, however, taken its physical toll of Hoare. In April, in the middle of the committee stage, he was taken seriously ill with congestion of the lungs. It was not until 16th May that he was able to return to the India Office and to see the Bill through its last stages in the Commons. On 6th June it was introduced in the House of Lords. On the following day Hoare became Foreign Secretary in the government changes resulting from the long-expected supersession of MacDonald by Baldwin as Prime Minister of the National Government. When the Bill received the royal assent on 2nd August he was deep into the intricacies of his new portfolio.

So what must be accounted the greatest achievement of Hoare's career had been completed. There was much accomplishment (and a disastrous disappointment) still ahead but India was undeniably the peak, even more considerable than his stewardship of the Air Ministry in the 1920s. Without any prior emotional or political commitment to Indian advance he had assumed the onerous and, in party terms, thankless task at the India Office in 1931 and, by dint of hard work and a mastery of his brief, had translated what before had been a mixture of vague aspirations and rather incoherent plans into firm legislative reality. He had grown perceptibly in political stature in the process. The minister who was prepared to withstand the assaults of a Churchill and the sullen opposition or, at best, weary resignation of the great mass of his own party, was very different from the opposition representative at the first round table conference who had expressed grave reservations about the wisdom of responsible central government in India. Yet even in 1930 Hoare had seen that the Simon commission's prescription for responsible government only in the Indian provinces did not come anywhere near to meeting the expectations of moderate opinion in India, let alone those of the Indian Congress. But he knew, too, that the prospect of a Congress-dominated unitary British India, which might well insist on seceding from the British Commonwealth, was anathema to the Conservative party and was probably unacceptable to British public opinion as a whole. Hence the importance of the federal idea, the full implications of which Hoare saw perhaps more clearly than any other leading British politician. The federation of British India and the Indian princely states would allow for constitutional advance at the centre but at the same time provide institutional restraints on the actions of any potentially secessionist or communally discriminating Indian government. It was the only kind of constitutional framework that had any chance of acceptance in the circumstances of British politics.

In the face of a reluctant party Hoare ensured that it was accepted.

Yet this mammoth Government of India Act on which Hoare and many others had laboured so long and so hard was never to be fully implemented. Provincial self-government came into operation in 1937, providing Congress politicians among others with their first experience of the problems of governing, but insufficient princes had executed instruments of accession for their states to make it possible to establish the federation before the outbreak of war in 1939 intervened to bring constitutional development to an abrupt halt. The key factor in this delay was the failure to convince the princes of the benefits of federation and here the Viceroys — Willingdon until 1936, and then Linlithgow — must bear much of the responsibility. Hoare had done his best from London before June 1935 but this was essentially a task which had to be left to the man on the spot. Perhaps, as Lord Templewood and Lord Halifax both felt in retrospect, diehard tactics were also to blame in delaying the progress of the reforms and thus reducing the time available for their implementation before the war came.[92] Churchill and his friends certainly made Hoare's task infinitely more arduous but it seems doubtful whether they were able to effect a substantial delay in its completion. The group to which Hoare's attention was mainly directed was not the diehards but the centre group headed by Austen Chamberlain. The long joint select committee stage was primarily a device to secure the adherence of this group — and, with it, that of the great mass of the Conservative party — to the government's Indian policy. After the publication of the committee's report in November 1934 the progress of the Government of India Bill to the statute book was quite remarkably speedy for so complex a piece of legislation.

When constitutional advance was resumed in India after the war it was in quite different circumstances and produced quite different results: instead of one federation for the whole of India, the sub-continent, after incalculable human suffering, was to be divided between two mutually antagonistic federal states. It seems reasonable to assume that India's post-war development would have been far smoother had the federation provided in the 1935 Act been set up before 1939. This was what Hoare believed and so did most of those associated with him in devising the Act. Many years later Lord Hailey told him that:

> I am convinced that if events had made it possible to pursue
> the policy you had initiated in the Act of 1935, we should
> today be able to look back on a final chapter in our Indian his-
> tory that would have brought infinitely more satisfaction
> both to India and Britain than anything we can now hope to
> see.[93]

This view was not confined to British administrators. A few
months before Indian independence was achieved in 1947
K. M. Panikkar — a former state chief minister and distinguished Indian historian and diplomat — wrote to Lord Templewood: 'I have never failed to regret that the Act of 1935 was
not given effect to at the Centre in 1937. If it had been what an
easy and peaceful transition there would have been to freedom.'[94] But as Panikkar then went on to point out, and as
Nehru himself affirmed to R. A. Butler, the Government of
India Act provided a model for the post-independence constitution makers in both India and Pakistan. The Act was, in
the words of a leading historian of British India, 'an organic
connecting link between the old and the new [and] ... contained within itself the seeds of independence'. No doubt it was
this that Lord Templewood had in mind when he wrote to L. S.
Amery in February 1954 that, 'there are no clear-cut successes
or failures in political life, and in this case, the indirect results
of the Act may have been as permanent as its direct results
would have been.'[95]

5

Foreign Secretary

In May 1929, near the end of Hoare's long term at the Air Ministry, Trenchard had reported to Hankey, the Secretary of the Cabinet, that 'Sam Hoare was dying to go to the Foreign Office'.[1] It was an understandable ambition. To attain one of the two or three most important posts in any Cabinet was reason enough but in Hoare's case there was the experience he had gained during his wartime intelligence missions to Russia and Italy and his continuing interest in central European affairs, particularly those of the Czechoslovak nation he had helped to found. Moreover, his first two ministerial offices had each brought him into contact with much wider concerns than a purely domestic department would have done. The Foreign Office represented a perfectly natural progression for a highly successful senior minister like Hoare.

But when, with the reconstruction of the government which was expected to follow MacDonald's imminent retirement from the prime ministership, the opportunity for fulfilling his ambition seemed to have arrived, Hoare did not find the choice easy. In April 1936 Willingdon's term as Viceroy was due to end and a decision about his successor had to be taken in the summer of 1935. Hoare, who had once been tempted by the thought of an Indian governorship, was greatly attracted by this, the most prestigious of all overseas appointments. Having seen the Government of India Bill through virtually all its stages he relished the challenge of attempting to implement his policy in India itself. A month or so before Hoare left the India Office rumours were circulating that his next appointment might be to India although at the same time it was widely thought that

Linlithgow would get the job.[2] The Indian posting would have
the added advantage of giving Hoare a few months respite
from arduous official duties in which to recoup his health since,
unlike a ministerial reshuffle which would immediately involve
him in fresh responsibilities, the Viceroyalty would not be taken
up until the following year.[3]

India had obvious disadvantages for his future career, however. Having controlled policy-making for so long the transition to mere implementation, subject to the oversight of his own
ministerial successor, might in practice have been unpalatable.
It is curious, indeed, that Hoare should have coveted the post
when he knew better than most what a relatively small part
Willingdon had played in the shaping of policy: perhaps he felt
that with the Government of India Act on the statute book there
was no new Indian policy to be formulated in Whitehall and
that he would be virtually free from ministerial direction. But
if Hoare was temporarily seduced by the pomp and trappings
of the Viceroyalty, Lady Maud was not. Her advice was firmly
against a step which she thought would be inimical to her husband's political career. Not that that career need necessarily be
ended (although any opportunities arising during the five-year
term would be missed): Reading and Halifax had both provided
recent examples of Viceroys resuming a career in British politics on their return. But acceptance of the peerage which was the
necessary concomitant of becoming Viceroy would effectively
bar him from the office on which Lady Maud, perhaps even
more than Hoare himself, had set her heart — the prime ministership.[4]

During May Baldwin, even before taking over from Ramsay
MacDonald, seems to have put to Hoare the choice between the
Foreign Office or India. By the end of the month Hoare had
apparently firmly, if with some reluctance, decided on the
Foreign Office. He explained his motives to Butler (who relayed
them to Brabourne in India):

... he had had a long talk with [Findlater] Stewart, and had
told him the worst, and that he did not want to move from a
good Office with an exceptional staff before the end of his
job was completed, but that he had always said that if he was
offered the Foreign Office he would go there. He himself was

really in favour of accepting the Viceroyalty, because he felt
he could manage Indian politicians, he liked the heat and
hated the House of Commons ... He would enjoy the pomp
and ceremony. But there were stronger forces at home keeping
him here. Maud did not like the idea of India, and S.B. and
Neville, with whom he has worked so closely for so long, said
they could not afford to lose him during the next five difficult
years in England.[5]

But matters were by no means completely settled, even at that
comparatively late stage — just a week before Baldwin assumed
the prime ministership. One complication was that there was the
possibility of a highly popular alternative appointment to the
Foreign Office, that of the young and apparently dynamic and
idealistic Anthony Eden, who as Lord Privy Seal was Simon's
ministerial no. 2 and had been particularly active in League of
Nations questions. On 16th May Eden had sought an interview
with Baldwin in which he told him that he did not wish to carry
on at the Foreign Office under a new chief: a clear indication
that if Baldwin wanted to retain Eden in a post concerned with
foreign affairs it had to be as Foreign Secretary.[6] Eden's appointment could have been made without creating any difficulties for
Baldwin with Hoare since the latter was so clearly in two minds
as to which he really preferred between the Foreign Office and
India; the only problem then would be that the King, who still
exercised considerable influence over Indian appointments, had
told Baldwin that Hoare's immediate translation from the India
Office to the Viceroyalty would create an unfortunate prece-
dent.[7] On 3rd June Baldwin warned Linlithgow that he was not
assured of the Viceroyalty[8] and on the same day he consulted a
friend in whose judgement he placed much reliance: Geoffrey
Dawson, editor of *The Times*. Dawson thought that the patient
skill Hoare had shown in bringing together the disparate elements of Indian policy might be beneficially employed in
solving European problems. The decisive advice probably came
from the colleague who was clearly going to be the 'strong man'
of Baldwin's Cabinet, Neville Chamberlain. Chamberlain was
reluctant to see his friend Hoare apparently passed over for so
senior a post in favour of a junior minister aged only 38; in any
case, he felt that Eden needed the experience of another de-

partment before he could be considered Foreign Secretary material.[9] Some uncertainty about the final dispositions seems to have continued. On 4th June Baldwin definitely offered the Foreign Office to Hoare and the latter accepted, only stipulating that Eden should continue to serve at the Foreign Office with him, if willing to do so.[10] But on the following day someone normally very much at the centre of things – Hankey, the Cabinet Secretary – told Eden quite confidently that it had been decided he should go to the Foreign Office. That same afternoon, however, Baldwin gave Eden the unwelcome news that although he was now to enter the Cabinet it was still as no. 2 at the Foreign Office, this time under Hoare.[11] On 7th June the appointments were publicly announced, along with all the other appointments in Baldwin's third Cabinet. Hoare was to be the Foreign Secretary, with the Cabinet assistance of Eden as 'Minister without Portfolio for League of Nations Affairs'.

Among those who offered their congratulations to Hoare on his promotion none was more enthusiastic than Beaverbrook:

> You have been raised on high by capacity and character. I am convinced that you will be raised higher still, maybe to the highest place of all, by the same qualities.
>   Your stay at the Foreign Office will be memorable. Your problems are great. Your opportunities are greater.[12]

This was the judgement of a loyal friend but there would have been many others less partial who would still have forecast that the new Foreign Secretary, at the relatively youthful age (for a major politician) of 55, and with a splendid parliamentary achievement to his credit, was standing on the brink of an even more brilliant career. Hoare's stay at the Foreign Office was indeed to be memorable, but not quite in the way Beaverbrook had anticipated.

In all his first three ministerial appointments, covering the years from 1922 to 1935, Hoare succeeded to what in a moment of retrospective gloom he referred to as a *damnosa hereditas*.[13] At the Air Ministry it was the sentence of death which in 1922 hung over both the department and the separate service it supervised. At the India Office it was the almost insuperable problem of trying to devise a programme for constitutional advance acceptable both to articulate (and heterogeneous) political opinion in India and to the broad mass of the Conservative party. In both departments Hoare succeeded in surmounting his inheritance with a degree of success which probably no other politician would have exceeded. But the *damnosa hereditas* of the Foreign Office in June 1935 was of a quite different order of magnitude and complexity. Its demands were so urgent that Hoare hardly had time to come to grips with them before disaster struck. He was unable this time to surmount his departmental inheritance.

Hoare's difficult legacy at the Foreign Office had several elements, some organisational and some – the most intractable – in the realm of policy. To take over the Foreign Office in June 1935 was to take over a ship far from happy and far from united. Part of the problem arose from the incumbency of Hoare's immediate predecessor, Sir John Simon, who had been Foreign Secretary since the post-electoral reshuffle of the National Government in November 1931. Although a man of formidable intellectual and forensic gifts Simon owed the eminence of his Cabinet position primarily to his being the leader of the National Liberal group in a government at pains to demonstrate its inter-party character. But the dominant Conservative element in the National Government, and particularly its backbenchers, became progressively dissatisfied with Simon's seemingly indecisive conduct of affairs, the more so as they felt that so important a portfolio should be in the hands of a member of their own party. The Conservative attack on Simon came from both extremes of the party. Those on the left who placed their faith in the League of Nations and the concept of collective security blamed him, albeit unfairly, for the collapse of the disarmament conference (whose opening Hoare had attended in January 1932) and for the failure of the League to deal with Japanese aggression in Manchuria and the Yangtse Valley in 1931–3. Right-wing Conservatives, on the other hand, were critical of Simon for dealing with the League at all, to the detriment, as they saw it, of the country's sovereignty. For them, one of the final straws was the admission of the Soviet Union to League membership, with the approval of Simon and the National Government, in September 1934. Soon afterwards the crisis provoked by Italian designs in Abyssinia was progressively to involve both the League and British policy in a situation from which it was almost impossible that either could emerge with credit. As the going got rougher so Conservative disquiet was augmented. In April 1935 a group of some 70 Conservative M.P.s protested against Simon's retention of the Foreign Office, and Baldwin admitted to the Conservative *emeritus* Foreign Secretary, Austen Chamberlain, that the Cabinet no longer had confidence in Simon in that post.[14] His name was at the head of everyone's list for the expected Cabinet reshuffle on the retirement of MacDonald and it became only a question of which Conservative would succeed him. The appointment of Hoare gave wide satisfaction, even if the younger element in the party would have preferred Anthony Eden.

Eden in fact provided another factor in Hoare's difficult inheritance. Elected an M.P. at the age of 26 in 1923, his political advance had been sensationally rapid but had taken place almost entirely within the ambit of the Foreign Office and foreign affairs, particularly the affairs of the League of Nations, of which he was widely regarded as one of the foremost champions in British political life. Parliamentary private secretary to Austen Chamberlain as Foreign Secretary from 1926 to 1929, Eden graduated to ministerial rank as parliamentary undersecretary at the Foreign Office on the formation of the National Government in 1931 and remained there on his promotion to Lord Privy Seal at the end of 1933. Apart from a few months in 1931 his entire ministerial service at the Foreign Office had been under the aegis of Simon. With his full ration of personal ambition, and perhaps a not insignificant quota of youthful arrogance, Eden was understandably reluctant to remain in double harness when Simon's departure became inevitable. Hoare, however, was anxious to retain his services there, and Eden's pill was sugared by his membership of the Cabinet and the designation of particular responsibilities in his ministerial title.[15]

It was nevertheless an administratively clumsy arrangement. This was symbolised at the outset by difficulty over the wording of Eden's appointment. It was at first announced as 'Minister without Portfolio for League of Nations Affairs' but then had hastily to be amended when the Law Officers pointed out that a minister without portfolio could not very well be a minister with a special portfolio. The post then became 'Minister for League of Nations Affairs (without portfolio)'. As usual with such dyarchical ministerial arrangements in single departments M.P.s professed to a concern about which minister would be responsible for answering which parliamentary questions, and Hoare had to resist attempts to put down questions directly to the Minister for League of Nations Affairs. As he told Austen Chamberlain:

> As you know better than anyone, it is in practice impossible to distinguish between League of Nations questions and questions dealing with general foreign affairs ... there is no League of Nations Department ... It is a section of the Foreign Office and on no account ought we to admit the existence of a separate organisation. If we once make this admission there is bound to be divided responsibility at the Foreign Office.[16]

But the impression that there was indeed divided responsibility was not diminished by the appointment of Lord Cranborne as parliamentary under-secretary for League of Nations Affairs, and thus apparently more Eden's subordinate than Hoare's. In this case there was an additional impression of some administrative muddle when it was discovered that Cranborne's post needed legislative sanction and Hoare, in addition to all his other departmental cares, had to pilot a special Bill through the Commons.[17]

In the short time that they had to operate the ministerial arrangements probably worked as well as could have been reasonably expected, given that Hoare and Eden were by no means ideally suited in temperament and experience for a close ministerial relationship. Hoare was careful to give the younger man his head when it seemed appropriate to do so and Eden's official loyalty to his ministerial superior was impeccable. But yet it remains curious why Hoare should have advocated the arrangement and that Baldwin should have effected it. On Hoare's part it was no doubt a desire to get expert assistance in an onerous job when his own health and strength had been under such prolonged strain with the India Bill. Baldwin had, however, been complaining at the beginning of June about the confusion that seemed to reign at the Foreign Office and the fact that 'he did not know where he was' with the department.[18] To promote to Cabinet status a minister who had been in the department for four years continuously — in which time he had inevitably attracted personal loyalties — and place over his head a senior colleague with whom he had had no previous contact seemed a poor way of trying to end the confusion. Although Hoare brought his considerable administrative skills to the Foreign Office — the staff there soon having the opportunity of contrasting his speedy and efficient treatment of the papers submitted to him with the dilatory and unmethodical approach of his immediate predecessor[19] — these were in part offset by the existence of two Cabinet ministers in the same department. Inevitably the ministerial dichotomy came to be matched by a kind of official one, with some of the staff reporting normally to Eden (and Cranborne) rather than to the Secretary of State and his 'general' under-secretary, Lord Stanhope.

The Foreign Office was quite unlike the two other departments over which Hoare had presided and, despite his long-standing ambition to become Foreign Secretary, it was not long before he came to pine for the more stable virtues of the India Office where, 'surrounded by advisers who were all agreed upon the same policy, I could devote myself to a single purpose'. The change, typically for one who, like Hoare, was so sensitive to his working environment, was symbolised in the contrasting styles of the Secretary of State's room in each department.

> In the India Office, there was the intimacy of a small study, the comfort of the eighteenth-century mahogany from East India Office, and the delight of the Persian miniatures from Moghul Delhi; in the Foreign Office, a vast and draughty saloon with windows too big either to shut or to open, a writing-table in the middle of the room that made conversation difficult, and the atmosphere of a pretentious hotel lounge.[20]

But the contrast was not confined to the interior decoration. The Foreign Office staff, unlike their counterparts in most of the 'home' departments (with the possible exception of the Treasury) considered themselves not so much as the generalist administrators of Civil Service tradition as experts in their field of foreign affairs, with all the expert's enthusiasm for propagating his own views. In place of the wise, discreet and immensely able Findlater Stewart at the India Office, Hoare now had as his permanent secretary that extraordinarily gifted but volatile character Sir Robert Vansittart who, as Lord Avon later recalled, was more 'a sincere, almost fanatical, crusader' than 'an official giving cool and disinterested advice'.[21] But the important point (which Lord Avon omitted to make) was that Vansittart was not unique in the Foreign Office of the 1930s. As Hoare later observed: 'Everyone seemed to be over-excited. There appeared to be no generally accepted body of opinion on the main issues. Diametrically opposed views were pressed upon me, and sometimes with the intolerance of an *odium theologicum*.'[22] In the Foreign Office, reversing the traditional precept of the British Civil Service, the experts were on top rather than on tap and, as is the way with experts, found it difficult to submerge their expertise in a departmental consensus. It placed a more than usually onerous burden on the department's political leadership, in a sense depriving ministers of the full ballast that sound generalist senior officials can give.

If the Foreign Office was internally divided as to what the main lines of British foreign policy should be it reflected the confusion and uncertainty of British public opinion. There was the understandable if naive belief, almost universally held, that another war was totally unthinkable and could best be prevented by disarmament all round, combined with the pursuit of 'collective security' through that apparently most hopeful feature of the 1919 peace settlement, the League of Nations. Britain was still expected to play a world role but membership of the League would enable it to do so without all the disagreeable — and expensive — paraphernalia of armed strength that had traditionally been thought an essential bulwark of international influence and the preservation of national integrity. The British penchant for laying down the law to lesser breeds could be indulged at a cut price. This appeared to make some sort of sense in the 1920s with an unarmed Germany still painfully trying to build up a democratic polity and only Japan, for long Britain's faithful ally until American jealousy of its rising strength forced Britain to end the alliance, as a possible potential threat to world peace. In Europe the real threat for many in Britain, including most of the Conservative party, seemed then to be posed by the Soviet Union, but even here it was a threat perceived more in terms of internal subversion than armed aggression requiring large forces to deter or repel. But the rise of Hitler and the Nazis in Germany in the early 1930s fundamentally altered the situation. This was in part recognised by the National Government when in March 1932, on the insistence of the Chiefs of Staff, it agreed in effect to end the ten-year rule — the assumption that there would be no major war for a period of ten years ahead — which had so bedevilled defence planning.[23] Even then it was many months before the financial constraints on any real rearmament began to be removed and then the emphasis was much more on defence against air attack than the other basic strategic necessities for fighting a continental enemy: a strong mobile army and a powerful navy to protect essential sea routes. Nor was enough done to keep vital alliances in good repair. British attitudes to the potential dangers of German resurgence were equivocal, evincing both a widespread feeling of guilt about the supposed harshness of the Versailles terms and a concomitant readiness to condone German breaches of them when they could be represented as the mere assertion of national independence. French policy, despite the country's endemic political and social instability, was in principle much more realistic: so much so that for much of the 1920s it was France rather than Germany which seemed to constitute the greater danger of European peace. Failing any firm British guarantees of assistance in the event of German aggression — the fine sentiments of the Locarno agreements of 1925 notwithstanding — France desperately sought compensation in a series of ineffectual and in the end highly embarrassing alliances in eastern Europe. The other wartime European ally, Italy, felt it had done almost as badly out of the war as the defeated Germany, above all in falling far short of the colonial spoils which the secret Treaty of London of 1915 had seemed to promise, in return for its intervention in the war. The Italian fascist regime under Mussolini certainly did not lack its admirers in all political strata in Britain, but its concern with national glory and the rather belated and anachronistic fulfilment of colonial ambitions in Africa had diminished its value as an ally, had Britain been seriously looking for one. Nevertheless, Italy in 1934 demonstrated its concern with the European balance when Italian troops were sent to the Brenner Pass at the time of the abortive Nazi coup in Austria.

With a reviving and brutally nationalistic Germany in Europe and a now unfriendly and aggressive Japan threatening British interests in the Far East and the Pacific, allies were what Britain needed above all. The need was, however, masked by the existence of the League of Nations and the confidence placed in the collective security which membership — against all the evidence of past and present international conflict — was supposed to achieve. Collective security had failed its first major test against Japan from 1931 onwards but there were still those who felt that the League might have more success in Europe.

Moreover, few in British public life at this time, inside or outside the Foreign Office, agreed with the insistence of Vansittart, Hankey and Amery (and, at a later stage, Churchill) that Germany was the cardinal danger, to meet which all other policy should be subordinated. There was still the hope that Germany could be persuaded to engage in general disarmament in exchange for a lifting of the restrictions on its rearmament imposed by the peace treaty. Thus in March 1934 a close Cabinet ally of Eden (who was not himself then a member of the Cabinet) was calling privately for 'a clear view of a Foreign Policy that was not Vansittart's': in other words, a policy of general disarmament and conciliation of Germany rather than a firm Franco-British (and, if possible, Italian) front against Germany.[24] Eden agreed with the attempt to conciliate Germany and so did Hoare at this time. When in the same month (March 1934) a report by the Defence Requirements Committee of the C.I.D., established under Hankey's chairmanship in November 1933, came up for discussion in the Cabinet, Hoare criticised as premature its assumption that Britain should prepare for war against Germany; other ministers argued that even if Germany were to be regarded as the ultimate potential enemy Britain should be wary of accepting any military commitment to the French.[25]

A year later it looked as if British policy might be taking a new direction. In March 1935 a British defence white paper launched a modest plan for Britain's rearmament and in the same month came the unilateral renunciation of the Versailles treaty's rearmament restrictions by Germany. Hoare was moved to recognise that 'The only course for us to take is to prevent any breach between ourselves and the French and the Italians.'[26] In the following month the government, through the agency of MacDonald and Simon, took steps at the Stresa conference to form the so-called Stresa front with France and Italy in order to protest against the recent German action in defiance of the peace treaty and, by implication, to guard against future infringements. Britain at last seemed to be looking to its alliances, as well as trying to provide itself with the defence capability on which the achievement of any of its foreign policy aims depended. Appearances, however, were deceptive, and Hoare's policy inheritance at the Foreign Office – the chief element in his *damnosa hereditas* – had already gravely threatened the frail fabric of the Stresa front.

Although Germany had unilaterally seized what was to have been the quid pro quo for its agreement to general disarmament – the abrogation of the restrictive clauses of the peace treaty – the British government had not given up hope of limiting the scale of German rearmament by conciliation. On 4th June, 1935, three days before Hoare took over at the Foreign Office, a German delegation led by Hitler's special envoy, Ribbentrop, began talks in London on a naval agreement between the two countries. This rather surprising (and to the French, at least, disturbing) development had in fact been foreshadowed in talks which Simon and Eden had had in Berlin at the end of March and a much-publicised speech by Hitler on 21st May, in which he had offered to limit the expansion of the German navy to 35 per cent of the British fleet, had given it added impetus. Right at the beginning of the London talks, however, Ribbentrop startled the British delegation by demanding immediate British acceptance of the 35 per cent ratio proposal before he would continue the discussions: Hitler's offer had now become a demand rather than a subject for negotiation. The British representatives objected that there was a tacit understanding with the other naval powers, including the United States and France, that there should be no bilateral arrangements in advance of a general naval conference, due to be held at the end of the year, but Ribbentrop brushed the objection aside. The next day the Cabinet empowered its ministerial naval committee to give appropriate instructions to the British delegates and the committee decided that the offer should be accepted, in view of the Admiralty's overwhelming desire to seize this opportunity of limiting British naval commitments in home waters when at any time Japanese aggression might compel the dispatch of a fleet to the Far East. On 6th June, in one of his last acts as Foreign Secretary, Simon announced Britain's acceptance at the Anglo-German naval talks, and on the following day telegrams were sent informing the American, French, Italian and Japanese governments of the British decision and inviting their reactions: but they were quite clearly designed more to give information than the opportunity for prior consent before the decision was finalised.[27]

Hoare took over as Foreign Secretary the day the telegrams were sent out. It was thus hardly possible for him to change the policy — and there is no evidence to show that he was anything but in complete agreement with it.[28] He did not take part in the remaining discussions with Ribbentrop's delegation (which were interrupted for six days for the Whitsun holiday) but was present at the last meeting on 18th June, when the agreement was finally ratified by Ribbentrop and a Foreign Office official, R. L. Craigie. Hoare's retrospective account (written after consultation with Vansittart and Sir Robert Craigie) was a spirited justification of the Anglo-German Naval Treaty. There was no question, he wrote,

of placating Hitler. Seeing, however, Hitler's growing strength in the air and on land, and our serious weakness, we were forced to play for time. The Agreement might not last for ever — no international agreement was ever permanent — but it would at least have the effect of slowing down the construction of a formidable German Fleet and giving us time to rebuild and strengthen our own. Having taken this first step we hoped to follow it up with an Air Pact on the basis of parity for ourselves, France and Germany, and we believed that we were more likely to succeed with the second stage when once we had shown Hitler that an agreement upon naval armaments was possible. The alternatives were either drift or preventive war. No one in Great Britain was prepared to go to war with Germany in order to stop German rearmament. A preventive war, therefore, was out of the question. The alternative of drift had let him build up an army as strong as the French and an air force as strong as ours.[29]

Nevertheless, had Hoare had time to consider all the implications of a formal naval agreement with Germany it is conceivable that he might have attempted to guide the Cabinet into a different decision. He was not, of course, to know that the hopes placed in it would not be realised: the agreement did not lead to an air pact (mainly, it must be said, because of French opposition) and the advantages it was supposed to secure for the British navy were probably illusory. The German navy was much less important in Hitler's plans than the army and air force and the scale of German naval rearmament may well have been unaffected by the naval treaty with Britain. The immediate diplomatic disadvantages were, however, easy to discern at the time. France, in particular, was offended by the formal approval Britain thereby gave to German infringement of the arms limitation clauses of the peace treaty. Moreover, such a bilateral treaty with Germany seemed hard to reconcile with the recent Stresa front, which had been explicitly designed as a tripartite protection against German aggression. The conclusion of the naval agreement with Germany undoubtedly complicated even further the crisis over Italian ambitions against Abyssinia, any solution of which depended utterly upon French co-operation.[30]

The Abyssinian crisis was the most intractable policy element in Hoare's departmental inheritance and after six months it left his political career apparently in ruins. So much has been said and written about the affair that it is difficult, forty years on, to disentangle fact from fiction, the stark realities of the situation from moralistic tub-thumping. Fortunately several scholarly treatments of the crisis have appeared in recent years and from these it is clear that, while British policy failed, it probably had no real chance of succeeding.[31] Moreover, the failure was not just of Hoare — so often made the scapegoat — but of the whole government, not least Hoare's successor as Foreign Secretary, Anthony Eden. Nor were the policy-makers helped by an extraordinary outburst of moral fervour on the part of articulate British public opinion which deserved a better cause and which had unfortunately mostly evaporated when, shortly afterwards, Britain had to confront sterner challenges to its resolution from a more formidable rival than Mussolini's Italy.

The parameters of British policy towards the Abyssinian crisis had been determined many years before Hoare became Foreign

Secretary. There was, above all, the long history of imperialist involvement of Britain, France and Italy in that area of Africa and the tacit acceptance of the primacy of Italian economic and other interests there by the other two powers — by Britain, as early as 1891. In 1896 an attempt by the Italians, from their coastal possessions in what later became Eritrea and Italian Somaliland, to establish a protectorate over the Amharic mountain kingdom of Abyssinia (whose able ruler, Menelik, was engaged in conquering neighbouring feudal fiefs in order to restore the glories of the ancient empire of Ethiopia) came to grief at Adowa, when an Italian army was routed by an Abyssinian army over four times its strength. Despite this reverse the three European powers concluded an agreement in December 1906 by which each recognised the others' special interests in Abyssinia: Britain, in the source of the Blue Nile at Lake Tana, on which Egypt and the Sudan depended; France, in the railway from Djibouti in French Somaliland to the Abyssinian interior built and operated by the French under concession from the Abyssinian emperor (it reached the capital, Addis Ababa, in 1917), which provided Abyssinia with its only outlet to the sea; and Italy, in a potential sphere of influence in north, south and east Abyssinia to protect Eritrea and Italian Somaliland, with a right to a 'territorial connection' between the two colonies through Abyssinia. After the First World War, disappointed of the colonial gains in east Africa it had expected to make, Italy turned to subtler methods to extend its influence over Abyssinia. When Abyssinia applied for membership of the League of Nations in 1923 it was Italy (and France) which sponsored the application and Britain which opposed it, on the grounds that the government in Addis Ababa appeared to exercise only exiguous control over large areas of the country and had made little effort to stamp out either endemic slavery or the widespread arms traffic. Energetic lobbying by Italy and France ensured the success of Abyssinia's application, although it was compelled to give certain undertakings with regard to slavery and the arms traffic; and it seemed that League membership left unaffected the rights over Abyssinian territory claimed by Britain, France and Italy under the 1906 treaty. Two years later Britain felt the need for Italian co-operation over its desire to build a dam at Lake Tana (in the Italian sphere of influence, according to the 1906 treaty) and was prepared to promise in return to support Italian efforts to obtain from the Abyssinian government a concession to build and operate a railway from the Eritrean frontier to the frontier of Italian Somaliland (the 'territorial connection' of the 1906 treaty), together with an exclusive zone of economic influence in the area to be crossed by the railway. The agreement was made in the form of an exchange of notes between Mussolini and Sir Ronald Graham, the British Ambassador in Rome, in December 1925, the contents of which were rather belatedly conveyed to France (which should have been consulted in advance under the 1906 treaty) and Abyssinia. The French response was remarkably mild but the Abyssinians chose the forum of the League of Nations to make a protest, pointing out that the Anglo-Italian plan was hardly consistent with the sovereignty of a League member. Britain and Italy put a bold front on it by replying in effect that just as they were free to grant concessions to each other, so the Abyssinian government was free to grant, or withhold, concessions to them. But both Austen Chamberlain, the British Foreign Secretary, and Mussolini were compelled to issue public assurances that neither of their countries had any intention of suggesting that Abyssinia was to be considered as subject to Italian economic influence.[32] Once again, Italy had to employ more ingratiating methods, especially when the main British motive for supporting Italy's claims seemed to have been removed by the Abyssinian government's unexpected action in granting permission to a Sudanese-sponsored American company to survey for the building of a dam on Lake Tana in November 1927. On 2nd August, 1928, Italy and Abyssinia signed a treaty of 'friendship, arbitration and sincerity' which declared that neither country would take any action that might 'prejudice or damage the independence of the other' and that both would submit all disputes which could not be solved through normal diplomatic channels to 'processes of conciliation and arbitration'. The treaty also bound both governments to develop and promote commerce between the two countries, and to facilitate this a supplementary economic convention was signed providing for the construction of a road from the port of Assab in Eritrea to a point 430 miles inside Abyssinia, each country undertaking to build that stretch of road which passed through its territory;

Abyssinia was to be given a lease of land for a wharf and a free zone at Assab. Little was done to give effect to this treaty, however, and by 1930 (the year Haile Selassie became emperor of Abyssinia) it had become practically a dead letter. The Italians attributed its failure to Abyssinian dilatoriness and intransigence, the Abyssinians to technical problems connected with the road scheme. But whoever was mainly to blame — and the fault was by no means all on the Italian side — the treaty did nothing to abate Italian encroachments into the indeterminate desert area of the Ogaden beyond the Italian Somaliland frontier or Italian efforts to encourage internal dissension against Haile Selassie's authority.[33] For a variety of reasons — the need for a safety valve for the domestic social and economic distress which fascist policy was powerless to alleviate, and the belief that Germany would in a very few years be strong enough to move against Austria, among them — Mussolini began to feel that the time was propitious for asserting by military means that dominance over Abyssinia which Italy had been seeking for half a century. From 1932 military preparations were made in Italy and its east African colonies: they needed to be careful plans since Mussolini wanted to avenge, not repeat, Adowa.[34] But by the end of the summer of 1934 they were still contingent plans 'until such time as Abyssinia provided the necessary provocation and the great powers the necessary acquiescence'.[35]

The event which is generally held to have precipitated Italian aggressive action — the Wal-Wal incident in early December 1934 — illustrated the ambivalence of the main participants in the Abyssinian affair. It was caused at least as much by the Abyssinians as by the Italians and it involved Britain in a very much more direct way than was clear at the time (or, for that matter, in many subsequent analyses of the crisis) since it occurred in an area which the Abyssinians were in the process of ceding to Britain. Early in 1934 the British Minister in Addis Ababa (Sir Sidney Barton) had been instructed to propose confidentially to Haile Selassie that Britain cede to Abyssinia the port of Zeila in British Somaliland, together with a corridor connecting it with the Abyssinian hinterland. In exchange for thus securing what land-locked Abyssinia had so long desired — a port under its own control — the emperor would cede to Britain an area in the Ogaden embracing roughly the grazing grounds of the British Somali tribes, agree to frontier rectifications with Kenya and Sudan and enter into a treaty of friendship. The region to be ceded included the watering spots of Wal-Wal and Wardair which were both effectively in Italian occupation, although their *de jure* status was obscure (the Foreign Office itself privately admitted that the whole of the area was 'within the Italian sphere of influence' and 'permanently occupied by Italy').[36] The negotiations were undertaken by Britain without notifying in advance either of its 1906 agreement partners; it is almost certain, however, that the Italians knew of them, either because such matters were almost impossible to keep secret for long or because the Italian secret service was already photographing the contents of the British embassy safe in Rome (as it was certainly doing in 1935). When, on 22nd November, 1934, a mixed British-Abyssinian boundary commission engaged in demarcating the territory to be ceded to Britain arrived at Wal-Wal, accompanied by 600 Abyssinian troops, the commander of the small Italian garrison of 160 native soldiers could be forgiven for feeling some alarm. The British section of the commission withdrew, leaving the Abyssinians and Italians to glower at each other. Perhaps inevitably in the circumstances serious fighting broke out on 5th December in which 150 lost their lives before the Abyssinians were put to flight. Abyssinia was furnished with a chance to bring the whole question of Italian encroachments before world opinion, in the shape of the League of Nations; Italy, with a flimsy — but in the current state of Mussolini's xenophobia, sufficient — pretext for war. Britain was left only with embarrassment and a fatally compromised role in the international crisis which was shortly to break.

Although Abyssinia early drew the attention of the League to the incident at Wal-Wal no League action was necessary for some time until the long process of negotiation between the two sides under the 1928 treaty was exhausted. Meanwhile Mussolini had irrevocably decided (as recorded in a secret memorandum he circulated on 30th December) on 'the destruction of the Abyssinian armed forces and the total conquest of Ethiopia'; operations were planned to begin on 1st October, 1935. It was now necessary to ensure the acquiescence of France and Britain — for the League Mussolini had nothing but contempt. France's tacit consent was secured in discussions between Laval and

Mussolini in Rome early in January 1935, France merely expressing its continuing interest in the Djibouti-Addis Ababa railway. At the end of January the Italian embassy in London informed the Foreign Office of the Franco-Italian agreement and invited British co-operation in the 'mutual and harmonious' development of their interests in Abyssinia. In effect Britain was being asked to terminate its discussions with the emperor on the Zeila-Ogaden exchange and to join France in giving Italy a free hand in Abyssinia.

The secret negotiations had proved so embarrassing in the event that it was not surprising that on 22nd January Barton was instructed to inform Haile Selassie that 'the present situation makes it inadvisable to pursue even informally the possibility of all around settlement, involving territorial adjustment'.[37] But the British government was anxious to retain the emperor's good will since it was still hoping that the long-term and as yet unfulfilled project to build a dam on Lake Tana would become practicable. It thus hedged on the Italian invitation to discuss their mutual concerns in Abyssinia, merely establishing an inter-departmental committee under Sir John Maffey to report on the extent of Britain's real interests there. It could not, however, openly countenance any military action by Italy which, it was becoming increasingly clear, would be anathema to a British domestic opinion alerted to the existence of the League's machinery for settling international disputes by the so-called Peace Ballot being undertaken by the League of Nations Union since November 1934. The Foreign Office gave several warnings to the Italian government about the seriousness with which any aggressive military steps would be viewed – the first by Simon to Grandi (the Italian Ambassador in London) on 11th February, after two Italian divisions had been mobilised for service in east Africa. Meanwhile the two contending parties were wrangling about Wal-Wal and, losing patience, Abyssinia on 17th March brought the dispute before the League, both to appeal to its arbitration machinery and to point out that the build-up of Italian armed forces in east Africa threatened its territorial integrity and political independence. Italy was able, however, to persuade the League Council – of which it was itself a permanent member – to taken no cognisance of the Abyssinian approach on the grounds that the possibilities of arbitration outside the League had not been exhausted.

The Abyssinian attempt to activate the League had come just the day after Germany's formal repudiation of the disarmament provisions of the Treaty of Versailles, an event which temporarily put the problems of a remote part of Africa in the shade. Much has been made of the fact that at the resultant Stresa conference in April between Britain, France and Italy the British delegates, MacDonald and Simon, made no overt attempt to apprise Mussolini of British disapproval of any Italian aggression against Abyssinia. The matter was certainly discussed at the official level — the Foreign Office official dealing with Abyssinia warning his Italian counterpart that 'it would be useless to expect ... that we could in any way actively assist Italy to attain her Ethiopian objectives'[38] — but it was omitted in the formal ministerial sessions. This was hardly surprising as the conference had been called to deal with the problem of European security in the light of Germany's infringements of the peace treaty: and the idea that Mussolini proposed adding the words 'in Europe' after the phrase 'maintenance of peace' in the Stresa declaration, and that the British and French delegates meekly agreed, is entirely without foundation — they had been in the British and French drafts from the first.[39]

But the British government could not remain silent on the question of Italian ambitions in Abyssinia which each day were becoming more noisily obvious. In May three more divisions were mobilised for service in east Africa, the militia placed on a war footing and further categories called to the colours; in the middle of the month secret orders were sent to the Italian commander confirming that operations would begin in October. It was an agonising decision for the British government, deeply involved as it was in any territorial settlement in east Africa, anxious to preserve the newly established Stresa front, but aware that the dispute between Italy and Abyssinia could not for much longer be prevented from coming substantively before the League of Nations. Vansittart had no doubt as to how British policy should proceed. It should seek to take the heat out of the situation for fear that harm would be done to the over-riding objective of keeping Germany in check. As he minuted at the end of February, Britain should try to dissuade Italy from 'going the full length' because that country ought to 'have her hands free for greater matters'. Italian aggression would deal the League a 'deadly blow' and an adverse reaction could be expected from British public opinion. But British dissuasion of Italy should be done in 'the quietest, most friendly way' so that Britain would not have to play 'an isolated and futile role of opposition' to Italian designs in Abyssinia. If peace were to be maintained in Europe Britain 'cannot afford to quarrel with Italy and drive her back into German embraces'. Such a quarrel would 'break the European harmony' of Britain, France and Italy and result in Italy leaving the League as Germany had done in 1933. Vansittart even contrived to find some sort of moral justification for Italian policy: he always believed, he wrote, that Italy would eventually expand somewhere, and the present crisis would have been avoided if Britain had not been so 'impudently greedy' in 1919 and had let Italy have a German colony then.[40]

Vansittart's political masters did not see matters in quite this *Realpolitik* way and were most anxious about the domestic impact of seeming to condone Italian aggressive designs. At a League Council meeting in April, immediately after the Stresa conference, Simon attempted to put a term to Italian delaying tactics designed to prevent the League from considering the Wal-Wal affair. Simon was unsuccessful in this attempt but he did succeed in alerting the Italians to the fact that they could in no way assume tacit British consent to their Abyssinian ambitions. Further warnings which both Simon and Vansittart delivered through Grandi served only to strengthen Italian resolve to bring things to a speedy conclusion, and a speech by Mussolini on 14th May indicated that war was virtually inevitable. On the following day the affair first became the subject of a full-scale discussion in Cabinet, which continued in a further Cabinet meeting two days later (17th May), when Sir Eric Drummond, former League Secretary-General and now British Ambassador in Rome, was present. Simon, with the assistance of Vansittart and G. H. Thompson, prepared a memorandum for the guidance of his colleagues (who did not include Hoare since he did not return from his Norfolk convalescence until the evening of the 15th). On the only too firm assumption that Italian military operations would start in October, with the end of the rainy season, Simon outlined the unpalatable choices facing the British government:

> If they support against Italy the practical application of
> League principles, their action is bound greatly to compromise
> Anglo-Italian relations and perhaps even to break the close
> association at present existing between France, Italy and the
> United Kingdom ... On the other hand, if the United King-
> dom acquiesces in a misuse of League machinery, His
> Majesty's government will undoubtedly lay themselves open
> to grave public criticism.

It was no doubt Vansittart's influence which made the Foreign
Secretary's memorandum seem to lead to the conclusion that,
in the last analysis, Italian co-operation in Europe was more
vital than the preservation of Abyssinia's territorial integrity.
Abyssinia should be persuaded, in effect, to give what Italy
seemed to want without the necessity of war, namely 'to follow
a policy more in accordance with modern conditions by recognising Italy's claim to taking fuller part in increasing the trade
between Abyssinia and the outside world and in assisting the
development of the economic resources of the Abyssinian
Empire'.[41] While it did not dissent from this analysis the Cabinet
felt that Italy should not be allowed to delay League consideration of the dispute indefinitely on the pretext that attempts at
conciliation between the two parties were still not exhausted and
then launch a war in September or October, claiming that
conciliation had failed. Eden was instructed to try to secure a
terminus ad quem to Italian delaying tactics at the imminent meeting of the League Council and this he was able to do in the
resolutions adopted on 25th May.[42] It was hoped that Anglo-
Italian relations would not be seriously damaged by so doing,
but the risk, the Cabinet felt, had to be taken. To underline that
risk a well-orchestrated campaign of anti-British propaganda
began in the fascist-controlled Italian press.

This was the stage the affair had reached when Hoare took
over at the Foreign Office on 7th June. The British government
had already embarked on its ambivalent course of overt support
for League procedures coupled with a concern to keep Italy as
an ally in Europe. So had the government of Britain's even more
essential European ally, France, although here the balance between keeping Italy's friendship by turning a more or less blind

eye to its Abyssinian ambitions and fidelity to the League was, since the Laval-Mussolini agreements of January 1935, much more heavily weighted in Italy's favour: had it not been that the government Laval formed on the very day Hoare became Foreign Secretary was dependent on Radical party support the League element in French policy might have been even smaller.[43]

The Anglo-German naval discussions necessarily preoccupied Hoare in his first few days in office, but as soon as he was able to do so he took stock with his advisers of the Italo-Abyssinian imbroglio and Britain's role. He had numerous discussions with Vansittart, sometimes alone, sometimes with Eden present. Hoare was very ready to agree with Vansittart as to the basic strategic facts of the situation: that German strength was daily becoming more formidable; that Japanese aggression in the Far East at any moment might threaten Britain with war on a second front when it was incapable of fighting on more than one; that a friendly Italy was essential to guarantee British lines of communication to the Far East and enable French forces to concentrate on France's border with Germany; and that the current Italian suspicions of German designs in Austria made Italy a willing partner in the Franco-British effort to contain Germany.[44] At the same time another piece of information highly relevant to British policy-making was just becoming available. The Maffey committee presented its draft report on 18th June, but its main conclusion was undoubtedly known in the Foreign Office before then. This was that 'No such vital British interest is concerned in and around Ethiopia as would make it essential for His Majesty's Government to resist an Italian conquest of Ethiopia'; and while British interests in the Nile basin were substantial these would not be threatened by Italian aggression in east Africa except in the 'improbable' event of war between Britain and Italy. Effective Italian control in place of the present inefficient central administration in Abyssinia might even have advantages for Britain since unruly border tribes would be curbed, slave raids eliminated and the pasturage rights of the British-protected Somali tribes assured.[45] If Britain were to oppose Italy in Abyssinia, the message of the Maffey report seemed clear, it would have to be on grounds other than national self-interest.

But perhaps there might yet be a chance of diverting Mussolini from the collision course with the League of Nations and world opinion on which he seemed set. So Vansittart thought, and he suggested to Hoare and Eden that the scheme discussed with Haile Selassie for the exchange of the British Somaliland port of Zeila and a linking corridor for territory in the Ogaden should be revived, but now the Abyssinians would transfer the Ogaden, not to the British, but to the Italians and would also make economic concessions to Italy elsewhere. In this way, according to Vansittart, Mussolini would be allowed to 'obtain something substantive for the shop window without fighting or fever'.[46] According to Hoare it was while the three men — Eden, Vansittart and himself — were spending the weekend at Sir Philip Sassoon's country estate at Trent Park in the middle of June that they decided the offer should be made.[47] Vansittart telegraphed Drummond in Rome on 17th June and the Ambassador expressed the view that there was a good chance of success. On the 19th Hoare sprang the proposal on a rather surprised Cabinet. He apologised for bringing it forward without background papers and at such short notice, but said that the circumstances were such that he had no alternative. The situation had deteriorated and large Italian forces were on their way to the Red Sea. The French government which 'should in the last resort have supported the League in the event of a clash, were showing that in that case they would be on the side of Italy'. There was every prospect of Britain being placed

in a most inconvenient dilemma. Either we should have to make a futile protest, which would irritate Mussolini and perhaps drive him out of the League into the arms of Germany, or we should make no protest at all and give the appearance of pusillanimity.

Hoare's Cabinet colleagues were at first reluctant to make a decision involving the cession of part of a British protectorate without lengthy deliberation, but recognised that the gravity of the situation required Britain to show its domestic and world public opinion that a substantial effort had been made to avert the approaching catastrophe. It was agreed to send Eden to Rome with the proposal.[48] On the following day Hoare sought

to smooth Eden's path by writing to Mussolini to recall their indirect wartime association:

> ... As your Excellency may perhaps recall, I had the honour
> of serving for two years in Italy during the War. In the course
> of that time I had many opportunities of admiring the manner
> in which Italy and her people discharged the heavy tasks
> which they were called upon to assume. The happy recollec-
> tions of that period are still vividly in my mind, and the
> experience which I was then enabled to gain will be of the
> greatest value to me in my endeavour to maintain and
> strengthen the traditional friendship between our two
> countries ...[49]

But Hoare's diplomatic civilities were to no avail, and by the
time that Mussolini had replied in kind (a warm message was
sent to Hoare on 28th June) Eden had come and gone and completely failed to change the dictator's resolve to subjugate
Abyssinia. The proposal was spurned: indeed it only deepened
Mussolini's suspicions of British motives.[50] Italy was already in
de facto occupation of most of the territory it was proposed to
transfer to it, while the Zeila project appeared to Mussolini not
only to increase Abyssinia's economic independence but to be
designed to further Britain's own aims in the area. Britain was
too deeply implicated in Abyssinia to be accepted by Mussolini
as an honest broker, even if he had been prepared for a peaceful
settlement.

The whole idea, in fact, seemed ill-judged. It had no real
chance of success (Drummond's belief that it had was only one
of many examples of his unreliability as a source of insight into
Italian policy), and it was broached with Mussolini without any
prior consultation with the French, who would obviously feel
their interests in the Djibouti-Addis Ababa railway challenged
by a new coastal outlet for Abyssinia. Coming within a few
days of the conclusion of the Anglo-German naval agreement it
jeopardised the prospect of co-operation with the French on
which any hope of a reasonable resolution of the crisis depended.
Hoare must have longed, after his first few days at the Foreign
Office, for the calm judgement and sage counsel of Findlater
Stewart. Vansittart – the main originator of the Zeila offer –
may have had a strong strategic sense but he was clearly

deficient in tactical sense. Although Hoare was ministerially responsible he can perhaps be forgiven so early in his tenure and in the midst of a serious international crisis for placing reliance on the advice of the official head of his department, especially when Eden seemed to concur in it.

Eden's Rome visit marked the end of a phase in British policy in the Italo-Abyssinian dispute. Thereafter British initiatives aimed at conciliation took place either within the framework of the League or in attempted partnership with France. But the French, for reasons which do not necessarily reflect on French policy, were unreliable partners. Laval, as Foreign Minister and now as Prime Minister once again, had done more than any other Western statesman to secure the adherence of Italy to the anti-German front and was unwilling to imperil this by a forward policy against Italy in east Africa. French policy would overtly support League actions, if only because the Radicals on whom Laval depended were advocates of 'collective security'; but it was support for conciliatory measures, not coercion. And even before Italian forces invaded Abyssinia on 3rd October it was coercive measures which League members were actually considering. In British policy, unlike the French, there was a fatal ambiguity. Conciliation stood little chance of success, given Mussolini's militaristic mood, but had to be tried. But so also had coercion, and this, in the current state of Britain's armed forces, was not viable without French assistance, which — it was soon clear — would not be forthcoming. An element of bluff became almost inevitable, but unfortunately the bluff was called and in the end Hoare came to believe that only a return to the policy of inducing Abyssinia to make territorial and other concessions to Italy — but on a much more considerable scale than was contemplated in Eden's June visit to Rome — could save anything of Abyssinian sovereignty. At no stage did Hoare either say in public or contemplate in private that Britain, singly or with France (these being the only two countries which counted in this context), would engage Italy in war, although he naturally had to ensure that prudent precautions were taken in case Italy should itself engage in war against Britain.

The Cabinet had an opportunity of examining the situation in the light of the failure of Eden's Rome talks at its meeting on 3rd July. The discussion turned on the application of the

Covenant of the League of Nations to the aggressive act which Italy, it was becoming increasingly obvious with each day that passed, was intending against Abyssinia. Such an act (besides breaching the 1906 agreement between Britain, France and Italy) would constitute an infringement of article 10 of the Covenant, which declared that 'Members of the League undertake to respect and preserve as against external aggression the territorial integrity and existing political independence of all Members of the League.' It would, moreover, bring into play the 'sanctions' provisions of article 16, as further defined by the League's General Assembly in October 1921. The original article spoke of resort to war by any League member being deemed as act of war against all other members,

> which hereby undertake immediately to subject it to the severance of all trade or financial relations, the prohibition of all intercourse between their nations and the nationals of the Covenant-breaking State, and the prevention of all financial, commercial or personal intercourse between the nationals of the Covenant-breaking State and the nationals of any other State, whether a Member of the League or not.

But the 1921 gloss watered this down considerably, in particular transforming League Members' obligation to take action against an offender 'immediately' into a lengthy procedure whereby

> If the Council [of the League] is of the opinion that a State has been guilty of a breach of the Covenant, the minute of the meeting at which the opinion is arrived at shall be immediately sent to all Members of the League, accompanied by a statement of reasons and by an invitation to take action accordingly.[51]

It was the implications of article 16 which mainly occupied the Cabinet's discussion on 3rd July. The inescapable dilemma once again presented itself. On the one hand, if the collective commitment of League members under the Covenant were ignored or evaded

> a heavy blow would be struck at the whole of the Pacts and agreements on which the post-war system of Europe had been built up. It would amount to an admission that the attempt to

give the League coercive powers was a mistake — an admission that would have serious effects in increasing the existing confusion abroad, as well as on public opinion at home.

On the other hand, however,

> The responsibility of the Powers on which the burden of fulfilling Article 16 would fall was recognised to be a heavy one, since it involved not only the present dispute and relations with Italy, but also the whole of the existing international system. If France was prepared to honour its obligations, other nations would probably follow. Without French cooperation the application of Article 16 was out of the question, and as yet the attitude of France was uncertain.[52]

Britain's League role, the Cabinet was clear, could be only as a partner, albeit a leading one, in collectively agreed and implemented policies. This point Hoare made strongly in his first major Commons speech as Foreign Secretary on 11th July, when he asserted his country's willingness to share in the responsibility for a system of collective security under the League. 'As things are, and as long as there is an effective League, we are ready to take our full share of collective responsibility. But when I say collective responsibility, I mean collective responsibility.'[53] The clear implication was that there was no question of independent British action against Italy. To this position he kept consistently throughout the crisis, not least in his speech to the League General Assembly in September.

The Cabinet did not discuss Abyssinia again substantively until 22nd August, by which time there had been a number of inconclusive further developments.[54] In the middle of August, for example, representatives of the three signatories of the 1906 agreement on Abyssinia met in Geneva in an attempt (at least on the British and French side) to combine some satisfaction of Italian ambitions in Abyssinia with the continuance of the country's national integrity. The Italian representative (Aloisi) suggested on 16th August that there should be a tripartite declaration in favour of Italian political and economic preponderance in Abyssinia. The counter-proposals of the Anglo-French representatives (Eden and Laval) would have granted Italy practically complete economic suzerainty but fell short of recognising its political dominance. Accepting that the internal situation in Abyssinia left a lot to be desired they suggested League assistance to enable the country to carry out wide measures of internal reform. While territorial rectifications in Italy's favour were clearly envisaged in the Anglo-French proposals they nevertheless stipulated the continuation of Abyssinian independence and sovereignty. On the following day the conference was vouchsafed Mussolini's intransigent reply: the proposals were 'absolutely unacceptable' and merely designed 'to humiliate Italy in the worst possible fashion'.[55]

Vansittart, who had accompanied Eden, had never had any hope of the tripartite talks succeeding but thought they were justified in helping to establish the government's 'rather lonely record' for 'fertility and perseverance in endeavouring to avoid a catastrophe'.[56] Hoare, too, had had little confidence in the prospect of their success but nevertheless their failure came at a bad time for his morale. In the dog days of summer, with colleagues scattered on holiday or otherwise engaged, he could be forgiven for finding irksome his exposed position in the centre of a disagreeable international crisis. Matters were made no better by a serious attack of arthritis in his foot which virtually immobilised him at times. On 18th August he unburdened himself to his closest Cabinet colleague, Neville Chamberlain, holidaying in Switzerland:

> I believe we have done everything possible to keep in step with the French and to do nothing that will provoke the Italians. None the less ... it looks to me as if the Italians will be entirely unreasonable and as a result there will be a first-class crisis in the League at the beginning of September.

Hoare believed that it was urgently necessary for the Cabinet to determine its policy on the assumptions that either the French were completely with Britain or that they had backed out of co-operative action. It was equally urgent for the Cabinet to consider contingency plans to meet 'a possible mad dog act by the Italians'. Here Hoare had been confronting great difficulties:

> On the one hand I was anxious to suggest no action which would even give the impression of provocation to the Italians

or of war to the British public. On the other hand I have been very nervous of leaving undone anything that might make a mad dog act more dangerous. In the circumstances it seemed to me that I could do no more than get the Chiefs of Staff and the Planning Committee to investigate the position and to leave it to the Cabinet to decide upon what action should be taken.

The two most senior members of the government had given Hoare little help in coping with the difficult situation. Baldwin 'would think about nothing but his holiday and the necessity of keeping out of the whole business almost at any cost' while MacDonald had merely sent 'a curious and almost unintelligible letter' gratuitously warning Hoare of the dangers of the situation. Hoare was convinced that the only viable British policy was 'to keep in step with the French and, whether now or at Geneva, to act with them'.[57]

A special Cabinet was summoned for 22nd August, and a meeting of Eden and Hoare with their most senior Cabinet colleagues for the preceding day. Just before these meetings were held Hoare took an important initiative in an attempt to ensure that the government would have the widest possible political support in the steps it might be compelled to take: he and Eden consulted in turn some of the leading political figures outside the government's own ranks. Austen Chamberlain, Winston Churchill, Lord Cecil, George Lansbury (soon to lose the leadership of the Parliamentary Labour Party), Sir Herbert Samuel (for the official Liberals), Lloyd George – all these came to the Foreign Office on 20th and 21st August to hear the government's views on the developing crisis and to express their own. For so distinguished but idiosyncratic a group there was a surprising unanimity of view that there needed to be genuinely collective action on the basis of full Anglo-French co-operation. Austen Chamberlain, according to the account Hoare wrote for his Cabinet colleagues, was 'most clear and insistent that, provided that the action was collective and that we and the French were keeping in step, economic sanctions of some kind were inevitable'. Samuel, too, agreed that 'the two assumptions of economic action must be, firstly, collective action, and secondly, full Anglo-French co-operation', while Lloyd George envisaged that only in the event of collective League action should Britain make it clear that 'we are prepared to take our part'. Churchill's advice was remarkably unbellicose. He thought that 'the extremely difficult position of France' should be recognised and that the British government should not make 'impossible requests to M. Laval'. At the appropriate time it should be made 'perfectly clear to the world that ... we are prepared to carry out our League obligations even to the point of war with all our military resources, provided that other members of the League are prepared to take the same action'. It was quite clear that none of these leading politicians, Churchill included, contemplated for a moment that Britain should at any time be involved in a single-handed war with Italy over Abyssinia. The emphasis was wholly on Anglo-French co-operation, preferably within a League framework.[58]

The ministers who foregathered with Hoare and Eden on 21st August, the day before the specially convened Cabinet, were Baldwin, MacDonald, Chamberlain and Simon. After hearing from Eden of the abortive tripartite talks in Geneva and from Hoare of the conversations with the political leaders, this 'inner Cabinet' for the first time gave serious consideration to the implications of a policy of League sanctions against Italy. On the basis of investigations by the Foreign Office it seemed feasible to apply economic sanctions in two separate stages, the second more stringent than the first and involving the possibility of belligerent action (such as the searching of Italian ships). There was no reason, Hoare thought, why non-members of the League should not join in the first stage by, for example, agreeing to prohibit Italian imports into their countries. But sanctions of some kind seemed inevitable if Italy went ahead with an invasion of Abyssinia. Hoare said he

had been left with the impression that there would be a wave of public opinion against the Government if it repudiated its obligations under Article 16 — that was to say, its obligations under the principle of collective responsibility, on the assumption that France would go as far as we were prepared to do. It was abundantly clear that the only safe line for His Majesty's Government was to try out the regular League of Nations procedure.

Neville Chamberlain pointed out that 'even the mildest economic sanctions might in the end lead to war' and hence the British armed forces ought to be put in a state of readiness. Hoare agreed: Mussolini might well launch a 'mad dog' attack against Britain. MacDonald hoped it would be possible, however, 'to discover a completely pacific method of applying economic sanctions against Italian trade'.[59]

It was the state of Britain's armed forces, particularly the navy, which occupied much of the five-hour discussion at the full Cabinet on the following day. Several members drew attention 'to the grave effects on our diplomacy of our present military weakness'. The Cabinet had before it two reports from the Chiefs of Staff. The first, dated 3rd August, listed the air, sea and land reinforcements required in the Mediterranean and the Middle East and emphasised the need for plenty of advance warning of an Italian attack to enable the forces to make their dispositions. The second report, of 9th August, dealt gloomily with the strategic implications of any military involvement with Italy which would be bound 'to leave the British Fleet temporarily weakened to such an extent as to be unable to fulfil its worldwide responsibilities'. The dispatch of air reinforcements to the Mediterranean would weaken Britain *vis-à-vis* Germany and gravely set back the aim of reaching parity with Germany in the air by April 1937; and it would not be possible to reinforce the air force at Singapore. The Chiefs of Staff warned against any precipitate rush into sanctions and stressed 'the assured military support' of France as an essential prerequisite.

The Cabinet nevertheless decided that while a war with Italy would be a 'grave calamity' the British delegation at Geneva should be instructed to 'reaffirm that Great Britain would fulfil its obligations ... following closely the procedure laid down in the Covenant, not in any quixotic spirit, and with due regard to the many difficulties'. Any unnecessary provocation of Italy must, however, be avoided and it was taken for granted that there could be no overt military action against Italy such as armed blockade or closure of the Suez Canal. And France must be kept up to scratch: no commitment, particularly as regards sanctions, could be entered into which France was not equally prepared to assume. As purely precautionary measures the Cabinet decided to order units of the Home Fleet to be ready to sail to Gibraltar (two battlecruisers, three cruisers and some smaller craft arrived there on 17th September), to send anti-aircraft units to Malta and Alexandria and to reinforce the R.A.F. in the Middle East. It turned down a naval request for the mobilisation of naval reserves, however, because of 'the resounding effect it would have on public opinion both at home and abroad'. Further consideration of military precautions was left to the recently constituted Defence Policy and Require-ments Committee of the Committee of Imperial Defence.[60]

The stage was thus set for the meeting of the League early in September. Hoare approached it with some misgivings. He was clearly hoping that sanctions, with all that they might imply in terms of an Italian 'mad dog' act against the British navy and air installations in the Mediterranean, could be avoided. But yet there was the strong, if muddled and uninformed, public demand for something to be seen to be done to stop Italy. As he told Sir George Clerk, the British Ambassador in Paris, on 24th August:

> The general feeling of the country, fully reflected in the Cabinet, can, I think, be summarised as one of determination to stick to the Covenant and of anxiety to keep out of war. You will say that these feelings are self-contradictory. At present at least the country believes that they can be re-conciled. Most people are still convinced that if we stick to the Covenant and apply collective sanctions, Italy must give in and there will be no war. You and I know that the posi-tion is not as simple as this and that the presumptions that, firstly, there will be collective action including full collective action by the French, and, secondly, that economic sanctions will be effective are, to say the least, very bold and sanguine.

Nevertheless, 'it is essential that we should play out the League hand in September'.

> The British Government will certainly have to make its posi-tion clear in public at a suitable time in Geneva. We shall have to say that we are prepared to do our part if others will do theirs, and that if sanctions are not applied, it will not be because of our failure to carry out our obligations. It will either be because the members of the League will not play

their full part or because the non-members of the League would make the application of sanctions futile.[61]

In order the better to 'play out the League hand' and to make the British government's policy clear at Geneva Hoare decided that he would himself address the League's General Assembly at the session due to open on 9th September, leaving it to Eden to attend the earlier Council meeting from 4th September. The day before the Council met the arbitrators who had eventually been appointed to examine the overt cause of the crisis – the Wal-Wal incident – submitted their unanimous judgement that neither Italy nor Abyssinia was to blame for the accidental and now rather distant events of early December 1934. But the arbitration did have one implication for the current situation: it deprived Italy of any justification for its military build-up in east Africa on the grounds of Abyssinian armed provocation. The Italian response was to table at Geneva on 4th September a lengthy memorandum, supported by a collection of photographs of revolting brutalities, alleging Abyssinia's unfitness to be a member of the League and its consequent ineligibility for the privileges of membership. Slavery was rampant, Abyssinia's neighbours were never safe from border raids, while the present Abyssinian empire was the result of the unbridled aggression of the Amharic denizens of the Abyssinian highlands against non-Amharic neighbouring tribes – and much more in the same vein. Italy, far from being an aggressor, was in fact claiming to be defending the League's civilised values against barbaric oppression.[62] While there was a good deal of truth in the Italian charges (Vansittart had early warned Hoare of the danger of public opinion 'misrepresenting Abyssinia as a kind of oppressed paradise'[63]) they did not justify unilateral action by Italy, and neither Eden nor Laval commented on the memorandum at the Council meeting. Both instead supported a proposal on 6th September to refer the whole dispute to an *ad hoc* Committee of Five, consisting of themselves as representatives of Britain and France, together with representatives from Poland, Spain and Turkey. The committee's report was presented a mere twelve days later: but by that time Hoare had made his League debut as British Foreign Secretary.

Hoare devoted considerable care to the preparation of his

Assembly speech, conscious of the opportunity it presented for demonstrating to Italy the strength of world opinion against what it was planning to do in Abyssinia. Although Vansittart prepared a draft, and Hoare discussed the speech's contents with Baldwin and Neville Chamberlain at dinner at his house in Cadogan Gardens on 5th September, the final version — as with all Hoare's speeches — was very much his own.[64] On 9th September he flew to Geneva in an R.A.F. aircraft (fitted with a special sling to support his arthritic leg) and on the following day — the day before his Assembly appearance — he had two discussions with Laval, who had come to Geneva earlier than he had intended to take part in them.

The meetings with Laval on 10th September were fated to assume an almost malign significance in the light of subsequent events. It was there, so most accounts have it, that the two men began to betray the League by agreeing not to take any action to support really effective League measures against Italy and, above all, abrogated in advance any military steps to make Italy disgorge the fruits of its clearly meditated aggression. It is certainly true that Hoare counselled caution while Laval made no attempt to conceal his belief that economic sanctions might provoke Italy into attacking the League member or members who imposed them. But there seems no support in the contemporary record for the widespread belief that military measures against Italy were excluded in all circumstances, despite the fact that Laval himself, in a speech in the Chamber of Deputies less than four months later, said that war with Italy was specifically ruled out at the talks (at that time — in the wake of the Hoare-Laval pact fiasco — he was fighting for his government's life and had all sorts of ulterior motives for giving refurbished accounts of past actions).

The talks began in Laval's hotel at 11 a.m. Hoare was accompanied by Eden and a Foreign Office official, William Strang; Laval, by two senior Quai d'Orsay (Foreign Ministry) officials, Léger and Massigli. Laval could find little to dissent from in Hoare's analysis of the relationship between the Italo-Abyssinian crisis and the European situation: indeed, Hoare undoubtedly made it to reassure his French partner. The chief consideration he had in mind, Hoare said, was the problem posed by German rearmament:

Throughout the whole Abyssinian conflict he had been thinking not so much of an Italian dispute with a backward
country, as of the reactions of the dispute on the European
position, with Germany rearmed and under the temptation
to make a threat to European security some time during the
next ten years.

On the Abyssinian affair itself Hoare did not disguise the fact
that the British government had no particular sympathy with
Abyssinia (not that Laval was tempted to disagree with him).
The British had had just as much trouble from the Abyssinians
on the Sudan frontier as the Italians had had on the Eritrean.
Things had perhaps become a little better in the last few years,
but there was still no effective central government and Abyssinia
remained a bad neighbour. British public opinion was, however,
'impressed with the need for collective security under the
League'. Hoare felt that the object of any League action should
be

> to secure adequate agreement on measures which would
> mark the disapproval of all members of the League, and if
> possible of the world at large, of what the League would
> consider a flagrant violation of its principles, and if war broke
> out [between Italy and Abyssinia], to put an end to it as soon
> as possible.

It should be made clear that all the participating governments
stood together, and that any mad dog act by Italy against any
of them would be resisted by all; and, above all, there was a
clear need for Anglo-French agreement in all the steps taken.

It was to this last point that Hoare returned when the discussion was resumed in his hotel in the evening. The essential
thing was to avoid action 'which was likely to be ineffective and
to make the League ridiculous'. If the two governments gave
the world the clear impression that they were acting together
and had no intention of abandoning the Covenant it might be
possible to influence Mussolini. It was, in any case, the only
course of action open to them in the coming weeks before Italy
actually launched its attack. Laval, in the main, agreed but he
was patently concerned about the dangers of provoking Italy
by extreme League actions. France would be faithful to the

Covenant, he pointedly assured Hoare, 'in the measure in which His Majesty's Government would be moderate in their application of it'.[65]

The Assembly speech which Hoare delivered on the following day, 11th September, was aimed at several different targets. One, apparently introduced into the draft of the speech at a late stage, was the rather naive hope that a proposal that European powers with colonial territories should make the raw materials those territories produced available to powers with few colonies or none would reduce European colonial ambitions and rivalries. The world economic conference of 1933 had discussed such a scheme, and a further discussion on the matter was being bruited.[66] Another of Hoare's objectives was to give some sort of public assurance to the French that British policy was not so obsessed with the Abyssinian crisis that it had forgotten — what for Laval was the over-riding factor in foreign policy — the threat posed by German expansionism in Europe, and that France could count on British support in steps to deal with it. Vansittart, in particular, was anxious to strengthen this aspect of the speech and had included in his draft a reference to Britain standing with the League for 'resistance to all unprovoked aggression in whatever quarter such a danger to the peace of the world may arise'. Hoare himself changed this passage to read 'the collective maintenance of the Covenant in its entirety, and particularly for steady and collective resistance to all acts of unprovoked aggression'. As late as the afternoon of 10th September Vansittart telegraphed from London to try to persuade Hoare to amend the reference, conscious as he was that the French were really seeking a bilateral undertaking from Britain, not what to them was an empty commitment to collective League action. Hoare was not persuaded, however, and, indeed, when he came to this passage in the actual delivery of his speech he repeated the word 'collective' in 'the collective maintenance of the Covenant'.[67] He may well have thought that he had already given sufficient assurance to Laval in his private talks that the German problem was in the forefront of British policy, despite the current preoccupation with the Abyssinian crisis.

A third aim of Hoare's Assembly speech, implicit rather than explicit (since there was only one, incidental, reference to the current crisis), was an eleventh hour attempt to dissuade Mussolini from invading Abyssinia. It was a vain hope since the Italian dictator, who had been deaf to the many private diplomatic representations made to him, was not likely to accede to a public appeal made in an international forum which he despised. And in so far as the appeal could be backed by threats of penalties for non-compliance Hoare, as a responsible minister rather than an impractical idealist, was forced to emphasise the essentially collective nature of any sanctions which the League might impose if Italy went ahead with its aggression. If the sanctions were genuinely collective then Britain would go along with them as energetically as any member: but it would have been the height of irresponsibility for Hoare to have suggested that Britain was prepared to act alone. That he went to great lengths to make this clear is apparent from even a cursory reading of his speech.

It would not be appropriate here to reproduce that speech in full.[68] He promised at the beginning that he would 'speak freely, avoiding rhetoric and general sentiments' and on the whole he was as good as his word, giving a clear and well-constructed analysis of the nature of the League and of the obligations of the Covenant. There was, for example, a restatement of an obvious truth that was sometimes forgotten in the heady atmosphere of Geneva:

> ... let us clear our minds as to what the League is and what it is not. It is not a super-State, nor even a separate entity existing of itself, independent of or transcending the States which make up its membership ... The League is what its member States make it. If it succeeds, it is because its members have, in combination with each other, the will and the power to apply the principles of the Covenant. If it fails, it is because its members lack either the will or the power to fulfil their obligations ... If this national support is strong, the League will be strong. If it is weak and uncertain, the policy of the League cannot be firm and consistent ... the League is nothing apart from its members.

On collective security Hoare was equally clear, although he could not escape the essentially self-contradictory nature of the concept (which envisages states at one and the same time being irresponsible enough to create the problem of war and responsible enough to solve the problem through collective security) :[69]

> Collective security, by which is meant the organisation of peace and the prevention of war by collective means, is, in its present form, not a simple but a complex conception. It means much more than what are commonly called sanctions. It means not merely Article 16, but the whole Covenant. It assumes a scrupulous respect for all treaty obligations. Its foundation is the series of fundamental obligations, freely accepted by members of the League, to submit any dispute likely to lead to war to peaceful methods of settlement according to the procedure provided by the Covenant, and not to resort to war for the settlement of disputes in violation of the Covenant.

There were, Hoare pointed out, two principal conditions in which the collective security system was originally designed to operate: the reduction of national armaments and the enforcement by common action of international obligations; and the existence of League machinery for the modification, by consent, of international conditions dangerous to peace. The system was completed by 'the obligation to take collective action to bring war to an end in the event of any resort to war in disregard of the Covenant obligations'. Underlying all these obligations 'was the expectation that this system would be subscribed to by the universal world of sovereign states, or by far the greatest part of it'. It was 'an inspiring conception' but its realisation would not have been easy even in the most favourable circumstances. And the circumstances had been far from favourable in the event. The fear of war was growing and with it came an increase in national armaments. The League from the outset lacked the membership of certain powerful nations and had since lost the membership of others. There followed a passage which was subsequently much quoted (although the explicit qualifications in it were often ignored):

> These, then, are the conditions in which we find ourselves. The obligations of the Covenant remain; their burden upon us has been increased manifold. But one thing is certain. If

the burden is to be borne, it must be borne collectively. If risks for peace are to be run, they must be run by all. The security of the many cannot be ensured solely by the efforts of a few, however powerful they may be. On behalf of His Majesty's Government in the United Kingdom I can say that, in spite of these difficulties, they will be second to none in their intention to fulfil, within the measure of their capacity, the obligations which the Covenant lays upon them.

Hoare then widened the discussion to consider steps which might help to remove some of the causes of war. Without specifically mentioning the Abyssinian dispute he clearly had it in mind when, after referring to the development of self-government in the British Empire and to his own Government of India Act, he went on to express the British belief 'that backward nations are, without prejudice to their independence and integrity, entitled to expect that assistance will be afforded them by more advanced nations in the development of their resources and the building up of their national life'. Italy, so the implication seemed to be, might expect to play a leading role in this process as regards the development of Abyssinia's resources. The lengthy passage which followed on the need to make raw materials more generally available to colonial and non-colonial powers alike also had obvious reference to Italy's oft-proclaimed needs.

Hoare's peroration, which perhaps did not altogether avoid the rhetoric which he had said he would eschew, ran:

It has been not only suggested that British national opinion, as well as the attitude of the United Kingdom Government, is animated by some lower motive than fidelity to the League, but also that even this fidelity cannot be relied on ... The attitude of His Majesty's Government has always been one of unwavering fidelity to the League and all that it stands for, and the case now before us [his only direct reference to the Italo-Abyssinian dispute] is no exception but, on the contrary, the continuance of that rule. The recent response of public opinion shows how completely the nation supports the Government in the full acceptance of League membership ... In conformity with its precise and explicit obligations the League stands, and my country stands with it, for the collective maintenance of the Covenant in its entirety, and particularly for steady and collective resistance to all acts of unprovoked aggression. The attitude of the British nation in the last few weeks has clearly demonstrated the fact that this is no variable and unreliable sentiment, but a principle of international conduct to which they and their government hold with firm, enduring, and universal persistence.

Hoare was understandably amazed at the almost universally rapturous reception which greeted his generally restrained and carefully qualified speech, both at the League itself and even more in press comment around the world. 'I felt it would make an impression. I had no idea, however, that it would make so big an impression', he told the King's private secretary a few days later.[70] For a man with a rather precise and unexciting manner of delivery such acclamation was a new experience. Retrospectively, he felt that this very matter-of-factness, contrasted with the verbose rhetoric of many Assembly speeches, may have contributed to the success of the speech, added to the fact that he was 'a new actor in the Assembly'.[71] But at the same time the attention was embarrassing in policy terms since he had no wish to lead other League members to 'avoid their own responsibilities by making them think that it was British rather than League policy that they ought to accept'.[72] There was a danger, he felt, that the League would leave the running in the Abyssinian crisis to Britain, with all the dangers that spelt for Britain's long-term strategic interests.

On the evening of the 11th Hoare had a third conversation with Laval, in which he again attempted to reassure him on British policy towards Germany. He told Laval that throughout his speech he had been thinking primarily, not of the current crisis but of the German danger. If collective action by the League could really be made to work over Italy and Abyssinia then Germany might be dissuaded from 'embarking upon some aggressive act'.[73] It is extremely doubtful whether this argument convinced the shrewd and practical Laval, who believed that German aggressive acts were only likely to be restrained by strengthening the Stresa front of France, Britain and Italy rather than by running the real risk of breaching the Stresa front by two of its members taking the lead in the League to restrain the third from doing in faraway Africa what it was clearly going to do anyway. But when Laval's turn came to address the Assembly two days later it looked as if Hoare (and perhaps Laval's Radical Cabinet colleagues) had persuaded him, too, to 'play out the League hand'. France, he said, 'cannot fail to carry out her obligations ... France's policy rests entirely on the League'. He was at pains, however, to place emphasis on the League's conciliatory, rather than its coercive, role in a crisis involving a major European power with which France had recently settled all its differences. Laval said:

> ... in the supreme effort being made by the Council, I shall have the satisfaction of once more fulfilling my duty as the representative of a Member of the League, and that dictated to me by friendship [with Italy] ... we are studying every proposal likely to satisfy Italy's legitimate aspirations so far as is compatible with respect for the sovereignty of another State Member of the League.[74]

Hoare was well pleased with his hours of talk with Laval and considered the French Prime Minister's Assembly speech (which he heard just before returning to London) ample reward. He had decided to hide nothing from his French colleague – a course which was not without its dangers since the French 'invariably let everything out in the Press' – and at the end Hoare felt that they were on very good terms with each other. Laval, he told his friend Sir Clive Wigram for the King's ears, 'is a queer card ... he is by origin a peasant from the Auvergne and he has all the cunning of a French peasant'. He rather reminded him of Lloyd George, 'with his incessant desire to do a deal of some kind behind everybody else's back'. But with rather more optimism than was justified by the facts of the situation or his own assessment of Laval's character Hoare allowed himself the conclusion that 'there is now no danger of our finding ourselves in an isolated position without French support'.[75]

A week after Hoare's Assembly speech a last opportunity for a peaceful settlement of the dispute before the Italian forces marched was presented with the proposals of the Committee of Five, in which Eden and Laval participated. The committee's report tacitly subscribed to the Italian allegation that Abyssinia had not fulfilled the conditions on which it had been admitted to

League membership by recommending a comprehensive system of League supervision and control in the country – a kind of international mandate which was, however, subject to the agreement of the Abyssinian government. League advisers were to reorganise the administration of finance, justice, education and public health, and other overseas specialists were to help create a police force and gendarmerie capable of suppressing slavery, the illicit traffic in arms and frontier raids. In all this outside assistance Italy would play a leading, although not necessarily an exclusive part; on the other hand, the report included a postscript in which Eden and Laval, on behalf of their respective governments, promised 'to facilitate territorial adjustments between Italy and Abyssinia ... and to recognise a special Italian interest in the economic development of Abyssinia'. The proposals were still-born. The Abyssinian government signified its willingness to accept them but only because it felt certain that Italy would reject them and wished the onus of blame for their failure to fall on Rome rather than Addis Ababa; Mussolini was prompt to oblige, and the report of the Committee of Five joined the limbo of fruitless League initiatives.

In the weeks that followed three themes were uppermost in Hoare's mind. Two were inextricably linked: to strengthen Britain's defence posture in the Mediterranean while trying to avoid giving Mussolini the opportunity to plead provocation for any mad dog act he might undertake. The third was the perennial one of keeping the French up to scratch, both in agreeing to sanctions against Italy when the time came and, even more importantly for British interests, guaranteeing support for Britain if Italy were to launch an attack on British positions. Detailed military plans were made in the Defence Policy and Requirements Committee and here Hoare was very much the moving spirit against what he felt to be the defeatist attitude of the Service chiefs. He wrote to Eden in Geneva, just after coming away from a committee meeting on 17th September: 'You will be glad to hear that they were all in a much better mood. The soldiers, sailors and airmen are gradually beginning to show signs of no longer being the worst pacifists and defeatists in the country.'[76] And at the meeting on 23rd September the decision to reinforce the British garrison in Egypt by a brigade, as a counter to the patent threat to Egypt posed by the sending of two

Italian divisions to Libya, was taken (according to the committee's secretary, Major H. R. Pownall) 'in spite of the opposition of the C.I.G.S. and, I believe, the opinion of other members of the Committee. It was only Hoare's insistence which saw it through.'[77] But on the very same day he dispatched a personal message to Mussolini, through Drummond, to assure the Italian leader that Britain did not want to humiliate Italy, destroy the Italian fleet or lower the Duce's prestige. There had been no discussion, Mussolini was told, of 'closing the Suez Canal or military sanctions' against Italy. Nevertheless Britain would fulfil its obligations as a League member if the League agreed upon collective action. Vansittart thought there was a faint chance of the message saving the situation 'if means can also be devised for saving Mussolini's face'.[78] Laval had wanted the British government to go further and definitely assure Mussolini (as he had already done informally) that there had never been any question of closing the Suez Canal or of military sanctions but Hoare was careful to phrase his reference to these steps so as not to exclude them altogether, remote though their application might in fact be.[79]

On 24th September the Cabinet had its first meeting for over a month and examined exhaustively the recent developments in the crisis. In advance of an actual Italian attack on Abyssinia there was no certainty as to how the League would react in terms of the imposition of sanctions. Hoare told his colleagues that he thought League members would be prepared to agree to sanctions but only 'on a moderate basis'. There could, however, have been no disposition in the Cabinet to exaggerate the effect such sanctions would have since it had before it the report of a committee, with a membership drawn from the Board of Trade, Foreign Office and Treasury, which had concluded that Italy had the resources to sustain an east African war for a year to eighteen months, and that even a successful League boycott of Italian exports would reduce this period by no more than three or four months.[80] There was little sign of other nations at Geneva supporting tougher measures 'in spite of bold speeches', and there was the risk that Britain might find itself bearing alone all the economic and strategic consequences of opposing Italy. What this meant for the navy in the Mediterranean was spelt out by the First Lord, Eyres-Monsell, who bemoaned the deficiencies in the fleet's anti-aircraft equipment and the danger of air attack in the Mediterranean's narrow waters. It was agreed, once again, that the fulfilment of Britain's obligations to the League depended upon the French doing likewise. Members of the Cabinet 'repeatedly emphasised that we must be clear as to the French attitude' and Baldwin, summing up the discussion, commented that:

> it was essential that Signor Mussolini should be made to know that any action he might take against us would be met equally by France ... He thought all were agreed that the last thing that must be allowed to happen would be a single-handed war between this country and Italy.

The Cabinet expressed its satisfaction with the way the Foreign Secretary was handling the difficult situation and several tributes were paid to him on his Assembly speech.[81]

The Cabinet's next meeting took place on 2nd October, on what proved to be the very eve of the Italian invasion of Abyssinia. Even at this late stage Hoare was expressing the hope that a settlement would be possible which, 'without destroying Abyssinian independence, would give Italy some satisfaction'. It was still considered impossible to make a firm policy decision about sanctions but the Cabinet did agree to back 'the maximum of economic sanctions on which agreement could be secured', while firmly excluding sanctions involving military measures 'in view of the attitude of the French Government'.[82] There was not long to wait before at least one decisive, if disagreeable action was to be taken beyond the Cabinet's control.

6

The Hoare-Laval 'Pact'

The Italian invasion of Abyssinia in the early hours of 3rd October represented more than the actual occurrence of a long-anticipated event. It meant also the end of any hope that there could be a solution mediated through the League and thus virtually sounded the death-knell of the policy which Hoare had taken over. The principal intention of the framers of the League Covenant (as Vansittart reminded ministers, too late, in July 1936) 'was not to support the victim of aggression against the aggressor ... [but] ... to marshal such overwhelming force against the potential aggressor that the aggression would not take place at all'.[1] The League, lacking the universality of membership which had underlain this intention, had tried to prevent Italy from resorting to war — Hoare's Assembly speech was perhaps the high water mark of this attempt — and had failed. Now Italian forces were on the march the inadequacy of 'collective security through the League' would be exposed for all to see.

On the face of it, however, the League acted with some speed on the news of the Italian invasion. Italy was designated the aggressor and article 16 was invoked on 7th October. Between 11th and 19th October the Assembly Committee of Eighteen adopted various sanctions proposals covering such matters as the lifting of the embargo on arms to Abyssinia (effected by Britain on 11th October) and the parallel tightening of the embargo on arms to Italy; the prohibition of loans and credits and of certain raw material exports to Italy (but not, at this stage, oil, coal, iron and steel) and the import of Italian goods; together with provisions for mutual support between League members to offset the economic losses they would incur by enforcing sanctions against Italy. All these measures necessarily had to be left to the discretion of individual governments, and at least two European countries with close trade links with Italy — Austria and Hungary — gave early notice that they had no intention of implementing them.[2] Meanwhile the Italian invasion was proceeding with the success to be expected of a well-equipped modern army against an unsophisticated ill-armed one. The main problems for the Italian forces were more those of terrain and communications than enemy resistance, brave and resolute though that often was. Within a few days Adowa was 'avenged' by the town being captured and most of the province of which it was the capital — the Tigré, bordering on Eritrea — had been overrun.

At a meeting on 9th October the British Cabinet gave its approval to British participation in sanctions on the lines proposed by the League Committee of Eighteen. It also looked ahead to a further stage of more rigorous measures and agreed that 'if oil-producing or supplying Member States, such as Romania, were prepared to impose an embargo on oil, His Majesty's Government would be prepared to join in this and to consider further an embargo on exports of coal'.[3] But by the time the Cabinet next considered the crisis, on 16th October, more cautious counsels prevailed and it was considered wise 'to postpone the application of any new sanctions until the position with the French Government had been cleared up'.[4] Franco-British relations — despite Hoare's optimism after his September talks with Laval — were in fact at this point probably at the lowest ebb they reached during the whole of the crisis. Discussions on naval co-operation in the Mediterranean had been allowed to peter out and the French government, in addition to demanding from the British a guarantee of support if the Covenant were to be breached in Europe (that is, by Germany), had intimated that it felt the level of British naval reinforcements in the Mediterranean might, with justice, be considered a provocation by Italy since they exceeded what the situation required.[5] At the same time a fierce anti-British campaign had been launched in the French press (subsidised, it was widely thought, from Italian sources), with the redoubtable commentator 'Pertinax' (Henri Béraud) in the van with a savage article in *Gringoire* on

10th October entitled 'L'Angleterre doit-elle être réduite à l'esclavage?' On the day the Cabinet met (16th October) Vansittart told Corbin, the French Ambassador, that there was 'now more Anglophobia in France than at any time since Fashoda'.[6] Hoare, clearly near the end of his patience, complained to his colleagues that Laval 'seemed to be constantly intriguing behind the back of the League of Nations and ourselves with a view to some accommodation with Signor Mussolini'; while the First Lord of the Admiralty expressed his profound disquiet at the lack of co-operation in the Mediterranean by the French, when guaranteed use of French bases was essential to the safety of the British fleet. Nevertheless, in tacit recognition of the force of the objection to recent British naval moves in the Mediterranean, the Cabinet agreed that two battlecruisers could be withdrawn; but, in a telegram delivered in person to Laval by Clerk, the British Ambassador, on the same day, it demanded 'an unqualified assurance of immediate military support in its widest sense in case we are attacked'. Two days later Laval gave what were considered to be satisfactory assurances and the crisis in Franco-British relations eased (although the anti-British press campaign continued).

A domestic political development was now to cut across the international crisis. On 19th October Baldwin revealed that a general election (statutorily due within the next year) was imminent and four days later, in the course of a three-day foreign affairs debate in the House of Commons, he announced that it would take place on 14th November. The move was no doubt shrewdly timed in an attempt to limit the almost inevitable loss of seats to the Labour Opposition after four years in government but, in view of what has since been learned about British electoral behaviour (not least the lack of salience of particular issues, above all, foreign policy issues) there is little reason to believe that it was in fact an especially favourable moment for the government's appeal. In his own contribution to the debate in which the election date had been announced Hoare was deliberately low-key, making no attempt to extract political capital from the crisis. As he had done in his Assembly speech he emphasised that economic measures against the aggressor had to be genuinely collective, with all member states taking 'their share of the risks, the inconveniences and the losses'.

Britain had no intention of acting alone. Moreover, sanctions of a military nature had not been considered at any stage of the Geneva discussions and 'no such measures ... have formed any part of our policy'. Hoare reminded M.P.s that the purpose of collective action was 'not to expand but to limit the war; not to extend its duration but to shorten it' and that such action did not obviate the 'need to search for some means of an honourable settlement within the framework of the League'.[7]

In the event the National Government, while it secured 89 fewer seats in the election than in 1931 (432, compared with 521), retained an overwhelming Commons majority; Labour trebled its 1931 representation (from 52 to 154), at the expense of both Liberal and National Government candidates, and could not realistically have envisaged circumstances over the year Parliament still technically had to run in which it would have been likely to do significantly better. For Hoare it proved to be the last election he fought and while there was a slight swing against him in Chelsea he still managed to capture 75 per cent of the votes cast in a contest with a single rival, a Labour candidate.

The election campaign and Baldwin's subsequent concern with the reconstruction of the government made no easier Hoare's pressing responsibilities at the Foreign Office. He was left very much to his own devices, with the minimum of counsel from senior colleagues, all involved in the election. Although there was a meeting of the Defence Policy and Requirements Committee on 5th November the full Cabinet did not meet for well over a month after 23rd October. Like every government facing an imminent election, the National Government was not anxious to be confronted with the necessity of major policy decisions until it had been confirmed in office with a comfortable majority. Although Hoare and his colleagues could hardly have anticipated a National Government defeat on 14th November a sizable loss of electoral support was certainly possible, casting doubt on the government's ability to pursue its policy. It was natural for the government to want to go as slow in the Abyssinian crisis as circumstances would permit.

Circumstances did not permit of complete quiescence, however. From Paris, where Laval maintained a close contact with Mussolini, came indications that the Italian dictator might be prepared to consider terms for the ending of Italian action in Abyssinia. The French were in possession of a plan, said to have been drawn up by Mussolini himself on 13th October, providing for an Italian mandate over the non-Amharic regions of Abyssinia, together with those parts of the Tigré province occupied by the Italians since the invasion was launched; a joint League-Italian mandate over the Amharic core of the country, the settlement of the disputed frontiers with Eritrea and Italian Somaliland in Italy's favour; and the disarmament of Abyssinia.[8] While these proposals, as they stood, hardly qualified as that 'honourable settlement within the framework of the League' of which Hoare spoke in the Commons on 22nd October it was considered appropriate to send a Foreign Office official — Maurice Peterson, head of the recently formed Abyssinian department — to confer in Paris with his opposite number in the Quai d'Orsay, the Comte de St Quentin. The two officials were to take as their text, not the Italian plan, but the report of the Committee of Five of the previous month, and to fit into it a detailed scheme that both Italy and Abyssinia might conceivably accept. It was clearly understood that the two governments were acting on behalf of the League (and its conciliation committee, the Committee of Five) and that any plan which emerged from the discussions would be *ad referendum* to the League itself and be submitted to the parties to the dispute. Peterson's instructions made it plain that the British government was

> only prepared to continue negotiations on the basis, first of a definite exchange of territory that gave Abyssinia a port, and secondly, of a formula that, whilst accepting Italian development in the southern [non-Amharic] provinces, maintained Abyssinian sovereignty under League supervision.[9]

After only a few days' discussion Peterson brought back a draft to London. When, however, it was considered by Hoare, Eden and Vansittart at a Foreign Office meeting on 28th October doubts were expressed about its suitability.[10] It was decided that when Eden returned to Geneva on 1st November to resume his place in the Committee of Eighteen he would be accompanied by Hoare (and Hankey, the Cabinet secretary). It was a brief and perhaps ill-conceived visit by Hoare which seemed to accomplish very little. In the course of two days he had discussions with Laval, Titulescu (the Foreign Minister of Romania, which supplied Italy with a substantial quantity of its oil) and Mussolini's representative, Aloisi. With Aloisi he tentatively agreed to ease British-Italian tension in the Mediterranean by the withdrawal of the two battlecruisers at Gibraltar (a step already approved by the Cabinet) in exchange for the recall of an Italian division from Libya — but this was soon repudiated by Mussolini. The one clear result of Hoare's visit was that he and Laval agreed to support a definite date for the bringing into force of economic sanctions: and on 2nd November the Committee of Eighteen fixed on 18th November.[11]

At the same meeting the Committee of Eighteen, as the result of a curious and almost unintentional procedural gambit, agreed to propose the addition of oil — and coal, iron and steel — to the list of commodities whose export to Italy might be embargoed.[12] The proposal was put to governments on 6th November and on 22nd November the committee agreed to consider, and make a definite decision on, these additional sanctions at a meeting on 29th November. Immediately a new urgency was given to what was already a fevered atmosphere of international debate centred on Geneva. This was not so much because an oil embargo would have any marked effect on the course of the Italian campaign in Abyssinia — the Italians had been building up large oil stocks in east Africa and the export of American-controlled oil to Italy had substantially increased since the crisis began, trebling the normal levels by the end of November[13] — but because it would inflame still further an Italian public opinion which was now for the first time unitedly behind the Abyssinian adventure as a result of the original decision to impose sanctions and would make considerably more likely the much-discussed 'mad dog act' by Mussolini. This had obvious implications for Britain, which was looked on both by Italy and other League members as the main policeman of sanctions; and for France, so reluctant to be nailed down to firm military support if Britain were attacked by Italy.

On 21st November Peterson had been sent back to Paris with fresh instructions, drafted (with Hoare's approval) by Eden, to renew his discussions with St Quentin. These were still to be based on the Committee of Five's report, but the British government was now prepared 'to consider putting Adowa and Adigrat [in Tigré] into the scale for Italy, with a corresponding reduction in what had been proposed for her in the south'. Abyssinia must, however, receive at least one outlet to the sea, preferably at Assab in Eritrea; and Italy was to be offered no more than a proportionate share 'in any plan of assistance the League might propose for Abyssinia'.[14] On the 25th Peterson telegraphed through Clerk to say that the French side was putting the terms which it thought Italy might be induced to accept considerably higher than this. He mentioned the cession by Abyssinia (in exchange for a port and a connecting corridor), not only of Adowa and Adigrat but also the province of Danakil, adjacent to Tigré province and bordering Eritrea, French Somaliland and British Somaliland, and 'most if not all of Ogaden'. There was also to be, as in the Committee of Five report, an area of unspecified size in the south in which it was accepted that Italy had 'special interests' in terms of economic development and settlement. Some of the officials who minuted on this telegram had reservations about these additional concessions but Vansittart, Eden and Hoare all approved them in principle subject, as Eden minuted, 'to the proviso that we have always made and must always maintain that a settlement must be acceptable to the three main parties, Italy, Abyssinia and the League'. Eden also commented, and Hoare agreed, that the proposal for Italian special interests in the south — which might cover a third or more of Abyssinian territory — 'would certainly have to be combined with non-Italian League control'.[15] Armed with this new authority, Peterson resumed his negotiations in Paris.

Meanwhile there was feverish activity to attempt to secure the other flank of the government's policy: protection for Britain's strategic position in the Mediterranean. And over all hung the damoclean sword of the oil sanction. Vansittart, in particular, was deeply concerned over the likely consequences of any hasty agreement to take such a step. Minuting on 23rd November on a message from the Rome embassy which had expatiated on the danger that Mussolini might be prepared to fight even in the certainty of eventual defeat rather than accept 'humiliating' terms, Vansittart urged Hoare not to 'proceed or allow others to proceed at Geneva with measures against oil imports into Italy' until British defences were adequate and the support of France and other states assured. 'To run the risk alone and unprepared would surely be unthinkable', he concluded.[16] At a meeting of the Defence Policy and Requirements Committee on 26th November there was a general consensus that Britain could not rely on French co-operation and that the government should go slow on giving its approval for additional sanctions until the extent of the French commitment was precisely known. The committee approved Hoare's suggestion that Laval should again be pressed to make it clear to Italy that France would 'automatically and at once give us assistance and that, consequently, she should now take material steps to ensure that her assistance would be effective'. The Chiefs of Staff were asked to set out what help was needed from other powers, and in particular France, in case of an Italian attack; while at the same time Hoare strongly pressed the Services to expedite their own preparations, including an increase in the supply of anti-aircraft ammunition.[17]

Hoare had in fact already been in contact with Laval, through Clerk, both on the subject of the oil sanction and on French assistance in the event of an Italian attack. As soon as Laval had heard that the Committee of Eighteen was proposing to come to a decision on an oil sanction on 29th November he asked for British support in seeking a postponement. The overt reason was his own parliamentary difficulties – and his government was indeed fighting for its life in the Chamber of Deputies – but Laval's fears of Italian reactions to an oil sanction almost certainly loomed larger in his mind. Vansittart backed the idea of a postponement enthusiastically and even suggested immediately telegraphing to Rome the information that the British were taking part in the postponement so that the French did not gain all the credit in Mussolini's eyes. This stratagem was too much for Hoare, but he did, on 25th November, agree to support Laval's proposal for a delay; on the same day Clerk was asked to persuade Laval to inform Mussolini 'in whatever form may be thought best' that any attack upon Britain would lead to war with all League members including France. Laval seems to have given some such message through the Italian ambassador in Paris but, at least up to 5th December, none had been sent through the more authoritative and certain channel of the

French ambassador in Rome.[18]

Laval was successful in inducing the Committee of Eighteen to postpone its consideration of oil sanctions but the period of delay could clearly not be for more than ten days or so (12th December was the date eventually fixed). Meanwhile the Peterson-St Quentin talks, which had been proceeding in Paris continuously from 22nd November, were running into difficulties. Despite the further concessions the British government had been prepared to make in response to Peterson's message of 25th November, Laval still considered the package insufficiently attractive to satisfy Mussolini (there is no evidence that either side, perhaps realistically, considered in any detail what Haile Selassie's attitude might be). Apparently in order to avoid having to call on Mussolini to cede Italian territory Laval returned to the proposal, rejected by Mussolini in June, for the transfer of Zeila in British Somaliland rather than Assab in Italian Eritrea; moreover, he added for good measure a purely French stipulation against the building of any railway to the port likely to compete with the Djibouti line. The British side insisted that Italian and not British territory must be used in the exchange and that the connecting corridor to the port should be sufficient in extent to enable a railway to be built if the Abyssinians so wished. There were also differences on the extent of the territorial transfers to Italy, particularly in the Tigré.[19]

To the French at least it seemed at this juncture, with a League oil sanction in prospect, even more important that Hoare and Laval should meet to iron out the difficulties than it had been when they last met at the beginning of November. On 28th November, Léger, Vansittart's opposite number at the Quai d'Orsay, pressed strongly through Clerk for a Hoare-Laval meeting; it seemed clear that he was acting on Laval's instructions and that this time Laval wished to come to London. This, however, presented difficulties, since Hoare — whose never really certain health had recently been showing alarming signs of the enormous burden he was bearing (he had had several complete blackouts) — had just arranged, under his doctor's advice and with Baldwin's active encouragement, to take a much-needed skating holiday in Switzerland with Lady Maud. It was thus decided that Hoare should stop off in Paris on 7th December, on his way to Switzerland. The decision was probably effectively taken when Hoare and Vansittart discussed the Léger suggestion on the 29th, for when, later that day, Neville Chamberlain, Hoare, Simon, Eden and Runciman met in Chamberlain's room in the House of Commons, it was agreed 'to hold up the [oil] sanction long enough to allow further conversations in Paris to test out the possibility of a general settlement'.[20] Since Hoare wished Vansittart to be with him at the talks it was necessary to secure specific royal approval for the absence abroad at one and the same time of the Foreign Secretary and of the permanent under-secretary. The letter Hoare wrote to Wigram, the King's private secretary, on 2nd December to ask for royal permission gives a clear account of the antecedents of the visit which was to have so profound an effect on his career:

> As you know, I have had no proper holiday for several years. My doctor has been insistent upon my getting off as soon as possible, particularly as I have recently had a series of fainting fits, one of which took place last night. I have discussed the question with the Prime Minister and Vansittart, and we are agreed that, whilst there are always difficulties in the way of my getting away, the difficulties are less if I get away quickly rather than if I stay longer. Moreover, if I leave at the end of the week, I shall be passing through Paris and can accept M. Laval's urgent invitation to have a talk with him on Saturday [7th December]. If I postpone my departure, this talk will be impossible before the important meeting of the League [Committee of Eighteen] on 12th December.

Since Hoare anticipated that his visit to Laval might be very important he was proposing taking Vansittart with him.

> If, as I hope, M. Laval and I agree upon a basis for a peace negotiation, Vansittart will stop on in Paris for a day or two in order to clinch the details. I hope that His Majesty will approve of this exceptional arrangement ... The special importance, however, of this meeting makes, I suggest, it necessary to take him.

It was clear that Hoare looked upon his talk with Laval, however successful it might be, as just one stage in a whole series of

international discussions. ' ... it looks to me', he told Wigram,
'as though the next few weeks are going to be a period of intensive negotiation for a settlement. We intend to go all out for
bringing the conflict to an end.' He himself would be in Switzerland for at least a fortnight but as he was taking with him a
Foreign Office private secretary and a cypher he would be able
to keep in close touch with developments and could 'always get
back if anything that necessitates my return arises'.[21]

On the day Hoare wrote to the Palace the Cabinet met for its
first full-scale consideration of the Abyssinian crisis since
October. It had plenty of documentation before it. There was,
for example, a Foreign Office paper on oil sanctions which Hoare
and Eden had approved on 27th November. This noted that the
Committee of Eighteen, in response to its approach to governments, had been informed by those of the Soviet Union,
Romania, India and Iraq that they were prepared to operate
the proposed new sanctions on oil, coal, iron and steel but that
the first two governments had made this agreement conditional
upon the co-operation of all the producing countries. A 'complete and immediate embargo' on oil was in any case out of the
question 'owing to the lack of control over the American
supplies'. Britain had still to furnish its reply to the committee
and the Foreign Office paper suggested that the government's
attitude should, in effect, be the same as that of the Soviet
Union and Romania: that it would be prepared to participate
in an oil embargo provided all the producing states co-operated.
At the same time the paper stressed the two desiderata of
French conduct: that Laval should make it abundantly clear to
Mussolini that an attack on Britain would automatically involve
France; and that joint Franco-British naval, military and air
talks should be instituted to plan the necessary co-operation.[22]

The Cabinet also had the record of conversations that Vansit-
tart and Hoare had had in London on 25th and 28th November
with an unofficial emissary of Mussolini, General Garibaldi,
who was the son of Hoare's wartime friend, Riciotti Garibaldi.
Although the sort of terms for a settlement Garibaldi represented
Mussolini as seeking were considered by both Hoare and
Vansittart as unacceptable by the League, Abyssinia or the
British government, there were some indications that, as
Garibaldi claimed, Mussolini was shifting 'from the rigid posi-

tion that he had at first adopted' and that the terms were a bargaining counter rather than a final demand. Hoare owned to being impressed by Garibaldi's 'obvious sincerity and fervent desire to find some basis of agreement'; the question was how influential he could be in persuading Mussolini to moderate his demands.[23]

The Cabinet was to meet once again before Hoare departed for Paris and Switzerland but it was the Cabinet of 2nd December (rather than that on the 4th, which dealt with other matters) which enabled Hoare's colleagues to survey the situation to date in the Italo-Abyssinian crisis, in the light of Hoare's forthcoming talk with Laval and of the decision which would soon have to be made about the oil sanction. Retrospectively Hoare felt that he should have insisted upon the summoning of a special Cabinet to hammer out a clear agreement 'as to how far I could go with Laval'.[24] In spite of the rather muddled way Hankey recorded the minutes (no doubt an apt reflection of the discussion itself) the Cabinet of 2nd December – entirely devoted to the Abyssinian question – seems in fact to have been just that.[25] There was, it is true, nothing specific about the terms of a possible agreement but members of the Cabinet could have been under no illusions that these would not involve the recognition of a predominant Italian interest in Abyssinia and some transfer of territory: these had both been accepted in the Committee of Five plan of September and underlay the Peterson-St Quentin discussions and other, more informal, contacts (such as that with General Garibaldi) of which the Cabinet had been made aware. There were clearly some differences of opinion in the Cabinet on particular aspects of policy, a fact not always obvious from the secretariat's record. Hailsham, Eyres-Monsell, Cunliffe-Lister, Runciman and Londonderry (until he was dropped from the Cabinet in the post-election reshuffle on 22nd November), for example, were all unhappy about the imposition of any sanctions let alone one on oil, while others (apparently including Oliver Stanley and Walter Elliot) thought the dangers of an Italian attack resulting from a British agreement to an oil embargo had been exaggerated. But unless the minutes ('conclusions') of the Cabinet of 2nd December are a complete travesty of the discussion that took place Hoare was being abjured by the Cabinet collectively (a) to press on with peace talks; (b) to secure the essential prerequisite of full French co-operation; and (c) to avoid British involvement in war. This was a lot to expect of a sick and tired man on his way to a convalescent holiday especially in the complete absence of any constructive advice or suggestions from his colleagues, but it was nevertheless a mandate which Hoare fully discharged in his Paris agreement with Laval.

The Cabinet, which was attended by all its twenty-three members, opened with a long statement by Hoare. He stressed that the British government could not adopt a negative attitude to an oil sanction nor refuse to play its part in genuinely collective action to effect it, having fought the election on that basis (Hoare had confided to Hankey on 25th November that he 'would resign if the oil sanction was not accepted' by the Cabinet).[26] But there were all the concomitant dangers. Britain needed to be sure of French and, if possible, American support for an oil embargo. At the same time 'We must press on with the peace negotiations as rapidly as possible, with a view to bringing the conflict to an end.' The Peterson-St Quentin talks in Paris had not made much progress as yet but he (Hoare) 'had to go away for reasons of health for a short time, and he proposed on his journey to see M. Laval and to try and press peace talks with him'. It was now a question of whether

> it might not be better to keep the prospect of an oil sanction hanging over Signor Mussolini's head rather than fix a date at once, in which case, as Signor Mussolini's own agents represented, he would become more intransigent. On the whole he thought the issue depended on the prospect of the peace talks. If the discussions were going well ... the League Committee [of Five] might meet and be told that the peace talks were going satisfactorily and that for that reason we and the French were not asking for the immediate imposition of an embargo.

There would thus be a two-stage decision on an oil sanction: first a decision in principle and then a decision about its actual implementation. On the whole, Hoare thought it would be wise, if the peace talks were going well, to proceed with the sanction on this basis.

Hoare's statement was followed by a general discussion, during which Baldwin asked the opinion of every member of the Cabinet (although the minutes rarely identify individual views). Two of the Service ministers, Eyres-Monsell (Admiralty) and Cunliffe-Lister (Air) had gloomy reports to give on the naval and air situation in the Mediterranean. While there was no doubt that the fleet was strong enough to obtain command of the Mediterranean it might sustain serious losses in doing so 'since our forces were not in a proper state of readiness for war in a land-locked sea'. And war in the Mediterranean would have serious repercussions on imperial defence as a whole, with the defences of Singapore still incomplete and the whole British position in the Far East depending on the navy. But if the naval position was bad, the air position was even worse. No anti-aircraft guns would be available for the defence of Alexandria and the only thing which could deflect an Italian air attack would be attacks on Italian bases and on northern Italy. 'That depended on complete co-operation by France. We should require not only facilities for our own aircraft but active co-operation by the French Air Force ...' Among the Service ministers only Duff Cooper, who had taken over at the War Office less than a fortnight before, professed to feel any sort of optimism. For his two colleagues, on the other hand, it was clear that 'The gap between our foreign policy and the state of our defence forces was too wide':

> ... our defence forces and defences in the Mediterranean were not in a proper condition for war, and from this point of view it was urged that an effort should be made to obtain peace, holding the threat of the oil sanction over Italy, and that the fixing of the date should not be decided until after the failure of peace discussions.

Some Cabinet members, the minutes record, thought the risk of an Italian attack on British forces was remote. But others — who would certainly have included Eyres-Monsell — referred to secret intelligence reports which indicated that the Italians were making active preparations for a military response to the imposition of an oil embargo, while Baldwin at one point observed that 'in dealing with Signor Mussolini we were not dealing with a normal kind of intellect'.[27] If Italy should indeed attack Britain there must be satisfactory and binding arrangements with France. Until such arrangements had been made it was urged once more that we ought not to fix the date of the oil sanctions. If the negotiations showed that France was not willing to co-operate, the whole matter would have to be re-considered.

To ensure full co-operation between British and French military authorities the conversations already begun between the Admiralty and the French navy should be extended to the air force and, if necessary, to the army.

All this was a tall order if the League decision about the additional sanctions was not to be held up for more than a few days. The suggestion was made that 'a week was a very short time to establish whether the peace conversations were going well or not and to clear up the military point'. Then came a most significant request to the Foreign Secretary, illuminating in a few words the intense desire of his colleagues that he seize any opportunity to secure peace and avoid the possibility of Britain's involvement in what, in the long term, could be a disastrous war: 'It was hoped that the Foreign Secretary would take a generous view of the Italian attitude'. Hoare responded to this virtual diplomatic *carte blanche* by agreeing that the peace talks must be given the best possible chance. The subject of further military conversations with France could, he thought, be opened up when he saw Laval on 7th December. It was then again pointed out that this did not allow much time before the Geneva meeting on the 12th, the clear implication being that Hoare should depart even earlier for Paris. Hoare explained that the French government's current preoccupation with its internal political troubles made this difficult. But it was evident that his colleagues wanted results, and quickly, from his talk with Laval.

Baldwin summed up the discussion, observing that there was general agreement 'on broad lines'. If Britain were to be involved in hostilities as a result of any action it now took

the situation for the Government would be a bad one unless everything possible had been done to avoid them, especially when the detailed facts of our defensive preparations became known ... It had to be remembered that it was this country that would have to withstand the first shock of an Italian forcible reaction to sanctions. He himself was not willing to be committed at this moment to ... the date of the application of oil sanctions.

The specific conclusions of the three-hour debate were that Hoare was to bring the question back for further consideration by the Cabinet in either of two contingencies: '(i) If the peace talks did not offer any reasonable prospect of a settlement (ii) If the military conversations showed that France was not willing to co-operate effectively.' Thus did the Cabinet set the stage for the Hoare-Laval agreement. As Zetland, Hoare's successor as Secretary of State for India, wrote to the Viceroy after the Cabinet meeting: '... it is quite possible that there may be interesting developments during the next week or ten days.'[28]

The five days which elapsed between this Cabinet meeting and his departure for Paris served to reinforce for Hoare the necessity of finding quickly some kind of solution to a crisis which threatened Britain's whole strategic position. On 4th December the Chiefs of Staff produced their collective view of the situation in military terms. After detailing what they considered to be essential co-operative action from other League powers in the event of an Italian attack (the French were expected, among other things, to capture or paralyse Italy's northern industrial area and to bomb its air bases) the Chiefs of Staff concluded:

... we wish to emphasise the danger which would arise if political arguments on the application of fresh sanctions outrun arrangements for co-operation between the forces of the powers concerned. We submit that it is essential that this country, alone, should not be committed to risks for which other Members of the League are militarily unprepared. Powers agreeing to sanctions should be ready to meet the situation which may arise therefrom. When, therefore, further discussions take place likely to lead to fresh pressure on Italy, we urge that steps be taken simultaneously to initiate military discussions with all those Powers whose duty it is to co-operate in the Mediterranean in the event of Italian aggression.[29]

This was to expect a great deal — indeed virtually the impossible — and seemed more the result of Service reluctance to become embroiled with Italy than a realistic evaluation of what was needed in terms of international support. Hoare, who had done more than anyone else to try to activate Service preparations, was gravely disappointed at the dilatoriness with which the Services had responded (Pownall's diary records him as 'continually' complaining about 'the limitations placed on him by our known weakness' and 'pressing the Service Depts to do this, that, and the other').[30] Nevertheless he had to accept the expert opinion of the government's military advisers, with all their faults of omission and commission. One of the major aims of Hoare's Paris mission was to expedite military discussions but only two days before he left he heard through the British military attaché in Paris, who had been talking with General Gamelin, Chief of the French General Staff, that while the French would assist 'in the event of war' they could not 'take any precautionary measures for fear of compromising a settlement' with Italy.[31] This was not a good augury for meeting the stringent desiderata laid down by the British Chiefs of Staff.

Such strategic factors were usually notable by their absence from the political debate outside government circles. This was partly because, as Baldwin had indicated in his summing up at the Cabinet on 2nd December, the government had no wish to reveal the inadequacy of its defence preparations; partly also because the Labour Opposition and enthusiasts for 'collective security' in general saw no incompatibility between demanding at the same time both disarmament and the rattling of sabres at Italy. The Abyssinian crisis figured prominently in the first foreign affairs debate of the new Parliament on 5th December.[32] Hugh Dalton, leading for the Opposition, abjured Hoare to tell Laval 'that this country is not favourable to, is not even interested in, any terms of settlement of this war which allow the Italian dictator to profit by reason of his aggression'. Hoare, in reply, made clear that France and Britain

> were working within the framework of the League, that we wished at the earliest possible moment to share our special responsibility with other members of the League, and that any proposals that might emerge from these or other discussions must be acceptable to the three parties to the dispute — the League, Italy and Abyssinia.

The delay in the meeting of the Committee of Eighteen had

given a further opportunity to bring about a peaceful settlement. Hoare continued:

> It may be that we are engaged upon a hopeless task. It may be that it is impossible to reconcile the divergent aims of Italy, Abyssinia and the League ... None the less, the French and we intend not only to go on trying but to redouble our efforts during the short period of time that is still open before the Geneva meeting [on 12th December] ... [and] acting on behalf of the League and in the spirit of the League ... to make another great effort for peace.

While he did not wish to minimise the great difficulties in the way of a reasonable settlement he was sure 'we must not despair of surmounting them' and that 'a particular effort to surmount them' must be made 'in the course of the next few days and the next few weeks'. The clear implication of this repeated refrain was that the meeting with Laval would be dealing with substantive issues (as Hoare expressed it to the Dominion high commissioners the same day, he was going to see whether he and Laval could reach agreement 'on joint proposals').[33] This was certainly accepted by the respected elder statesman Austen Chamberlain, who stressed in the debate that a solution acceptable to Italy and the League should not be held up by objections from Abyssinia, a country which

> is not a client for whom I would have chosen to fight a test case. It is a slave-holding State; it is a slave-raiding State ... I do not think that you can say to Abyssinia: 'We will continue indefinitely our pressure on Italy and go on heightening it until you agree'. I think it must be until the League of Nations agree and a satisfactory solution is accepted by Italy.

Inside the Foreign Office itself there was divided counsel on how far it was possible to go in appeasing Italian ambitions in Abyssinia. Some officials thought that any cession of Abyssinian territory, particularly Tigré province, would 'in the eyes of the world, inevitably put a premium on the aggression of which Italy has been guilty'.[34] On the other hand, the most experienced official on Abyssinian questions, G. H. Thompson, observed (in a minute on 1st December) that

we may have to recommend to the League — lest worse befall
— the basis of a settlement which, while not giving Italy
nearly all she sought, may yet be more favourable than anything she could have secured purely by negotiation ... [and
involve] ... some compromising with the spirit of the Covenant, a slight sacrifice of principle.[35]

Vansittart signified his assent to this assessment and, shortly
afterwards, in conversations with Grandi at the Foreign Office
on 3rd, 4th and 5th December, had direct evidence of the current
state of Italian ambitions. When, however, he saw Corbin, the
French Ambassador, on the morning of the 6th he thought it
wise to indicate through him to the French government that
there must be a 'limit to appetite on one side and connivance on
the other'.[36]

Later that day (Friday, 6th December) Vansittart left for
Paris by the boat train to take part in the talks which were to be
held on the following day. While there he was also to take the
opportunity, he told Corbin, 'of endeavouring to form some
judgement of the state of Anglo-French relations' in the light of
the continuing anti-British campaign in much of the French
press, for 'any successful settlement depended upon full Anglo-
French co-operation'.[37]

Lady Maud Hoare also departed for the Continent on 6th
December, but without her husband. The plan was for Hoare to
fly to Paris on Saturday the 7th, arriving in time for lunch, and
then, after his discussion with Laval, to leave on the night train
to join Lady Maud at Zuoz in the Engadine, where a rink had
been specially opened for them. But things did not go according
to plan. Thick fog on Saturday morning made an air flight impossible and Hoare and his private secretary, Paul Mason, had
to take the boat train. The result was that Hoare did not arrive
in Paris until about 4 p.m. He was met at the station by Clerk,
Vansittart and Peterson and went with them briefly to the
British Embassy, where Peterson went over some of the points
arising from his negotiations with St Quentin, before leaving for
the Quai d'Orsay and the meeting with Laval soon after 5
p.m.[38] The discussions between the two statesmen and their
advisers (like Hoare, Laval had three — Léger, Massigli and St
Quentin) did not begin until 5.30 p.m., several hours later than

they would have done had Hoare been able to travel by air.

Laval opened by deploring the fixing of even a relatively remote date for the implementation of an oil sanction which, he was certain, would precipitate a 'desperate act' by Mussolini. Hoare then expressed the view of 'many people' that France was neither able nor willing to assist if Italy were to attack another League member. Laval declared that the French people would stand by their obligations but that they must feel that everything possible was being done by way of conciliation 'to find a way out of the present crisis'. Hoare, however, was concerned about convincing Italy that Britain and France were united, without which no negotiations could be successful. At this point Vansittart observed that the three essential processes — fixing the date for the oil sanction, peace negotiations and Franco-British military staff talks — should be carried on simultaneously. He suggested that the staff talks should begin early in the following week, and to this Laval readily agreed (they were in fact held in Paris on 9th and 10th December). Hoare stressed that any impression that the League was weakening must be avoided at all cost. Laval concurred, but at the same time asserted that 'Geneva would accept whatever France and Great Britain approved'. He felt that British reservations on the terms were too severe and appealed to Britain 'to be more generous'. Hoare replied that it was 'essential not to offer the appearance of rewarding aggression': the proposals must be kept within the framework of the Committee of Five report. Abyssinia must have a definite outlet to the sea and there could be no question of an exclusively Italian mandate. The aim should be 'a judicious mixture of an exchange of territory and the conferring of economic concessions'. To go too far in the cession of Abyssinian territory 'would lead to the Emperor's overthrow and provoke the accusation that all the League had managed to do was to ruin Abyssinia'. Vansittart intervened to express his agreement with his minister. It was essential to remember, he said, that 'there must be some limit set to what Abyssinia could be expected to cede even in return for a port; to exceed the limit would be to expose the League itself to the gravest danger'. Laval said he accepted the Committee of Five principles but maintained that the idea of an international mandate, as opposed to an exclusively Italian one, did not interest Mussolini.

It was now late and Laval suggested that they end the discussion for the night and resume at 10.30 on the following (Sunday) morning. Hoare was longing to get to Zuoz and to start his much-needed holiday, but he recognised that Laval had shown sufficient movement in his position, particularly his swift agreement to immediate staff talks and his acceptance of the Committee of Five report as the basis of any proposed settlement, to make further discussion worth while. Reluctant though he was to do so he agreed to spend a further day in Paris, no doubt cursing the while the morning airport fog which had, in effect, made the adjournment necessary. A short communiqué was issued to the press announcing the existence of complete agreement between the two governments and the intention of the ministers to continue their exchange of views on the following day 'in order to determine the bases which might be proposed for the friendly settlement of the Italo-Ethiopian dispute'.[39]

When Hoare, Laval and their advisers met again on Sunday morning they immediately plunged into the details of the proposed territorial exchanges and the economic concessions to Italy. As far as cessions of Abyssinian territory in the north and west were concerned Hoare felt that in the course of the discussions he succeeded 'in reducing very greatly their scope', thus making it possible to extend the area of Italian economic monopoly in the south — an economic monopoly which he was emphatic was not another name for the transfer of sovereignty or the institution of an Italian mandate, since it would be under League auspices and supervision. The territory proposed to be ceded (mainly in Italian-conquered Tigré but also substantial 'rectification of frontiers' with Eritrea and Italian Somaliland) would be in exchange for a port — either Assab or, if the Abyssinians preferred it, Zeila (although if it were to be Zeila Laval was strongly against a concomitant right to build a railway). Some two-fifths of Abyssinian territory, including the central highlands area, remained unaffected by either cession or the granting of an economic monopoly to Italy.

The discussion then turned to the procedure to be followed if the two governments agreed to the proposals that their representatives had hammered out. Hoare proposed that they should be taken, without delay, to a reconvened Committee of Five. If the committee gave its approval it would either continue negotiations to settle final details, or ask the British and French governments to do so. Laval agreed, rather to Hoare's surprise. But he insisted that the draft proposals should be telegraphed to Mussolini before they were sent to Geneva or Addis Ababa, arguing that Mussolini would be more likely to accept them if he had no cause to think that 'we are doing anything behind his back'. Haile Selassie, on the other hand, was to be told 'in an appropriate form' and in much less detail that an attempt at peace was being made. Hoare agreed to this unfortunate act of discrimination in the belief that Anglo-French agreement on an actual plan was more important than procedural details. On the oil sanction there was to be no bargain with Mussolini. But if the Committee of Five agreed to the proposals then the two ministers considered it would be advisable for the Committee of Eighteen, dealing with sanctions, not to meet until a further opportunity had been given for the negotiations to succeed. In this way the 'very dangerous responsibility' which had devolved upon Britain and France would be shared with other members of the League.[40]

The main discussions ended in time for lunch at the Quai d'Orsay, but it took the afternoon for officials to prepare type-written drafts of the proposals and the suggested procedure for Laval and Hoare to agree and initial. When all was settled another short communiqué was issued which, apart from the usual banalities of such official statements ('Animated by the same spirit of conciliation and inspired by close Franco-British friendship' and so on), gave a frail hostage to fortune by stating that it was not intended to publish at present 'the formulae' for a friendly settlement of the dispute which had been worked out: 'The British Government has not yet been informed of them and once its agreement has been received it will be necessary to submit them to the consideration of the interested governments and to discussion by the League of Nations.' In a concluding section, which Hoare soon had cause bitterly to regret, both ministers expressed satisfaction with the result which had been achieved.[41] Hoare then took his leave of Laval and left for the British Embassy where he met the press for about a quarter of an hour, dealing with generalities and asking the journalists to refrain from detailed comment until the terms of the agreement could be released. At some stage, too, in this hectic day, he drafted a hasty note on the discussion for the Cabinet, had a message transmitted to the Foreign Office requesting a meeting of the Cabinet for the following day (Monday, 9th December), and instructed Peterson to leave for London forthwith with all the documentation so as to brief the Cabinet when it did meet. Hoare's final message to his Cabinet colleagues was an urgent one:

> I would strongly recommend the action that I have described to the Cabinet and that it should be taken at once. It is essential in my view that the communication about the basis of the negotiation should be confidentially communicated to Signor Mussolini at once. By this I mean tomorrow afternoon. The recommendations in my view have two great advantages. In the first place, they reduce the question of territorial cessions to a minimum. In the second place they bring back the League into the front of the picture and put the responsibility for the settlement where it should lie — upon the shoulders of of the League rather than upon the French and ourselves.[42]

Soon after meeting the press Hoare, absolutely exhausted (his private secretary thought he would have to support him, he seemed so near collapse),[43] took the night train for Switzerland, arriving at Zuoz the next afternoon. By that time the proposals had been extensively and tendentiously leaked in the French press — by whose agency it is now impossible to determine — and the first signs of popular reaction against them were beginning to appear.

At such short notice it was not possible to gather the Cabinet together until 6 p.m. on the 9th, and then it met at the House of Commons rather than its normal venue. There was understandable disquiet about the inevitable 'reward for aggresssion' which the proposals represented but it agreed that they should go forward, subject to one proviso as to procedure. Acting on Eden's suggestion the Cabinet decided that the proposed peace terms ought to be communicated to Abyssinia at the same time as to Italy, and that Haile Selassie 'should be strongly pressed to accept them as a basis for discussion, or at least not to reject them'.[44] Vansittart was instructed to see Laval and did so at 2 a.m. that night. Laval agreed that Abyssinia should be informed simultaneously with Italy but asked for assurances, which Vansittart strongly urged his government to give, that there would be no question of enforcing the oil sanction if Abyssinia turned down the proposals and Italy accepted them.[45] The Cabinet met again at midday on 10th December. It confirmed its decision of the previous day that the Paris terms were 'the best, from the Abyssinian point of view, that could be obtained from Italy' and agreed that Eden should support them at Geneva. It refused, however, to give Laval the assurances he was seeking: Laval then reluctantly withdrew his condition and telegrams were sent later that evening to Rome and Addis Ababa, where Barton was instructed by Eden to 'use your utmost influence to induce Emperor to give careful and favourable consideration to these proposals and on no account lightly to reject them'.[46]

Despite its rejection of Laval's request the Cabinet clearly had no intention of expediting the oil sanction. At a further Cabinet meeting on the morning of 11th December Baldwin expressed the general view by saying that additional sanctions 'ought not to be undertaken unless we were assured that they would be effective' and 'until we knew what America was going to do we should hold our hand'. It was a view not unaffected by the report that Eden — who was to leave for Geneva later that day — had given on the support from other League members Britain might expect if attacked by Italy because of sanctions. Eden said he had no news from France, but Greece and Turkey had promised their full co-operation, while the answer from Yugoslavia had been less satisfactory: in all, a rather slender tally from an organisation of some fifty states. On the Hoare-Laval proposals the view of the Cabinet now seemed to be shifting perceptibly, and no one disagreed with Eden when he expressed the hope 'that he would not be expected to champion the proposals ... in detail at Geneva'; members felt that it was the zone of economic expansion and colonisation allocated to Italy in Abyssinia which was likely to be the most criticised part of the plan, most public comment having ignored the provision for League supervision.[47]

The reason for the shift in the Cabinet position was undoubtedly the unprecedented campaign against the Hoare-Laval proposals (or what was known of them on the basis of the French press leaks) being mounted in the editorial and correspondence columns of most of the press (with the notable exception of the Beaverbrook and Rothermere papers), in Parliament and in members' postbags. The *News Chronicle* of 10th December, for example, spoke of a 'Secret plan to reward Mussolini' and 'A flagrant betrayal of the League', while its leader was headed 'Peace with dishonour'. *The Times* became unmistakably hostile on the 13th, when it said that the terms would be acceptable neither to Abyssinia nor the League and that too much had been sacrificed in the effort to reach common ground with France; and on the 16th came Geoffrey Dawson's famous editorial headed 'A Corridor for Camels' (a scornful reference to Abyssinia's proposed outlet to the sea) and declaring that the proposals were dead from the moment their general tenor was known, because there had never been the slightest chance that British public opinion would support 'an unjust peace'.

Hoare had arrived in Zuoz on 9th December believing, as Clerk and Vansittart had assured him, that he had secured a major diplomatic triumph. An analogy had even been drawn — no doubt for its especial appeal to Hoare, who was a devotee of Napoleon and the Napoleonic age — with the sense of triumph Napoleon felt on first seeing the cupolas of the Kremlin.[48] Hoare's exultation was, however, doomed to a much earlier end than Napoleon's. News of the leaks in the French press and of the beginnings of the resultant storm had reached Zuoz by the time he arrived there, but there was reassurance that evening when he received a message that the Cabinet had unanimously approved the proposals, subject to their transmission to both Italy and Abyssinia. Shortly afterwards he had a telephone conversation with Eden who, while clearly not enthusiastic about the developments in Paris,

> did not seem much worried. The only part of the scheme he disliked was the big economic area in the South. I told him to repudiate me [on the extent of the area] if he wished and that I fully agreed with the Cabinet decision to inform Abyssinia and Italy simultaneously.[49]

Nevertheless he considered returning home, only to be dissuaded from doing so by Lady Maud insisting that he continue the desperately needed holiday only just begun — and by the difficulty of making quick travelling arrangements. The following morning (Tuesday, 10th December) a bizarre accident ended all possibility of an immediate return. In the course of his first skating session on the specially opened rink he had another fainting fit and in his fall broke his nose in two places. The result was that, on doctor's orders, he was confined to his hotel room for several days in order to recover from the physical shock and avoid any infection of the fractures.

His enforced confinement in a Swiss hotel was made no easier by the news coming in of the gathering press and parliamentary campaign against the Paris agreements. He was understandably chagrined that in a brief debate on a highly critical Labour motion on the very day of his accident

> Baldwin, instead of insisting that the plan had been prepared at the request of the League as the basis of a compromise to stop the war, talked of facts that, if they were fully known, would convince the whole House of the wisdom of what had happened. 'My lips are not yet unsealed. Were the trouble over, I would make my case and I guarantee that not a man would go into the lobby against me.'[50]

On Thursday the 12th Hoare's P.P.S., Mark Patrick, wrote to warn him of the divisions in the ranks of government supporters:

> I certainly don't mean to suggest ... that we are faced by a party revolt. I don't think so for a moment ... I do, however, feel very sure that there is great uneasiness, deeper and more widespread, for instance, than anything we had over the India Bill at its worst moments. I am certain I am not wrong in thinking that the state of opinion is serious.[51]

On the same day Eden, who telephoned from Geneva soon after his arrival there, and Vansittart, just back in London from Paris, both advised Hoare to return, although there is no evidence that Baldwin did the same, troubling though the political situation was obviously becoming. Hoare now desperately wanted to take the advice but his doctor absolutely forbade him to travel until the 15th (Sunday), and then only by a daytime flight.

Even when Hoare had arrived back in London the agonising experience of being at the centre of a crisis without being able effectively to influence its course continued. He was confined to his house and allowed only a few visitors until, at the very earliest, 19th December — such was the medical directive. He was thus unable to attend the vital meetings at which the Cabinet decided, in face of the mounting political opposition — and, above all, the dissatisfaction in the ranks of the government's own parliamentary supporters — to renege on its original decision to back the proposals. Of the visitors Hoare did receive at Cadogan Gardens the two most helpful were Neville Chamberlain, who acted as his spokesman in Cabinet, and his old and loyal friend Beaverbrook, who had early written to assure him that 'My desire is to back you up, to support and sustain you in the present difficulty ... to stand unswervingly in support of you in this crisis'.[52]

Chamberlain called on the 16th, the day after Hoare's return, and heard from him a confident justification of the Paris proposals, which Chamberlain then recounted at the meeting of the Cabinet on the following morning, the 17th. There could be no further sanctions, in Hoare's view, unless all League members were prepared to back them up and face the possible military consequences. At present there was no indication that any other nation had made any preparations, with the result that the consequences would fall on Britain alone. The kind of peace terms envisaged by those who condemned the Hoare-Laval proposals could be obtained only 'as a result of a League success equivalent to great victories in the field'. Since such terms could not be dictated to Italy, those hammered out in Paris were the best available. It was time, Hoare thought, that the League faced up to the realities of the situation.[53]

Hoare's Cabinet colleagues were less confident, however. Their main concern now was to devise a formula which Eden could announce at the meeting of the League Council on the afternoon of the 18th to extricate them from the exposed position in which they found themselves. A meeting of ministers was held late on the 16th and the discussion was resumed in full Cabinet the next morning. The Cabinet — which had only a few days before urged the acceptance of the proposals on the parties concerned — now agreed that Eden should make it clear that the British government was no longer recommending acceptance if (as was now increasingly obvious) they did not meet the agreement of Abyssinia, Italy and the League. But the Cabinet was still at this stage prepared for the actual negotiation of the Paris proposals to be defended in the Commons debate on an Opposition censure motion arranged for 19th December. Baldwin, Chamberlain and Eden were deputed to see Hoare both to secure his agreement to the League Council formula and to determine with him the general line to be adopted in the debate.[54]

When his three colleagues saw him on the 17th (Eden only briefly since he was catching the boat train for Geneva) Hoare readily agreed to the League formula, which in no sense conflicted with the principles on which he had acted in Paris, one of which was that the British and French governments were acting on behalf of the League and that it was for the League, as much as for Italy or Abyssinia, to accept or reject the plan. Both Baldwin and Chamberlain departed with the assurance, according to Hoare's retrospective account, that 'we all stand together'.[55] That evening Hoare sent over to Chamberlain a copy of the speech he had been drafting (with help from Vansittart and Beaverbrook) for the coming debate; and Chamberlain sat up late studying it in preparation for the Cabinet meeting on the following morning.[56]

But when the Cabinet met on the morning of Wednesday, 18th December, it was soon clear that, far from all standing together with the Foreign Secretary, a decisive number wanted to repudiate him. It became not just a question of acknowledging that the public opposition to the Hoare-Laval proposals made their implementation virtually impossible but that Hoare had been wrong to enter into them in the first place and had exceeded his Cabinet authority in doing so. The practical conclusion to that was Hoare's resignation.

No one can be certain what led to this *volte-face*. Hoare himself felt in retrospect — and it seems a reasonable supposition — that the decisive factor was a meeting of the Conservative backbench Foreign Affairs Committee, under the chairmanship of Sir Austen Chamberlain, on Tuesday afternoon (the 17th). Chamberlain had gone to the meeting, so his brother Neville told Hoare, with the intention of supporting the agreement as 'the least bad of several bad alternatives' and initially spoke in this vein. But the feeling in the committee had been so strongly against the proposals that Chamberlain changed his mind and spoke a second time to join in the condemnation. His revised verdict was immediately carried to a simultaneous meeting of National Liberals (from which Simon, the party leader, absented himself) and fanned the flames of opposition there. With such a demonstration of backbench feeling, the next day's Cabinet became what Hoare later described as 'a stampede'.[57]

The discussion in Cabinet on 18th December must rank as one of the most unprepossessing of modern times. Almost to a man Cabinet members turned on an absent colleague unable to defend himself in an attempt to saddle him with the sole responsibility for their present discomfiture. With understandable discretion Hankey permitted only a brief and bowdlerised version of the minutes (conclusions) to be circulated, keeping a much fuller account – parts of it not even committed to the typewriter, but indited in his own hand – under lock and key.[58] Neville Chamberlain began the discussion by giving a résumé of what Hoare was proposing to say in the debate, from which it was clear that, although the Foreign Secretary was prepared to accept that, in view of public opinion, the government could not continue to support the plan, he had not changed his mind about the rightness of his action: the peace proposals were dead but they had been the best that could be obtained through negotiation. In the subsequent discussion all but five of the ministers present (Eden was in Geneva) are recorded as having participated. Only Zetland felt that the Cabinet should not repudiate the responsibility for the Paris proposals it had accepted nine days before. All the others were acutely unhappy about the parliamentary situation (itself a reflection of the pressure of opinion outside) and of the effects on it of an unrepentant speech by Hoare; Baldwin spoke of 'a worse situation in the House of Commons than he had ever known' and forecast a drop in the government's normally massive majority to a mere 100 in the debate. At the very minimum Hoare must recant and disown the Paris proposals along with the rest of the Cabinet, but at least four members (J. H. Thomas, Ormsby-Gore, Halifax and Walter Elliot) suggested that this was not enough and that there was really no alternative to his resigning and delivering his speech as a backbencher. The main lines of the cover story that government spokesmen were to deploy in the parliamentary debates on the following day (particularly Halifax in the House of Lords)[59] and subsequently were then in effect sketched out: that the Cabinet had not authorised Hoare to discuss peace proposals with Laval and had accepted them initially, against widespread doubts, only because of their confidence in Hoare, a confidence which — such was the implication — had been sorely abused. As Lord Swinton (as Cunliffe-Lister had just become) said in the discussion: 'They would never have approved negotiations on those lines if they had been asked to do so before the Foreign Secretary went to Paris; nor could they ever agree in the Paris communiqué expressing satisfaction with the terms.' It was not clear whether the Cabinet as a whole would now be content with a recantation from Hoare or whether his resignation was required, but undoubtedly Halifax struck a receptive chord when he commented that much more was at stake than the loss of the Foreign Secretary, 'namely, the whole moral position of the Government before the world', and that he thought the Foreign Secretary should resign; he omitted to point out how the government's moral position might be affected by so obviously bowing to ill-informed public pressure.

Chamberlain was once again the intermediary between Hoare and his Cabinet colleagues. According to Hoare's published account Chamberlain

> had been asked to tell me that my proposed statement did not go far enough, and that it was necessary for me to say that the plan was bad, that I had been mistaken in accepting it, and that in view of the general opposition I withdrew my support of it. I told him at once that I was not prepared to make any such recantation. I was convinced that nothing short of the proposals would save Abyssinia and prevent Mussolini from joining the Hitler front. This being so, resignation, not recantation, was the only course open to me.

Chamberlain's own brief diary account of this conversation merely records that he had the 'distasteful task' of reporting the Cabinet discussion to Hoare, who 'said he must make his speech and would announce his resignation'.[60] In his resignation speech in the Commons next day Hoare said that he could not 'honestly recant' from the view that 'the course I took was the only course that was possible in the circumstances' but that as soon as he realised that he had lost 'the confidence of the great body of opinion in the country' he decided to resign 'without any prompting, without any suggestion from anyone'.[61] The decisive influence, however, must surely have been the attitude of his colleagues. While Chamberlain may have spared Hoare the knowledge that several Cabinet members felt that only resignation would suffice he did apparently show him a slip of paper, passed to him during the Cabinet, on which Halifax had written the suggestion that Hoare should resign in his own interests (a rather different emphasis from Halifax's spoken concern with 'the whole moral position of the Government').[62] It is thus impossible to determine whether Hoare resigned because he refused to subscribe to the new Cabinet line or because he realised that his continued presence was no longer desired by a substantial number of his colleagues; but in either case he could have no reason to be impressed by their loyalty, and it says much for the intensity of his political ambition that he was eager to rejoin them six months later. Hoare's resignation was finalised when Baldwin came to see him at six that evening, after which Hoare wrote to Wigram to place his resignation in the hands of the King;[63] the official announcement was made from Downing Street at 9.30 p.m.

The speech on which Hoare had been working for the last few days had now to be substantially revised. Sentences like 'I felt and my colleagues felt that the situation was so acute that it was necessary to make a serious attempt for a negotiated peace' and 'I must now summarise the Government's position' clearly had to go.[64] What was to have been a defence of the government had now to become the speech of a resigned minister. But it was a resignation speech with a difference. Whereas most such speeches are vehicles for the ex-minister to explain the policy difference or differences with his colleagues which had caused him to resign rather than sink his doubts in the anonymity of Cabinet collective responsibility, Hoare's speech studiously refrained from mentioning his colleagues directly at all. Its chief concern was to do what the Cabinet had now decided it could not do — to defend the Paris agreement as a reasonable, if doomed, attempt to provide a peaceful solution to the crisis provoked by Italy's invasion of Abyssinia.

The debate on 19th December would have attracted enormous attention even if the Foreign Secretary had not resigned only a few hours before it was due to begin. But now that that resignation had taken place the debate became the most dramatic parliamentary occasion in the experience of most of the M.P.s present. In the view of friends and critics alike Hoare, never an inspiring speaker and now seriously inconvenienced by his broken nose, rose to the occasion and delivered perhaps the most effective speech of his career.[65] For the first time for thirteen years he had to address the House elsewhere than from the front bench — he was in the traditional third bench below the gangway — but he gave, nevertheless, the best kind of front bench speech: authoritative, closely argued and, for all the three quarters of an hour it took to deliver, succinct. It was all the more dramatic since, as a personal statement, it preceded the debate whereas if Hoare had still been Foreign Secretary it would have followed Attlee's speech moving the censure motion.[66]

Hoare first described at some length the events leading up to his discussions with Laval in Paris. Despite all efforts to avoid it, including his own attempt to 'mobilise world opinion' in his Assembly speech, war had broken out over Abyssinia and every day that it continued it involved the world in greater and more dangerous problems.

> There was trouble in the East; there was trouble in Egypt; there was trouble brewing in more than one quarter of Europe; and, not least, there was the depressing fact that the war seemed to be compromising British relations with a large body of public opinion in France.

As Foreign Secretary Hoare had done everything in his power to make a settlement possible while, at the same time, ensuring that Britain played its full part in League action against the aggressor. A turning point in both aspects of this 'double task' had come about a fortnight ago with the new situation created by the possibility of an oil embargo.

> From all sides we received reports that no responsible govern-ment could disregard that Italy would regard the oil embargo as a military sanction or an act involving war against her. Let me make our position quite clear. We had no fear as a nation whatever of any Italian threats. If the Italians attacked

us we should retaliate ... with full success. What was in our mind was something very different, that an isolated attack of this kind launched upon one Power, without ... the full support of the other Powers, would, it seemed to me, almost inevitably lead to the dissolution of the League.

It was in these circumstances that ten days ago, reluctantly but in response to an urgent request, he went to Paris. His conversations there with Laval took place

in an atmosphere of threatened war ... in which the majority of member States — indeed, I would say the totality of member States — appeared to be opposed to military action. It was a moment of great urgency. Within five days the question of the oil embargo was to come up at Geneva, and I did not feel myself justified in proposing any postponement of the embargo, unless it could be shown to the League that negotiations had actually started. It was a moment when it seemed to me that Anglo-French co-operation was essential if there was to be no breach at Geneva.

The proposals that emerged from two days of strenuous discussion contained features which neither he nor Laval liked. But they seemed to provide 'the only basis upon which it was even remotely likely that we could start a peace discussion' and they were the minimum upon which the French government was prepared to proceed. Hoare had felt that 'the dangers of the continuance of the war were so serious that it was worth making an attempt, and that it was essential to maintain Anglo-French solidarity'. It was in this spirit that he had agreed to the suggestions and (referring to one of the most criticised features of the events in Paris) had subscribed to the final communiqué expressing satisfaction with the terms.

Hoare then went on to examine the proposals themselves. His conclusion was that as a whole they were 'immensely less favourable to Italy' than the demands Mussolini had made to Eden in Rome in June. And Hoare maintained that he had not neglected the Abyssinian side of the controversy. His chief fear had been

that we might lead Abyssinia on to think that the League could do more than it can do, that in the end we should find a terrible moment of disillusionment in which it might be that Abyssinia would be altogether destroyed as an independent State.

He recognised that 'the present peace negotiations have failed' but the problem of settlement remained, made all the more difficult and dangerous by that failure.

> Now that we are entering upon this new chapter it is essential, if collective action is to be real and effective, that we go beyond the period of general protestations and that we should have actual proof of action from the member States that are concerned ... We alone have taken ... military precautions ... Not a ship, not a machine, not a man has been moved by any other member State.[67] Now that negotiations have failed, we must have something more than these general protestations of loyalty to the League.

It was, in fact, a choice between the full co-operation of all League members and 'the kind of unsatisfactory compromise that was contemplated in the suggestions which M. Laval and I put up'. In the situation with which he was confronted a fortnight ago, in the absence of any assurance of the full co-operation of other League members, 'the course I took was the only course that was possible in the circumstances'.

Hoare ended by emphasising how essential it was for a Foreign Secretary, more than any other minister,

> to have behind him the general approval of his fellow-countrymen. I have not got that general approval behind me today. As soon as I realised that fact, without any prompting, without any suggestion from anyone, I asked the Prime Minister to accept my resignation.

Then, betraying by a catch in his voice the only overt sign of the emotional strain he was undergoing, Hoare wished his successor, whoever he might be, 'better luck than I have had in the last two weeks' and sat down. As he did so, he felt a sudden shoot of pain in his nose which made him instinctively to put a hand to it — an action which caused some onlookers to think that he was weeping. The myth that he burst into tears at the end of his speech dogged him to the end of his life and is still perpetuated.[68]

The subsequent debate was of variable quality, and rarely matched the drama and quality of the speech which had immediately preceded it. Baldwin was singularly ineffective but in a sense the very abjectness of his contrition served to turn the wrath of his backbenchers. He was helped by Attlee's accusation against his honour for having followed a policy inconsistent with his election pledges. This apparently led the always chivalrous Austen Chamberlain to fall in line behind his party leader. His support for the government was thought by many to be both crucial (as Hoare had considered it to be in the Indian debates) but, in this instance, uncertain. In view of his contribution to the debate on 5th December, however, it would have been difficult for him to do other than support it, unless he had upbraided the government for not continuing to support the Hoare-Laval proposals.[69] In the division the government had a majority of 232, only the independent Liberals and a few unaffiliated M.P.s (including Eleanor Rathbone) voting with the Labour Opposition. The sacrifice of Hoare had clearly paid handsome dividends for the Baldwin government.

Hoare had not heard the debate. He left the House just as Attlee began to speak and three days later left London with Lady Maud to resume the holiday in Switzerland which had begun so disastrously. The loss of high office, and in such circumstances, could not be anything but a bitter blow to a politician as ambitious as Hoare. But there were consolations. One was the shower of letters he or Lady Maud received — some 200 of them — expressing both sympathy and admiration for the dignity of his resignation speech.[70] They came, among others, from Sir Clive Wigram on behalf of the King (with whom Hoare had the usual audience to surrender his seals and who was to die four weeks later); from Cabinet colleagues and other political associates, including Neville Chamberlain, Halifax (who discreetly omitted any reference to his own, possibly decisive, share in Hoare's downfall and spoke as an 'old friend' in congratulating him on the 'Courage: Candour: Sincerity: and great dignity' of his speech), Runciman ('Your speech was not only dignified and ... lofty in tone, but also so wise in its frank recital of our position and of the necessity for an early peace that you can await the verdict of the future calmly'), Duff Cooper, Churchill (from Tangier), Amery and Winterton; political opponents

(Attlee and Stafford Cripps); foreign diplomats (Maisky, the Russian Ambassador, Grandi and Jan Masaryk); and friends and colleagues from various phases of his career, including Peter Struve, Findlater Stewart, the Archbishop of Canterbury, Osbert Sitwell and the young journalist Malcolm Muggeridge, who had met and corresponded with Hoare while working for an Indian paper ('... when you became Foreign Secretary I thought there was just a chance of our being saved from the idealogues, at least in foreign affairs; now that you've been thrown to them — a malicious angry pack — I know there isn't'). Perhaps even more impressive were letters Hoare did not see. Two old India Bill colleagues, for example, commiserated with each other on his resignation. Linlithgow wrote to Lothian to say that 'the Government has lost one of its best men, and the man best equipped for the very difficult job of Foreign Secretary', while Lothian agreed that the loss of Hoare from the Foreign Office was 'a calamity' and doubted whether his successor, Eden (whose appointment was announced on 22nd December) was 'a big enough man for the job'.[71]

Many of the letters — including those from Wigram, Attlee, Duff Cooper, Neville Chamberlain, Churchill and Winterton — anticipated Hoare's early return to the government: indeed Winterton quoted people as saying 'He'll be Prime Minister in two years' time', while Chamberlain expressed to Lady Maud his hope 'to live to see him P.M. yet'.[72] Hoare's courage in resigning was frequently contrasted in public comment — even in those parts of the press hostile to the Hoare-Laval proposals — with the pusillanimity of the government which had made him the scapegoat for its own shortcomings. The implication of this, too, was that there could be no final exclusion of so able and experienced a politician from future office. It remains a matter for speculation whether there was in fact a firm arrangement for Hoare's return. According to a retrospective account of the affair by Beaverbrook, Baldwin — initially through Chamberlain — offered Hoare Cabinet office at the earliest possible moment provided he resigned without compromising the government and later followed this up with a confirmatory letter.[73] This letter seems to have disappeared but there is in the Baldwin Papers a letter from Hoare, dated 22nd December, which could well have been a reply to it. In it Hoare wrote:

Thank you very much for your letter. I believe I have succeeded in doing what you wanted me to do. I have kept the country out of war. The result is an immense relief to me and I care not what may be the personal consequences to me ... [74]

Hoare's P.P.S., Mark Patrick, quoted Baldwin as saying openly that 'it won't be six months before Sam is back,' while Baldwin told Austen Chamberlain on 21st December that:

his only comforting reflection as regards Sam Hoare's resignation was that he might now entirely recover his health and give many more years of service to the country, whereas if he had continued in office he would have had a permanent breakdown.[75]

Hoare, as he finally went off to recuperate, had thus every reason for believing that his traumatic experience was only a temporary interruption in a political career which might yet encompass the highest office of all. That was certainly the view of a young colleague who knew him well. R. A. Butler wrote to Brabourne on 19th December:

Sam's resignation is of course a great blow to me since he was my patron in politics, and I owe him a great deal. He has shown his usual acumen and courage in getting in his resignation quickly, and I think that if his health improves, and he is able to reduce the tempo of his life, and be patient, it may make a very great man of him, since he has not had to take this sort of step previously in his career. There is no doubt that he will have a strong body of opinion in the country ready to face realism with him, and if his future conduct is impressive, he will remain the kind of 'spear-head' modern leader, as against the lumbering democratic one who will remain Head of the Government after his departure.[76]

However sympathetically Hoare's part in the chain of events leading up to his resignation as Foreign Secretary is viewed, especially when set beside the extraordinary contortions of his Cabinet colleagues in seeking to place what was a collective responsibility on his individual shoulders, it is nevertheless difficult to acquit him of a serious error of judgement in concluding what could so easily be represented as a hard and fast agreement

to secure peace by the dismemberment of Abyssinia. His retrospective account acknowledges this and is here in refreshing
contrast to the general run of self-exculpatory political memoir-
writing. He blamed himself, as we have already noted, for not
having insisted on a special Cabinet, in advance of the Paris
visit, to come to a clear agreement 'as to how far I could go
with Laval'[77] — apparently forgetting that the Cabinet on 2nd
December had given him virtually *carte blanche*, with the emphasis on taking 'a generous view of the Italian attitude'. He
also blamed himself for not being in closer touch with public
opinion and thus failing to realise the need for a long effort of
preparation before approval of the plan could be expected (but
here the premature leak hardly helped the process).

> The details of the actual position should have been stated and
> re-stated for weeks on end — how we and the French were
> only making recommendations ... for submission to the
> League, how much of the territory involved was unadminis-
> tered and unpopulated desert, and finally how formidable
> were the risks to Europe of a complete break with Italy. The
> facts of a grim situation needed to be faced in concrete form.
> The trouble was that there was little or no time for this full
> explanation, and my impatience for a settlement suppressed
> my natural instinct for caution.[78]

But one rather painful truth Hoare did not admit: that the
plan, like all its predecessors, had no real chance of acceptance
by the parties concerned. Although there were indications that
Mussolini might be prepared to consider the plan — and Drummond in Rome was insistent that he would have done but for the
British and League public reaction against it — it would at the
most have been as the basis for further negotiation in which he
would have demanded more concessions. Having rejected previous plans before the Italian invasion he was hardly likely to be
content with little more now that Abyssinia was militarily at his
mercy. Haile Selassie, who had provisionally accepted the
Committee of Five plan in September only because he was certain of Italian rejection of it, was equally unlikely to accept the
Hoare-Laval proposals, being understandably unwilling to
recognise that half a loaf might be better than no bread. For
other League members the inevitable fact that aggression must

seem to have been rewarded would at that time have been difficult to swallow, unaware as they were that in six months' time
the aggressor's reward would become complete, with the total
subjugation of Abyssinia. Vansittart at the time argued that
Laval had said in Paris that before the French people could be
brought to face the possibility of war it was essential for a reasonable offer to have been made to Mussolini and refused by
him: in other words, that an Italian rejection of the Hoare-
Laval proposals might have provided a French *casus belli*.[79] But
whatever Laval may have told Hoare and Vansittart, it seems
inherently improbable that this could have been a genuine
motive for his eagerness to settle terms for an agreement with
Hoare; nor is it an argument that Hoare himself ever used.

Part of the explanation for Hoare's lapse from his normally
shrewd and politically sensitive caution has been sought in the
influence over him of the extraordinary man who was officially
his chief Civil Service adviser. At least one newspaper (the
News Chronicle) claimed at the time to see in Vansittart 'The
Man Behind It All', and so have other commentators since. A
letter which Vansittart wrote, five days after the Paris talks, to a
sympathetic member of the Cabinet (Runciman) seems to
suggest that he even thought so himself. 'I am indeed distressed
to think that I have been responsible for embarrassing any of
you, and of course particularly Sam', Vansittart wrote on 13th
December.[80] This was a curious apology to make, even from so
politically committed a civil servant. As Foreign Secretary
Hoare would never have attempted to evade his ministerial
responsibility for the results of the Paris talks, however much
he might have listened to, and agreed with, the assessment of his
chief adviser, and all his subsequent actions, including his resignation, gave proof of the fact. It may have been that Vansittart
was referring to something rather different. On three days immediately before departing for Paris he had discussed the details of Italian territorial ambitions in Abyssinia with Grandi.
The departmental minutes of these conversations (which were
seen by both Hoare and Eden) show them to have been ex-
ploratory, with no agreement reached. But the reports that
Grandi sent back to Rome indicated that Vansittart played a
much more active, even compromising, role than his superiors
realised. In fact, after the Hoare-Laval proposals were known

Grandi was claiming that they were 'halfway between the proposals which Vansittart made him on 3rd December and the concessions which Vansittart had been induced to accept on 5th December'.[81] Perhaps Vansittart was troubled lest these talks with Grandi, which Laval would almost certainly have heard about from his Italian contacts, had made it difficult for Hoare to induce Laval to agree to more equitable terms for a settlement.[82]

Some people who knew Hoare well — including Trenchard and Liddell Hart as well as several of his Cabinet colleagues — believed that his recent ill-health and the strains of office over many months had influenced his actions in Paris.[83] But again Hoare himself never attempted to plead ill-health, either at the time or subsequently, although he was clearly far from fit and, as we have seen, was absolutely exhausted when the talks were over.

To attempt to seek such explanations is, however, to ignore how much the Hoare-Laval proposals were really implicit in the policy which Hoare had been bequeathed as Foreign Secretary and which he was virtually powerless to alter, even if he had wanted to. The Paris agreement can be seen as a last desperate effort to make that policy viable by saving Abyssinia from complete extinction but yet avoiding any danger of British involvement in an isolated war with Italy. Hoare failed, but so did his successor, and perhaps even more lamentably. Within six months of Eden's assumption of the Foreign Secretaryship Abyssinia had surrendered and all League sanctions against Italy had been lifted (the oil sanction was never imposed, Eden having failed to persuade either the Cabinet, the French or the League to accept it); the warning Hoare had given Laval on 7th December of the danger of provoking 'the accusation that all the League had managed to do was to ruin Abyssinia' had become stark reality. A shrewd German diplomatist had forecast in February (1936) that this would be the outcome of the expenditure of moral fervour over the Hoare-Laval pact. 'You have found a whipping-boy for Mussolini in Hoare', Hans Dieckhoff told Arnold Toynbee. 'Now that you have relieved your feelings at Hoare's expense you will not feel any impulse to save Ethiopia by having a showdown with Mussolini'. For Sir Maurice Peterson, intimately involved in the negotiations at the time, 'the real appeasement lay not in trying to save what could be saved but in the subsequent letting-go of the whole'.[84] But during the same period an event took place of much greater importance to the peace of the world than Italy's brutal and anachronistic war in an insalubrious corner of tropical Africa. In March 1936 Germany, once again in defiance of the Versailles treaty, remilitarised the Rhineland – an action unopposed (except verbally) by Britain or France and made all the easier by the disarray among the Stresa allies caused by the Anglo-French quarrel with Italy over Abyssinia. It was the Rhineland occupation rather than the essentially peripheral crisis over Italian aggression in Abyssinia that led to the holocaust of 1939 and after. And in March 1936 the Germans were felt by many in Britain, including some of those most exercised over Abyssinia, to be merely regaining full possession of 'their own backyard'.

> History has perhaps never played a stranger trick upon Man [a perceptive observer has written] than to allow British indignation against [Italy's] international lawlessness and imperialist and racial bullying to have smoothed the path for Adolf Hitler. Out of this misconception was born that deformity, the Italo-German alliance, of which Hitler had so long dreamed.[85]

The failure of Hoare, Eden and their colleagues did, however, have the merit of finally exposing the limitations of the League of Nations as a substitute for the traditional methods of international diplomacy.[86] The policy adopted towards German expansionism between 1937 and 1939 was open to the gravest criticisms but at least it was free from the cant of confronting an aggressive major power with 'collective security through the League'.

7

Return to High Office

The Hoares spent some six weeks in Switzerland after returning there in the wake of the traumatic events that had ended their first attempt at a convalescent holiday. Now the convalescence was needed as much for mental and emotional bruising as for physical exhaustion. Hoare's vaulting political ambition had received a possibly fatal check and while he had much to rue in his own conduct he could also legitimately lament the supineness and disloyalty of Cabinet colleagues and the sheer malignancy of fate.

The cure was effected by frequent, and this time undramatic, recourse to the skating rink, by wide reading and by work on the political memoirs that he always intended to write whenever the time-consuming rigours of political life permitted. He had one or two visitors of some political importance, including his old Oxford friend Lord Astor, owner of the *Observer*, and his M.P. wife, Nancy, and maintained a friendly correspondence with the two key figures among his former colleagues, Baldwin and Neville Chamberlain. He also, inevitably, sought advice from Beaverbrook as he had done at all other crucial stages of his political career. Beaverbrook clearly saw no future in any kind of splendid isolation on the backbenches and counselled Hoare to do all that he could to assist Baldwin and his government when he returned to the political scene.[1]

Hoare was back in London on 8th February. Reading the British newspapers on the journey home he was horrified to find that much was being made of the monthly newsletter which had just been distributed to his Chelsea Conservative association members (several weeks late owing to the death of the King) and which contained his personal explanation of the Hoare-Laval affair and his resignation. The newsletter's contents seemed innocuous, merely a chattier version of his resignation speech (and including a rather maladroit phrase about the Laval meeting in Paris involving the inconvenience of 'separating myself from Lady Maud and the luggage') but *The Times* chose to see in it a reprehensible attempt to justify the Hoare-Laval proposals and to denigrate the League. Hoare wrote immediately to both Baldwin and Chamberlain to disabuse them of any idea that he was trying to make trouble: distribution of the newsletter had been by the constituency association, not by himself, and in it he had explicitly disclaimed 'any sort of criticism of my former colleagues'. He also wrote to *The Times* to assert his continued belief in the League and collective security — and in the necessity for the re-equipment of Britain's defence forces to help to make it a reality.[2]

Hoare had in fact returned at the moment when a debate on the effectiveness of British higher organisation for defence, originally sparked off by a leader in *The Times* on 2nd December, 1935, and continued in the press by correspondents as distinguished and experienced in defence matters as Lords Trenchard and Salisbury, was impinging upon internal government policy-making. The chief organisational reform — pressed in debates in both Houses on 11th and 14th February — was seen by most of the critics to be the creation of a Ministry of Defence with a full-time minister to take over and expand the existing work of the Committee of Imperial Defence under the often nominal chairmanship of a hard-pressed Prime Minister. Inside the government this proposal was fiercely contested by Hankey (virtually the creator of the existing C.I.D. system), among others, but on the whole the Cabinet was coming round to the view that some ministerial change was necessary, even if it did not go as far as a Minister of Defence *tout court*. The favoured course was a co-ordinating minister who would act as deputy to the Prime Minister in the chairmanship of the Committee of Imperial Defence, but leaving intact the autonomy of the service departments.[3] The question then arose of whom to appoint to the new post. Hoare's name, with several others (including Churchill's), was canvassed in the press and, more significantly, was advanced within the Cabinet not only by his

friend Chamberlain but by one of the bitterest Cabinet critics
of the Hoare-Laval proposals: William Ormsby-Gore, who had
virtually demanded Hoare's resignation at the Cabinet meeting
on 18th December. The desirability of instituting the new post
depended entirely on who was available to fill it, Ormsby-Gore
said in a letter to Baldwin on 11th February.

> If you are willing to consider taking Sir Samuel Hoare back
> into the Cabinet to do this job, I think he would be the right
> man in the right place, and the only man at present available.
> I would rather have no Ministerial appointment of this kind
> if it were to anybody else than Sir Samuel Hoare.[4]

Baldwin saw Hoare on 11th February for the first time since
his return and discussed generally with him the possibilities of
his return to the government. At their second meeting on 23rd
February, however, he placed before Hoare the definite prospect of appointment either to the defence co-ordination post or to
the Admiralty. The former depended upon further inquiries
which he still had to make, but he knew the Admiralty was to be
vacated by Monsell (who had recently gone to the Lords) by
Whitsun at the latest. Baldwin's own preference seemed to be for
Hoare to take the defence post and Hoare, too, found the prospect of its 'more general and less departmental duties' attractive
after his onerous departmental stints of the past thirteen years.[5]

It is not altogether clear why it was Sir Thomas Inskip, the
Attorney-General, who was appointed Minister for Co-ordination of Defence on 13th March rather than Hoare. Some felt it
was due to what was considered a premature intervention by
Hoare in a debate on the government's defence white paper on
9th March and, perhaps even more, to a rather contrived
reference to Baldwin at the end of his speech which was interpreted by some as a public solicitation to be taken back into the
government. Hoare had been arguing that the rearmament programme embodied in the white paper needed to be supported
on a national rather than an exclusively party basis, and he
concluded:

> If the Prime Minister will use his great influence upon these
> broad lines, if he will impress on the country the great urgency
> of the problems that face us, he will find a great body of sup-

port in the country, and among his followers there will be none more willing to give him support than a very old friend and former colleague who has just had the privilege of addressing the House this afternoon.[6]

Even so sympathetic a colleague as Neville Chamberlain confided to his diary that this 'sounded like an obvious and clumsy bid' for office 'and created a thoroughly bad impression', while R. A. Butler regretted that 'Sam's inability to sit back and wait has seriously prejudiced his future'.[7]

But the decisive factor in Baldwin's mind in relation to Hoare and the defence post may well have been a conversation he had with Eden, Hoare's successor as Foreign Secretary, several days before the defence debate. Eden had expressed concern at any imminent return by his predecessor in a post which so obviously overlapped with his own ministerial responsibilities; he was, however, in favour of Hoare's appointment to the Admiralty at a later date.[8] Clearly someone like Inskip, a lawyer with no known alignments in (or, indeed, without much knowledge of) defence or foreign policy questions was much less likely to cross the Foreign Secretary than so senior and experienced an ex-minister as Hoare.

On the day Inskip's appointment was announced Baldwin wrote to Hoare with the definite offer of the Admiralty to begin sometime between Easter and Whitsun, which Hoare accepted with alacrity. A month later Baldwin wrote again to say that the appointment would actually take effect at the later rather than the earlier date and Hoare, reluctantly it was clear, expressed himself as willing to 'possess my soul in quietness'.[9] Two months later, on 5th June, 1936, he returned to high office as First Lord of the Admiralty. His period of exile had lasted less than six months.

The press gave a warm welcome to the appointment of the man it had, in general, so recently vilified. The *Glasgow Herald* considered that the Cabinet had gained in prestige by Hoare's return to it, while the *Manchester Guardian* even thought the occasion an appropriate one to tip him as 'Mr. Chamberlain's most dangerous rival for the Premiership'. In the *Observer* Garvin, who had strongly supported the Hoare-Laval plan, now proclaimed that 'Seldom has the resignation of any Minister been so bitter at the moment and never has vindication been at once more swift and more complete.'[10]

The Admiralty was certainly no inappropriate department for the former Foreign Secretary whose actions had been so strongly influenced by the possible effects on Britain's strategic position of a war with Italy in the Mediterranean. One of his first ministerial duties was to supervise the run-down of the naval operation in the Mediterranean following the Cabinet's decision on 17th June (twelve days after Hoare had rejoined it) to recommend to the League Assembly that it lift sanctions against Italy (which the Assembly did on 3rd July).[11] This at once ended the enormous strain imposed on the fleet and its manning by months of war-readiness (as recently as 19th May the First Sea Lord had told a Cabinet committee that four battleships had had to be paid off to furnish men for the Mediterranean fleet, leaving the navy with only seven capital ships in operational condition[12]). At the same time, as Hoare informed the Defence Policy and Requirements Committee on 22nd June, he was able to secure an acceleration of the naval construction programme launched by his predecessor: two more cruisers (making seven in all) were to be built in the coming year and destroyer-building was to be doubled. A supplementary naval estimate was presented to the Commons on 7th July and passed on 20th July.[13] The building of further battleships was still barred under the London Naval Treaty of 1930 but as soon as this treaty expired on 31st December, 1936, Hoare ensured the two new battleships were laid down early in 1937.

As at the Air Ministry Hoare developed excellent relations with his chief professional adviser, in this case Sir Ernle Chatfield, the First Sea Lord. Chatfield later recalled how speedily Hoare got to grips with the work of the Admiralty ('in a month he knew more about our Admiralty and Fleet problems than a First Lord usually learns in six')[14] – in part, no doubt, the result of his enforced rest from the pressures of office as well as from his long familiarity with the affairs of a sister service department. And again as he had done as Air Minister Hoare informed himself about the operational side of service activities, and a well-publicised visit to the Mediterranean fleet in the Admiralty yacht *Enchantress* in September was followed by visits to Home stations and to Admiralty dockyards.

One major issue with which Hoare was concerned at the Admiralty inevitably reminded him of his Air Ministry days. Some months before Hoare became First Lord, the Admiralty had begun a campaign, in which Chatfield was very much the moving spirit, to reopen the question of the control of the Fleet Air Arm which Hoare's long tenure at the Air Ministry had seen apparently finally settled in the air force's favour. When Inskip became co-ordinating minister the problem, not inappropriately, was placed in his lap. After much effort, exchange of departmental memoranda, personal representations to Inskip and the Prime Minister by ministers and service chiefs, and at least two quite separate investigations, Inskip delivered a report on 21st July, 1937, which recommended that responsibility for selecting and training personnel and generally for the organisation of the ship-borne Fleet Air Arm should be transferred to the Admiralty but that the Royal Air Force should continue to control shore-based aircraft. The proposals were approved by the Cabinet on 29th July.[15]

Two months before this more or less final solution of what had been so fertile a source of inter-service acrimony for two decades Hoare had left the Admiralty for yet another department. But the main lines had been clearly demarcated before he did so, and as First Lord he had fully backed his First Sea Lord in all his many initiatives. Nevertheless he was obviously in a delicate position as a former Air Minister at a crucial stage of the Fleet Air Arm's development. As Chatfield later expressed it:

> Loyal as [Hoare] proved himself to the Navy, he could not be expected to conduct effectively and with conviction the case for the removal of a control that he, in earlier times, had been partly instrumental in imposing on the Service of which he had now become the political head.[16]

Thus, while Hoare provided effective support and counsel to Chatfield (as the latter's own account makes clear) he felt he could not take an active part in the various inter-departmental discussions. He recognised, however, that the situation was now quite different from that in the 1920s, when the air force was so small that any loss of aircraft and personnel might have endangered its independent existence. There was no longer any risk of a concession to the navy leading to the disruption of the independent air force: in fact, as he told an anxious Trenchard, he thought 'the R.A.F. would now be well quit of the sea-borne units'.[17] Moreover, there was a clear advantage in any step which would mitigate a bitter inter-departmental controversy. It was not difficult for Hoare thus to rationalise a decision which was so much at variance with the campaign he led at the Air Ministry in the 1920s, especially when he had not himself initiated the new naval demand nor remained at the Admiralty when the change was actually put into effect.

With what at the time seemed the dominating domestic political event of 1936 – the abdication of Edward VIII, less than eleven months after he had succeeded to the throne on the death of his father George V – Hoare had both personal and departmental connections. He had first met the then Prince of Wales during the war and had developed friendly relations with him in the intervening years. 'We had often met in London', Hoare later recalled, 'and he had dined with us in Chelsea and we with him at York House.'[18] As First Lord of the Admiralty and political head of the service in which the new King, as a one-time naval cadet, retained a continuing interest, Hoare's royal contacts were quite frequent. In October he was invited to a four-day shooting party at Sandringham and in the middle of November attended the King on a two-day inspection of the Home fleet at Portland. On both occasions he was asked by Baldwin to attempt to dissuade the King from proceeding with his plan to marry Mrs Simpson but on neither, apparently, did a suitable opportunity for such a delicate mission present itself. But when the King sought and obtained Baldwin's agreement to his seeking the advice of other members of the Cabinet Hoare was one of the two ministers he chose to consult, the other being Duff Cooper. The King saw Hoare at Buckingham Palace on 21st November, shortly before he saw Duff Cooper. His subsequent recollection of the interview agreed substantially with Hoare's. The Duke of Windsor wrote:

The First Lord of the Admiralty's temperament was not such as to encourage the belief that I might convert him into a champion of my cause. The most that I hoped from our meeting was that after hearing my story he would understand the compulsions working upon me, and might be moved, when the matter came up for formal discussion in the Cabinet — as soon it must — to speak up in defence of my right to marry. But I failed to win him as an advocate. Mr. Baldwin, he warned me, was in command of the situation: the senior Ministers were solidly behind him on this issue. If I were to press my marriage project upon the Cabinet, I should meet a stone wall of opposition.[19]

This was the last direct contact Hoare had with the King until his abdication less than three weeks later. There was indirect contact, however, through their mutual friend Beaverbrook, whom Hoare left in no doubt about the Cabinet's inflexible attitude towards the proposed marriage to Mrs Simpson, whether morganatic or otherwise. But Hoare was grateful to the crisis for bringing him once again in close touch with Beaverbrook, for the first time since his resignation the year before. As he wrote to Beaverbrook on 10th December.

> ... I am glad and grateful that another crisis brought us together again. It is almost a year to a day since my resignation. The first friendly word from the outside came from you. I never forget these things nor shall I forget our talks of the last fortnight, and your manifest wish to help me in my career.[20]

As a service minister Hoare could hardly avoid involvement in questions of foreign policy, despite any reluctance he may have had to be 'pushed back into the Foreign Office orbit' or the rather curious assurance Lord Avon claims Baldwin gave him, when he told him of his predecessor's imminent appointment to the Admiralty, that he 'need not be worried that Hoare would interfere with foreign affairs'.[21] As First Lord Hoare automatically became a member of the new Foreign Policy Committee of the Cabinet, which had met for the first time at the end of April.[22] The outbreak of civil war in Spain on 18th July — six weeks after Hoare's return to office — provided a major foreign policy issue on which the political head of the service which was expected to protect British interests in the face of the attempted blockade of the Spanish coast by the insurgents under General Franco, and other interference with peaceful trade from both sides, could not be expected to remain dumb. Hoare later recalled:

Scarcely a day passed in the autumn of 1936 and throughout 1937 that did not involve discussions with the Foreign Office over the many problems raised by incidents in Spanish waters and our policy of Non-Intervention. The Cabinet was unanimously agreed upon doing everything possible to localise the Spanish conflict. When, however, non-intervention led to interference with British shipping, complicated questions arose over belligerent rights and specific breaches of international law. Should we, for instance, escort British ships into Spanish harbours and retaliate at once against Spanish attacks? Should we sink unidentified submarines as soon as they were sighted? These were the kind of questions that were constantly arising.[23]

On at least one occasion Hoare felt it necessary to argue against a recommendation from the Foreign Secretary. A continuing and, in the end, insoluble problem was posed by the attempt to make the internationally agreed policy of non-intervention effective, in view of flagrant breaches by Italy and Germany on behalf of the Franco nationalists and, to a lesser extent, Russian aid to the Popular Front government. In January 1937 Eden proposed to a meeting of ministers that Britain should unilaterally make itself responsible for monitoring non-intervention by checking the movement of ships in and out of all Spanish harbours. There had been no prior consultation with the Admiralty about this rather ill-considered proposal and not surprisingly Hoare, on behalf of the navy which would have to put the plan into effect, opposed it. As Lord Avon later recalled:

> Hoare produced every kind of technical argument to invalidate my plan: the Spanish coast was very long, with many ports; a large number of ships would be required to examine the many neutral vessels; it would involve mobilising the Home and Mediterranean Fleets exclusively for the purpose and calling up the naval reserve; it was very difficult to carry out a blockade on the high seas, no blockade was ever watertight; and further chatter of this kind.

But it was Hoare's 'chatter' which convinced their colleagues, several of them concerned about the possibility of provoking an international incident with Italy or Russia. 'I destroyed it',

Hoare later remarked of Eden's plan.[24] Subsequently a scheme was agreed with France, Germany, Italy and the Soviet Union under which the five powers were each responsible for a portion of the Spanish coast. It may not have been very effective but at least it avoided the obvious dangers of Eden's unilateral plan.

In January 1937 also Hoare as First Lord had to deal with an issue very similar to those which arose almost as a matter of routine in his next ministerial office. He was advised by his staff to dismiss five workers in the Admiralty dockyards at Devonport and Chatham on suspicion of acts of sabotage against naval ships. Since the information on which the action was recommended came from confidential sources, including the secret service, it was not possible either to put the men on trial or inform them of the basis of the accusations against them. In consultation with Fisher, the official Head of the Civil Service, Hoare referred the evidence to a committee of three senior civil servants, which reported unanimously in favour of the men's dismissal. The Cabinet came to the same view, and Hoare then authorised the step. As in all 'civil liberties' cases there was a good deal of press criticism, while the Opposition put down a motion of censure. When the motion came to be debated on 26th January Hoare was acutely conscious of the impossibility of making a convincing reply, being unable to divulge the full details of the cases against the men without compromising the sources of information. It was, as he later recalled, 'A very sticky wicket but all our party [was] solid', defeating the Labour motion by 330 votes to 145. He was not, however, content with this technical victory. He immediately instituted discussions with the trade unions and the relevant joint industrial council (in which the formidable Ernest Bevin participated) to ensure that union representatives would be associated in any future dockyard dismissals on security grounds.[25]

As 1937 proceeded it was merely a matter of time before Baldwin resigned from the premiership and handed over to the leading member of his Cabinet and most obvious heir apparent, Neville Chamberlain. Baldwin, in his seventieth year, was determined to go and, according to Hoare, was 'Like a schoolboy counting the days to the holidays'.[26] Procedural constraints made it difficult to time the takeover before the end of May, and in particular the coronation of George VI on 12th May and the opening of the Imperial Conference (which Hoare addressed on naval questions) immediately following this on 14th May. But ambitious politicians were jockeying for position in the new administration well before Baldwin's actual retirement on 28th May. Despite the relative recentness of his return to the government and the equivocal circumstances in which he had originally left it, Hoare was very definitely of that number. Chamberlain was Hoare's closest Cabinet colleague and on several occasions had advanced his claims to promotion when others had the final decision. With Chamberlain as Prime Minister Hoare could clearly look forward to preferment. The Admiralty was not the office he would have chosen for himself had the field been wider in March 1936 and it was understandable that he should seek other opportunities in the coming Cabinet even if it might have been better for his reputation if he could have contained his ambition a little longer (he himself later regretted his tendency 'to tire of an enterprise before it was fully completed'[27]). His sights were set on the Chancellorship of the Exchequer, not so much for its intrinsic interest to him as for what it meant in terms of the eventual succession to the highest office of all. Others, too, including some press comment (as in the *Morning Post* on 15th March) and the head of the Treasury, Warren Fisher, also assumed that Hoare would have the reversion of the post that Chamberlain would vacate on becoming Prime Minister. But Chamberlain had other ideas: he decided that the Chancellorship must go to the leader of the only remaining recognisable group of non-Conservatives in the exiguously National Government, Sir John Simon. When Chamberlain discussed a new appointment with Hoare it was to offer him any post other than the Treasury. After a day's reflection Hoare chose the Home Office, a choice which had Chamberlain's full approval since, as he told Hoare, 'he wanted me for general policy'.[28] On 28th May, 1937, the day Chamberlain at last succeeded Baldwin, Hoare thus became 'His Majesty's Principal Secretary of State for the Home Department'.

The Home Office was in many ways a most appropriate department for Hoare at this stage of his career. All his previous extensive departmental experience had been in service and overseas departments. For his first home departmental appointment nothing, apart from the Treasury, could have been more prestigious than the Home Office. And although the Home Office was the traditional 'rag bag' of departments, with multifarious as well as onerous responsibilities, there were among its functions challenges to Hoare's skills in departmental administration, legislation and policy-making more personally agreeable to him than anything the Treasury would have been able to offer.

But in the first few months of his new portfolio it was perhaps onerousness rather than personal satisfaction that was more to the fore. There was, immediately, an immensely complicated piece of factory legislation (for which the Home Office was still then responsible) to see through its final stages in the Commons, and Hoare's ability to read and master briefs rapidly was put to an early test among its 300 clauses. The major legislative task, however, concerned one of the newer responsibilities of the department, that for what was then known as Air Raid Precautions, and later as Civil Defence. When the creation of a special A.R.P. department within an existing department was being considered in 1934 the chief candidates had been the Ministry of Health, the department most closely concerned with the local authorities which would necessarily play a leading part in the administration of any comprehensive A.R.P. scheme, and the Home Office, with its responsibility for the police. The Home Office, with no great enthusiasm on its part, was the ministry finally selected and in April 1935 an A.R.P. department was formed under its aegis.[29] It was something of a sickly infant. On the one hand it was not considered wise to advertise or speedily develop its activities for fear of spreading alarm and despondency among the population while on the other – on the strength of grossly exaggerated official estimates of the effects of aerial bombing – there was a widespread feeling that the likelihood of a 'knock-out blow' from an enemy strong in the air made any attempt at civilian defence both costly and probably ineffective. The Abyssinian crisis gave a mild fillip to A.R.P. work since reports that the Italians had used gas in the campaign led to an intensification of anti-gas preparations. It was not an unmixed blessing, however, since it led to the diversion of very limited resources to what was certainly a soluble danger (in the sense that a 'knock-out blow' was not) but one which, in the event, never materialised.

When Hoare became Home Secretary the A.R.P. organisation was thus extremely small-scale, mostly concerned with the supply of gas respirators. In addition it had become bogged down in a dispute between the Treasury and local authorities about finance. Hoare lost little time in coming to grips with the problem, in contrast to the indecision of his two immediate predecessors, Gilmour (1932–5) and Simon (1935–7),[30] and before 1937 was out an Air Raid Precautions Act had been passed to provide local authorities with a 60 per cent grant, rising to 75 per cent for the poorer authorities. At the same time Hoare introduced an organisational strengthening with the appointment of an able senior civil servant, Wilfrid Eady (then Secretary of the Unemployment Assistance Board) as head of the A.R.P. department with the rank of deputy under secretary of state. The following year saw an intensive drive for volunteers for the A.R.P. service, which reached the million mark soon after the Munich crisis. Hoare led the way with speeches, broadcasts and well-advertised visits to A.R.P. exercises and the like, while his young and energetic parliamentary under secretary, Geoffrey Lloyd, was particularly active on this side of the department's work. Hoare obtained the highly experienced services of Sir John Anderson, a former permanent head of the Home Office who had recently returned from the Governorship of Bengal and entered the House of Commons as Scottish Universities' M.P. in January 1938, to chair a committee to advise on evacuation policy in the event of air attack — a feature of A.R.P. organisation which came in for particularly harsh criticism during the Munich crisis when war, and heavy air attacks on London, had for a time seemed imminent.[31]

But perhaps Hoare's most distinctive personal contribution to Air Raid Precautions lay in the creation of a special corps of women volunteers — the Womens' Voluntary Service (W.V.S., later W.R.V.S.) — and, not less important, in persuading Lady Reading to head it. The inaugural meeting of the new organisation was held, under Hoare's chairmanship, at the Home Office on 16th May, 1938. The move was by no means welcomed by the Home Office staff, especially when Hoare insisted on giving Lady Reading the status of a deputy under-secretary and accommodating her small headquarters staff in the Home Office itself.[32] When, nine years later (and two years after the end of the war), the W.V.S. was put on a permanent basis, Lady Reading wrote to Lord Templewood:

> ... I hope and believe that you have still a strong paternal interest in this body of yours, which you brought into the world with such farsightedness and wisdom, and I cannot tell you how deeply I feel at realising that we have been given the privilege of service ... I, personally, can never thank you enough for the results that have come of that decision you made nine years ago, and for that reason I do want you to know that the W.V.S. is to continue and will play its part for the community.[33]

The expansion of A.R.P. services naturally meant a greater load on the responsible minister and immediately after the Munich crisis Hoare sought to divest himself of it. He wrote to Chamberlain in October 1938 to complain that 'the burden of A.R.P. is too heavy for me with all my other work' and at the end of that month, at Hoare's suggestion, Sir John Anderson was appointed Lord Privy Seal to take over the supervision of the A.R.P. department and the co-ordination of inter-departmental policy on all aspects of civilian defence.[34] Until the outbreak of war, however, Anderson exercised these functions by delegation from the Home Secretary and his staff in their official correspondence had to employ the cumbrous periphrasis, 'I am directed by the Lord Privy Seal in the exercise of the functions of the Secretary of State for the Home Department.' But thereafter Hoare, although he still had to give Anderson — a poor parliamentary performer — a certain amount of political assistance, was relieved of the major administrative load.

Hoare's most demanding but absorbing policy and legislative concern at the Home Office — almost on the scale of the Government of India Bill — was fated not to come to fruition, cut off by the advent of the war to which the expansion of civil defence had been directed. As a lineal descendant of one of the founders of what became the Howard League for Penal Reform and a great-grand nephew of Elizabeth Fry he could not fail to respond to one of the most basic of his department's responsibilities, that for the penal system. By convenient chance, the prison vote had to be moved in the Commons just a week after Hoare became Home Secretary and he was able, in what he later considered to be his most successful speech in the House, to give a sympathetic and well-received account of recent reforms in prison regime. He described, for example, experiments with a new approach to the granting of privileges to prisoners. Traditionally the full rigours of prison discipline were inflicted upon new inmates, who only slowly and precariously gained the small privileges that brought them nearer to normal life. But reformers had urged that the better course was to leave them from the first in possession of certain privileges, with the knowledge that they would lose them on bad behaviour. The experiments, on a limited scale, had proved successful in terms of prison morale and discipline and it was now proposed to extend the system.[35] In recent years there had been a number of reports by royal commissions or departmental inquiries on various aspects of the treatment of offenders – probation, approved schools, Borstal treatment, preventive detention, corporal punishment and mental responsibility among them – and the question Hoare had to decide early in his term as Home Secretary was whether action should be taken on them and, if so, in what form. On the one hand it was urged by some of his advisers that each separate issue could best be tackled in the form of private members' bills, minimising the calls on the government's legislative timetable and perhaps minimising also governmental involvement in the popular controversy that social reform measures so often provoke. On the other, there were those who favoured an overtly government-sponsored and comprehensive bill, and it was this course that Hoare himself favoured and with little hesitation decided to adopt. There was his genuine family and personal commitment to penal reform, coupled with a perfectly reasonable ambition to be associated with a major piece of domestic legislation – as a counterpart, so to speak, to the Government of India Act; there was also a desire on Hoare's part to provide some sort of ideological bridge between an overwhelmingly Conservative administration and the Labour Opposition – and, indeed, the real opposition to the measure was to come, not from the Labour or Liberal parties, but from Conservative backbenchers, including many of those who had been such thorns in Hoare's flesh during the Indian debates.[36]

In November 1937 Hoare was able to circulate the general lines of a comprehensive Criminal Justice Bill to the Cabinet and soon secured its approval for the introduction of legislation. His legislative zeal did not go unmarked by his colleagues, however. As Butler (then junior minister in the Ministry of Labour) reported to Brabourne,

> Sam has caused a good deal of antipathy by managing to crowd out some other Cabinet Ministers at the gate and get in with his Prison Reform Bill, when he had hardly finished with his Air Raids Precaution Bill. There is naturally a good deal of jealousy but he is increasing daily in administrative ability, not concealing that he does not suffer fools gladly.[37]

There followed several months of wide-ranging consultations with the various expert and interested bodies and individuals. 'I imagine', Hoare later wrote, 'that few Ministers have ever had more interviews about a single measure than I had in connection with the Criminal Justice Bill.'[38] As at the India Office, with the Government of India Bill, he worked in close partnership with his permanent under-secretary, who at the Home Office from early in 1938 was Sir Alexander Maxwell. Hoare had himself secured Maxwell's appointment, on the retirement of Sir Russell Scott, despite fierce opposition from Warren Fisher. Fisher had favoured the appointment of a Treasury man; Maxwell, on the contrary, had served his whole career in the Home Office, latterly as Chairman of the Prison Commission and then as deputy under-secretary. Maxwell, who retired in 1948, was one of the Home Office's most distinguished permanent heads and his appointment, against the advice of the Civil Service establishment, was further evidence of Hoare's ability to pick the right man for the job.[39]

The Bill, with 83 clauses and ten schedules, was ready for its second reading at the end of November 1938. Under its provisions such long-established but now rather disagreeable terms of the language of penal deterrence as 'penal servitude', 'convict', 'convict prison', 'criminal lunatic' and 'hard labour' were to be abolished. Two new types of prison sentence were proposed: 'corrective training' for between two and four years for those between the ages of 21 and 30; and 'preventive detention' for persons over 30 for periods between two and four years but up to ten years for certain types of offenders with long criminal records. Corporal punishment, or 'judicial flogging', was to be abolished, except for attacks on prison staff. In the treatment of young offenders even greater changes were proposed, involving the establishment of remand centres, regional remand homes for 'problem' children and 'Howard Houses' for offenders between the ages of 16 and 21; the ultimate object being the abolition of sentences of imprisonment for the young.

The Bill's reception in the Commons in the second reading debate on 29th November and 1st December was almost wholly favourable and the stage was passed without a division.[40] But this appearance of unanimity was deceptive and the detailed committee stage in standing committee proved a long-drawn out process, against a background of mounting opposition in some sections of the press, among Conservative backbenchers and in the party organisation, to the abolition of corporal punishment. Although abolition was passed in committee by 32 to 17 in March 1939, the managers of government business became worried about the possibility of backbench rebellion when the measure returned to the floor of the House for the report and third reading stages: the Chief Whip told Hoare he estimated that nine-tenths of Conservative backbenchers were against the abolition of corporal punishment. At the very least it seemed inevitable that the clause would have to be the subject of a free vote. But it never got to this point. There were all sorts of measures, some of them the responsibility of the Home Secretary, that could colourably be given priority in these last few months before the outbreak of war, and the remaining stages of the Criminal Justice Bill were deferred until the new parliamentary session due to begin in October 1939. In November Hoare (now Lord Privy Seal) announced that the Bill would not be proceeded with, it being impossible either to complete its last stages or to implement it even if time could have been found to pass it. But the months of drafting and discussion were by no means wasted for nine years later Hoare's abandoned Bill formed the basis of the Criminal Justices Act of 1948 and Hoare, as Lord Templewood, was able to contribute actively to its examination in the House of Lords.[41]

Other aspects of his departmental responsibilities for law and order were much less congenial to Hoare than major legislative reform of the penal system. There was, for example, the continuing problem of the deliberately provocative demonstrations by the British Union of Fascists under Mosley and the left-wing reaction to them which so often, especially in the East End of London, erupted into violence. It was a situation in which it was virtually impossible for the impartiality of the police to remain unquestioned and Hoare, as the responsible minister, had to answer many attacks. Then from the beginning of 1939 came another threat to law and order even more dangerous than that posed by fascists and communists, with the launching of an Irish Republican Army campaign of bomb outrages in Britain. Between January and July there were 127 bomb incidents, 57 in London and 70 in the provinces, injuring 56 people; a bomb explosion in Coventry in August killed five people. Although 65 people were convicted for these offences it was felt that police powers of search and arrest were insufficient to cope with so comprehensively organised a campaign of violence; and there was no way of deporting an Irish terrorist. On 24th July, 1939, Hoare introduced the Prevention of Violence Bill to give the police wider powers and to enable suspects to be deported; five days later — helped by a bomb explosion at King's Cross station which occurred during the debates — the Bill had become law.[42]

The post of Home Secretary, then as now, makes more onerous personal demands on its holder than almost any post in the government. In addition to a full ration of major issues of departmental policy he is likely to be much more involved than other ministers in the minutiae of departmental administration since the Home Office works in such sensitive areas that at any moment a seemingly trivial matter may become of intense public controversy. A successful Home Secretary needs to be richly endowed with the gift of imaginative sympathy as well as with the more obvious political and administrative skills and as a result more political reputations have been tarnished than enhanced among occupants of the office. Hoare's two-year term undoubtedly ranks among the successful. The imaginative sympathy he displayed was to be seen not so distinctively in the more dramatic instances of a Home Secretary's personal actions — the decision, for example, on the exercise of the royal prerogative of mercy in capital cases (where Hoare gave no particular hint of the ardent abolitionist he was later to become) — as in his response to a completely uncovenanted human predicament: the mass flight of Jews from Nazi oppression.

The problem of Jewish refugees seeking entry into Britain (and, of course, anywhere else that offered a safe haven) had intensified after the promulgation in September 1935 of the notorious Nuremberg Laws against 'non-Aryans' living in the Reich. But the really massive flight and expulsions of refugees — most of them stripped of virtually all their possessions — came in 1938 with, first, the German occupation of Austria in March and then, in November, after the horrifying Jewish pogrom in Germany known as *Kristallnacht*. Czech Jews began joining the rush after the Munich settlement at the end of September and were vastly augmented after the complete German takeover of their country in March 1939. The threatened Jewish populations of Poland and Romania also participated in the panic-stricken effort to escape from state-ordained racial bestiality. By October 1939 Britain's contribution to the solution of this appalling human problem had been to give sanctuary to some 50,000 refugees from Germany and Austria and 6,000 from Czechoslovakia.[43]

As Home Secretary during the most intense period of Jewish immigration Hoare had to balance his generous instincts (which had been nurtured by his direct contact with the sad plight of Russian refugees in Constantinople sixteen years before) with considerations of the 'public interest'. He had to bear in mind, for example, the continuing high rate of domestic unemployment (12·6 per cent in 1938) and the traditionally restrictive attitude to foreign immigrants of trade unions and professional associations. More than once, he later wrote

> I received an unpleasant shock to my humanitarian sentiments. When, for instance, I attempted to open the door to Austrian doctors and surgeons, I was met by the obstinate resistance of the medical profession ... It was only after long discussions that I was able to circumvent the opposition and arrange for a strictly limited number of doctors and surgeons to enter the country and practise their profession. I would gladly have admitted the Austrian medical schools *en bloc*.[44]

There was also the consideration — urged by British Jewry as strongly as any other group — that mass immigration would lead to an unacceptable growth in domestic anti-semitism: indeed,

Hoare had been told by the secret service that 'the Germans were anxious to inundate this country with Jews, with a view to creating a Jewish problem in the United Kingdom'.[45] And there was always the problem of financial constraints, in face of an influx of refugees made destitute by their oppressors.

There were no easy solutions and the government's policy, for which Hoare had the major individual responsibility, was criticised in Britain both for being too liberal and for not being liberal enough. A recent authoritative study has, however, concluded that 'When a balance sheet ... is drawn and Great Britain's refugee policy is compared with that of other countries it emerges, in the context of the pre-war period, as comparatively compassionate, even generous.'[46] Most of the individual immigrant cases were, of course, dealt with by officials, under regulations which Hoare ensured were constantly kept under review. But on a number of occasions, as in the case of the Austrian doctors, Hoare himself took the effective decision. It was he who, on the representation of Ernest Jones (a fellow skating enthusiast), agreed in March 1938 to allow the aged Sigmund Freud to settle and work in Britain, for what proved the last year or so of his life, together with his family, his servants, his personal doctors and a number of his pupils, accompanied by their families; and, in a case involving no such figure of international distinction, allowed entry to the widow and son of a man who had recently committed suicide in a German concentration camp.[47] Lord Templewood's papers contain evidence that those who had most reason to know of his efforts were deeply grateful. In December 1951 the secretary of the Association of Jewish Refugees in Great Britain wrote to him to place on record

> our gratitude for your unforgettable services in those days of anxiety. Tens of thousands would have shared the fate of their fellow-Jews on the Continent if they had not found admission to this country. They owe their lives to the generous immigration policy of the Government with which you, My Lord, at that time served as Home Secretary. We know that it was mainly due to your influence and guidance that the rescue work was carried out with speed and energy and in a spirit of human understanding. We shall always remember with

deepest gratitude the decisive part you thus played in the history of our community and in the life of each of its members.[48]

Any Home Secretary in a British government in the late 1930s would inevitably have been drawn into the discussion of foreign policy issues, as Hoare necessarily was in dealing with the refugee problem. Moreover, as the minister responsible for Air Raid Precautions he was a constant attender at meetings of the Committee of Imperial Defence, where Hoare in fact hammered away at the need for more resources to be devoted to anti-aircraft protection, if need be, at the expense of the capacity of the British army to provide an expeditionary force for a continental war.[49] But Hoare — as other Home Secretaries might not have been — was also a member of the Cabinet's Foreign Policy Committee and when, at the height of the Czechoslovak crisis in the second half of September 1938, that committee was temporarily superseded by a small inner group of Chamberlain and three others who planned British policy during the crisis Hoare was included in this 'Big Four'. He thus became, in the eyes of contemporaries and many later commentators, an archetypal 'appeaser', an uncritical supporter of Chamberlain's policy of trying to remove the causes of European conflict and avoid war by conciliating dictators whom those with the benefit of hindsight know to have been beyond conciliation; according to one 'rebel' Conservative backbench M.P. at the time (Harold Macmillan), Hoare was 'one of the worst and most sycophantic of Neville Chamberlain's advisers'.[50]

Hoare's loyalty to Chamberlain in the pursuit of his policy shines through his published memoirs of the period, widely held to be one of the most cogent defences of appeasement and of Chamberlain. The opening of the relevant public archives have, however, shown that Hoare was by no means the sycophant Macmillan accused him of being, particularly in the last six months before the outbreak of war. He might well have attempted to restore his own reputation at the expense of Chamberlain's by explicitly revealing those occasions when he differed from the Prime Minister: the fact that he did not do so was no doubt in part the result of his devotion to Chamberlain's memory and of what must now seem a very old-fashioned belief in the confidentiality of Cabinet discussions.

It is certainly true that up to and including the Munich settlement of the Czechoslovakian crisis in September 1938 Hoare's agreement with the policies and actions of the Prime Minister was virtually absolute. He had no hesitation, for example, in joining the rest of the Cabinet in supporting Chamberlain in his difference with Eden over the timing of negotiations with Mussolini on the withdrawal of Italian troops from Spain and recognition of Italian occupation of Abyssinia which was the ostensible reason for Eden's resignation as Foreign Secretary on 20th February, 1938; Hoare felt at the time that the difference between the two men was procedural and that Eden's resignation was induced more by personal vanity than by any substantive policy issue.[51] The German occupation of Austria on 11th March came as a shock to Hoare, as to the rest of the Cabinet, but it was not such as seriously to shake the belief that it was still possible to negotiate specific agreements with Hitler since it could be argued that the aggression was confined to a German-speaking people and apparently (according to a Nazi-run plebiscite a month later) had their consent. But it clearly had strategic implications for the European balance and Hoare recognised that it was necessary 'to hurry on even more determinedly with our military preparations'.[52]

One of the most serious implications of the extinction of Austria was, of course, for the defence of Czechoslovakia, the western and most important half of which (containing Bohemia, Prague and the Skoda munitions works) was now surrounded on three sides by German territory. In the anxious discussions on the situation which took place in Cabinet and Foreign Policy Committee from March onwards Hoare did what he could for the multi-national state with whose foundation he had been so closely associated and whose leading statesmen, Thomas Masaryk (who had died in October 1937) and Beneš, he counted among his friends, as he did Masaryk's son Jan, who was Czechoslovak envoy in London. When, in April 1938, the crude Nazi-inspired campaign to exploit the supposed grievances of the $3\frac{1}{2}$ million Sudeten Germans in Czechoslovakia began in earnest Hoare, alone in the Cabinet, had the knowledge which enabled him to expose the hollowness of the charges against the Czechoslovak government, whose treatment of its several minorities, while certainly not faultless, was far superior to that of any of its neighbours.[53] At an early stage of the crisis Hoare seems to have contemplated the possibility of Britain's undertaking a new commitment to France in respect of French treaty obligations to come to the defence of Czechoslovakia if the country were attacked;[54] but later he was in complete accord with British efforts to ensure that France joined in bringing pressure to bear on the Czechoslovak government to settle with Germany and thus avoid the need for any French implementation of treaty obligations. However sympathetic Hoare may have been to the Czechoslovak cause he felt that the brute strategic facts could not be ignored: that Czechoslovakia was, in the last resort, incapable of being defended, and that in any case no British government could at that time have counted on popular support for entering a war in its defence. Thus, in the last stages of the crisis which in Britain centred on Chamberlain's three flights to see Hitler in September 1938 (at, successively, Berchtesgaden, Godesberg and Munich) Hoare's role as a member, with Halifax and Simon, of the small inner group of ministers with whom Chamberlain was in closest touch from about 10th September to the Munich agreement three weeks later was not a particularly distinctive one (although Hoare's colleagues capitalised on his friendship with Beaverbrook to make him during the crisis the main ministerial point of contact with newspaper proprietors and editors). He accepted his full share of collective responsibility at every stage of the negotiations which culminated in the dismemberment of Czechoslovakia by the incorporation of Sudetenland into the German Reich.[55]

It is difficult to envisage any final resolution of the often passionate debate on the rights and wrongs of the Munich settlement which has raged almost continuously since 1938. Did it avoid virtually inevitable war and provide an indispensable breathing space before Britain and France finally had to stand firm against the aggressive designs of Hitler's Germany a year later, or was it an abject and unnecessary surrender — at the expense of a small and recognisably democratic country — to a gigantic campaign of bluff which would have been called had determination been shown? One's attitude to these and other questions thrown up by the Czechoslovak crisis of 1938 must in

large part be a matter of subjective evaluation. Hoare himself —
at the time and subsequently — looked on the settlement much
more as a painful necessity than as a triumph of diplomacy.
Czechoslovakia, he frankly admitted to the House of Commons
on 3rd October, four days after Munich, 'has received a stagger-
ing blow'; nevertheless, the provision in the agreement for an
orderly transfer of Sudetenland was far better than the immediate and perhaps bloody military occupation of the whole of
Czechoslovakia that had been threatened. Now Britain must
look to the future. Hoare continued:

> We have to take stock of the position and whilst we are pre-
> pared to go on the line set by the Prime Minister of attempt-
> ing wherever it is possible to find a peaceful solution to the
> problems which confront Europe, we are not going into the
> future blindfold ... we shall continue our preparations to
> keep ourselves, and to make ourselves, strong.[56]

There is evidence in the Templewood Papers that after
Munich Hoare, while still fundamentally at one with Chamberlain on major policy issues, was increasingly impatient with
what he considered to be the Prime Minister's negativeness. One
way in which Chamberlain demonstrated this, Hoare felt, was in
his reluctance to introduce new blood into his government. Six
days after Munich Hoare was urging Chamberlain to hold a
general election, not only to affirm general popular support for
the double policy of appeasement and rearmament, but also to
provide an opportunity for broadening the government and,
perhaps, persuading Eden to return to it (but not the government's most formidable Conservative critic, Churchill, with
whom Hoare thought there was 'little or no common ground').
But instead Chamberlain announced that there would be no
election in the immediate future, a decision which, Hoare told
Beaverbrook, came as a surprise to the Cabinet.[57] The broadening which Hoare seems to have had in mind was not in any sense
the creation of an inter-party coalition with Labour but rather
the introduction of respected, experienced and primarily non-
partisan figures like Sir John Anderson, Lord Chatfield (the
recently retired First Sea Lord) or Lord Trenchard. At the end
of October it was only after considerable effort that he succeeded
in getting Anderson appointed as Lord Privy Seal; at the same

time he had pressed Chatfield's qualifications to replace Inskip as Minister for Co-ordination of Defence but this change did not take place until January 1939.[58]

Chamberlain's negativeness, in Hoare's retrospective view, extended to measures as well as to men. By October 1938 Hoare had become convinced that the rearmament programme, particularly on the army side, called for a ministry of munitions or supply; the possibility of setting up such a ministry was debated in the Commons in November and the idea clearly had widespread support.[59] But Chamberlain set his face against it and a Ministry of Supply was not established until July 1939. Nor did Hoare feel that Chamberlain showed sufficient urgency on the manpower front where the logic of events pointed to conscription. It was only with the greatest reluctance that Chamberlain could be brought (in November 1938) to allow the compiling, on a voluntary basis, of a national register of service – to conscription itself he was, until April 1939, as much opposed as the trade unions.[60]

The final shattering of the Munich settlement with the German takeover of the rump of Czechoslovakia on 15th March, 1939, came as a bitter blow to Hoare who up to that time, as he later confessed, had believed that there were limits to Hitler's ambitions and 'that he would not go beyond the German race'.[61] Moreover, only five days before he had, after consultation with Chamberlain, included a reference to the European situation in a widely reported annual address to his Chelsea constituency association which now looked singularly inept. Chamberlain had suggested that Hoare should in his speech 'discourage the view that war was inevitable, and insist upon the great possibilities of peace'. Following this advice Hoare proclaimed on 10th March the possibility of a golden age of prosperity for the world if only the five leading statesmen in Europe – Chamberlain, Daladier, Hitler, Mussolini and Stalin – could work together in peace and friendship. Although this was clearly a contingent prophecy only (albeit a rather vacuous one) and directed to the dictators as much as to the domestic audience, it was easy to misrepresent it as an unqualified heralding of a golden age on the eve of a world war and Hoare's reputation undoubtedly suffered then and subsequently from such misrepresentation.[62] To make matters worse soon after delivering his Chelsea speech Hoare succumbed to a bout of the influenza to which he was constantly prone. In the depression induced by the collapse of his hopes for peace, his seeming public gaffe and the effects of his viral infection Hoare even contemplated resignation: 'I felt that my part in the Government was finished,' he later wrote, 'and that I had better retire from public life.'[63]

Hoare was roused from his depression and restored to his faith in his political future by the man to whom he had turned so often in the past — Beaverbrook. Hoare wrote:

> He, like me, had set his heart on peace. None the less, his advice was against my leaving the Government, although he fully realised the magnitude of the change that had come over the political scene. After all, war had not started, and there was still a chance of preventing it. It might well be that when we had become militarily stronger, we should be able to resume our efforts for a peaceful settlement with a better chance of success.[64]

Beaverbrook still believed that Hoare would become Prime Minister in succession to Chamberlain: he told a Canadian correspondent in June 1938 that Hoare had 'something like first claim to the crown' and the same impression was fostered in his newspapers.[65] Moreover, just four months before Beaverbrook had taken steps to see that Hoare did not lack the resources to remain in politics.

Although in terms of capital ownership (particularly by virtue of his Norfolk property)[66] Hoare was a wealthy man he was always concerned about the maintenance of his income amid the vagaries of political life. This was a factor in his eagerness to return to office after his resignation but even after he had done so there was at least one occasion, in the spring of 1937, when he seriously thought of leaving politics altogether for the attractive financial prospect of a directorship of the Midland Bank, with the possible reversion to the chairmanship shortly afterwards.[67] It was a topic which Hoare undoubtedly discussed with Beaverbrook, whom he had seen frequently during the last stages of the Czechoslovakian crisis in September. On 4th November (1938) Lady Maud took a hand and — almost certainly without the knowledge of her husband — plucked up courage to write to the immensely rich Beaverbrook what can only be described as a begging letter. 'Sam must soon make up his mind whether he goes on in active politics after the next election or whether he tries to make a new career', Lady Maud told Beaverbrook. After more than thirty years of politics he was naturally very tired and could do with a change and a rest. Lady Maud continued:

> But this is only one side. The other is financial. Sam is convinced — and I believe rightly so — that we can hardly afford to go on in office and certainly can't survive a time in opposition. He is never able to look into our affairs. We grow poorer every year and that is worrying all enjoyment out of him ... and makes him long for a fresh career with greater leisure, some financial security and perhaps less strain ... Which is he to do? If he is not to retire at this election, he must be relieved of financial anxiety. The double burden is too heavy. If he goes, I believe it will be a great loss to the country ... but unless my belief is shared by those who can and will help, go he must. What is your advice? I should be more than grateful for it ...[68]

Beaverbrook's response, four days later, was to see Hoare and then on 22nd November he wrote to him:

> My long experience in public life has given me a very brilliant picture of the financial misfortunes of the man who takes office. He not only loses his income from directorships and other employments, but he invariably neglects his investments, and loses his Capital. A very superficial inquiry has disclosed to me that you conform in every respect to this picture of the man who takes office.

It was on this account that he was sending Hoare, 'out of a full pocket', a sum which he variously described as 'very small' and 'a dribble' but which his biographer has identified as a cheque for £2,000. He intended, he said, to repeat the payment 'this time next year & for the rest of this Parliament, & for the next Parliament, if you still decide to stay in office, & I still have the necessary money'. The next cheque came, however, less than a year later, on the day Germany invaded Poland, and within a few weeks it was followed by another.[69] There is no record in either the Beaverbrook or Templewood papers of any further payment being made, presumably because Hoare's ministerial career came to an end in May 1940.

In thus being the object of Beaverbrook's generosity Hoare was in no way exceptional for, as Beaverbrook told him when sending the second cheque, 'I have always opened my pocket books to my friends ... I am not taking any special or particular place in your life that might single you out from others.' Nor were the payments made in the expectation of services to be rendered, although had they been publicly known at the time the accusation of corruption would undoubtedly have been made. The relationship between the two men had always been of benefit to both, Beaverbrook deriving (in no sense improperly) a special insight into governmental thinking, and Hoare finding in Beaverbrook his most valued source of political advice. In this context it is perhaps significant that Hoare apparently made no attempt to exercise his considerable influence to assist Beaverbrook in achieving a ministerial ambition. In early March 1939 Hoare was charged with the task of setting up the 'skeleton' organisation for a Ministry of Information which was intended to come into actual operation with the outbreak of war.[70] It is clear that Beaverbrook, who had been Minister of Information in the First World War, would dearly have liked to have been minister again when the Second World War came. 'I would have been the best man for the job at the outset', he later told Hoare. 'I have the experience in journalism and propaganda. And in character I am just the type to have made a success, and a real success at that.' But the post went to Lord Macmillan, a distinguished judge whose experience of both journalism and propaganda was limited, and Beaverbrook consoled what looks suspiciously like wounded pride by protesting that the new ministry was now 'nothing more than a minor department'.[71]

When, with Beaverbrook's help, Hoare had surmounted the depression which afflicted him immediately after the Prague coup he began thinking of the implications of this sombre development for both domestic and foreign policy. From his sickbed he wrote a 'line of affectionate encouragement' to Chamberlain:

There is nothing on your side that you need regret and I do

not believe on looking back over the last six months there is
anything you could have done substantially differently. As it
is, there is nothing much to be done except an intensification
of the re-armament programme.

He then made an important suggestion:

Perhaps you or Edward [Halifax] or both would do well to
see the party leaders. Whilst I do not think that the kind of
National Government that Anthony [Eden] wants would be
in the least likely to emerge from it it does seem to me to be
important, if we can, to diminish the bitterness of party
politics at the moment.[72]

The suggestion fell on deaf ears. Chamberlain had profound and
undisguised contempt for the Labour Opposition and little
more regard for the independent Liberals or his critics within
the Conservative party. It was yet another aspect of what Hoare
felt was Chamberlain's negativeness. In the absence of a lead
from the Prime Minister there was little that an individual
Cabinet minister could do to reduce the acerbities of political
debate at a time of increasing national peril. Nevertheless, the
fact that Hoare was proceeding with the Criminal Justice Bill,
much more popular with Labour than with many of his own
party, was a positive contribution to the reduction of the level of
political partisanship.

But it was in the major reorientation of British foreign policy
precipitated by the Prague *coup* that Hoare played his most
significant role and — in contrast to the usually accepted view
of him as a devoted follower of Chamberlain — it was one in
which, almost alone in the Cabinet, he was firmly opposed to
the Prime Minister. Following the German takeover of Czechoslovakia it was considered essential to build up an anti-German
alliance in eastern Europe, both to protect countries like Poland
and Romania which seemed marked down as the next victims of
German aggression and to ensure that if, as appeared increasingly likely, Britain and France were to be involved in war with
Germany it would be a war in which Germany was engaged on
at least two fronts. This immediately posed the question of the
part to be performed in the alliance by the power which, although almost ignored by Britain and France in the Munich

crisis, could obviously not now be left out of account: the Soviet Union.[73] But quite apart from what the Soviet attitude might be to any western approach there were varying views among British policy-makers on the desirability of joint steps, let alone an alliance, with the Soviet Union. Some of the difficulty derived from conflicting intelligence about the strategic worth of Russia as an ally, but much more was a consequence of the ideological revulsion against Russia which had characterised the Conservative party since the 1914–18 war. None in the Cabinet felt this revulsion more strongly than Chamberlain and for several weeks after Prague, with the full support of Halifax as Foreign Secretary and most of the Cabinet, he opposed any real attempt at close co-operation with the Soviet Union. This line was made more tenable by the fact that the Poles (and other east European countries) strenuously resisted the prospect of Soviet entry to, or passage through, their territory in fulfilment of commitments under an anti-German alliance. Since most British policy-makers considered Poland to be a more valuable ally than Russia, ideological predilection and respect for Polish wishes could be happily married. Thus instead of a four-power guarantee in which the Soviet Union would participate there was the extraordinary unilateral British guarantee of Poland announced on 31st March, when a German attack seemed imminent.

Hoare was certainly not against specific agreements with powers under threat of attack – indeed he unsuccessfully argued for a guarantee for Turkey as well as for Greece after the Italian invasion of Albania on 7th April.[74] But in Cabinet and Foreign Policy Committee he consistently stood out against his colleagues' under-valuation of the importance of a Soviet alliance (and concomitant exaggeration of the value of the Poles, whom Hoare considered 'politically unstable and un-reliable' allies).[75] Until the decision was taken, late in May, to begin serious negotiations for a Soviet alliance Hoare's stand was supported at various times by Oliver Stanley, Chatfield (the Minister for Co-ordination of Defence), Walter Elliot and Malcolm MacDonald but by no one else in the Cabinet. It is not too much to say that his was one of the greatest individual contributions to that decision; it was no fault of his that it was taken probably too late to prevent the Soviet government from perceiving, in the end, a greater expediency in concluding an alliance with the poacher rather than the gamekeepers.

Hoare's ideological revulsion against Soviet communism was no less than his colleagues'; in fact it may well have been more deeply entrenched as a result of a personal experience of Russia greater than that of any other Cabinet member and his early post-war involvement in the attempt at a White Russian counter-revolution. But he also knew the great strengths of the Russian people and he had read history, not least Napoleonic history. He saw also that an accommodation with the Soviet Union would have domestic political advantages in helping to secure Labour party support for the government's policy. He warned Chamberlain and the Foreign Policy Committee on 27th March that the omission of Russia from the proposed moves in eastern Europe 'would be regarded in many quarters as a considerable defeat for our policy'. 'No one', he is recorded as saying, 'could accuse him of any predilections in favour of Soviet Russia' but he firmly believed that 'Russia constituted the greatest deterrent in the East against German aggression' for 'All experience showed that Russia was undefeatable.' The rest of the committee, however, followed Halifax's lead in thinking that Poland was a 'sounder, more reliable ally than Russia' and too important to be offended by an Anglo-French agreement with the Soviet Union.[76] The committee was still maintaining the same line at its meeting on 19th April but Hoare was able to achieve a minor success for realism when he expressed concern that:

> Poland would be able to offer little military resistance to German invasion, and would soon come to an end of her munitions. We should be in no position to supply her, and Russia was the only source of munitions to Poland and the other countries of Eastern Europe.

He urged that the Chiefs of Staff be asked to report on the military value of Russian assistance and to this the rest of the committee agreed, though no doubt with differing expectations as to what the examination would reveal.[77]

Hoare continued to argue for a Soviet alliance at the Cabinet on 10th May and the Foreign Policy Committee on 5th and 16th May, and by the time the committee met on 19th May there were signs that the battle was nearly won. Halifax was clearly wavering and only W. S. Morrison and Chamberlain himself remained in intransigent opposition. Chamberlain tried to argue that a triple alliance between Britain, France and the Soviet Union would unite all Germans behind Hitler, including the moderate elements whom it was desirable for Britain and France to foster and encourage. To this Hoare replied that the German government would be deterred only by fear; when the emergency arrived the moderate elements would disappear.[78] On the following day (20th May) Cadogan, the permanent head of the Foreign Office, recorded in his diary that Chamberlain had said that he would 'resign rather than sign alliance with Soviet' but only three days later Cadogan was writing to Halifax in Geneva that the Prime Minister had come 'very reluctantly' to the view that it might be necessary to accept a triple pact with the Soviet Union, although he was 'very disturbed by all it implies'.[79] The major personal reverse which a decision to seek alliance with Russia would represent for Chamberlain was partially covered by his insistence that the terms of the pact should be tied in with the now almost forgotten Article 16 of the Covenant of the League of Nations — on the rather devious ground that since the article might soon be fundamentally revised the British commitment to Russia would in consequence take on a temporary character. A suitable formula was manufactured in the Foreign Office and a copy of it was sent to Hoare as well as to Halifax and Chamberlain. When the Cabinet met on 24th May to set the seal on the new course of action Hoare, for so many weeks the Prime Minister's chief critic within the Cabinet, spoke in favour of the League Covenant link. This time there was no dissent and the Cabinet unanimously approved the conclusion of an alliance with the Soviet Union.[80]

Just three months after this decision was taken the Russians did the very thing that Hoare and others had hoped an early British initiative might prevent. But although the tortuous course of the British negotiations in Moscow could have given little grounds for hope of a successful outcome Hoare retained his dedication to the idea of a Soviet alliance down to the final act of betrayal with the signature of the Soviet-German non-aggression pact on 23rd August. When, in the middle of July, Molotov, the new Soviet Foreign Minister, demanded that military staff talks must accompany any political agreement the immediate response of the majority of the Cabinet and the Foreign Policy Committee, guided by Halifax and Chamberlain, was to reject the demand. At a Foreign Policy Committee meeting on 19th July, however, Hoare emphasised the disastrous effects a breakdown in the negotiations would have on Britain's allies in eastern Europe (which had now accepted, if reluctantly, the necessity of Soviet participation). Chamberlain was unconvinced: must Britain agree to Molotov's demands simply to keep its allies 'sweet and happy' he asked? Nevertheless a week later the Cabinet agreed that military talks could even precede the conclusion of an alliance and on 5th August an Anglo-French military mission departed by sea for Moscow.[81] But by the time it arrived there on 11th August the Russo-German pact had become virtually inevitable. Whether an Anglo-French alliance with Russia was ever really a practical proposition in the light of what is now known of Russian motivations at the time is doubtful. But on the basis of the information available to the British government it is difficult not to conclude that Hoare showed more prescience than either Chamberlain or Halifax, the ministers most directly concerned, in early urging the approach to Russia. The Prime Minister and Foreign Secretary were not reluctant because of any special insight into the practicability of the policy but because they thought a Russian alliance less important as well as far more ideologically distasteful than one with Poland. For Hoare ideology took second place to realism. His retrospective self-evaluation of his role seems vindicated by the contemporary record:

> So far as my influence counted, I was persistently on the side of making every effort to bring Stalin over to the Allies, and if that was impossible, at least to keep him from throwing the weight of Russian power, whatever it might be, on to the enemy's side.[82]

The British response to the shock of the Russo-German pact was the final signature, delayed by the Moscow negotiations, of the formal treaty with Poland committing Britain to its defence. With a German invasion of Poland clearly imminent so was Britain's involvement in war, whatever evanescent hopes might have been raised in some breasts by, for example, the last minute activity of various emissaries from an apparently peace-loving Goering and a suggestion from Mussolini for another Munich-style conference. During the last few hectic days of peace Hoare was fully occupied with the many war preparations which came within his ample ministerial scope. Among other things he had to see rapidly through Parliament (after consultations with the Labour Opposition and the trade unions) legislation providing for sweeping governmental emergency powers, supervise the final arrangements for the new Ministry of Information, brief press proprietors, editors and lobby correspondents on developments in the crisis, and discuss with the Palace plans for the possible evacuation of the King and Queen from London.[83]

When German forces finally invaded Poland on 1st September Hoare expected a British declaration of war to follow immediately and, like many others, he was surprised to hear Chamberlain, at the first of two Cabinets on 2nd September, describe the note which the British government had sent to the German government the previous day as a 'last warning' rather than an ultimatum. Hoare protested that 'this communication had been generally regarded as in the nature of an ultimatum. There would be tremendous risks in accepting any delay'. Neither he nor several other Cabinet members (let alone a restless House of Commons) were prepared to attach the weight that Chamberlain and Halifax evidently did to the French desire for a 48 hour delay to enable them to complete their mobilisation before France became liable to German air attack, and the desirability of giving time to see whether the Germans would withdraw from Poland in order to secure Anglo-French participation in an international conference.[84] Nevertheless Chamberlain soon afterwards made a merely holding statement in an angry House of Commons which had been expecting a firm declaration. This led a group of dissident ministers, meeting at various times during the evening of the 2nd under the surprising chairmanship of Simon, to bring pressure to bear on the Prime Minister, resulting in the calling of a further Cabinet at 11.30 p.m.[85] Hoare had not participated in the meetings of the Simon group, not because he did not share his colleagues' anxiety over the delay in declaring war — for his intervention at the earlier Cabinet had made his position crystal clear — but almost certainly (like Kingsley Wood, another dissident who absented himself from the Simon meetings) to avoid an embarrassing confrontation with his friend and closest Cabinet colleague. He was in fact in bed when the summons to the 11.30 p.m. Cabinet arrived. Lady Maud drove him through a thunderstorm to Downing Street where he joined with the rest of the Cabinet in approving the issue of a British ultimatum, independently of the French, at 9 a.m. the following morning to expire two hours later. At 11 in the morning of 3rd September Hoare was again at No. 10 and there heard Chamberlain make his broadcast announcing that Britain was at war.[86] Before the day was out he had become a member of Chamberlain's nine-man War Cabinet.

8

From War Cabinet to Madrid Embassy

Chamberlain had been considering the nature and composition of his War Cabinet at least eleven days before Britain declared war. On 23rd August he asked Lord Hankey, with his encyclopaedic knowledge of the higher organisation of government, to brief him on Lloyd George's War Cabinet of 1916.[1] At first Chamberlain seemed to be aiming for a very small group of ministers, perhaps five at most, predominantly free from departmental responsibilities. When, on 1st September, Churchill accepted office in the new administration it was still uncertain whether he would be a member of the War Cabinet as a departmental or non-departmental minister. Chamberlain's decision that Churchill would be a safer colleague as a service minister than as a minister with a roving commission seems to have been the main factor in determining that the War Cabinet, when finally unveiled on 3rd September, should be primarily departmental and rather larger than had been anticipated. With Churchill included as First Lord of the Admiralty there had to be places for Sir Kingsley Wood as Secretary of State for Air and Leslie Hore-Belisha as Secretary of State for War — as well as for the defence co-ordinating minister, Lord Chatfield. Halifax, as Foreign Secretary, and Simon, as Chancellor of the Exchequer, retained their offices in the War Cabinet. This left only two of the nine War Cabinet posts (apart from Chamberlain and Chatfield) for ministers explicitly relieved of departmental burdens. One of them was Hankey, as Minister without Portfolio. The other was Hoare who, according to his own account, was not approached by Chamberlain on the question of his wartime office until the early afternoon of 3rd September. He was then given the choice between joining the War Cabinet as Lord Privy Seal and chairman of its Home Policy Committee or continuing as Home Secretary outside the War Cabinet but resuming in addition his former civil defence responsibilities — now vastly augmented — in the new office of Minister for Home Security.[2] It was not a difficult choice, and Chamberlain could hardly have been in doubt as to what it would be. Hoare would obviously want the more prestigious and apparently more influential post, and would not be anxious to be involved once again in those civil defence duties which less than a year before he had been so relieved to delegate to Sir John Anderson, the Lord Privy Seal. So, on 3rd September Hoare exchanged ministerial titles with Anderson and entered the War Cabinet.

Before many weeks were out he had reason to regret his choice. In the British Cabinet system the way of a co-ordinating minister without department is hard: so often limited, as Churchill has described it, to 'exalted brooding over the work done by others', with 'the privilege to talk at large' rather than the ability to give directions and to act, even in a limited sphere, which a departmental minister possesses.[3] From the ample accommodation and large staff of the Home Office Hoare moved to a small suite of rooms in the Treasury, where he presided over an office establishment of less than half-a-dozen. Initially there were his excellent Home Office principal private secretary, Arthur Hutchinson, an assistant private secretary and two or three typists. Within a few days he had persuaded his old friend J. T. C. Moore-Brabazon to join him as parliamentary private secretary. Walter Layton gave him informal advice on statistical matters and at the end of the year R. B. Bennett, a former Canadian Prime Minister now living in Britain, joined his staff as adviser on economic questions.[4] But his personal staff resources could not begin to compare with those available to even the humblest departmental minister.

Hoare's primary functions were concerned with domestic policy but they were not exclusively so and in fact one of his first and perhaps most far-reaching assignments was as chairman of a War Cabinet committee set up on 6th September to plan for the further development of the army. Called the Land Forces Committee it contained the service ministers, with Chatfield, Burgin (Minister of Supply) and Hankey, and met on several occasions before the end of 1939, when it appears to have lapsed.[5] The vital decisions about the army were taken at the first and second meetings of the committee on 7th and 8th September, and were approved by the War Cabinet on 9th September: a speed of decision-taking owing much to Hoare's incisive chairmanship (to which Churchill later testified). It was Hoare who, after discussion principally with Hankey, put forward the proposals which formed the basis of the committee's first report. These were (as he later recalled):

First, that we should assume that the war would last three years, and that the greatest possible publicity should be given to this assumption. An explicit declaration to this effect would, I felt sure, convince the world in general and Germany in particular that we intended to mobilise our total resources for victory. Secondly, that we intended to have an army of fifty-five divisions by the end of the second year of the war, and a minimum of twenty divisions at the end of the first year. Thirdly, that the necessary priority for labour and materials for completing this programme should be guaranteed. Fourthly, that we would at once use every possible method, whether by foreign purchases or improvisation at home, to increase our strength in big guns.

A further conclusion was arrived at by the committee in its second report, and approved by the War Cabinet on 22nd September:

that we should state categorically that our national effort would in no way fall behind the effort that we made in the First World War, and that the immediate programme of army expansion would be only the first chapter of still greater developments.[6]

Subsequent meetings of the committee were not so uniformly harmonious, and Hoare must once again have been reminded of his earlier ministerial battles when a dispute arose between the army and the air force about the control of air units assigned to army co-operation. The end result was that the current position was confirmed, with each service controlling its own units, but not before Hoare had been stimulated to make a possibly contemporary private note that the 'Army [was] very stupid and ignorant [and the] R.A.F. obstructive and secretive'.[7]

Army and War Office stupidity seems to have contributed to a domestic policy crisis which involved Hoare in considerable embarrassment within a few days of the outbreak of war. Although the Ministry of Information whose establishment Hoare had planned over several months had come immediately into being with the declaration of war, under its own minister, Hoare was by no means rid of his responsibilities for its activities. The minister appointed — Lord Macmillan — was a member of the House of Lords and no junior minister had initially been designated; thus Hoare had still to answer for the ministry in the Commons, as well as representing its interests in the War Cabinet. He retained, moreover, the related role of main Cabinet link with the press which he had assumed during the Munich crisis. The new department could not fail to be unpopular: it was generously staffed (much of the staff being assigned to the regional organisation it had been thought would be necessitated by the expected devastating air raids which had so far not materialised); it was responsible for press censorship; and it distributed news about Britain's war effort which, in this early 'phoney war' period, was notably sparse. One piece of news it was decided could not be released at the time was the transporting of the British Expeditionary Force of two divisions to France. Instructions were given to the British press to suppress any reference to the operation until it had been completed. But, on the other side of the Channel, the French authorities — to the consternation of those in London — published on the evening of 11th September information about the B.E.F. crossing while it was still in progress. Hoare subsequently recorded:

> The story was cabled to America and spread at once over the world. In the circumstances the Ministry of Information, with the approval of the War Office, told the British press that the embargo was removed. The papers therefore printed their morning editions with the news prominently featured.

But the War Office had second thoughts and demanded that all publicity should once again be prohibited. The Ministry of Information could not very well ignore 'so serious a representation upon a question of military security' and reimposed the

11 The National Government, August 1931, *front row, left to right,* Snowden, Baldwin, MacDonald, Samuel and Sankey; *back row, left to right,* Cunliffe-Lister, Thomas, Reading, Chamberlain, Hoare

12 The Second Indian Round Table Conference September–December 1931. On the right of the chairman (Lord Sankey) is Hoare; on the left, Gandhi

13 Hoare being greeted by Anthony Eden on his arrival in Geneva, 9th September, 1935

14 Hoare addressing the Assembly of the League of Nations, 11th September, 1935

embargo. In the meantime, however, the early morning editions had gone out, proclaiming the forbidden news. Hoare's own account continued:

> There followed several hours of complete confusion, in the midst of which an official of the War Office, without any authority, instructed Scotland Yard to seize any papers which contained the news. Upon the strength of this instruction, the police visited the newspaper offices and waylaid early morning travellers in order to obtain possession of the papers. Scarcely, however, was the perquisition completed when the French Director of Information released a further and fuller account of the transport of the Expeditionary Force that made our embargo more than ever futile. Almost, therefore, before the editions had been suppressed, the papers were once again given liberty to publish their stories.[8]

Such a saga of muddle and divided counsels provided rich fuel for the critics of the Ministry of Information, both inside and outside the government. A Commons debate on the war situation on 13th September gave the critics their parliamentary opportunity to score easy points and Hoare was in the uncomfortable position of having to reply.

> My main difficulty was that I could not say that the whole trouble was due first, to the French, and then, to the War Office. All that was possible was to apologise and promise that it would never happen again. The House, having lectured the Ministry officials for a crime they had not committed, never afterwards abandoned its prejudice against the new office.[9]

Hoare looked to some relief from his exposed position in relation to this unloved government department by pressing for the appointment of a parliamentary secretary to represent it in the Commons. His own choice for the post would have been Brendan Bracken — chairman of the *Financial News* and loyalest of supporters of Churchill in his years of political exile — whom Hoare had got to know well in his various contacts with newspaper proprietors over the past few years. But Chamberlain would not hear of the appointment (perhaps his willingness to admit former opponents as colleagues extended only to those who, like Churchill, were too important to exclude) and Sir

Edward Grigg was appointed instead on 19th September.[10] Shortly afterwards a major change in the functions of the Ministry of Information from those envisaged in the immediate pre-war plans was announced by Hoare, who had to admit that it had been necessitated by the loss of public confidence. Henceforth the service departments and other functional departments would be responsible for policy relating to news and censorship in their departmental fields, leaving the Ministry of Information only with that for publicity overseas.[11] But well before the war ended this decision was again reversed and the Ministry of Information became the central department for all government news and censorship in the way that Hoare had originally planned; and the man who presided over the restored department was Brendan Bracken.

Part of the problem with the Ministry of Information had been the clash of inter-departmental interests which its responsibilities involved, particularly with the service departments. Another inter-departmental clash in which Hoare was intimately involved as chairman of the Home Policy Committee concerned a subject as intensely unpopular as government control of news: food rationing, which on Hoare's advice was accepted by the War Cabinet in respect of butter, bacon and sugar in December. The Ministry of Agriculture and Fisheries and the new Ministry of Food were both, from varying viewpoints, departmentally engaged in the question of food supply and Hoare was deputed to attempt to co-ordinate their activities. Unfortunately, Hoare's role as chairman of the Food Policy sub-committee (of the Home Policy Committee) had been publicly announced and M.P.s disposed to be critical, particularly Lloyd George, 'made great play with my obscure and anomalous position, and dragged me into controversies about which I knew little'.[12] But on broader topics Hoare's interventions were happier, as when the War Cabinet accepted his recommendation of a ploughing programme of an additional two million acres to supplement the seven million acres already under cultivation. Another of his inquiries was into merchant shipping needs, which again involved an inter-departmental clash — between a Ministry of Shipping demanding more shipping tonnage and an Admiralty anxious that nothing should imperil the naval shipbuilding programme and insisting that the trouble was not shortage of tonnage but delays in turning round merchant ships. Hoare's investigations and subsequent report to the War Cabinet

> showed that although submarine sinkings were at the time well below our pre-war estimates, there was urgent need not only for making better use of the Merchant Navy and for further restrictions in non-essential imports, but also for a greatly increased programme of new construction. Our target at the time was a yearly output of 800,000 tons, and that only to be reached at the end of August 1940. I was convinced that this figure was altogether inadequate. I therefore proposed that it should be raised to a million and a half tons, and equal priority given for steel to both the Merchant and Royal Navies.[13]

Hoare's report was accepted in January, although Churchill successfully insisted that the Admiralty should be responsible for all shipbuilding, including that for the merchant navy which the new Ministry of Shipping had only just taken over from the Board of Trade.[14] Nevertheless Hoare had the satisfaction of mediating an amicable settlement of an all-important question which could well have led to prolonged controversy and delay.

But many matters could not wait for detailed inquiry and report: Hoare's co-ordinative field was peculiarly prone to *ad hoc* crises and the necessity for instant parliamentary explanation. The intense cold weather of mid-February 1940, for example, precipitated an unexpectedly large demand for domestic coal and, in London, as a result of the shortage of railway rolling stock for transporting coal, there was a prospect of an immediate coal famine. Hoare knew nothing of the crisis until he was asked to clear it up, by arranging for a concentration of all available rolling stock on the single objective of supplying London. The incident provoked from him on 21st February a *cri de coeur* to the Prime Minister:

> Several times since the war started, I have been called in at a moment's notice to deal with some urgent domestic situation about which I had never been kept regularly informed. It happened more than once with food. It happened again with agriculture and now it has happened with coal. Until late last night I did not even know that there was a really serious

coal crisis. In the meanwhile, the House of Commons assumes that all these questions are within the purview of the Home Policy Committee and that I am in some way responsible for them. As a matter of fact many important domestic questions have never come before the Home Policy Committee at all, e.g. ... the present coal situation. I do feel most strongly that domestic questions of importance ought to be regularly brought to the Home Policy Committee in the same way as they would normally be brought to a peace-time Cabinet and that Ministers ought to let me know when big questions affecting their Departments are blowing up ...[15]

Hoare was clearly suffering from his decision to take a co-ordinating office rather than remain content with an executive one. He was later to believe that it was the unpopularity he incurred both in Whitehall and at Westminster as a result of his inter-departmental activities which led to the general expectation 'that when Chamberlain resigned ... I would not be a member of any new War Cabinet'.[16]

As a senior member of Chamberlain's government Hoare was, of course, concerned in most of the major discussions on the general conduct of the war. An insight into his attitude after a month or so of the phoney war (which was so unlike his or anyone else's anticipated scenario for the early stages of a new world war) is provided by a letter he wrote on 7th October to his old friend Lord Lothian, now the British Ambassador in Washington.[17] The day before Hitler had put out ambiguous peace feelers — which were rejected within a few days by Chamberlain and Daladier, the French Premier — and Hoare thought it appropriate to assure Lothian that:

no one here or in America should have any anxiety as to the country's morale or the Government's determination. There are, of course, a number of people who are asking whether it is worth while going on with a war that started to save Poland and has seen Poland's destruction in the course of three or four weeks ... and those who are irritated by the smaller vexations of war, and who have not been braced up to them by any great demand for patriotic sacrifice ... They do not, however, alter the fact that the morale of the country as a whole is good.

The one exception among well-known political figures was Lloyd George who, in a speech in the Commons on 3rd October, had, according to Hoare, 'implied that we were certain to be defeated, and that we must make peace from weakness and not from strength'; but Hoare was sure 'that there is no big body of support that would influence the conduct of events in this direction'.[18] He felt that the present strategy was the right one, namely, 'that we should not fritter away our resources, but have them concentrated ready for the decisive moment'. The 'first and predominant war aim' (he told Lothian on 21st November) must be to win the war in Europe.[19]

At the end of November, however, the war took a new turn which led Hoare to believe that some frittering away of resources from the central aim might be justified. With the Russian invasion of Finland the prospect arose of both driving a wedge between Russia and Germany (several of whose military leaders, including Admiral Raeder, were known to be sympathetic to the Finns) and, of great significance, enlisting the neutral Scandinavian nations on the allied side. Sweden was a major source of iron-ore for Germany, the ore being transported by ship across the Baltic for most of the year but when that sea was blocked by winter ice (January to March), via the Norwegian port of Narvik and down the Norwegian coast. Churchill, who at this time showed little of the strategic flair he was later to display as Prime Minister and was clearly a sore trial to his colleagues (Hoare included) had unsuccessfully proposed as early as 19th September that — regardless of the claims of neutrality — the Norwegian coastal waters should be mined. He now urged that allied troops be sent to help Finland by way of Narvik, thus conveniently achieving two objectives at the expense of flouting both Norwegian neutrality and world opinion.[20] Hoare was also in favour of aiding Finland, although more circumspectly. He was not able to attend the War Cabinet on 27th December at which British policy towards Finland and Scandinavia generally was to be discussed since he was visiting the French front for a few days in company with Hankey. But he wrote to Chamberlain to reiterate the policy he had earlier advocated:

that (1) we ought to help Finland as much and as quickly as

possible, even at some risk to our preparations in France and
the Middle East (2) that we ought to try to get Sweden into
the war on our side. I know how difficult this will be, but there
is a chance now in the Swedish fear and hatred of Russia.

Sweden, he was convinced, was now the key place in the war,
both for its own importance (including its iron ore) and its
influence on other neutrals, particularly the United States. He
even, in a half-jocular way, offered himself as Minister to
Sweden, where his friendship with King Gustav, a frequent
tennis partner, might stand him in good stead.[21] The suggestion
– jocular or not – was taken up and on 12th January Chamberlain proposed to his War Cabinet colleagues that Hoare should
lead a mission to Norway and Sweden. The proposal seems at
first to have been accepted but soon opposition developed and
on the 17th it was put into cold storage. Chamberlain did not
altogether abandon the idea, however, and he discussed it again
with Hoare on 13th March but the final collapse of Finnish
resistance on that very day put paid to any hopes of inducing
Norway and Sweden to renounce their neutrality.[22] Within a
few weeks rather more aggressive tactics were to be employed –
disastrously – in Scandinavia but by then Hoare's role in the
War Cabinet had completely changed.

If Hoare had been unhappy about Chamberlain's reluctance
to recruit new talent into his government immediately before the
war, he was doubly so now that war had imposed so many more
burdens on the governmental machine and increased the
opportunity for damaging criticism from disgruntled politicians
outside government. He would have liked Labour – who were
particularly captious critics in Parliament on supply and manpower questions – to have been in the government from the
beginning of the war, but he believed that the animosity of the
party (not least that of Attlee himself) against Chamberlain
made this impossible.[23] Hoare would have been surprised had
he known that one leading Labour politician at this time, far
from denigrating Chamberlain as Prime Minister, had been
privately expressing concern that Chamberlain's health might
not prove equal to the strain of war and that, if he were to resign, he might be succeeded by Hoare. At the end of November
Herbert Morrison confided to Charles Peake, the head of the

Foreign Office News Department, that he was not in favour of Labour entering a coalition government, on grounds both of constitutional propriety and Labour's incompetence for office.

> An opposition was a functional necessity of the English constitution and should not be dispensed with unless those who composed it could bring exceptional and valuable gifts to a Coalition Government. Frankly, this was not the case with the present Opposition and he [Morrison] doubted whether there were half a dozen members of it who could add anything in strength or decision to the present Government. Most of the Labour Front Bench, he said, were frightened of power and few were capable of drive unless they had a strong committee behind them.

Peake's Foreign Office memorandum on this fascinating if indiscreet conversation continued:

> Mr. Morrison spoke in praise of the Prime Minister and said that if the war continued as it had begun he thought the Prime Minister would see it through in his present office and he doubted whether there was a better man. He regretted that the acerbities of debate before the war should have caused sore feelings in his party which still rankled. These might yet smooth out. If this country were heavily attacked, or if the Prime Minister's health proved unequal to the strain upon it, he said ... that he supposed the Lord Privy Seal [Hoare] would succeed him, a decision which he thought would be unwelcome to all Opposition parties. The Opposition disliked the idea of the Lord Privy Seal, feared the prospect of the First Lord [Churchill] succeeding as Prime Minister, and would welcome the Foreign Secretary [Halifax] in that capacity, though he feared it was constitutionally impracticable ...[24]

The reasons why Hoare — a man well to the left of his party on most policy matters — should have been so particularly the object of Labour's animus are obscure. It would seem, however, that he had not been forgiven for the Hoare-Laval agreement which, despite all that had happened since, was still considered by pacifists and the political left as a dire betrayal of the holy grail of collective security; and it was significant that Simon, who had also been thought to have offended against collective security while Foreign Secretary, was usually paired with Hoare as unacceptable to the Labour politicians whose governmental abilities Herbert Morrison found so deficient.

The first opportunity for a major reconstruction of the government came with the resignation of Hore-Belisha as Secretary of State for War early in January. Hoare thought the opportunity should be taken to secure the adherence of at least one of the political groups outside the government and suggested that Sir Archibald Sinclair, the Liberal party leader, be invited to take Hore-Belisha's place at the War Office; but Chamberlain thought the move would offend Labour and the only outsider figuring in the governmental changes was Lord Reith. At about this time Hoare himself (with no great enthusiasm on his part) was being canvassed as co-ordinating minister for economic policy but the project was dropped when Simon, as Chancellor, steadfastly opposed any such appointment within the War Cabinet while he was a member.[25] Towards the end of March several factors impelled a government reconstruction. In the War Cabinet there was the growing disillusionment of Lord Chatfield with his role as Minister for Co-ordination of Defence in the presence in the War Cabinet of the political heads of the service departments: he felt very much the fifth wheel of the defence coach, even though since November he had been acting as chairman of the Military Co-ordination Committee which included the three service ministers. Then there was Sir Kingsley Wood's ill-health and increasing unwillingness to continue at the Air Ministry; and the illness and death (on 30th March) of Sir John Gilmour, the Minister of Shipping. Once again the chances of a coalition with Labour were discussed but Chamberlain told Hoare that he did not want to run the risk of their refusing or asking impossible terms. Instead Chamberlain sought to prevail on a reluctant Hoare to change places with the ailing Wood and return to the department over which he had presided so successfully, although in vastly different circumstances, eleven years before. It was an agonising choice and, as so often in the past, it was eventually made on the advice of Beaverbrook, whom Hoare was now seeing with all the old frequency. It would be a great relief to him to be rid of his well-nigh impossible task as domestic policy overlord, but the Air Ministry was not the alternative he would have chosen. There had been much recent criticism of the department over such matters as aircraft production (which was still its responsibility) and its indeterminate bombing policy, and the Chief of the Air Staff, Newall, was clearly no Trenchard. Moreover, the job would involve Hoare in uncomfortably close relations with the volatile and unpredictable Churchill, whom Chamberlain was making Chatfield's successor as chairman of the Military Co-ordination Committee while retaining the office of First Lord of the Admiralty. Before finally accepting the job Hoare, with Chamberlain's approval, tried to induce Trenchard, now 67 years of age, to resume their old partnership by accepting a place on the Air Council. Trenchard refused but his refusal, as Hoare told Chamberlain,

> was solely due to the obvious embarrassments of anyone like himself being in an organisation without real responsibility. As to myself he said that he would rather see me there [i.e., at the Air Ministry] than anyone else, though it might be my funeral in a year's time![26]

This rather dubious encomium, added to Beaverbrook's enthusiastic advice to accept the post, may have served to overcome Hoare's reluctance and his appointment to the Air Ministry was announced with the other changes on 3rd April.[27]

Hoare could hardly have taken over at a more unfortunate time. Within a few days the ill-advised Norwegian adventure — for which Churchill, above all, had been pressing for so long — was launched and Hoare had to assume ministerial responsibility for an R.A.F. operation which, without possession of any Norwegian airfield, was bound to fail. As a first step the navy mined Norwegian coastal waters on 8th April. That evening Churchill and Oliver Stanley (who had succeeded Hore-Belisha at the War Office) dined with Hoare at his house at 2 Chester Place, off Cadogan Square.[28] Hoare's note of the occasion and its immediate sequel ran:

> Winston very optimistic, delighted with minelaying, and sure that he had scored off the Germans. He went off completely confident and happy at 10.30. At 5.a.m. [9th April]

Newall rang me from the Air Ministry saying that the
Germans had occupied Denmark and were invading Norway.[29]

The phoney war had ended, and the initiative was firmly in
German hands.

It is not proposed here to attempt to follow the complicated
and depressing course of the British intervention in Norway,[30]
much of which turned on the method of attacking the key port of
Trondheim: whether by direct assault – a 'hammer blow' by
troops or battleships; or by a 'pincers movement' from Namsos
to the north and Andalsnes to the south. Strategic indecision at
home and inadequate resources on the spot were more than
enough to decide the issue. Hoare's notes show quite clearly
where he felt the main individual responsibility for the fiasco
lay: in Churchill's 'meddling' and 'complete wobbles' over
tactics and strategy. At one point Hoare wrote of 'endless meetings' of the Military Co-ordination Committee with 'Winston
in the chair, nagging everybody' which eventually led to a
decision for a hammer blow operation against Trondheim. But
later Churchill informed his fellow service ministers that he and
the Chiefs of Staff considered a frontal assault on Trondheim too
risky and had, with the Prime Minister's agreement, settled on
the pincers alternative: indeed the landings at Namsos and
Andalsnes had already taken place. Hoare and Stanley had no
alternative but to accept the accomplished fact but, as Hoare
recorded, 'From that day on, everything went wrong'.[31] (On
25th April, less than a fortnight after the landings, the decision
was taken to evacuate the troops – successfully accomplished on
1st and 2nd May – and the Norwegian adventure was virtually
over.) Churchill's two service colleagues were understandably
chagrined when the Prime Minister proposed that this and other
high-handed actions by Churchill should, in effect, be legiti-
mised by giving him powers of direction over the Chiefs of Staff
(to be joined by his own representative, General Ismay) and
the right to summon them independently of the other service
ministers. Hoare and Stanley protested strongly, as Chamberlain reported to his sister:

> They said they would rather he became Defence Minister
> while they resigned and were succeeded by Under Secretaries

so that everyone should know where responsibility in fact lay. It was only when I said that I would rather resign myself and let W.C. be P.M. as well as Defence Minister that they said that would be too great a disaster and they would do what I asked them.[32]

The new arrangement came into effect on 1st May. Nine days later Churchill had indeed become Minister of Defence and much else besides; his own heavy responsibility for the Norwegian failure being, as Hoare recognised, 'rightly ignored in the unprecedented conditions of the time'.[33]

Although the Norwegian campaign dominated Hoare's six weeks' tenure of the Air Ministry it did not prevent him making a distinctive contribution to a department which had lacked effective political leadership since Kingsley Wood became minister in 1938. A by no means friendly critic detected the difference at once. To Hugh Dalton, who had been acting for some time as a kind of Labour 'shadow' Air Minister, Hoare — at his first interview with him on 19th April — 'gave the impression of knowing much more about the air than Kingsley Wood ever did'.[34] It was, however, a very different department from the one Hoare had left in 1929.

The Air Ministry and Air Force that I had known had been a new and struggling department and a small *corps d'élite* that Trenchard and I had managed almost as a family party. The Department was now one of the largest in Whitehall, and the Air Force fast becoming the predominant fighting service. Aircraft production, not yet allocated to a special department, which in the early days had meant little more than the ordering of a few score machines, had become the most complicated and urgent of the Government's responsibilities. Whilst in the past the Secretary of State had been able to control practically all the details of administration, he now seemed little more than a passenger in a coach driven by staff officers and technical experts ... I had ... become not so much an initiator of Air policy as an interpreter of air operations, first to the Cabinet, and next the House of Commons and the public.[35]

There were, nevertheless, notable developments during Hoare's brief final incumbency, in some of which the change of minister played a part. April saw the highest aircraft production figures yet and there were significant organisational changes on both air staff and supply sides: the Chief of the Air Staff (like his colleagues in the other services) was now 'double-banked' by a Vice-Chief of the Air Staff and Sir Charles Craven, managing director of Vickers-Armstrong, was brought on to the Air Council by Hoare in the post of Civil Member for Development and Production. Hoare remedied the absence of centralised statistical information in the department by establishing a statistical unit within the private office; and, in addition to much else, was deeply involved in discussions on the further expansion of R.A.F. training overseas.[36]

But any success Hoare achieved, or might have achieved, at the Air Ministry was engulfed by the failure of the Norwegian expedition. On 29th April, when it was known that Namsos and Andalsnes were to be evacuated, Hoare's friend and Indian collaborator Leo Amery warned him with rather brutal conciseness that it 'meant the end of H.M.G.'[37] and the immediate aftermath of the damaging Commons debate on 7th and 8th May was soon to reveal the truth of Amery's prophecy. Hoare himself spoke on the second day of the debate, immediately after listening to a blistering attack on Chamberlain, Simon and himself from Herbert Morrison, who had said:

The fact is that before the war and during the war we have felt that the whole spirit, tempo and temperament of at least some Ministers have been wrong, inadequate and unsuitable. I am bound to refer, in particular, to the Prime Minister, the Chancellor of the Exchequer and the Secretary of State for Air. I cannot forget that in relation to the conduct of British foreign policy between 1931 and 1939, they were consistently and persistently wrong. I regard them as being, perhaps more than any other three men, responsible for the fact that we are involved in a war which the wise collective organisation of peace could have prevented, and just as they lacked courage, initiative, imagination, psychological understanding, liveliness and self-respect in the conduct of foreign policy, so I feel that the absence of those qualities has manifested itself in the actual conduct of the war. I have the genuine apprehension that if these men remain in office, we run [a] grave risk of losing this war.[38]

This, of course, was a gross distortion, coming ill from a leading member of a Labour Opposition that for so many years after 1931 had set its face against equipping Britain with the military resources necessary to confront aggressive powers in Europe (and in its references to Chamberlain it conflicted with what Morrison had been saying in private only six months before). It was also inconsistent in excluding Halifax, Chamberlain's chief foreign policy agent before and after Munich, from the collective condemnation: it almost beggars belief that after this kind of blanket attack on the National Government's foreign policy Halifax should have been Labour's first choice for the leadership of an all-party government. But distorted and inconsistent though it was Morrison's attack undoubtedly reflected the feelings of most of the Opposition and not a few of the government's own supporters. Hoare's speech, which tried to give an account of the difficulties with which the R.A.F. had had to contend in Norway, was not a success, and even as recorded in *Hansard* seems to justify Amery's harsh description of 'Sam ... maundering away inaudibly about the gallant exploits of our airmen in Norway which nobody wished to listen to because it was all irrelevant to the issue which was the general competence of the Government.'[39] It was difficult to see what else Hoare could have done: as he later commented, there was 'A good answer for every detail, but not for failure'[40] — and the failure in Norway was plain for all to see. He was well aware that his days in office were probably numbered. As he drove home with Lady Maud after his speech he prophesied: 'That is not only the last speech I shall make as a Minister, but it is the last speech that I shall make in the House of Commons.'[41]

For the second time in his ministerial career Hoare was to experience the frailty of political loyalties and to become the scapegoat for collective failings. While the final stages of the Norwegian debate were taking place in the Commons on the evening of 8th May, broad hints were being dropped to dissident government M.P.s outside the chamber by Chamberlain's P.P.S., Lord Dunglass, and government whips (conceivably without Chamberlain's direct knowledge) that there would be a reconstruction of the government involving the departure of Hoare and Simon if the government were supported in the division lobby.[42] The choice of scapegoats may well have been determined by what it was considered the Labour party would require before entering the all-party government which now seemed both essential and inevitable. But despite the bitterness of Morrison's attack on Chamberlain, Simon and Hoare, it is by no means certain that Hoare was an indispensable sacrifice to enlist Labour's support. That same evening of 8th May Dalton went to see R. A. Butler (as ministerial assistant to Halifax, the man the Labour party wanted to see as Prime Minister) to say that Labour 'would enter a government under Halifax, but not under Chamberlain or in company with Simon'. No mention of Hoare in this context is made in Lord Butler's retrospective account of the conversation while Dalton's makes a distinction between Chamberlain and Simon — whose departure was essential in view of their long record of failure in peace and war — and Hoare, whom Dalton himself did not 'put in the same class', possibly because of the insight he had gained into Hoare's administrative ability during his brief spell at the Air Ministry.[43] But whatever their motivation the blandishments of Chamberlain's entourage did not prevent 33 government M.P.s from voting against the government and almost double that number abstaining, thus precipitating a decline in the government's normal majority from some 250 to 81.

For the next two days Chamberlain was fighting against all the odds to retain the premiership. His closest colleagues, including Halifax and Kingsley Wood (now busily advising Churchill on tactics) were rapidly deserting him. But not Hoare. He repaid the treachery of Dunglass and the whips with absolute loyalty to Chamberlain. On 9th May he was still hopeful that Chamberlain's resignation could be avoided and discussed with Beaverbrook 'ways and means of protecting [Chamberlain] from his enemies'.[44] Early on the 10th the German invasion of the Low Countries deepened the military as well as the political crisis and led Chamberlain to propose to the War Cabinet that morning that he delay his resignation until the battle for France had been decided. Only Hoare spoke in favour. Halifax, according to Hoare, was 'quite heartless' and Wood was 'against delay, evidently pushing for Winston'.[45] Later in the day Chamberlain finally resigned in favour of Churchill, having failed to persuade Halifax to take on the task. There followed several days of rather unseemly scrambling for posts in the new coalition government while the battle for France became ever more grave ('Complete confusion between fighting the battle and making the Cabinet', Hoare noted). By 16th May all but one of the full ministerial appointments had been announced. For all Labour's tirades, the list included Chamberlain himself as Lord President inside the War Cabinet and Simon as Lord Chancellor outside it. But the names of the two members of the previous administration who had most reason to know how uncomfortable a colleague Churchill had been during the Norwegian campaign – Stanley, the Secretary of State for War, and Hoare himself – were conspicuous by their absence. There is among Hoare's notes on this hectic period a reference to suggestions that he might go to the Dominions Office or return to the India Office but it is not clear from whom they emanated: it may have been that the matter was mentioned in a lengthy conversation he had with the King (whom he knew well) when delivering up his seals of office on 12th May. Whether or not a definite invitation ever came Hoare had made up his mind, after receiving Beaverbrook's firm advice, not to accept a lesser post outside the War Cabinet.[46] On the morning of 12th May he went to the Air Ministry to say his farewells and to end a ministerial career which had begun in the same department 18 years before.

However much he may have been prepared to accept the loss of ministerial office when the formation of a coalition government became inevitable Hoare could not fail to be depressed when the blow actually fell. He was the only one of the four leading members of the pre-war government to go into the political wilderness – along with the new posts for Chamberlain and Simon, Halifax remained Foreign Secretary – and this very isolation intensified the blow to his pride and, he believed, to his reputation in the eyes of the world. He wrote to Chamberlain on 14th May:

Unlike almost all my colleagues I have not gone into the Government, and I greatly fear that the world at large will explain my exclusion as evidence of weakness and incompetence. No one has said a word in my defence. You know my

record, and if it were generally known, it would need no
defence, but it is not known and I alone of the four of us who
went through Munich am left isolated to stand this unjust
criticism ...[47]

There was some consolation, however, in the private unsolicited
testimonials from colleagues who did indeed know of his record
and valued it at its true worth. Hankey, for example, wrote on
12th May:

> I could not believe my ears or eyes when I learned that you
> were leaving the Air Ministry, where you were doing such
> magnificent work ... that the man who has mastered the
> problems of the key service of all should be replaced by an un-
> tried and wholly inexperienced politician [Sir Archibald
> Sinclair], and who has made no mistake and shown how to
> combine initiative and daring with prudence – well it just
> beats the band.[48]

On the following day, Leslie Hore-Belisha, the former Secretary
of State for War, wrote:

> I felt a pang of deep sympathy when I learned of your
> sacrifice. From my personal experience I know that you de-
> served this fate least of all. You showed vision in many of the
> things that were wanted and I look back with real apprecia-
> tion on the help you gave me in the first stage of the war ...
> Your able chairmanship of Committees over which you
> presided left me with keen admiration of your practical and
> businesslike gifts.[49]

Moore-Brabazon (who had accompanied Hoare to the Air
Ministry in April to continue as his P.P.S.), told him on the same
day:

> I am so upset that the world did not appreciate your great
> initiative and wisdom, for you have drive and initiative and
> were always right. What more is asked of a minister? ... It
> has been wonderful being with you. I have enjoyed every
> moment of it, but I could cry that the country has you no
> longer at Air ...[50]

Most welcome also was a brief note on 17th May from a young

Conservative backbencher who had helped Hoare in the India
Bill debates – Godfrey Nicholson:

> I should like to tell you that, although I voted against the
> Government and against Chamberlain [on 8th May], I am
> sincerely and truly sorry *you* have left office.
>
> I have had much kindness from you and I should like you
> to consider me a loyal friend.[51]

Nor was his work with the press unappreciated. Maurice Webb,
secretary of the Parliamentary Lobby Journalists (and future
Labour minister) was unanimously requested by his colleagues
to convey to Hoare

> … our most sincere thanks for all your assistance to us in the
> past, particularly in recent months.
>
> We have appreciated the ready way in which from time to
> time you have met us, taken us into your confidence and given
> us invaluable guidance.
>
> We shall all most certainly miss the contacts with you,
> which constituted, as we all agree, a really distinctive period
> in the history of the Lobby …[52]

Hoare was not to be left unemployed for long. He was now in
constant touch with Beaverbrook, both at Beaverbrook's
London residence, Stornoway House, and at the Ministry of
Aircraft Production, which Beaverbrook had been appointed to
head on 14th May and where Hoare's recent departmental
knowledge was invaluable to the new minister. They both also
saw a good deal of Brendan Bracken, now P.P.S. to the new
Prime Minister. The three of them came to the speedy conclusion that Hoare must have a job of importance and that the
most appropriate would be that of Viceroy of India, due to be
vacated by Linlithgow at the end of his normal term in the
spring of 1941. On 15th May Bracken wrote to Hoare:

> In my small way I shall strive for yr. appointment to the great
> job which you are supremely competent to do. If it comes
> your way don't kick. Take it for the good of England and
> India.
>
> You, of course, know that I am a mere bellhop. Sometimes
> such poor creatures are listened to.[53]

This, undoubtedly, was the post Hoare now wanted above all others. Lady Maud was less enthusiastic — as she had been in 1935 — but her initial reluctance gradually changed into conviction that India would be best for her husband's career.[54]

There was, however, another plan afoot for Hoare. It had been decided in April 1940 that in view of the strategic importance of ensuring the neutrality of Spain — on France's southern flank and commanding the entry to the Mediterranean — that Britain needed to be represented in Madrid by a more prestigious public figure than the normal career diplomat, especially as the current British Ambassador, Sir Maurice Peterson (the former head of the Foreign Office Abyssinian department) seemed to be falling foul of the Spanish authorities.[55] Lord Chatfield had been offered the post after ceasing to be Minister for Co-ordination of Defence in April and it appears that his departure for Spain was merely a question of selecting the most suitable time. But then came the German invasion of the Low Countries and with it and its immediate aftermath a shift in the whole balance of the war in Germany's favour. On 13th May Attlee reported to the War Cabinet that he had heard from an unimpeachable source that Spain would attack the allies within 48 hours and that that attack would be the signal for Italy to come into the war. Halifax said that he had been assured by the Spanish Ambassador, the Duke of Alba, that General Franco was determined to avoid getting involved in the war, but two days later the Foreign Secretary proposed to his War Cabinet colleagues, 'that some outstanding figure in public life should be asked to go to Spain in order to maintain our prestige. He had in mind that Sir Samuel Hoare might be invited to accept this mission.' The War Cabinet approved this suggestion and on 18th May Halifax was able to announce to it that Hoare had accepted his invitation. On 20th May Halifax told his colleagues that:

the Spanish situation was moving rapidly. With the approval of the Prime Minister, he had informed Sir Samuel Hoare that the sooner he reached Madrid the better. He [Halifax] had accordingly seen the Spanish Ambassador that morning and had asked him to obtain, as quickly as possible, the *agrément* of the Spanish Government for Sir Samuel Hoare's Mission.

On 23rd May Halifax reported that the Spanish government had conveyed its *agrément*. Hoare's appointment was publicly announced on the following day (it had been forecast in the press a week before) and on 29th May Hoare and Lady Maud were on their way by air to Madrid, via Bordeaux and Lisbon.[56]

The successive brief announcements in the War Cabinet concealed what was in fact a most difficult decision for Hoare to make. He had set his heart on the Viceroyalty, and could be forgiven for infinitely preferring that to the uncomfortable, probably dangerous and highly speculative assignment in Spain. He may have initially refused the latter. According to the contemporary diary of Sir Alexander Cadogan it was decided to offer the Spanish post to Hoare on 12th May — the very day he surrendered his seals of office as Secretary of State for Air — but that when the invitation was made by Halifax on the following day Hoare declined it. Cadogan's diary account is, however, so suffused with vituperative spite against Hoare as to make it an unreliable guide in the absence of any supporting evidence.[57] There is no reason (apart from Cadogan) to believe that Hoare received the Madrid offer before 15th May, the day the War Cabinet approved its being made. But between then and the 18th, when the War Cabinet was told that he had accepted, Hoare needed a good deal of persuading. Apart from Beaverbrook and Bracken he discussed the Spanish mission with Chamberlain, R. A. Butler, Lord Tyrrell and Admiral Tom Phillips, the Deputy Chief of Naval Staff, whom he had got to know well as First Lord. Chamberlain (who was to die five months later) was gloomy about the prospects of Hoare's being able to achieve anything in Spain, which he felt certain — now that France seemed doomed to collapse — would come under German domination, but he expressed admiration for Hoare's courage in contemplating so unpleasant a public duty.[58] Admiral Phillips was much more positive. As Hoare later recalled his advice it was that:

> You must go at once. It is essential that the Atlantic ports of the Spanish Peninsula should not fall into enemy hands. With the probable loss of France and the French fleet we are stretched to the utmost in our battle with the U-boats. If the Atlantic ports of the Peninsula and with them the coast of

north-west Africa go over to the enemy, I do not know how
we shall carry on. It is essential also that the naval base of
Gibraltar should remain available for our Mediterranean and
eastern communications. If you can do anything in support of
these fundamental needs of the war, your mission will be of
the highest strategic importance.[59]

Hoare, then, could feel that a 'special mission' to Spain ('special',
since a normal diplomatic post would have constituted an office
of profit under the Crown and necessitated his giving up his
parliamentary seat) was not just a convenient way of disposing of
a recent ex-minister in what was little more than a routine
diplomatic post closely controlled by the Foreign Office, but the
opportunity of making a real contribution to the prosecution of
the war. The decisive factor for his acceptance, however, seems
to have been that it did not necessarily rule out the Viceroyalty
since that would not have to be announced before the autumn
and would not commence until April 1941. After some six weeks
to three months in Madrid he could hand over to Chatfield and
return in time for the announcement of his appointment as
Viceroy. Such was the plan that was hammered out by Hoare
in discussion with Bracken and Beaverbrook, and to which
Halifax was privy. What is more doubtful is whether Churchill
— the man in whose gift the Viceroyalty lay and whom Hoare
saw on 24th May — had entered into any commitment to
appoint Hoare Viceroy when the time came. It seems unlikely
that he did so but Hoare seems to have gone to Spain convinced
that there was at the very least an informal understanding that
he would be the next Viceroy.[60] The conviction did not prevent
him from feeling, as he departed for Spain, an overwhelming
sense of impending isolation from the political life in which he
had for so long played a leading part. Just before boarding the
aircraft on the morning of 29th May he sent a brief note to
Beaverbrook. 'Do send me a line sometimes & don't forget me',
he beseeched his friend, 'I feel this morning as if I were going
into exile.'[61]

Spain was indeed a kind of political exile for Hoare. This in
every way surprising appointment — which he could never have
visualised when mapping out his political career ahead in, say,
1922, 1931, June 1935 or even December 1935 — was to be his

last full-time public appointment. Except for periods of home leave he was to remain in Spain for four and a half years and when he returned at last his political involvement was confined to a seat in the House of Lords. The Viceroyalty he yearned for never materialised. Although Halifax raised the question of Hoare's appointment to India with Churchill at the end of July 1940 and again in the middle of August, with apparently favourable responses, and while Beaverbrook assured Hoare early in September that 'So far as I know you are going to get India', Churchill himself wrote to Hoare towards the end of October to tell him that he had decided to renew Linlithgow's term and 'must in no wise be considered as committed to any particular solution of the personal and political issues involved in the selection of a new Viceroy'.[62] Despite the rather ominous ring of this sentence Hoare continued to nourish hopes as long as no successor to Linlithgow was named. It was not until June 1943 when, after an incredibly extensive Viceregal search lasting almost a year, Lord Wavell was nominated to succeed Linlithgow, that Hoare finally abandoned hope. His candidature as a man who had 'not only the knowledge but also courage and, in his own way, personality' had more than once been vigorously pressed by the Secretary of State for India, his friend and India Bill ally, Leo Amery (and was apparently favoured by Linlithgow) but each time met Churchill's immovable opposition. As Amery explained in a telegram to Linlithgow on 10th June, 1943, it had in the end been necessary to go outside political life to find an acceptable Viceroy:

[The] Prime Minister has definitely decided that he cannot spare Eden in view of peace conference, etc. He feels Anderson who is very useful here has aged latterly and would be regarded as a rather negative appointment. [Oliver] Lyttelton [Minister of Production] who also would be difficult to spare has not got the right kind of personality for India and might be erratic. Nothing will induce him to look at Sam Hoare. There is nobody else in the political stud who is either big size in himself or in public estimation.[63]

On the same day Amery wrote sympathetically to Hoare in Madrid:

I am afraid the announcement about the Viceroyalty will
have saddened you. I know it has always been the goal at the
back of your mind, and the succession of postponements over
the last 18 months may have made you feel that the door was
not finally closed. But there it is. Even as late as yesterday I
had some hope of persuading Winston to reconsider his view
of the matter, but he was entirely unconvinced. He recognises
your abilities and special knowledge of India ... But nothing
will shake his view that there is a sentiment here and also in
America over the Hoare-Laval Agreement and over Munich
which would prejudice the appointment from the start and
afterwards. As for Hoare-Laval, I have never doubted myself
that you were right then and that it might have saved much
trouble afterwards, and that only the chapter of accidents and
Baldwin's feebleness wrecked that situation. Over Munich we
differed, but history alone will be able to balance what we
lost and what we gained by the delay.[64]

Over ten years later Amery was still regretting that Hoare had
not been 'allowed to follow up [the Government of India Act]
in India itself during the war'.[65]

Churchill's objection to Hoare because of his association with
the pre-war appeasement policy was hardly relevant to the work
of a Viceroy of India in 1943 and looks suspiciously like a
rationalisation. The continuing animus of Churchill against
Hoare, deriving from their confrontation over the India Bill, in
which Churchill came off a decided second best, was revealed
even more in his rejection of him as Viceroy than in his failure
to include him in his government in May 1940. The latter was
by no means unexpected or undesired by Hoare himself and
clearly provided a convenient sop to the Labour party. But to
refuse to appoint Hoare Viceroy after the enthusiastic and
repeated recommendation of the responsible minister and in the
light of Hoare's obvious qualifications for the post was a much
more considered act. The widely held view of Churchill as a
man without rancour seems in need of some revision.[66]

It was certainly not Hoare's record in Madrid which told
against him in the Viceroyalty stakes, either in the autumn of
1940, when he was thought by all important members of the
government (including Churchill) to have turned with great

success a potentially dangerous phase of Anglo-Spanish relations, or in 1942-3 when, among other things, his advice and diplomatic skill had done much to prevent any Spanish threat to the allied invasion of North Africa ('Torch') in November 1942.[67] Indeed in his letter of 23rd October, 1940 (already quoted) Churchill implied that Hoare's continued presence in Madrid was necessary for the war effort:

> I really do not think there is anyone who could serve us so well as you, and the work you have done already has given great satisfaction to the Cabinet. I hope therefore that you will persevere in your difficult task, standing as you do in one of the key posts of Imperial Defence.[68]

Churchill did not exaggerate. Within days of Hoare's arrival in Madrid on 1st June circumstances had made it the most important embassy in Europe. On 10th June Italy, Britain's chief rival in the Mediterranean, entered the war on Germany's side, on 22nd June France was forced to accept surrender terms and by the end of June German forces were at the Franco-Spanish frontier. The possibility that Spain — ideologically aligned with Germany and Italy, obligated to them for help received during the Civil War and subject to direct German influence in many aspects of its governmental, cultural and commercial life — would not throw in its lot with the Axis seemed remote. And if it did so Gibraltar and the whole strategic position in the Mediterranean and North Africa, already imperilled by Mussolini's act of treachery, would be in the gravest jeopardy.

Hoare's assessment of the situation can be gauged from the voluminous correspondence he maintained (in addition to the normal ambassadorial reports to the Foreign Office) with his former ministerial colleagues, especially with the Foreign Secretary, Halifax (until the latter went to Washington as ambassador in December 1940).[69] His responsibilities as ambassador, unlike those in his political offices, were now primarily executive, but his performance of them (admirably documented in his book *Ambassador on Special Mission*) was clearly influenced — in a way which would not have been open to an ordinary career diplomat — by his recent high-level ministerial experience and by his familiarity with the political world. He immediately saw that however odious the Franco nationalist regime was it was secure in the saddle for the immediate future (in the long term Hoare placed his hopes in the restoration of constitutional monarchy as the cure for Spain's political ills[70]). The problem was thus how to try to ensure Spanish neutrality, or if — from its ideological and geographical propinquity to Germany this was too much to expect — its essential 'non-belligerency'. This needed, among other things, a recognition of Spain's neutral rights in the British enforcement of the economic blockade against Germany and, in the early stages at least, a willingness to help restore a Spanish economy which had been shattered by the Civil War.[71] But this was not a policy likely to be popular with British opponents of the Franco regime, some of the most prominent of whom were now members of the government (with Hugh Dalton, the Minister of Economic Warfare, Hoare crossed many swords through the agency of the Foreign Office). Hoare put the problem to Halifax, in a dispatch dated 26th July, 1940. He believed, he wrote, that Spain could be kept out of the war.

> This is why I ask His Majesty's Government so to apply our economic policy as not to give the impression that Spain is or will be our enemy. To adopt a fatalist attitude and to assume that Franco is bound to go in with Mussolini and Hitler is playing directly into the hands of the German *agents provocateurs*. The one thing above all others that these propagandists wish is to create an atmosphere of hostility in which incidents will arise that will inevitably lead to war.

But if he were to be proved wrong in his prognosis and Spain did eventually decide to enter the war he

> would be in favour of postponing the day as long as possible. Every month may now bring changes in the situation and … make this entry less likely. Spain will be constantly influenced by our failures or our successes. If the war goes better for us, we may see a surprising expression of feeling that is now suppressed below the surface. It will show itself first in the traditional xenophobia of the nation [i.e., against the many Germans in Spain]. Then, if we play our cards cunningly we may be able to make use of this xenophobia for drawing the coun-

try gradually out of the range of the Axis. It seems to me that this policy is worth trying, for even if it fails, I do not see what we lose by the attempt. The policy does not mean approval of Franco and the methods of his Government. My friends of the Left are fully entitled to continue to hold their views on this issue. It means one thing and one thing only: namely, the most effective way of keeping Spain out of the war altogether if possible, and if that is not possible, for as long a period as we can.[72]

Despite his belief that Spain would probably not commit itself to the Axis Hoare wanted the British government to confront the possibility of itself having to declare war on Spain. He wrote to Halifax on 1st October, 1940:

Supposing that a German ultimatum comes to Spain making either or both of these demands: the right of passage to the Mediterranean and the occupation of certain naval and air bases in Spain. Suppose further that the Spanish Government is too weak to resist the ultimatum, are we ready at once with a plan of action? For instance, if the Germans occupied bases and the Spaniards claimed that the transfer of bases need not be a *casus belli* and that we had already given away the case of the right of passage in allowing German troops to pass through Sweden, should we at once declare war on Spain? I myself think that the answer should be 'Yes' and that I should continue to make this clear to everyone ... I still believe we can keep Spain out of hostile action of this kind, but we have to take everything into account in this world of surprises and I should like to think that you have clearly in mind what you intend to do supposing the unlikely happened.[73]

But a policy designed to prevent or delay Spanish warlike involvement against Britain required endless patience and an insight into the stark facts of the Spanish situation. In December 1940 the illegal incorporation of the International Zone of Tangier into Spanish Morocco led Hoare to send Halifax (just before he left the Foreign Secretaryship) a clearly exasperated but none the less percipient appraisal. The 'Tangier business', he wrote, was typical of the methods of Serrano Suner, the new Spanish Foreign Minister and former Minister of the Interior.

If it is any comfort to us, they treat their own people even worse than they treat foreign Governments. Anybody, man, woman or child, may at a moment's notice be thrown into prison or shot without anyone having the chance of investigating or even discussing the case. Not a day passes without my having some new example of this complete want of balance. In normal times I should say that it was impossible to deal with a Government and country which behaves like this. Perhaps in these abnormal times we must deal with them but how to do it is difficult beyond imagination. If you take a conciliatory line, they think you are giving way. If you take a strong line, they say that you are threatening them and start kicking against you like mules. I should have given up the attempt some time ago if I did not feel that the Spanish people, like the French people, are becoming more and more anti-German. Unfortunately neither in France nor in Spain is there any means for public opinion to make itself felt. Unfortunately also, apart from their inherent vices, both Governments, French and Spanish, are captive Governments, the French Government entirely and the Spanish Government to a considerable degree so long as the Germans are on the Pyrenees. I am not sure whether in London everyone fully realises the implications of this position. It means that with the Germans on their back, there are many things that they cannot do and indeed it is almost essential for them to maintain an appearance of hostility against us ... It is no good Whitehall expecting from them the kind of conduct you would demand from a free government ... So far as Spain is concerned we cannot expect gratitude or common sense, and much less political sense. We must rather be ready to face endless gaffes and provocations. Indeed, we must steel ourselves to the fact that what we do for Spain we do for our own advantage, namely for keeping the war out of the Iberian Peninsula and not for the *beaux yeux* of this rash and irresponsible country.[74]

Hoare's task in Madrid was in large part an exercise in public relations: to project to the Spanish authorities and people the inevitability of Axis defeat and the necessity for Spain to maintain friendly relations with Britain and its allies. In the first part of his mission his hand was painfully, almost derisively weak, with the Dunkirk evacuation, the fall of France and Italy's entry into the war. The only items on the credit side were Spain's parlous economic state and need for such commodities as wheat and oil which only America — a very active pro-allied 'neutral' well before it entered the war at the end of 1941 — could provide in sufficient quantities; and the potential damage that a complete British blockade could inflict on Spain. But weak or not, Hoare played his hand with great skill, and with an unorthodox panache that would not have come easily to a more conventional diplomat. The first need was to raise the morale of the British Embassy itself, which had sunk to the depths in the face of the succession of allied defeats and uncertainty about the future. The appreciation of the situation Hoare got from his naval attaché, Captain A. H. Hillgarth, in a memorandum dated 2nd June, 1940 (the day after Hoare arrived in Madrid) was quite clear on this point:

> The British Embassy in Spain, as a whole, has until recently refused to take into practical account the fact that we are at war. Now that the Allies have suffered a defeat ... complacency has given place ... to a belief in ultimate Allied defeat. In effect, the Embassy Your Excellency has come to command is defeatist. This is not only patent in private conversation but is evident in the general interpretation of policy. As it is Spain with whom we have to deal and the Spanish viewpoint is very largely influenced by German and Italian propaganda, our belief in ourselves, which must betray itself in our words and actions, is of supreme importance. The Spanish opinion of our policy is governed to a certain extent by the interpretation the whole Embassy puts on the progress of the War. It cannot be confined to the Ambassador ... [75]

On Hillgarth's advice Hoare immediately put in hand an intensive review of embassy security procedures. Although the several German secret services had made Madrid their chief centre outside Germany, the British embassy almost invited burglary: there was no organised control of the entrance, no night watchman and no up-to-date safe for the custody of secret papers. The measures instituted under Hoare's instructions were instrumental in ensuring that no secret embassy papers ever fell into enemy hands, with the exception of the false reports about allied intentions which the embassy deliberately circulated to mislead the enemy.

Of more direct importance to the morale and *esprit de corps* of the embassy was an administrative innovation for which Hoare was responsible. Like most foreign missions at the time, the Madrid embassy tended to be divided into watertight compartments that made any feeling of common purpose difficult if not impossible to achieve.

> The Service and commercial attachés regarded themselves as responsible to their departments in London, the Chancery tended to be sidetracked by the experts from the wartime offices in London who came and went as their ministers decreed, whilst the Ambassador remained on an eminence where he was expected to see everything, but was in actual practice so far removed from much that was going on that he was apt to see very little.[76]

Drawing on his ministerial experience Hoare introduced a kind of Cabinet system for the various sections of the embassy.

> All the heads of the civil and military departments met in my room every morning and discussed with me not so much their own sectional details as the general position and the collective action to be taken for the next twenty-four hours. I would, for instance, give the meeting full accounts of any important interviews that I might have had with Franco, Serrano Suner or other Ministers. We would study the latest instructions from London and consider how best to support them not only with specific representations to the Ministry of Foreign Affairs but with joint pressure upon other departments of the Spanish Government. We would discuss the various rumours that the Germans were spreading, and agree upon the best line to circumvent them.[77]

There was thus collective information and collective responsibility. Hoare freely acknowledged that any success achieved was a joint success of the whole mission, however publicly prominent his own role had necessarily to be. Above all, he recognised his debt to his able second in command, Arthur Yencken, tragically killed in an air accident in May 1944.[78]

Hoare's chief task was, quite simply, to keep the British flag flying in a capital and a country which was already German-dominated (above all, in the press which derived all its news of the war from German sources) and which, for several months at least, could easily have been subjected to German armed invasion. From the outset he 'assumed ... and steadily maintained with both suppleness and dignity, that he was a most distinguished representative of a truly Great Power which eventually and inevitably must defeat the Axis'.[79] This involved constant protests to the Spanish authorities, both over infringements of neutrality and over the treatment of British nationals – the latter including not only residents but also a steady stream of escaping prisoners of war (who, if unfortunate enough to be caught at the frontier before they could take advantage of the elaborate escape network operated by the British embassy, were thrown into the forbidding prison camp at Miranda del Ebro, where their freedom had to be painfully negotiated by embassy officials). Not a week went by when Hoare was not impelled to make strong representations about some matter or other: as he later wrote, 'with the Germans in virtual charge of Madrid, persistence was my stock in trade'.[80] His rather precise and meticulous personality here served him in excellent stead.

A typical instance of Hoare's assertion of his country's rights occurred just four weeks after he had arrived in Madrid and when British fortunes, with the fall of France, were at their nadir. On 27th June German forces arrived at the Spanish frontier, thus completing the total conquest of France. Immediately afterwards a German colonel at Hendaye arranged with the Spanish general at San Sebastian a ceremonial visit of German troops to the Spanish town. When Hoare got to hear of this he saw at once that quite apart from being a blatantly unneutral act such a parade – ceremonial or otherwise – could well lead to a much more general infiltration of German troops which would make it virtually impossible for Spain to remain outside the Axis camp. He went to the Ministry of Foreign Affairs and told the minister, Colonel Beigbeder – who had apparently been unaware of the proposed parade and clearly disapproved of it – that if it took place he would immediately end his mission and return to England. Beigbeder issued orders for the march to be stopped and later the Spanish general con-

cerned was censured and transferred to another post; but the
minister was not able to secure the total prohibition of the entry
of individual German soldiers in uniform.[81]

Hoare developed a close working relationship with Beigbeder,
who, like most of the professional army, was strongly in favour
of the maintenance of Spanish neutrality. In October 1940,
however, Beigbeder was replaced as Minister of Foreign Affairs
by Suner, the leader of the pro-German Falangist element in the
government, and the two years of Suner's incumbency, before
he in his turn fell from power, were perhaps the most uncomfortable of Hoare's mission. It was during this period, too,
that the embassy came under physical attack and Hoare staged
one of his most dramatic protests. On 24th June, 1941, a well-
drilled mob demonstrated in Madrid against the Soviet Union,
which just two days before had perforce become a British ally
with the German invasion of its territory. Stones were hurled
at the British embassy, breaking many windows, the Union
Jack was torn down and an attempt to storm the building was
fought off by the regular force of British army guards, supple-
mented by 16 escaped P.O.W.s who were sheltering at the embassy before being smuggled out of the country via Lisbon or
Gibraltar. It was half an hour before the Spanish police could
be induced to take much interest but when they did the crowd
soon dispersed without any arrests being made.

Hoare and his staff decided on an immediate protest. They
went *en masse* — the service attachés in full uniform — to the
Ministry of Foreign Affairs and demanded to see the minister.
Suner was, however, at a meeting of the Council of Ministers
but when his staff located him there he agreed to see the British
Ambassador at his private flat.

> When we arrived, the private secretary who received us pro-
> posed that I should see the Minister alone, and that my staff
> should wait outside. I replied that we had come as a body to
> mark the gravity of the occasion and that as a body we must
> see the Minister. Having gained my point, we filed into the
> Minister's room. In spite of his offer of chairs, we remained
> standing, whilst I first read and then handed him a strongly
> worded protest. When I had finished, the Minister attempted
> to make some explanation. I interrupted him, saying dryly

that we had not come to argue. We then bowed and walked out.[82]

Hoare later discovered that Suner had been in some fear of physical assault from the irate British diplomats and had hidden a marksman in the room to guard against the eventuality.

The published memoirs of one of the Madrid embassy staff give a vivid insight into Hoare's methods. Sir John Lomax, who retired from the diplomatic service in 1956 as Ambassador to Bolivia, was commercial counsellor in Madrid from 1940 to 1941. After Hoare had joined the embassy in the early summer of 1940 the contrast with the usual overseas diplomatic post was striking. Sir John Lomax wrote:

> Most diplomatic missions known to me marked time on a motionless scene. The British embassy in Madrid was different. The ambassador, Sir S. Hoare, had lived in the political world of partisans and elections, where inertia and drift are lethal. By second nature he weighed up objectives, planned campaigns and tried this means and that. He was not one to take it easy when ahead; to give an antagonist the benefit of the doubt, or spare the kicks on an adversary, fallen or erect.[83]

Among all the British representatives under whom Lomax served in a long diplomatic career Hoare was alone in being prepared 'to step out of routine to bend local events to his will'. He made it his business, for example, to gauge the balance of forces in the Spanish Council of Ministers on each issue that arose and the kind of arguments Suner would use to give the decision a pro-Axis bent. He 'would then see to it that the other ministers would be primed with a contrary version: if not pro-Allied, at least insinuating that Suner's reports were false'. Lomax, whose job brought him into contact with more Spanish ministers than most, was frequently used by Hoare to convey such messages and was carefully rehearsed by him in what he should say.

> ... 'Lomax, go and see the Minister of Public Works and offer to quote him for metalling the highways in northern Spain. When he asks why, tell him that you've seen German officers measuring up the roads (I had) and you supposed

Spain must be thinking of a new road project.' Or, 'Lomax, call on the head of state monopolies ... he's sure to complain about [allied-enforced] petrol rationing; tell him that the ration is cut because German vehicles are allowed to fill up in northern Spain — tell him that Suner has given the orders.'

Often the meaning purpose of the message was obscure but Lomax 'noticed that a minister who had shown but languid interest in the ostensible purpose of my visit, would leap into mental top gear when I trotted out the ambassador's item'.[84]

Hoare sometimes derived tactical advantage from the un-likeliest situations. Under an Anglo-Spanish agreement signed in March 1940 the British government had undertaken to assist Spain to obtain 100,000 tons of wheat from sources under British control but by August 1940 only about 15,000 tons had been shipped, owing principally to Spanish dilatoriness over payment. The 1940 harvest in Spain was, however, disastrously bad and at one time it looked as if there would not be enough wheat to maintain the bread ration. In response to the urgent request of the Spanish Ministry of Agriculture via Lomax two wheat ships from Argentina chartered by the British Ministry of Food were ordered to be diverted to Spain. Hoare received the telegram informing him of this move on the day the Spanish press reported that a tidal wave had destroyed the old town at Santander in northern Spain and that the Germans had sent in a relief train of wheat to the strickened area. He immediately instructed Lomax to arrange an interview for both of them with Carceller, the Minister of Commerce and Industry. Lomax recorded the ensuing dialogue between Hoare and the minister (carried on through a British embassy interpreter) as follows:

'Tell the minister', [Hoare] began abruptly, as a feudal lord might address a tenant through the bailiff, 'that I've come about the Santander disaster. It needs a prompt and efficient service of relief. I've ordered as a gift the diversion of two shiploads of wheat. Here, Lomax, show the minister that telegram.'

I gasped. The shipload had nothing to do with Santander, nor yet with the Ministry [of Commerce and Industry]. It had been begged off us by the Ministry of Agriculture, and was not a gift: the price was being argued with the Spanish

15 Departure of the Royal Family for Canada, May 1939. The King is talking to Lord Halifax, on whose right are Hoare, Neville Chamberlain and Lord Crewe

16 Hoare with Sir Robert Vansittart, August 1939

17 Hoare and Lady Maud leaving for Spain, May 1940

18 Lady Templewood

19 Lord Templewood, 1958

20 Hoare's Norfolk home: Templewood, Northrepps, near Cromer

Treasury; it was to be discharged at Cadiz. Northern ports were too near the submarine bases ...

'There is one condition, minister [Hoare went on]. My announcement must be reported in the Spanish press in full and promptly, in tomorrow's papers in fact. The ships are still at sea you understand. I would not send them to your ports unless the facts are plainly stated in the press under a government communiqué. No thanks, just the facts.'

'But ... Senor Ambassador, I do not control the press ... you see ...'

'I see that everything done by the Germans in Spain is published under the headlines, like this trivial German wagon of wheat, and never a word about supplies and trade arranged by my embassy. I must know there will be full reports before I confirm the offer.'

The next day every Spanish morning paper carried the news, the first public announcement of the growing volume of supplies under the March 1940 agreement. But it did not alter the fact that the ships were bound for Cadiz and their cargo had to be paid for. Lomax was anxious about the repercussions when Carceller discovered that he had been tricked, but a colleague of Lomax more aware of the fierceness of the Spanish sense of pride assured him that Carceller would never mention the affair again, for fear of being laughed out of court. And apparently he never did.[85]

Hoare's chief antagonists in Madrid were the German ambassador and, until his removal from office in September 1942, Serrano Suner. Lomax was disposed to believe that Hoare was the victor in both battles. With the German ambassador, Hoare's

> favourite ploy was to pretend *sub rosa* contacts with him; or to praise his anti-Nazi sentiments ... two German ambassadors were removed from Madrid during Hoare's term there, and both transferred in circumstances suggesting that Hoare's hints had hit a Berlin target — as indeed anyone would expect who has had experience of the suspicions which pursue most notables in the totalitarian and police states.

Against Suner, Hoare, 'never ceased his war of subtle suggestion. Officially the occasion of his dismissal was a fracas between

Suner's falangist police and their political rivals but ... there is no doubt that the anti-Suner whispering began in Hoare's drawing room.'[86] Hoare disliked Suner intensely — he thought him 'without exception, the nastiest piece of goods that I have ever met'[87] — and was relieved that his successor as Foreign Minister, Jordana, was someone with whom, like Beigbeder, he could develop a relationship of mutual trust and understanding.

The essential basis of Hoare's 'confident and successful diplomacy' (in Sir John Lomax's phrase) was relevant knowledge.[88] He travelled widely in Spain — getting particularly good receptions in the north, where the nationalist influence was weakest — and cultivated extensive contacts among social and church leaders (his friendship with the Duke of Alba, combined with his shooting skill, gave him the entrée to many Spanish country houses). Among his fellow diplomats in Madrid, Theotonio Pereira, the young Portuguese ambassador, was a particular friend and ally, and he naturally worked closely with the American ambassador. For Hoare's first two years in Madrid Alexander Wedell represented the United States and while Hoare sometimes had doubts about his diplomatic competence he found himself a pleasant and agreeable colleague. But Wedell's successor, the distinguished historian Professor Carlton Hayes, was a different proposition. Hoare considered him difficult and unsympathetic, with little insight into diplomacy or official life; while Hayes clearly found it hard to accept the position of leadership which Hoare had established among allied diplomats well before Hayes arrived in Madrid in April 1942. And, as their subsequent accounts of their respective Spanish missions showed, they differed fundamentally about Franco's attitude to the war. Hoare believed that the Spanish dictator was always at heart one with Hitler and Mussolini and desisted from entering the war on their side only because he deemed it inexpedient to do so. On the basis of a much less extensive knowledge of wartime Spain Hayes came to the conclusion that Franco could never have contemplated voluntarily joining the Axis and that, at least after the fall of Suner in September 1942, he increasingly adopted a pro-allied position. It would seem that Franco observed the existence of some rivalry between the two main allied envoys and deliberately exploited Hayes' naivety by favouring him with personal invitations unusual in his relations with foreign diplomats. These culminated in Hayes' final leave-taking, in January 1945, when he was presented with a portrait of Franco valued at 100,000 pesetas.[89] Hoare — who had official interviews with Franco on only five occasions between presenting his credentials in June 1940 and taking his leave four and a half years later[90] — was in no danger of being vouchsafed so embarrassing a mark of esteem.

As well as being a diplomatic mission the wartime British embassy in Madrid was a vital point of personal and intelligence contact with occupied Europe. Among the mass of such contacts with which Hoare was concerned perhaps two stand out as providing at least footnotes to history. He had not been in Madrid three weeks when he was called upon to assist in the escape of the Duke and Duchess of Windsor from France, where the Duke had been attached to the British liaison mission to French G.H.Q. On 20th June, 1940, Hoare received a telegram informing him that the Windsors were at Perpignan, near the Spanish frontier, having left their Riviera villa in company with British consular staffs who were also leaving France in the wake of the German victory. Frantic activity then followed to get permission from the Spanish authorities for the Duke's party — some of whom had no diplomatic visas or documents for their cars — to cross into Spain. This eventually done, the Windsors arrived in Madrid, via Barcelona, on 22nd June, and were accommodated in the Ritz Hotel (the ambassador's residence being unsuitable for such distinguished visitors). From then until they departed for Lisbon on 2nd July Hoare was in constant discussion with the Duke, and the recipient and transmitter of many urgent messages to and from London on the Duke's future.[91] The King and the British government wished the Duke to return to England immediately and take up an appointment — the King suggested Civil Defence Commissioner for Wales might be appropriate. But the project foundered on Buckingham Palace's refusal to acknowledge the Duchess as 'Her Royal Highness' and certain difficulties about financial arrangements. In the meantime, the Germans were determined to exploit the Duke's presence in Spain. Hoare wrote to Churchill on 27th June:

Before [the Duke] arrived every kind of rumour was spread by the German embassy. Under the pressure of the German machine the Spanish press declared that you had ordered his arrest if he set foot in England, that he had come here to make a separate peace behind your back, that he had always disapproved of the war and considered it even a greater mistake to go on with it, etc. etc. I did my best to ridicule these stories and since he has been here I have gone out of my way to show to Madrid that there is not a word of foundation in them. I have had him constantly in and out of the Embassy and to luncheon and dinner ... Whenever I see him – and this is very often – he returns to the charge about being given a job in England ... [92]

Hoare sympathised with the Duke's desire for a worthwhile post and himself suggested to Churchill that he be offered a naval appointment: the eventual solution – the governorship of the Bahamas (which he would assume without setting foot in England) was hit upon after the Windsors had left Madrid for Lisbon. The day before they left Hoare telegraphed the Foreign Office to report that 'They have both been very discreet and have made a good impression on the Spaniards.'[93] But it may have been a close run thing. Wedell, the American ambassador, told Hoare that one of his staff had reported to him a conversation in which the Duke apparently said 'the most important thing now to be done is to end the war before thousands more are killed or maimed to save the faces of a few politicians': a remark which, if it had got to the ears of the German embassy or Serrano Suner, would have made splendid enemy propaganda.[94] Had Hoare then known of the rather comic opera plot that Ribbentrop and Suner had hatched up to have the Duke kidnapped and induced to take part in peace negotiations involving the fall of Churchill's government and the Duke's restoration to the throne he might have been even more anxious.[95] But he was in any case heartily relieved when the royal pair were safely out of Spain.

Some three years later Hoare received two visitors, also *en route* for Lisbon, whose mission had a rather more direct bearing on the conduct of the war. On 15th August, 1943, three weeks after the overthrow of Mussolini, two Italian visitors arrived at

the British embassy and revealed their identities to Hoare as
General Castellano, chief assistant to the Chief of the Italian
General Staff, and Signor Montenaro, an Italian Foreign Ministry official; they were travelling on false passports as members
of a mission to meet a returning Italian diplomat due to arrive
at Lisbon from South America on 20th August (the subterfuge
being necessary since the Germans controlled all the exits from
Italy). Their request to Hoare was a dramatic one: would he
accept an Italian surrender to take effect as soon as allied forces
(which were then completing the conquest of Sicily) had landed
on the Italian mainland? Castellano gave circumstantial details of German dispositions in Italy and emphasised the need
for speed since the Germans were already rushing reinforcements into Italy and a delay of even a few days might mean that
the Italian army would no longer be a free agent. Hoare had, of
course, to reply that he had no authority in the matter but
would transmit the offer immediately to the British government. Considerably disappointed, Castellano and his companion
rejoined their party for the journey to Lisbon. The telegram
Hoare then sent the Foreign Office was relayed to Churchill at
the Quebec conference and various negotiations were put in
hand. Eventually an armistice was accepted by Badoglio on 3rd
September, and on the night of 8th September, allied troops
landed at Salerno. But by that time the Germans were strongly
entrenched and any hope of a speedy victory in Italy had soon
to be abandoned. Hoare always regretted that, when every day
counted, it had not been found possible to exploit more quickly
and imaginatively the Italian offer which had come to him on
15th August.[96]

For some time before he finally left Madrid Hoare had become increasingly anxious about his long-neglected affairs in
England, not least his virtually disfranchised constituents in
Chelsea. He had discussed these matters extensively during his
home leave in the late summer of 1943 with his constituency
officers, old friends and advisers like Beaverbrook and Bracken,
and with Churchill and Eden. One possible solution, which
Churchill himself offered, was for him to take a peerage, but
Hoare was uncertain at that stage either whether he wanted to
say a final farewell to the House of Commons or whether he was
prepared to stay much longer in Spain now that, with the recent

improvement in allied fortunes and the virtual certainty of continued Spanish non-involvement, the main task of his mission seemed to have been accomplished. He returned from leave on 1st October, 1943, on the understanding with Eden that in January or February he would be coming back to England for a final decision on his future. This time-table was, however, delayed by the long-protracted negotiations between the American and British governments and Spain over the supply of Spanish wolfram to the allies and the related allied attempt to prevent the metal (used to harden steel) going to Germany (the American State Department favoured tough tactics, while the British, advised by Hoare and his staff, saw the uselessness of issuing ultimatums certain to stiffen Spanish resistance when the chances of significant quantities reaching Germany were in any case remote).[97] On 17th April, 1944, Hoare wrote to Churchill:

> When I was in England last summer I found my constituency of Chelsea in a very troubled state, air bombardment, migration of population, administrative difficulties of all sorts had created every kind of problem, and it was made clear to me that my friends there greatly missed the help of a member on the spot. I made it clear to them that I was torn between two loyalties, but that, appreciating their worries, I would discuss with them again at the beginning of this year the difficult question of my future and try and give them a definite answer ... Since then, however, the wolfram impasse, through no fault of our own, has continued week after week ... [as a result of] the completely negative attitude of the State Department.[98]

But a wolfram agreement was at last reached with the Spanish government at the beginning of May and a few days later Hoare flew to London for his much-delayed meeting with his constituency association. The result he conveyed to Beaverbrook on 10th May. He had told Churchill that he

> could no longer harmonise Madrid and Chelsea. The upshot of the conversation [with Churchill] was that, as he wants me to go back for this all important chapter of the war [i.e. the imminent landings in France], I have said I am ready to take a peerage. You will, I know, think me foolish, but I have had

to make a decision and I have come to the conclusion that in the circumstances it is the right one. I am at present keeping the decision absolutely confidential. [99]

At the end of May Hoare returned once again to Madrid, the more quickly as a result of the death of his indispensable second in command, Arthur Yencken. He left Brendan Bracken to make the necessary arrangements in Chelsea, including the finding of an alternative Conservative candidate, and on 27th June Churchill telegraphed to say that he was proposing to submit his name for a Viscountcy. On 1st July the news of Hoare's peerage and his letter of farewell to his Chelsea constituents were released to the press.[100] On 14th July Hoare, having chosen to use in his title the name of his beloved Norfolk home, became Viscount Templewood of Chelsea. Amid the chorus of congratulations he received on his ennoblement at least one old political friend regretted his departure from the Commons at a time when

> There are so few senior men in the [Conservative] Party to give a lead on constructive policy when we come back to party conflict, and the Party as a whole is all over the place as a result of these Coalition years ... Still, no doubt your voice can be effective in the country and in the counsels of the Party even if you are lost from the House of Commons.[101]

But L. S. Amery's hope was not to be realised. The political influence once wielded in his party by Sir Samuel Hoare was never recaptured by Lord Templewood.

With the successful launching of the allied invasion of Europe the necessity for Lord Templewood's continued presence in Madrid was clearly much reduced and he could be forgiven for believing that his long and in many ways disagreeable mission had in all essentials been completed. In June 1940 the German army had seemed on the point of crossing the Pyrenees into Spain: in August 1944 they were indeed crossing that frontier, but as fugitives, to be interned in Miranda del Ebro. Early in October Templewood flew to London to arrange the final details of his resignation and, sponsored by Trenchard and Fitzalan, to take his seat in the House of Lords on 11th October. The intention was for him to return briefly to Madrid to take official leave of General Franco. Templewood saw in this formal ceremony an opportunity to give Franco a warning about the conduct that would be expected from his regime if Spain were to be allowed to participate in the development of post-war Europe; and outlined his ideas in a memorandum dated 16th October.[102] The project gained fresh impetus when Franco himself wrote a letter to the Duke of Alba, dated 18th October, for transmission to the British Prime Minister. Franco's letter was an extraordinary compilation, blandly ignoring his and his regime's earlier pro-Nazi sympathies and blatantly unneutral acts and calling for the restoration of good relations between Britain and Spain which, according to Franco, had been injured by the activities of British agents in Spain and the British alliance with atheistic and communistic Russia.[103] The official leave-taking could now be used to convey Churchill's reply to this brazen communication, and Templewood drafted a notably trenchant version for the Prime Minister's consideration since, as he said, 'Nothing short of high explosive will have any effect upon General Franco's complacency.'[104] Understandably, however, Churchill had other things on his mind than letters to complacent but non-enemy dictators, and Hoare had to depart empty-handed on 30th November, 1944, for his final visit to Madrid. And — despite postponements of his return to London — he was still empty-handed when he paid his leave-taking visit to Franco on 12th December, the day before he flew back to England. Churchill's reply was not delivered until January, and represented something of a watering down of Templewood's draft.[105] But Templewood was able to get the substance of what he had wanted said in a debate he initiated in the Lords less than a week after his return, in which he emphasised that only countries which recognised fundamental human rights should be admitted to the economic and other privileges of reconstructed Europe.[106] He fervently hoped that allied pressure would soon bring about either a radical change in the Franco regime or its removal. He could hardly have foreseen that it would be another generation before the process would even begin to get under way.

But if Templewood's more long-term hopes about Spain were doomed to disappointment he had no need to be dissatisfied about the achievement of his short-term aims. The record there was succinctly summarised in a letter from Churchill on 23rd December, 1944:

> Your mission to Spain has been a far longer one than either of us supposed when you accepted the Embassy in 1940. I know that it has often been a trying position, but the skill with which you performed it is measured by our success in preventing Franco and the Falange from bringing effective assistance to the enemy during the period of our weakness, and neither I nor any of my colleagues in the Government underestimate your great personal contribution to the maintenance of our interests in Spain.[107]

It was a very different contribution to the war effort than the one the future Lord Templewood had visualised for himself when he entered the War Cabinet on 3rd September, 1939, but it may well have been of far greater importance to the eventual victory.

Epilogue:
The Last Years

To describe as retirement the fourteen years of Lord Templewood's life which remained after he relinquished his last full-
time public office in his 65th year would be an abuse of the
term. Retirement from front-bench politics it may have been —
although he used to the full his status as an elder statesman and
permanent member of Parliament to advance the causes which
he had at heart. But relieved of the burdens of ministerial office
— and the intense political ambition which accompanied them
— he could now engage in activities that had had to be crowded
out in over twenty years of public service.

He had first to ensure a regular source of income. His last
directorship he had given up on joining the National Government in 1931 but despite the gap city firms were not reluctant
to avail themselves of his services. In 1945 he became a director
of the Bank of London and South America and in April 1946
undertook for the bank a three-month tour of South America,
visiting Argentina, Chile, Colombia, Venezuela and Brazil;
although it was primarily a bank mission he was briefed by
government departments, including the Treasury, Board of
Trade and Ministry of Civil Aviation, on the problems of British
trade relations with the area, and the number of official engage-
ments the Templewoods fulfilled while there virtually converted
it into a government mission.[1] In 1946, too, he joined the London
boards of the Norwich Union Fire and Life Insurance Societies,
becoming chairman of both from 1950 to 1953.

The Templewood Papers contain hardly any material on his
business activities unless, like the 1946 South American tour,
they impinged upon wider events. Despite his family's banking

traditions he would appear to have become a businessman only reluctantly and on a strictly part-time basis. Before 1931 it had been an economic necessity, to make possible his backbench or Opposition frontbench career; now, in political retirement, the economic motivation may have been even greater, but not the commitment. Formerly business had been secondary to a political career. Now it was secondary to a new career Templewood carved out for himself as author and journalist. He was no tyro. He had written short books in the 1920s on his flights to the Middle East and India, and in 1930 a substantial volume on his wartime Russian experiences (*The Fourth Seal*) had appeared. In the intervals of a busy official life he had prepared material with a view to publishing volumes of memoirs when the time was appropriate. But his first book after the war in fact covered his most recent experiences, as Ambassador in Spain. *Ambassador on Special Mission* was published in 1946, after a highly successful serialisation in the *Sunday Dispatch* in March and early April of that year (sales of the paper increased by 90,000 a week during this period).[2] Then, in 1949, came an attractive family portrait, based on the Hoare game book, and entitled *The Unbroken Thread* (extracts from which had appeared before publication in the *Field*).[3] *Nine Troubled Years*, his memoirs of the 1931–40 period, was his most substantial work and took considerably more time in the preparation: consultation of his own papers and – as a privilege accorded to a former minister – the Cabinet Office and Foreign Office archives; extensive correspondence with former colleagues; and most diligent reading of secondary sources.[4] No sooner was that finished (it was published in 1954, after being serialised in the *Birmingham Post*) than he started work on his memoirs of the Air Ministry period, 1922–9, which appeared under the title of *The Empire of the Air* in 1957 (again after serialisation in the *Birmingham Post*).[5] He then began a volume which in part covered periods he had already dealt with in earlier books but on which a good deal of archival and secondary material had since appeared: to be called *Three Missions* it included accounts of his work in Russia and Italy in the First World War and in Spain in the Second World War and the typescript was virtually complete at his death.[6] All his volumes were the result of painstaking research aided, on occasion, by expert outside assistance (on a fee basis): Reginald Bassett, of the London School of Economics, provided much material for the section of *Nine Troubled Years* (pp. 110–48) dealing with disarmament in the 1930s; and the aviation writer Geoffrey Dorman supplied a good deal of historical material for *The Empire of the Air*. But there was no question of 'ghosting'. Templewood's books were his own, as were the numerous articles and book reviews he contributed to the newspaper and periodical press and his occasional broadcasts, all drawing on his unique knowledge of twentieth-century British politics.[7]

His skills as a publicist were by no means confined to recreating the events and experiences of his political past. He employed them, in conjunction with his seat in the House of Lords, in the service of a variety of causes he felt to be important. The Lords *Hansard* for 1944 to 1959 reveal Templewood as one of the House's most active non-ministerial members, participating in, and often initiating, debates on such topics as the post-war reconstruction of Europe, European defence, international human rights, India (initially critical of the Labour government's decision to set a date for Indian independence, he later came to accept it as inevitable in the circumstances), crime and the police, the magistracy (he was closely involved, as chairman of the council of the Magistrates Association from 1947 to 1952, in what became the Justices of the Peace Act of 1949), the air force, civil aviation and — close to his heart as a devoted ornithologist — the protection of wild birds (he initiated and saw through the House of Lords the Protection of Birds Act of 1954). But the subject to which he directed his particular attention was the one with which he had close hereditary links: penal reform and, in particular, the campaign for the abolition of the death penalty, for which Templewood — alone among Conservative peers — became a leading spokesman in the House of Lords.

He had always regretted that the advent of war had prevented his Criminal Justice Bill from coming to fruition. In November 1946 he introduced a motion calling on the Labour government to bring forward a comprehensive measure of penal reform.[8] The 1938 Bill had made no provision for the abolition of capital punishment, partly because Templewood was not then himself convinced of the wisdom of abolition or of the readiness of public opinion to accept it, and partly because he felt he had enough on his hands to get restless Conservative backbenchers to agree to the abolition of corporal punishment. In November 1946 he still did not specifically declare himself on the issue of the death penalty but he indicated in his speech that he thought public opinion might well be in process of change and that legislation to abolish capital punishment might become possible in a few years.[9] In February 1947 he became President of the abolitionist Howard League for Penal Reform — the lineal descendant of the body that his great-grandfather had helped to found in 1816 — and shortly afterwards he declared his support for abolition.[10]

The main grounds for Templewood's conviction that the death penalty must go were brief and simple, and derived from his practical experience as Home Secretary and that subsequent close study of penal questions in Britain and abroad which his Howard League appointment had recognised. Capital punishment was not, as had so often been claimed, a unique deterrent, any more powerful than a long period of imprisonment; it necessarily excluded the possibility of reformation of the murderer or of remedying any error subsequently discovered in his conviction; and the hideous paraphernalia of executions morally degraded those who carried them out and the society which tolerated them. As he told the Lords in April 1948:

> ... whilst I fully realise the gravity of the criminal statistics, whilst I feel as strongly as any noble Lord that it is essential that the community should be protected, whilst I agree with every noble Lord who has so far spoken that we must keep in mind the fate of the victim as well as the fate of the criminal, I feel profoundly the need for this country, in a brutal, disillusioned world, to set the highest standard of humane conduct and to show its respect for the sanctity of human life, not by following the example of those who take it, but by wise methods of preventing crime and redoubled efforts for reforming even the worst of criminals.[11]

From the introduction of the Criminal Justice Bill in November 1947 to the Lords' defeat of Silverman's Private Member's Bill to abolish capital punishment in July 1956 the battle went on virtually continuously. Like the 1938 Bill the 1947 measure made no reference to the death penalty; rightly, in Templewood's view, since he felt abolition should be the subject

of separate legislation. But when, in the course of the Commons'
debates, an amendment to include in the Criminal Justice Bill
a clause abolishing the death penalty for an experimental period
of five years was approved, Templewood felt he should support
the move as the likeliest means of achieving the objective of
abolition. He spoke strongly in favour of the new clause in the
debate in the Lords and was among the minority, along with
Labour and Liberal peers, when it was defeated by 181 to
28.[12] When, however, the government reacted by suggesting a
compromise clause abolishing the death penalty for certain
classes of murder only he ranged himself with the majority in
opposing it, believing it to be futile to have a half-way house
which was still based on the concept of the unique deterrent and
preserved all the degrading features of executions.[13] Templewood welcomed the government's decision to establish a Royal
Commission on Capital Punishment although, like all abolitionists, he regretted that its terms of reference excluded it from
recommending actual abolition. This restriction did not, however, apply to the evidence that the commission received and
Templewood submitted a memorandum and appeared before
it in November 1950 to give oral evidence in support of the
abolitionist case. Soon afterwards his influential book, *The
Shadow of the Gallows*, appeared (published in 1951 by Gollancz
rather than his usual publishers, Collins). When the report of
the Royal Commission was debated in the Lords in December
1953 Templewood naturally took part and in July 1956 he was
the obviously appropriate Lords sponsor of Silverman's abolition Bill.[14] After the Lords defeat of the Bill he was highly critical
of the Conservative government's subsequent legislation which,
like the Labour government's compromise clause of 1948,
attempted to categorise murder, retaining the capital penalty
for some categories only. But this time his opposition was confined to words and neither he nor his fellow abolitionists
attempted to divide the House against what became the
Homicide Act of 1957.[15] There the campaign had temporarily
to admit defeat. Victory was not to be achieved until six years
after Templewood's death. But his role as the most distinguished
and experienced Conservative advocate of abolition undoubtedly
contributed significantly to the ultimate success of the campaign.

It would be inappropriate to list all the public and private offices Templewood held in the post-war years. Some — like the presidency of the Howard League, the chairmanship of the Magistrates Association and the presidency of the Air League of the British Empire (1953–6) — were offices of his post-war 'retirement'. Others, including the presidency of the Lawn Tennis Association, to which he had been appointed in 1932, and the chancellorship of the University of Reading, in which he succeeded Sir Austen Chamberlain in 1937, he continued to hold from the pre-war period. One of his newer public appointments was peculiarly suited to the man who had led the 1922 parliamentary attack on the Lloyd George honours scandal. In March 1950 the Labour Prime Minister, Attlee, invited him to become a member of the three-man Political Honours Scrutiny Committee, which examines all nominations for honours for political services. Templewood accepted, and in October 1954 he was asked by Attlee's successor, Churchill, to become the committee's chairman, a post he held until his death.[16]

On their return from Spain the Templewoods had taken a flat in Eaton Mansions, Sloane Square, as their London *pied-à-terre*, but spent as much time as possible at Templewood, where their Palladian-style house and its superb grounds were a constant source of delight to them. Unfortunately, however, Lady Templewood's health was soon to restrict considerably the ease and frequency with which they could travel between London and Norfolk. While they were on a six-week visit to the United States early in 1948, Lady Templewood slipped while entering a lift, breaking an arm and, more seriously, chipping a bone in her hip. The hip injury never fully healed and the onset of arthritis largely confined her to a wheel chair. The Norfolk visits became virtually limited to the summer, with Templewood making occasional trips by himself in between. It was a sad deprivation for him and it says much for his dedication to his various London-based public commitments that he was prepared to forego the prospect of complete retirement in his beloved Norfolk.

The year 1959 opened for Templewood, who celebrated his 79th birthday in February, with no apparent diminution in his range of activities. In December 1958 he had accepted the chairmanship of a small committee to advise the Ministry of Works on the erection of a suitable memorial to his old friend and colleague Trenchard (who had died in 1956) and he presided over several meetings of the committee between February and April.[17] In January he made what was to be his last radio broadcast, recalling his earliest memories of British politics under the title 'Were those the days?'; in March he accepted an invitation (destined never to be fulfilled) to take part in a radio programme on the General Strike.[18] Then early in April he had a serious attack of the influenza which had so often afflicted him and from which he was still suffering when, on 8th April, he made his last speech in the House of Lords — appropriately on the subject which above all others had dominated his later years: penal reform.[19] The viral infection persisted for several weeks but Templewood seemed to have recovered when, late in the afternoon of Thursday, 7th May, soon after returning to his flat from the House of Lords, he suffered a sudden heart attack, collapsed and died almost immediately. His body was taken to Norfolk and buried on 12th May at Sidestrand parish church, beside his father, mother and two of his sisters. Lady Templewood was unable to travel to the Sidestrand funeral but she attended the requiem service held soon afterwards at St Barnabas Church, Pimlico, which was also attended by a representative of the Queen (Lord Bathurst) and of the government (the Secretary of State for Air), together with many friends and former colleagues, among them the man who had exerted the most important individual influence on the shaping of his political career — Beaverbrook.

So ended a life which had taken in some of the highest offices in the state during a political career spanning one of the most eventful half-centuries in British politics. Hoare was never a popular figure, either in the world of Whitehall and Westminster or with the public at large. He had absolutely no charisma, indeed his personality was to many irritating and unattractive; while the conjunction of obvious ability and intense ambition such as he displayed is rarely a prescription for popularity. But the contribution of a public servant to the welfare of his age is to be measured not by personal charm but by solid achievement. Hoare's ministerial career was one of the most impressive of any in the inter-war period. Under his aegis as Secretary of State for Air for most of the 1920s the separate existence of the Royal Air Force was finally secured from the assaults of the older services and the British public first made fully aware of the vast potentialities of civil aviation. As Secretary of State for India from 1931 to 1935 he placed on the statute book, against bitter opposition in his own party, what was at the same time the most complex piece of constitutional legislation ever to be considered by Parliament and 'the last major constructive achievement of the British in India'.[20] There followed the short and, for Hoare, ultimately disastrous tenure of the Foreign Office, culminating in the Hoare-Laval agreement and resignation from office. But the ministerial career was not yet over. In the years from 1936 to 1940 were crammed the Admiralty, two years as a reforming Home Secretary, the office of Lord Privy Seal and a brief return to the Air Ministry. In all his posts, not excluding the Foreign Office, Hoare showed himself to be an administrator of great competence, political astuteness and power of decision.

Hoare was a man of contrasts, and so was his career. In many ways he was an archetypal Conservative, born of and upholding privilege, passionately devoted to archaic causes like the maintenance of the established Anglican Church in Wales, skilled performer on the grouse moors. But in fact he was something of a rarity in the Conservative party, at least in his earlier days: a fully professional politician when so many still looked on politics as a kind of hereditary activity which came with membership of the ruling class. Well to the left of the party, with unfashionably liberal views on such matters as education and penal reform. Prepared, as with the Government of India Act and the Criminal Justice Bill of 1938, to defy right-wing elements in the party, although always striving for intra-party consensus. Sensitive to political nuances, consulted by Prime Ministers and other colleagues on electoral tactics, yet capable of completely misjudging the public mood, as in the Hoare-Laval agreement or in apparently forecasting a golden age of peace for Europe a few days before the Germans occupied Prague in March 1939. A lover of outdoor pursuits and, with his spare frame, an excellent athlete in such skill-demanding sports as tennis and ice-skating, yet of indifferent health almost amounting to hypochondria. A man extremely thin-skinned, desperately anxious to succeed and cast down by failure but yet of remarkable resilience, as when he rebuilt his political career, phoenix-like, from the ashes of Hoare-Laval or when he made the transition in 1940 from rejected minister to brilliantly successful wartime diplomat.

Hoare's achievement undoubtedly fell short of the hopes he had himself entertained at the high point of his career in June 1935. There was, too, and continues to be, a certain equivocality about the public estimation of his career. It was no doubt completely fortuitous but yet it seemed in some way symbolic that the House of Lords, which has marked with a few well-chosen obituary words the deaths of less notable members, should have allowed the passing of the first and last Viscount Templewood to go unrecorded in its deliberations. A leader in *The Times* commented on Templewood's misfortune in having his name linked with the controversial Hoare-Laval pact rather than with his constructive contributions to the Royal Air Force and to constitutional development in India:

> Politics and history are seldom fair in this way. Besides, there was always something missing to rob his labours of the sort of consequences that catch the popular imagination. What was the use of the Indian marathon, the fifteen million words of his speeches in Hansard, when India's fate turned out to be not federation but partition and independence? The outbreak of war robbed his Penal Reform Bill by a few weeks of a final reading. Even his mission to Spain had a negative criterion of success.[21]

But, as the leader went on to point out, this would be to take altogether too superficial a view of a man whose 'great merit as a politician was thoroughness' and whose 'claim to statesmanship was a humane and civilised approach to politics'. The last phrase, in particular, is a percipient one. For all the partisan passions some aspects of his career aroused — he commented in 1946 on how his personal history had been 'continuously disturbed by storms and commotions'[22] — and for all his skill as party analyst of the current political situation, Hoare was singularly open-minded in his attitude to the problems of politics and government. His own pen-portrait of himself is not over-drawn:

> A liberal amongst conservatives and a conservative amongst liberals, he has never been able to judge questions exclusively by their party colour. Nor has he ever entered willingly into

party battles. His dozen election fights he cordially detested. In the House of Commons it was the Committee discussions and not the heated scenes of partisan fury in which he felt at home. In the Departments over which he presided, it was the day to day administration that chiefly interested him. In all these activities he was anxious to see quick and concrete results, and to achieve even a part of his objective he was usually ready to accept a compromise. This very English habit of compromise has sometimes landed him in trouble, and it may be that [his] excessive sensibility has exaggerated the dangers of more resolute action.[23]

This may not be the stuff of which dynamic party leaders are made but it is a quality without which British representative government would be considerably the poorer.

Bibliographical Note

Note on Unpublished Sources

The following are the locations of the various unpublished collections referred to in the notes to chapters:

Amery Diary: In the possession of the Rt Hon. Julian Amery, M.P.
Baldwin Papers: University Library, Cambridge
Beaverbrook Papers: Beaverbrook Library, London
Brabourne Papers (MSS.Eur.F.97): India Office Library, London
Bridgeman Political Diary: In the possession of Major-General Viscount Bridgeman
Cabinet and Departmental Records: Public Record Office, London
    Admiralty (Adm.)
    Cabinet (Cab.)
    Dominions Office (D.O.)
    Foreign Office (F.O.)
    Prime Minister (Prem.)
Austen Chamberlain Papers: University Library, Birmingham
Neville Chamberlain Papers: University Library, Birmingham
W. P. Crozier Papers: Beaverbrook Library, London
Davidson (Indian) Papers: Bodleian Library, Oxford
Fisher Papers: Bodleian Library, Oxford
Halifax Papers (MSS.Eur.C.152): India Office Library, London
Hodsoll Papers: Churchill College, Cambridge
Lloyd George Papers: Beaverbrook Library, London
Lothian Papers (GD 40/17): Scottish Public Record Office, Edinburgh
Royal Archives: Windsor Castle
Runciman Papers: University Library, Newcastle upon Tyne
Sankey Papers: Bodleian Library, Oxford
Templewood Collection (MSS.Eur.E.240): India Office Library, London

Templewood Papers: University Library, Cambridge
Trenchard Papers: In the possession of Viscount Trenchard
Vansittart Papers: Churchill College, Cambridge
Weir Papers: Churchill College, Cambridge
Zetland Papers (MSS.Eur.D.609): India Office Library, London

Notes

Chapter 1 : Early Career

1 Richard A. Rempel, *Unionists Divided* (David & Charles, 1972), p. 45.
2 Templewood, *The Unbroken Thread* (Collins, 1949), p. 163.
3 The Templewood Papers in the University of Cambridge Library (from here on referred to as Temp. Pap.), XX/1, unpublished and incomplete typescript memoirs entitled 'At Home and Abroad', p. 2.
4 *The Unbroken Thread*, p. 302.
5 Sir Edward Cadogan, *Before the Deluge: Memories and Reflections 1880–1914* (John Murray, 1961), p. 90.
6 Henry Pelling, *Social Geography of British Elections 1885–1910* (Macmillan, 1967), p. 90.
7 Temp. Pap., I/2, Webb to Hoare, 24th February, 1910.
8 Temp. Pap., XIX/14, Cadogan to Templewood, 9th November, 1954.
9 *West London Press*, 11th December, 1908.
10 The wedding excited considerable interest in the press, largely because of the innovations Hoare and his bride, with their deep Anglo-Catholic sympathies, had introduced into the service. As one paper described it: 'Lady Maud Lygon and Mr. Samuel Hoare made a dozen departures from conventional wedding procedure. Their union took place at eleven o'clock on the moist, grey October morning in a church empty of flowers or other festal decorations; the music, specially chosen, was of the severest description, the service was followed by Holy Communion, and, most remarkable of all, the bride was escorted up the aisle by the bridegroom.' *Eastern Daily Press*, 18th October, 1909.
11 Temp.Pap., XX/1, 'At Home and Abroad', ch. 5.

12 14 House of Commons Debates, 5th Series (from here on referred to as H.C.Deb.), cols 1697–1702.

13 16 H. C. Deb., cols 2219–22.

14 Temp.Pap., I/4a, Note on meeting with the Prime Minister (which is substantially what appeared in the *Morning Post* and other papers).

15 Ibid., Balcarres to Hoare, 21st June, 1910.

16 Beaverbrook to Hoare, 10th September, 1935, quoted in A. J. P. Taylor, *Beaverbrook* (Hamish Hamilton, 1972), p. 53.

17 On the Board and the inspectorate at this period see Gillian Sutherland, 'Administrators in education after 1870: patronage, professionalism and expertise', in Gillian Sutherland (ed.), *Studies in the Growth of Nineteenth Century Government* (Routledge & Kegan Paul, 1972), pp. 263–85.

18 Edmond Holmes, *In Quest of an Ideal* (1920), pp. 16–17, quoted in Sutherland, p. 274.

19 See Asher Tropp, *The School Teachers* (Heinemann, 1957), pp. 199–203; Bernard M. Allen, *Sir Robert Morant* (Macmillan, 1934), pp. 254–63. The account that follows is based mainly on the material in the Runciman Papers (WR 46), in Temp.Pap., I/6, and in H.C.Deb.

20 For example, in the *Morning Post* and *Yorkshire Post*, 13th March, 1911.

21 22 H.C.Deb., cols 2050–1.

22 Trevelyan was referring, in a speech he made in the Midlands, to the popular agitation against the House of Lords.

23 23 H.C.Deb., cols 275–80.

24 Ibid., cols 280–5.

25 Ibid., cols 286–8, 297–9, 305–8.

26 Hoare's letter (the main purpose of which was to criticise Runciman for refusing to take ministerial responsibility for the memorandum) appeared in *The Times* and *Morning Post* on 27th March, 1911; Yoxall's, in the *Manchester Guardian* on 1st April.

27 Letter in the *Morning Post*, 27th March, 1911.

28 *The Nation*, July 1911, quoted in Tropp, op. cit., p. 183; Runciman Papers, WR 46, Massingham to Runciman, 21st April, 1911.

29 Runciman Papers, WR 46, Morant to Runciman, 23rd March, 1911.

30 Ibid., Runciman to Morant, 24th March, 1911.

31 Temp.Pap., I/6, C. James to Hoare, 22nd May, 1911.

32 28 H.C.Deb., cols 449–577, 595–626; *The Times*, 14th July,

1911; *Schoolmaster*, 22nd July, 1911.

33 Entry on Sir Robert Morant in *Dictionary of National Biography 1912–1921*, p. 387.

34 Temp.Pap., I/6, Percy E. Goatley to Hoare, 22nd March, 1911.

35 *The Schools and Social Reform*, reviewed in *The Times*, 3rd February, 1914.

36 The Conservative leader, Bonar Law, told Asquith in October 1913 that if the majority of his party had to choose the lesser of the two evils they would prefer Irish home rule to Welsh disestablishment. R. Blake, *The Unknown Prime Minister* (Eyre & Spottiswoode, 1955), p. 161, footnote. The story of Welsh disestablishment is traced in P. M. H. Bell, *Disestablishment in Ireland and Wales* (S.P.C.K., 1969) and K. O. Morgan, *Freedom or Sacrilege: A History of the Campaign for Welsh Disestablishment* (Church in Wales Publications, 1966).

37 38 H.C.Deb., cols 833–40.

38 47 H.C.Deb., cols 477–80 (22nd January, 1913).

39 54 H.C.Deb., cols 245–53 (17th June, 1913).

40 45 H.C.Deb., col. 1146 (16th December, 1912).

41 Temp.Pap., I/1, Lyttelton to Hoare, 6th February, 1913.

42 *Birmingham Daily Post*, 4th February, 1913; *Pall Mall Gazette*, 17th February, 1913.

43 (Morning) *Standard*, 28th December, 1912, and 11th April, 1913.

44 42 H.C.Deb., cols 2135–7 (22nd October, 1912).

45 *West London Press*, 3rd November, 1912.

46 43 H.C.Deb., cols 592–7 (31st October, 1912); *The Times*, 1st November, 1912.

47 Temp.Pap., XX/3, holograph chapter for 'new book', December 1955.

48 *London Magazine*, September 1913.

Chapter 2: Wartime Missions and Post-war Politics

1 Temp.Pap., II/1, J. L. Baird to Hoare, 13th February, 1916. This file, which contains material on Hoare's wartime intelligence work in Russia, and certain other files concerned with his similar work in Italy, have been closed on the instructions of the Cabinet Office for security reasons. Mr Clifton Child of the Cabinet Office has, however, written a memorandum summarising some of this material (which is filed with the Papers), and I have drawn on this in what follows: it will be referred to as 'Cabinet Office Memorandum'. Hoare wrote an account of his Russian experiences in *The Fourth Seal* (Heinemann, 1930);

it is surprisingly revealing about intelligence activities and, indeed, publishes some material which is in the closed Russian file of the Templewood Papers.

2 Temp.Pap., II/6, Hoare to Lady Maud Hoare, 28th March, 1916.

3 Ibid., Hoare to Lady Maud, 25th May, 1916.

4 Ibid.

5 Ibid., II/5, holograph notes by Hoare on his appointment to Russia.

6 Sir George Buchanan, *My Mission to Russia*, Vol. II (Cassell, 1923), p. 51.

7 *The Fourth Seal*, p. 53.

8 Ibid., p. 52.

9 Temp.Pap., II/1, Cabinet Office Memorandum.

10 Ibid.

11 Ibid., II/2, letter of 18th May, 1917.

12 *The Fourth Seal*, p. 102.

13 Ibid., pp. 156–7; Buchanan, op. cit., p. 51.

14 R. Bruce Lockhart, *Memoirs of a British Agent* (Putnam, 1932), pp. 137–8.

15 *The Fourth Seal*, p. 159.

16 Ibid., pp. 125–6.

17 Ibid., pp. 118–19.

18 George Katkov, *Russia 1917: The February Revolution* (Longmans, 1967), pp. 226–7.

19 Major-General Sir Alfred Knox, *With the Russian Army 1914–1917* (Hutchinson, 1921).

20 Temp.Pap., II/1, Cabinet Office Memorandum.

21 Ibid.

22 Russia was in 1917 still using the old style Julian calendar, which was 13 days behind the Gregorian calendar used in the West.

23 Temp.Pap., II/3.

24 Ibid., II/2, F. A. Browning to Hoare, 10th April, 1917.

25 Ibid., II/1, Cabinet Office Memorandum.

26 Most of these reports are filed in Temp.Pap., III/6.

27 Temp.Pap., XXII/1, typescript on Italy from Lord Templewood's unpublished book, 'Three Foreign Missions'.

28 Ibid.

29 Ibid. Sir Rennell Rodd, the British Ambassador, later described Mussolini at this period as 'one of the most strenuous propagandists of the cause of the Allies, who have every reason to be grateful for his potent advocacy'. Rodd, *Social and Diplomatic Memories 1902–1919* (Edward Arnold, 1925), p. 249.

30 Temp.Pap., II/1, Cabinet Office Memorandum, Hoare to Macdonogh, 3rd January, 1918.
31 Ibid., Macdonogh to Hoare, 8th January, 1918, Hoare to Macdonogh, 10th January, 1918, Macdonogh to Hoare, 23rd January, 1918.
32 Either then or afterwards Mussolini must have discovered the identity of his benefactor since when the two men met in 1925 (Hoare being on his way home from an official tour of the Middle East as Air Minister) Mussolini greeted Hoare as an old friend, alluding to their 'dealings with each other in the past'. Lord Templewood, *The Empire of the Air* (Collins, 1957), p. 113. See also Lord Templewood, *Nine Troubled Years* (Collins, 1954), p. 154.
33 Temp.Pap., III/6, report of 8th February, 1918.
34 E. Beneš, *My War Memories* (Allen & Unwin, 1928), pp. 209–10.
35 Temp.Pap., IV/2, Beneš to Hoare, 9th November, 1928; see also Beneš to Hoare, 6th March, 1919.
36 *The Times, Morning Post* and *Daily Mail* for 26th March, 1919; *Daily Express*, 4th June, 1919; 114 H.C.Deb., cols 26–7 (24th March, 1919), 696, 717 (27th March, 1919).
37 Temp.Pap., XX/5, Hoare typescript, 'The Coalition Parliament 1919–22'; *The Times*, 10th May, 1922.
38 Temp.Pap., II/8; *The Times*, 28th November, 1921 and 15th January, 1923 (letter from Hoare).
39 See, for example, Lloyd George Papers, F/8/3/63, Churchill to Lloyd George, 15th June, 1919, enclosing Hoare to Churchill, 10th June, 1919; F/9/1/7, Hoare *et al.* to Churchill, 14th July, 1919; F/9/1/11, Hoare to Churchill, 30th July, 1919; F/9/2/3, Hoare to Churchill, 18th January, 1920 (also in Temp.Pap., IV/3).
40 Temp.Pap., II/3, Hoare to Churchill, 31st May, 1919.
41 Churchill Papers, 16/9, Churchill minute of 23rd July, on a minute by the Director of Military Operations on a letter from Hoare to Churchill, 17th July, 1919 (I owe this reference to Mr Martin Gilbert).
42 Temp.Pap., II/5, typescript, 'The Coalition Parliament'.
43 *The Times*, 16th March, 1920 (letter from Hoare); article by Hoare, 'The Prime Minister and the Irish Settlement' in *Nineteenth Century and After* (October 1920); 133 H.C.Deb., cols 2014–8 (28th October, 1920) and 2132–3 (29th October, 1920); Hoare to Beaverbrook, 13th June, 1921, reproduced in Beaverbrook, *Decline and Fall of Lloyd George* (Collins, 1963), p. 282.
44 Temp.Pap., II/5, typescript, 'The Coalition Parliament'.

45 Robert Rhodes James, *Churchill: A Study in Failure* (Penguin, 1973), p. 166.
46 Hoare's speech is in 149 H.C.Deb., cols 6–12 (14th December, 1921).
47 See, for example, *Daily News*, 18th August, 1920 and *Time and Tide*, 7th January, 1921.
48 Hoare to Beaverbrook, 16th November, 1921, quoted in A. J. P. Taylor, *Beaverbrook* (Hamish Hamilton, 1972), p. 189.
49 Maurice Cowling, *The Impact of Labour 1920–1924* (Cambridge University Press, 1971), p. 56.
50 Beaverbrook Papers, Templewood file 1, Hoare to Beaverbrook, 7th October, 1921.
51 Temp.Pap., IV/5, Hoare to Lindley, 18th February, 1922.
52 Beaverbrook Papers, Templewood file 1, memorandum enclosed with Hoare to Churchill, 12th November, 1921.
53 Temp.Pap., II/8, Hoare to Lindley, 18th February, 1922.
54 For a popular account, especially of the brokerage services of Maundy Gregory, see Gerald Macmillan, *Honours for Sale* (Richards Press, 1954); the more recent account by Tom Cullen, *Maundy Gregory* (Bodley Head, 1974), adds little.
55 Lloyd George Papers, F/31/1/61, Law to Lloyd George, 11th July, 1922.
56 William (Viscount) Bridgeman, unpublished 'Political Diary', pp. 65–7.
57 156 H.C.Deb., cols 1745–1862.
58 See, for example, Beaverbrook, *Decline and Fall of Lloyd George*; L. S. Amery, *My Political Life*, Vol. II (Hutchinson, 1953); Robert Rhodes James, *Memoirs of a Conservative: J. C. C. Davidson's Memoirs and Papers 1910–1937* (Weidenfeld & Nicolson, 1969); Cowling, op. cit.; Michael Kinnear, *The Fall of Lloyd George* (Macmillan, 1973). Hoare's own account, the most detailed by any of the principal participants, appeared as the first chapter of *Empire of the Air*. His Papers contain two other retrospective typewritten accounts, both headed 'The Fall of the Coalition': one (beginning, 'During the recess ...') probably an earlier and rather fuller draft for what became the published version; the other (beginning, 'The fall of the Coalition') has a chronology of events sometimes at variance with the other versions. What follows is largely drawn from all three accounts, with conflicts between them reconciled on the basis of probabilities. The two unpublished versions are in Temp.Pap., XX/5 and will be referred to here as 'The Fall of the Coalition' (The fall) and 'The Fall of the Coalition' (During).

59 Temp.Pap., XX/5, 'The Fall of the Coalition' (During).

60 Ibid., 'The Fall of the Coalition' (The fall).

61 Kinnear, op. cit., pp. 120, 130–31. Kinnear attempts to show, from local press reports of members' constituency speeches, that all but a handful of members had made up their minds on the issue of the coalition before the Carlton Club meeting. But in advance of the meeting it was by no means clear how the issue would be formulated nor how the coalitionist leaders would react to it when the time came. Nor is there quite the complete correlation between prior public statements of intended action in hypothetical future circumstances and actual conduct in the event as Kinnear seems to predicate; in any case, as he himself admits, 80 of the 187 anti-coalition voters at the Carlton Club had made no public statement of their attitude. William Bridgeman, a junior minister in the coalition government, was in no doubt about Bonar Law's importance: '... if he had spoken for coalition they [the anti-coalitionists] would have lost'. 'Political Diary', p. 81.

62 Quoted in R. Blake, *The Unknown Prime Minister* (Eyre & Spottiswoode, 1965), p. 451.

63 *Empire of the Air*, p. 21; R. Rhodes James, op. cit., pp. 121–2.

64 *Empire of the Air*, pp. 21–2. The original draft is in Temp.Pap., I/2.

65 Temp.Pap., I/2.

66 *Empire of the Air*, p. 24; James, op. cit., p. 122. The list of M.P.s is in Temp.Pap., I/2. It contains 74 names, but three must have been included in error since one of them was a Labour M.P. and the other two coalition Liberals, including Lloyd George's faithful friend Sir William Sutherland (who was in any case a minister, not a backbencher). Another three were subsequently marked on the list as being out of the country and thus presumably did not have telegrams.

67 With the three non-Conservatives and the three known to be absent abroad excluded from Hoare's list the potential attendance becomes 68. But of these, 11 were unable to get to the Carlton Club on the following day because they were either out of London on business or out of the country: it therefore seems unlikely that they could have attended Hoare's meeting. That would leave 57. Hoare's own estimates in his three accounts were curiously inaccurate: in *Empire of the Air* (p. 26) he wrote that 74 signed the attendance list, but this must have been a confusion with the original list of proposed invitations; in one of the unpublished accounts he refers to 50 or 60, in the other 60,

invitations, but must have had in mind the actual *attendance*. This could be taken as negative confirmation of an attendance of about 57. On the other hand, press reports put the number attending at about 40, while two Conservative, junior ministers who were not, of course, present put it in the thirties (Bridgeman, 'Political Diary', p. 77; Robert Sanders's diary, quoted in Cowling, op. cit., p. 205).

68 *Empire of the Air*, p. 25.

69 Temp.Pap., XX/5, 'The Fall of the Coalition' (The fall). Cf. *Empire of the Air*, p. 27.

70 Ibid., 'The Fall of the Coalition' (During). Cf. *Empire of the Air*, pp. 28–9.

71 See, for example, R. T. McKenzie, *British Political Parties* (Heinemann, 1955), pp. 100–109; Cowling, op. cit., pp. 209–12; Kinnear, op. cit., pp. 123–4.

72 Temp.Pap., XX/5, 'The Fall of the Coalition' (During).

73 Ibid., 'The Fall of the Coalition' (The fall). Cf. *Empire of the Air*, pp. 31–2.

74 The accuracy of these figures has been questioned, although only marginally and quite unimportantly. In James, op. cit., the figures are given as 185 to 88, with one declared abstention, on the basis of voting cards among the Davidson papers (the list is reproduced on pp. 129–33, with that for the pro voters containing 184, not 185 names). Kinnear's study, *The Fall of Lloyd George* (pp. 131, 221–42), using voting lists in the Austen Chamberlain papers, produced the figures of 187 to 86, with some 13 abstentions. As Kinnear has pointed out, there are several inconsistencies between the Davidson-James list and the Chamberlain-Kinnear list which do not seem capable of resolution. In the meantime there seems no reason for substituting either for the long-accepted figures of the actual voting. The main value of Kinnear's researches here is that they provide some rough quantification of abstentions (and thus of the total attendance at the Carlton Club) which were not referred to at all in the official report but clearly must have occurred.

75 Keith Middlemas and John Barnes, *Baldwin* (Weidenfeld & Nicolson, 1969), p. 123; *Empire of the Air*, p. 33.

Chapter 3: Air Ministry and Shadow Cabinet

1 Hoare acknowledged Beaverbrook's influence in launching his ministerial career when he wrote to him on 25th May, 1923, just after he had entered the Cabinet under Baldwin: 'Looking

back over the last two years I can say without any doubt that the whole thing is chiefly due to you. For it was you that pushed my rather stolid self into the current, and it is thanks to you that the current has landed on such solid ground. You have been an extraordinarily good friend and I cannot sufficiently express my thanks.' Beaverbrook Papers, Templewood file 1.

2 Templewood, *The Empire of the Air* (Collins, 1957), p. 36; Temp.Pap., XX/5, 'The Fall of the Coalition' (The fall).

3 Bernard Shaw wrote to Russell to urge him 'not to waste any of your own money on Chelsea, where no Progressive has a dog's chance ... It is exasperating that a reasonably winnable seat has not been found for you ...' *The Autobiography of Bertrand Russell*, Vol. II (Allen & Unwin, 1968), p. 165. Russell stood again in the December 1923 election and managed to secure the equivalent of half the votes gained by Hoare. In the election of October 1924 he stood down in favour of his wife, Dora, who shared a third of the votes with a Liberal candidate in a three-cornered contest with Hoare.

4 Temp.Pap., XX/5, unpublished typescript by Hoare on 'First Baldwin Government. Fall of Labour Gov. Second Baldwin Government'.

5 Temp.Pap., XXI/5, Hoare's unpublished typescript on 'The Bonar Law Government', from internal evidence almost certainly written in 1936.

6 Basil Collier, *The Defence of the United Kingdom* (History of the Second World War, H.M.S.O., 1957), p. 3; Robin Higham, *Air Power* (Macdonald, 1972), pp. 39, 55.

7 For contrasting views of the value of Churchill's work at the Air Ministry see Robert Rhodes James, *Churchill: A Study in Failure* (Penguin, 1973), pp. 160–61, and Henry Pelling, *Winston Churchill* (Macmillan, 1974), pp. 259–61.

8 The most extensive account is in Stephen Roskill, *Naval Policy Between the Wars*, Vol. I: 1919–29 (Collins, 1968). See also, among many other relevant studies, F. A. Johnson, *Defence by Committee* (Oxford University Press, 1960), and Michael Howard, *The Continental Commitment* (Temple Smith, 1972).

9 For a general account of commercial air development see Robin Higham, *Britain's Imperial Air Routes 1918 to 1939* (Foulis, 1960). On airships see the same author's *The British Rigid Airship 1908–1931* (Foulis, 1961).

10 Trenchard Papers, C.H. II/27/143/2, Trenchard to Salmond, 9th November, 1922.

11 *Empire of the Air*, pp. 39, 40, 42.

12 Trenchard Papers, II/27/85, Hoare to Trenchard, 21st December, 1926.

13 *Spectator*, 11th January, 1957 (in a review of *Empire of the Air*).

14 Stanley Jackson, *The Sassoons* (Heinemann, 1968), p. 197.

15 *The Memoirs of Captain Liddell Hart* (Cassell, 1965), Vol. I, p. 152.

16 Temp.Pap., XVIII/9B, Bullock to Templewood, 23rd January, 1956.

17 Ibid., Bullock's memorandum of September 1946, enclosed with Bullock to Templewood, 24th October, 1955.

18 Temp.Pap., X/3, Bullock to Hoare, 9th and 21st June, 1938 and 31st March, 1939, Hoare to Sir Francis Lindley, 12th April, 1939, Sir Warren Fisher to Hoare, 12th April 1939, Hoare to Bullock, 18th April, 1939. Baldwin, who as Prime Minister sanctioned Bullock's dismissal, later recognised the decision to have been mistaken.

19 See, for example, Temp.Pap., V/1, Sutherland to Hoare, 16th November, 1927; V/2, Sassoon to Hoare, n.d. (? late 1925).

20 Templewood, *Nine Troubled Years* (Collins, 1954), p. 71.

21 *Empire of the Air*, p. 242.

22 Liddell Hart, *Memoirs*, p. 143.

23 Andrew Boyle, *Trenchard* (Collins, 1962), p. 461; Trenchard Papers, C.H. II/27/143/2, Trenchard to Salmond, 28th March, 1923.

24 Cab 24/158, Cabinet Paper 88(23), 'Air Policy and a One-Power Air Standard', February 1923. Much of its contents were made public by Hoare in his first Air estimates speech in the House of Commons on 14th March, 1923. 161 H.C.Deb., cols 1605–23. There were, for example, only 371 front line machines in service at home and overseas compared with 1,178 possessed by France, and even with the expansion programme announced in the previous August there would still be only 575 British front line aircraft compared with 2,180 in the expanded French air force. Anglo–French relations were at a particularly low ebb at this period, with differences over the Near East, and the French invasion of the Ruhr in January 1923.

25 Cab 21/225, Hoare to Law, 19th February, 1923; also in the Weir Papers, and much of it is quoted in W. J. Reader's biography of Lord Weir, *Architect of Air Power* (Collins, 1968), p. 103.

26 Cab 24/161, Cabinet Paper 270 (23) of 12th June, 1923; Kenneth Young, *Arthur James Balfour* (Bell, 1963), pp. 438–9; Roskill, *Naval Policy*, pp. 382–3.

27 Cab 24/161, Cabinet Paper 310 (23) of 5th July, 1923.

28 Ibid., Cabinet Paper 299 (23) of 30th June, 1923; Cab 23/46, Cabinet meeting of 9th July, 1923.
29 Cab 24/161, Cabinet Paper 349 (23); Cab 24/162, Cabinet Paper 461 (23); Roskill, *Naval Policy*, pp. 374–5.
30 L. S. Amery, *My Political Life*, Vol. II (Hutchinson, 1953), p. 265; Amery Diary for 27th July, 1st and 2nd August, 1923.
31 Temp.Pap., XX/5, 'Baldwin First Government, etc.' The minutes of the Cabinet meeting showed that the decision was indeed reached by a majority vote.
32 167 H.C.Deb., cols 1717–21 (2nd August, 1923); Amery Diary for 1st August, 1923.
33 Roskill, *Naval Policy*, pp. 473–84.
34 Roskill, *Hankey*, Vol. II (Collins, 1972), p. 417.
35 192 H.C.Deb., col. 719 (25th February, 1926).
36 Roskill, *Naval Policy*, pp. 517–18.
37 192 H.C.Deb., col. 768 (25th February, 1926); Collier, op. cit., p. 18.
38 Boyle, op. cit., pp. 518–19.
39 Temp.Pap., XX/5, 'First Baldwin Government, etc.'; Cf. *Empire of the Air*, pp. 195–9.
40 *Empire of the Air*, pp. 269–71.
41 Cmd. 1811/1923; H.C.Deb., cols 1618–21 (14th March, 1923).
42 Higham, *British Imperial Air Routes*, p. 80.
43 Hoare's account was published as *India by Air* (Longman, 1927), and much of it was reproduced in *Empire of the Air*, pp. 115–73. He also circulated a Cabinet paper on aspects of his flight, Cab 24/185, C.P. 62 (27) of 18th February, 1927.
44 On Hoare's key role in the development of the air route to South Africa see Robert L. McCormack, 'Imperial Mission and the Air Route to Cape Town 1918–32' in *Journal of Contemporary History*, Vol. 9, No. 4 (October 1974), pp. 77–97.
45 Higham, *British Imperial Air Routes*, p. 348.
46 Cab 24/161, Cabinet Paper 324(23); Roskill, *Naval Policy*, p. 364; 167 H.C.Deb., cols 700–1 (26th July, 1923); 173 H.C.Deb., cols 1344–9 (14th May, 1924).
47 Higham, *The British Rigid Airship*, pp. 251–322; Joseph F. Hood, *The Story of Airships* (Arthur Barker, 1968), pp. 81–6.
48 192 H.C.Deb., col. 777 (25th February, 1926).
49 *The Aeroplane*, 12th June, 1929. The journal also said that Hoare had either invented or at the very least put into general circulation the word 'airminded'. He certainly used it in the House of Commons on at least one occasion. 220 H.C.Deb., col. 1914 (30th July, 1928).

50 He created something of a stir by delivering his speech in reply to the address from the throne opening the special session of Parliament to debate the Irish treaty on 14th December, 1921, in the scarlet, silver-epauletted uniform of a deputy lieutenant of the County of Norfolk.

51 203 H.C.Deb., cols 1431–40 (10th March, 1927).

52 Temp.Pap., XX/5, 'First Baldwin Government, etc.'; *Empire of the Air*, pp. 205–9; Higham, *Air Power*, p. 79.

53 Temp.Pap., XX/5, 'First Baldwin Government, etc.'; *Empire of the Air*, pp. 200–204.

54 *Empire of the Air*, p. 295.

55 Temp.Pap., R.F.1, Hoare's unpublished typescript on 'Relations with King and Court – George V'.

56 *New Statesman*, 26th January, 1957.

57 Temp.Pap., V/3, Stamfordham to Hoare, 10th June, 1929.

58 Ibid., Moore-Brabazon to Hoare, 13th June, 1929, Bullock to Hoare, 7th June, 1929.

59 Ibid., VI/1, Trenchard to Hoare, 30th December, 1929.

60 See, for example, Robin Higham, *Armed Forces in Peacetime* (Foulis, 1962), p. 150, and the same author's *The Military Intellectuals in Britain 1918–1939* (Rutgers University Press, New Jersey, 1966), p. 199.

61 Temp.Pap., XX/5, 'First Baldwin Government, etc.'

62 For moderate critical views see, for example, Sir Charles Webster and Noble Frankland, *Strategic Air Offensive*, Vol. I (History of the Second World War, H.M.S.O., 1961) and Higham, *Air Power*. For a strident and clearly unbalanced attack see H. R. Allen, *The Legacy of Lord Trenchard* (Cassell, 1972).

63 Even one of the critics of the emphasis on strategic bombers has observed that when (as in the 1920s) 'home defences were not organised and populations unused to facing war' bombers had distinct advantages. 'Relatively small forces could be used ... the mere threat acted as a deterrent and an inhibitor'. Higham, *Air Power*, pp. 236–7.

64 Jon Jacobson, *Locarno Diplomacy: Germany and the West 1925–1929* (Princeton University Press, 1972), p. 17.

65 Temp.Pap., V/8, Hoare's holograph notes and typescript on 'The General Strike'.

66 Ibid.

67 Liddell Hart, *Memoirs*, p. 143.

68 Iain Macleod, *Neville Chamberlain* (Muller, 1961), p. 111.

69 Temp.Pap., V/2, Lloyd-Greame (later Cunliffe-Lister) to Hoare, 1st November, 1924.

70 Ibid., XX/5, 'First Baldwin Government, etc.'
71 Ibid.
72 Ibid., V/2, Chamberlain to Hoare, 23rd July, 1925.
73 Neville Chamberlain Papers, 18/1/931 and 934, Chamberlain to Hilda Chamberlain, 7th and 22nd September, 1935; *Nine Troubled Years*, pp. 36–7.
74 Thomas Jones, *Whitehall Diary*, Vol. I (Oxford University Press, 1969), p. 174.
75 Much of it is reproduced in Roskill, *Naval Policy*, pp. 471–94.
76 Keith Middlemas and John Barnes, *Baldwin* (Weidenfeld & Nicolson, 1969), p. 336; Robert Rhodes James, *Memoirs of a Conservative: J. C. C. Davidson's Memoirs and Papers, 1910–1937* (Weidenfeld & Nicolson, 1969), p. 213.
77 Bridgeman 'Political Diary', p. 195.
78 Temp.Pap., V/3, unpublished typescript by Hoare on the 'Resignation of the Second Baldwin Government', dated June 1929.
79 Beaverbrook Papers, Templewood file 1, Hoare to Beaverbrook, 24th April, 1929.
80 His return was clearly a welcome event. One of his fellow-directors, Sir Philip Waterlow, wrote to the chairman of the company, Sir Joseph Broodbank: 'Nothing could have given me greater pleasure than to hear that my old friend, Sam Hoare, was willing to come back to our Board. I am sure that you must know that it was always my wish that this would happen; and I know that you will find he will be a most able assistant to your responsible position as Chairman of the Company.' Temp.Pap., VI/1, Waterlow to Broodbank, 13th June, 1929, enclosed with Broodbank to Hoare, 14th June, 1929.
81 Baldwin Papers, Vol. 164, Hoare to Baldwin, 25th December, 1929. Middlemas and Barnes, in one of the most curious of the many factual errors in their monumental biography, state that Hoare was appointed to replace Younger as *Chairman* of the party, a post which Younger had vacated in 1923. *Baldwin*, p. 560.
82 Temp.Pap., VI/1, Davidson to Hoare, 30th December, 1929, and 24th January, 1930; Beaverbrook Papers, Templewood file 1, Hoare to Beaverbrook, 31st January and 9th March, 1930.
83 Macleod, *Neville Chamberlain*, p. 144. Copies of the committee's report, dated 9th March, 1931, are in Temp.Pap., VI/3 and Baldwin Papers, Vol. 53.
84 Macleod, pp. 132–3. The Conservative candidate at the Twickenham by-election in August had already espoused Empire

Free Trade and forfeited official support in consequence. Labour gained the seat. R. R. James, op. cit., p. 318.

85 Middlemas and Barnes, op. cit., pp. 560-62; L. S. Amery, *My Political Life*, Vol. III (Hutchinson, 1965), p. 24.

86 Beaverbrook Papers, Templewood, file 1, Beaverbrook to Hoare, 15th May, 1930 (also quoted in A. J. P. Taylor, *Beaverbrook* (Hamish Hamilton, 1972), p. 288), Hoare to Beaverbrook, 16th May, 1930, Beaverbrook to Hoare, 18th May, 1930.

87 The development of the Empire Free Trade campaign and its impact on the Conservative party is well described in Middlemas and Barnes, op. cit., pp. 545-602. See also Gillian Peele, 'St. George's and the Empire Crusade' in Chris Cook and John Ramsden (eds.), *By-Elections in British Politics* (Macmillan, 1973), pp. 79-107.

88 See, for example, Beaverbrook Papers, Templewood file 1, Hoare to Beaverbrook, 16th May, 1930.

89 Halifax Papers, Vol. 19, Hoare to Irwin, 17th May, 1930.

90 Bridgeman 'Political Diary', p. 235. On 17th March Baldwin had delivered his famous attack on Rothermere and Beaverbrook as seeking 'power without responsibility – the prerogative of the harlot throughout the ages'.

91 Macleod, op. cit., p. 144. Rothermere was not bound by the Chamberlain-Beaverbrook agreement and continued for several years his campaign against any Indian 'surrender'.

92 Beaverbrook Papers, Templewood file 1, Hoare to Beaverbrook, 28th March, 1931, Beaverbrook to Hoare, 30th March, 1930.

93 Temp.Pap., VI/1, unpublished typescript by Hoare on 'The Second Labour Government'; 247 H.C.Deb., cols 1467ff (2nd February, 1931); D. E. Butler, *The Electoral System in Great Britain since 1918* (Oxford University Press, 1963), pp. 59-83.

94 *Nine Troubled Years*, pp. 117-19, 123-5; Temp.Pap., C.VII/1, minutes and papers of the sub-committee on the Disarmament Conference (also in Cab 21/346).

95 R. Bassett, *1931: Political Crisis* (Macmillan, 1958), which is in no sense superseded by Robert Skidelsky, *Politicians and the Slump* (Macmillan, 1967). For Hoare's accounts see *Nine Troubled Years*, pp. 16-22; Temp.Pap., VI/1, typescript on 'The Second Labour Government'.

96 *Nine Troubled Years*, p. 21.

97 Temp.Pap., VII/1, unpublished Hoare typescript on 'The First National Government'; R. R. James, op. cit., p. 368.

98 Middlemas and Barnes, op. cit., p. 630.

99 Temp.Pap., VII/1, Chamberlain to Hoare, 24th August, 1931.

Chapter 4: India

1 Birkenhead, *Halifax* (Hamish Hamilton, 1965), pp. 237–9.
2 Quoted in Sir Maurice Gwyer and A. Appadorai, *Speeches and Documents on the Indian Constitution 1921–47*, Vol. I (Oxford University Press, 1957), p. 220.
3 Quoted in C. H. Philips (ed.), *The Evolution of India and Pakistan 1858–1947* (Oxford University Press, 1962), pp. 286–7.
4 Halifax Papers, Vol. 19, Churchill to Irwin, January 1930.
5 Temp.Pap., I/2, Peel to Hoare, 11th August, 1922.
6 Halifax Papers, Vol. 18, Hoare to Irwin, 28th October, 1929.
7 Gwyer and Appadorai, op. cit., pp. 146–7, 214, 216; Templewood Collection in India Office Library (hereafter 'Temp.Coll.'), Vol. 76, Irwin to Hoare, 10th June, 1930 (also in Halifax Papers, Vol. 19).
8 There is a good deal of material on these discussions in the Austen Chamberlain Papers, e.g., A.C.22/3/32, 34, 35, 39, 42; 25/6/29. See also Birkenhead, pp. 288–9.
9 Halifax Papers, Vol. 19, Baldwin to Irwin, 16th October, 1930.
10 Temp.Coll., Vol. 80, Stanley to Hoare, no date [September 1930]. Baldwin's correspondence with Salisbury and potential delegation members is in Baldwin Papers, Vol. 104.
11 Temp.Coll., Vol. 70, Hoare's note on 'Meeting with Govt. at Downing Street Nov. 16th 1930'; R. J. Moore, 'The Making of India's Paper Federation' in C. H. Philips and M. D. Wainwright (eds), *The Partition of India: Policies and Perspectives 1935–1947* (Allen & Unwin, 1970,) p. 61.
12 See D. A. Low, 'Sir Tej Bahadur Sapru and the First Round Table Conference' in D. A. Low (ed.), *Soundings in Modern South Asian History* (University of California Press, 1968), pp. 294–329.
13 It is so argued in Waheed Ahmad, 'The Formation of the Government of India Act, 1935' (unpublished Ph.D. thesis, University of Cambridge, 1969), pp. 292–3, 319–20.
14 R. J. Moore, op. cit., pp. 70–78.
15 Halifax Papers, Vol. 19, Hailey to Irwin, 6th January, 1931.
16 Temp.Coll., Vol. 80, duplicated copy of Hoare's memorandum for the Business Committee (or Shadow Cabinet), 12th December, 1930.
17 247 H.C.Deb., col. 689. On 19th January Churchill had sent a warm note of sympathy to Hoare ('My dear Sam') on the death of his mother. Temp.Pap., VI/1.
18 249 H.C.Deb., col. 1455 (12th March, 1931); Halifax Papers, Vol. 19, Irwin to Linlithgow, 13th March, 1931.

19 Baldwin Papers, Vol. 104, Hoare to Baldwin, 30th May, 1931; Austen Chamberlain Papers, A.C.22/3/23, Hoare to Chamberlain, 30th May, 1931.
20 See, for example, H. W. Richardson, *Economic Recovery in Britain 1932–39* (Weidenfeld & Nicolson, 1967); Derek H. Aldcroft, *Interwar Economy in Britain 1919–39* (Batsford, 1970); L. J. Williams, *Britain and the World Economy* (Fontana, 1971).
21 Temp.Coll., Vol. 1, Hoare to Willingdon, 17th September, 1931.
22 Temp.Pap., VII/1, 'The First National Government'.
23 Temp.Coll., Vol. 1, Hoare to Willingdon, 6th November, 1931.
24 Ibid., Hoare to Willingdon, 17th September and 19th November, 1931.
25 Lothian Papers, Vol. 149, T. H. Keyes (British Resident in Hyderabad) to Lothian, 30th August, 1931.
26 Templewood, *Nine Troubled Years* (Collins, 1954), p. 76. The Hoare-Willingdon correspondence is in the first eight volumes of the Templewood Collection.
27 Temp.Coll., Vol. 11, (telegram) Hoare to Willingdon, 18th September, 1931.
28 Ibid., Vol. 1, Hoare to Willingdon, 2nd September and 26th November, 1931; 260 H.C.Deb., cols 409–46 (25th November, 1931).
29 Temp.Coll., Vol. 1, Hoare to Willingdon, 17th September, 1931.
30 Temp.Coll., Vol. 11, (telegram) Willingdon to Hoare, 23rd September, 1931.
31 Royal Archives GV K2330(2)/111, Hoare to Sir Clive Wigram (the King's private secretary), 24th September, 1931.
32 Temp.Coll., Vol. 14 (b), R. A. Butler to Hoare, 5th February, 1932.
33 Ibid., Vol. 1, Hoare to Willingdon, 17th September, 1931.
34 Letter from Gandhi's great friend Horace Alexander to R. J. Stopford, in the possession of Mr Stopford (who was secretary to the Conservative delegation at the second round table conference as he had been at the first). Private interview with Mr Stopford, 25th October, 1973. See also John Gunther, *Inside Europe* (Hamish Hamilton, 1936), p. 239.
35 Temp.Coll., Vol. 16, Gandhi to Hoare, 28th February, 1932.
36 Ibid., Vol. 1, Hoare to Willingdon, 3rd December, 1931.
37 Ibid., Hoare to Willingdon, 19th November, 1931.
38 Ibid., Hoare to Willingdon, 26th November, 1931.
39 Gwyer and Appadorai, op. cit., pp. 237–8.

40 W. P. Crozier Papers, 4/16, Crozier interview with Hoare, 12th June, 1934.

41 Temp.Coll., Vol. 1, Hoare to Willingdon, 10th December, 1931.

42 Ibid., Hoare to Willingdon, 3rd December, 1931.

43 260 H.C.Deb., cols 1207–18; Temp.Coll., Vol. 18, Davidson to Hoare, 2nd December, 1931.

44 *Nine Troubled Years*, pp. 69–70.

45 J. R. M. Butler, *Lord Lothian* (Macmillan, 1960), p. 179.

46 Temp.Pap., VI/1, Lothian to Hoare, 12th November, 1931; *News Chronicle*, 12th November, 1931.

47 *Sunday Times*, 10th May, 1959. This point was also made by one of Hoare's assistant private secretaries at the India Office: although he served Hoare in a comparatively lowly capacity Hoare wrote him a warm letter of thanks and best wishes when he left his minister's private office for another post (private interview with Sir Frank Turnbull, 12th August, 1971).

48 Temp.Pap., VII/1, Baldwin to Hoare, 22nd December, 1932. Eyebrows were raised at the award since, as submissions for Indian honours were normally made by the Secretary of State for India, some assumed, understandably if incorrectly, that Hoare had recommended himself. Birkenhead had also received the honour during his much less distinguished tenure of the same office.

49 Temp.Coll., Vol. 2, Hoare to Willingdon, 14th October, 1932. The minutes and memoranda of the committee are in Cab. 27/520–1.

50 It is in Temp.Pap., VII/1.

51 For example, Temp.Coll., Vol. 2, Hoare to Willingdon, 5th May, 1932.

52 Ibid., Hoare to Willingdon, 22nd April, 1932.

53 Cab 27/520, committee meeting of 4th November, 1932; Keith Middlemas and John Barnes, *Baldwin* (Weidenfeld & Nicolson, 1969), pp. 701, 704.

54 Sankey Papers, C. 543, Sankey memorandum on India.

55 There was soon to be an improvement, however. The Congress campaign virtually petered out and between April and July 1932 the number of those imprisoned for political offences declined dramatically from 34,458 to 4,683 (and to a mere 76 by 1935). Thereafter 'the country remained sullen though peaceful'. Percival Spear, *The Oxford History of Modern India 1740–1947* (Oxford University Press, 1965), p. 354. Hoare made it his business to see the widows of British officials who fell victim to terrorist outrages during the Congress campaign (interview with

Sir Frank Turnbull, 12th August, 1971).

56 Temp.Coll., Vol. 1, Hoare to Willingdon, 3rd March, 1932.
57 Ibid., Vol. 2, Hoare to Willingdon, 12th May, 1932.
58 The statement is in Gwyer and Appadorai, op. cit., pp. 239–41 (where the Viceroy is wrongly identified as Irwin).
59 Ibid., pp. 261–6.
60 Temp.Coll., Vol. 2, Hoare to Willingdon, 14th October, 1932.
61 Ibid., Hoare to Willingdon, 18th November and 28th December, 1932.
62 Lothian Papers, Vol. 165, Lothian to Willingdon, 28th November, 1932. Another of Hoare's colleagues closely associated with the Indian policy – John Davidson, who, at Hoare's request, handled the publicity for the conference – recorded later that 'Sam Hoare, who was excellent ... worked himself to a frazzle' to ensure the success of the conference. Robert Rhodes James, *Memoirs of a Conservative: J. C. C. Davidson's Memoirs and Papers 1910–1937* (Weidenfeld & Nicolson, 1969), p. 394.
63 Temp.Coll., Vol. 78, Sankey to Hoare, 25th December, 1932, Simon to Hoare, 26th December, 1932, Liaqat Hyat Khan to Hoare, 23rd December, 1932.
64 Page Croft's press statement of 11th March, 1933. quoted in Lord Croft, *My Life of Strife* (Hutchinson, 1948), p. 222; Lord Butler, *The Art of the Possible* (Hamish Hamilton, 1971), pp. 48–9.
65 Temp.Coll., Vol. 3, Hoare to Willingdon, 10th and 17th March, 1933. Davidson wrote in similar terms to Sir Frederick Sykes, the Governor of Bombay: 'The Diehards, Page Croft, Gretton, etc., are out in full cry against the proposals, and they have been joined by Winston whose objective of course is to obtain if possible a reconstruction of the Government no doubt to include himself. He is using India as a stick to beat the Government's back, but there are very few in our Party who are not aware of his motive.' Davidson Papers, 3, Davidson to Sykes, 2nd March, 1933. See also *Economist*, 1st July, 1933, quoted in Neville Thompson, *The Anti-Appeasers* (Oxford University Press, 1971), p. 18; Robert Rhodes James, *Churchill A Study in Failure* (Penguin, 1973), pp. 268–9; Middlemas and Barnes, op. cit., p. 709.
66 Temp.Coll., Vol. 3, Hoare to Willingdon, 17th March, 1933.
67 Fisher Papers, Box 1, Hoare to Fisher, 16th March, 1933.
68 *Proposals for Indian Constitutional Reform* (Cmd.4268/1933).
69 Hoare used the phrase, taken from Defoe's *Robinson Crusoe*, in opening the second reading debate of the Government of India Bill. 297 H.C.Deb., col. 1149 (6th February, 1935). See also *Nine Troubled Years*, p. 68.

70 Temp.Coll., Vol. 3, Hoare to Willingdon, 17th March, 1933. Hoare's correspondence with Salisbury and others on the membership of the joint select committee is in Temp.Coll., Vol. 17.

71 Temp.Coll., Vol. 17, Chamberlain to Hoare, 23rd March, 1933 (also in Austen Chamberlain Papers 40/1/2).

72 Hailey Papers, Vol. 34, Hailey to Willingdon, 26th April, 1933.

73 Ibid., Hailey to Willingdon, 15th July, 1933; Temp.Coll., Vol. 78, Sankey to Hoare, 26th July, 1933, Salisbury to Hoare, 7th August, 1933, Vol. 3, Hoare to Willingdon, 11th August, 1933; Halifax, *Fullness of Days* (Collins, 1957), p. 124; *Nine Troubled Years*, pp. 90–91. A full transcript of each day's proceedings in the committee was issued to the press, including, of course, Hoare's evidence.

74 Lothian Papers, Vol. 167, Lothian to Reading, 8th September, 1933 (recounting a private dinner conversation with Hoare); Crozier Papers, 4/16, interview with Hoare, 12th June, 1934.

75 Temp.Coll., Vol. 4, Hoare to Willingdon, 16th February and 13th April, 1934; Hailey Papers, Vol. 27A, Hoare to Hailey, 15th February, Hailey to Hoare, 27th February, 1934. The Austen Chamberlain Papers, 40/1–3, contain much material on the activities of his group in the joint select committee.

76 Temp.Coll., Vol. 3, Hoare to Willingdon, 19th May, 1933.

77 *The Times*, 19th May and 23rd June, 1933.

78 Henry Pelling, *Winston Churchill* (Macmillan, 1974), p. 359.

79 Temp.Coll., Vol. 4, Hoare to Willingdon, 20th April, 1934; Royal Archives GV N24211/1, secret note by Hoare, no date; *Nine Troubled Years*, pp. 92–8; S. C. Ghosh, 'Pressure and Privilege: The Manchester Chamber of Commerce and the Indian Problem, 1930–1934' in *Parliamentary Affairs*, Vol. XVIII, No. 2 (Spring 1965), pp. 201–15; Martin Gilbert, *Winston S. Churchill*, Vol. V (Heinemann, 1976), pp. 511–48, deals in detail with the episode from Churchill's point of view.

80 Temp.Coll., Vol. 3, Hoare to Willingdon, 17th November, 1933.

81 Ghosh, op. cit., pp. 210–11.

82 Temp.Coll., Vol. 4, Hoare to Willingdon, 27th April, 1934.

83 L. S. Amery, *My Political Life*, Vol. III (Hutchinson, 1955), p. 100.

84 Brabourne Papers, Vol. 20, Butler to Brabourne, 19th April, 1934; Temp.Coll., Vol. 4, Hoare to Stanley, 17th May, 1934; 290 H.C.Deb., cols 1711–1808 (13th June, 1934); L. S. Amery, op. cit., Vol. III, pp. 103–4.

85 There is a useful comparison of the white paper with the joint select committee report – and of both with the subsequent

Government of India Act – in W. R. Smith, *Nationalism and Reform in India* (Yale University Press/Oxford University Press, 1938), pp. 420–49.

86 For an analysis of Conservative voting dissidence on India see John Malcolm McEwen, 'Unionist and Conservative Members of Parliament, 1914–39' (unpublished Ph.D. thesis, University of London, 1959), pp. 343–56.

87 For an excellent brief discussion of the dominion status issue in the Indian context at this time see Nicholas Mansergh, *The Commonwealth Experience* (Weidenfeld & Nicolson, 1969), pp. 261–8.

88 Temp.Coll., Vol. 4, Hoare to Willingdon, 31st January, 1935.

89 297 H.C.Deb., cols 1163–75 (6th February, 1935).

90 Temp.Coll., Vol. 4, Hoare to Willingdon, 13th February, 1935.

91 Ibid., Vol. 78, Grigg to Hoare, 5th February, 1935.

92 See, for example, the 1953–5 correspondence between them in Temp.Coll., Vol. 76, and Temp.Pap., XVII/8; cf. *Nine Troubled Years*, pp. 102–3.

93 Temp.Pap., XIX/14, Hailey to Templewood, 6th October, 1954.

94 Ibid., XVIII/6 (D), Panikkar to Templewood, January, 1947.

95 Butler, *The Art of the Possible*, p. 60; Spear, *The Oxford History of Modern India*, p. 369; Temp.Pap., XVII/8, Templewood to Amery, 23rd February, 1954; cf. *Nine Troubled Years*, p. 101.

Chapter 5: Foreign Secretary

1 Thomas Jones, *Whitehall Diary*, Vol. 2 (Oxford University Press, 1969), p. 184. According to Lord Butler the ambition to be Foreign Secretary had been nourished in Hoare by Sir Geoffrey Butler, his P.P.S. at the Air Ministry and Lord Butler's uncle. *Sunday Times*, 10th May, 1959.

2 Brabourne Papers, Vol. 20, Butler to Brabourne, 3rd May, 1935. Butler confided to Brabourne how well he thought both Hoare and Lady Maud would 'do the Viceroyalty'.

3 Templewood, *Nine Troubled Years* (Collins, 1954), pp. 108–9.

4 Private information from Mr Paul Paget.

5 Brabourne Papers, Vol. 20, Butler to Brabourne, 31st May, 1935.

6 Avon, *Facing the Dictators* (Cassell, 1962), p. 216; Keith Middlemas and John Barnes, *Baldwin* (Weidenfeld & Nicolson, 1969), p. 822.

7 Memorandum by Sir Clive Wigram (the King's private secretary), 20th May, 1935, quoted in H. Montgomery Hyde, *Baldwin*

(Hart-Davis, MacGibbon, 1973), p. 384. R. A. Butler thought 'it would be very unscientific and wrong to send as Viceroy the man who passes the Bill'. Brabourne Papers, Vol. 20, Butler to Brabourne, 31st May, 1935.

8 Baldwin Papers, Vol. 47, f. 75, Baldwin to Linlithgow, 3rd June, 1935.

9 Middlemas and Barnes, op. cit., p. 822.

10 Ibid., p. 823.

11 Avon, op. cit., 217–18.

12 Beaverbrook Papers, Templewood file 1, Beaverbrook to Hoare, 10th June, 1935.

13 Temp.Pap., XXI/5, unpublished typescript on 'The Bonar Law Government', probably written in 1936, soon after his resignation.

14 Neville Thompson, *The Anti-Appeasers* (Oxford University Press, 1971), p. 65.

15 Avon, op. cit., pp. 217–19; Templewood, *Nine Troubled Years*, p. 136.

16 Austen Chamberlain Papers, 41/1/62, Hoare to Chamberlain. 22nd July, 1935.

17 *Nine Troubled Years*, pp. 136–7. Cranborne did not officially take up his post until 2nd August, when the Bill received the royal assent as the House of Commons Disqualification (Declaration of Law) Act, 1935. The Act also covered the question of designated responsibilities in Eden's title as some doubts had been raised about this in terms of a 1919 ministerial offices Act.

18 Sir Walford Selby, *Diplomatic Twilight 1930–1940* (Murray, 1953), p. 46.

19 Hoare's P.P.S., Mark Patrick, told Butler that 'the Foreign Office is ecstatic about the return of papers to them within a few hours of submitting them to the [Secretary of State] ... ' Brabourne Papers, Vol. 20, Butler to Brabourne, 20th June, 1935. One of his two Civil Service assistant private secretaries recalls that Hoare would take files home at night and return them all minuted or initialled the next morning. When in the office he almost always worked in an armchair with a large writing pad rather than at a desk. Interview with Sir Paul Mason, 13th April, 1972.

20 *Nine Troubled Years*, p. 137.

21 Avon, op. cit., p. 242.

22 *Nine Troubled Years*, p. 137.

23 Cab. 23/70, 19 (32), meeting of 23rd March 1932.

24 Sankey Papers, 1934 file, Ormsby-Gore to Sankey, 7th March, 1934.

25 Cab. 23/78, 10 (34), meeting of 19th March, 1934.

26 Temp.Coll., Vol. 4, Hoare to Willingdon, 29th March, 1935.

27 W. N. Medlicott, Douglas Dakin and M. E. Lambert (eds), *Document on British Foreign Policy 1919–1939*, Second Series, Vol. XIII: *Naval Policy and Defence Requirements July 20, 1934–March 25, 1936* (H.M.S.O., 1973), pp. 340, 367–8 (footnote), 384; Roskill, *Hankey*, Vol. III (Collins, 1974), p. 171; Middlemas and Barnes, op. cit., pp. 827–8.

28 His retrospective account of his share in the decision to agree to a naval building ratio with Germany (*Nine Troubled Years*, p. 142) is inaccurate. It speaks of his urging the Cabinet on 11th June 'to authorise the signature of the Agreement'. There was no Cabinet meeting on 11th June and the decision to accept the agreement had been made before Hoare became Foreign Secretary.

29 *Nine Troubled Years*, p. 145; Temp.Pap., XIX/6, notes on talk with Vansittart, 14th May, 1953, and XIX/12, note by Craigie, dated 11th June, 1953, on the Anglo–German Naval Agreement.

30 See D. C. Watt, 'The Anglo-German Naval Agreement of 1935: An Interim Judgement', in *Journal of Modern History*, Vol. XXVIII, No. 2 (June 1956), pp. 155–75.

31 See W. N. Medlicott, *British Foreign Policy since Versailles 1919–1963* (Methuen, 2nd edn 1968), pp. 142–50; Neville Thompson, *The Anti-Appeasers* (Oxford University Press, 1971), pp. 66–101; Corelli Barnett, *The Collapse of British Power* (Eyre Methuen, 1972), pp. 350–82; C. J. Lowe and F. Marzari, *Italian Foreign Policy 1870–1940* (Routledge & Kegan Paul, 1975), pp. 240–90; Arthur Marder, 'The Royal Navy and the Ethiopian Crisis 1935–36', in *American Historical Review*, Vol. 75, No. 5 (June 1970), pp. 1327–56; R. A. C. Parker, 'Great Britain, France and the Ethiopian Crisis 1935–1936', in *English Historical Review*, Vol. LXXXIX, No. 351 (April, 1974), pp. 293–332; Aaron L. Goldman, 'Sir Robert Vansittart's Search for Italian co-operation against Hitler, 1933–36', in *Journal of Contemporary History*, Vol. 9, No. 3 (July 1974), pp. 93–130. A recent one-volume treatment, Frank Hardie, *The Abyssinian Crisis* (Batsford, 1974) reverts in the main to the earlier moralistic tradition, but an earlier study of the crisis down to the Italian invasion, George W. Baer, *The Coming of the Italian-Ethiopian War* (Harvard University Press, 1967), is extremely detailed and useful.

32 Lowe and Marzari, op. cit., pp. 243–4.

33 Ibid., pp. 245–7.
34 Baer, op. cit., pp. 25–44.
35 Lowe and Marzari, op. cit., pp. 249–50.
36 Foreign Office memorandum of 14th October, 1935, quoted in Lowe and Marzari, op. cit., p. 251.
37 Quoted in Lowe and Marzari, op. cit., p. 261.
38 Message from G. H. Thompson, 12th April, 1935, quoted in Lowe and Marzari, op. cit., p. 448, note 53.
39 Medlicott, Dakin and Lambert, *Documents of British Foreign Policy 1919–1939*, Second Series, Vol. XII, *European Affairs August 5, 1934–April 18, 1935* (H.M.S.O., 1972), pp. 910–11, note 43. One source for the story, who ought to have known better since he was present at the conference, was Vansittart, *The Mist Procession* (Hutchinson, 1958), p. 520.
40 F.O.371/19105, J 793/1/1, Vansittart minute of 25th February, 1935.
41 Quoted in Lowe and Marzari, op. cit., p. 265.
42 Lowe and Marzari, op. cit., p. 267.
43 Parker, op. cit., pp. 298–300.
44 *Nine Troubled Years*, p. 153.
45 F.O.371/19112, J 2268/1/1, and 19184, J 1509, 2381. The final report was printed in August. Copies were sent to the embassies in Paris and Rome, the latter being almost immediately copied for Italian secret intelligence and published in the Italian press in February 1936. Baer, op. cit., pp. 188–9.
46 Goldman, op. cit., pp. 114–15; Lowe and Marzari, op. cit., pp. 271–2.
47 *Nine Troubled Years*, p. 155.
48 Cab 23/82, 33 (35).
49 F.O.800/295, f.13a, Hoare to Mussolini, 20th June, 1935. Mussolini's reply at f.26.
50 Avon, op. cit., pp. 221–9; Mario Toscano, 'Eden's Mission to Rome on the Eve of the Italo–Ethiopian Conflict' in A. O. Sarkissian (ed.), *Studies in Diplomatic History and Historiography* (Longmans, 1961), pp. 126–52.
51 A convenient source for these texts is Ruth Henig (ed.), *The League of Nations* (Oliver & Boyd, 1973).
52 Cab. 23/82, 35 (35).
53 304 H.C.Deb., col. 518.
54 There were brief references in the meetings of 10th, 22nd, 24th and 31st July, after which there was the usual summer break, interrupted by the summoning of the special Cabinet on 22nd August.

55 Lowe and Marzari, op. cit., p. 279; Avon, op. cit., pp. 250–51.
56 F.O.800/295, ff.101–6, Vansittart to Hoare, 19th August, 1935.
57 Ibid., ff.98–100, Hoare to Chamberlain, 18th August, 1935 (reproduced in full in *Nine Troubled Years*, pp. 164–5).
58 Ibid., ff.108–19, Hoare's Cabinet memoranda on these conversations.
59 Cab. 23/82, FA(H) 7.
60 Cab. 23/82, 42 (35): Cab. 53/25, C.O.S. 388 and 392. The Defence Policy and Requirements Committee had its fifth meeting the day after the Cabinet of 22nd August. Cab. 16/136.
61 F.O.800/295, ff.125–8, Hoare to Clerk, 24th August, 1935; also in Temp.Pap., VIII/3.
62 Baer, op. cit., pp. 311–15; Lowe and Marzari, op. cit., p. 281; Avon, op. cit., pp. 258–9.
63 Temp.Pap., VIII/1, Vansittart to Hoare, 10th July, 1935. Two modern scholars have observed: 'There were many good points in the Italian case against Abyssinia … Slavery, the wild conditions on the frontiers, the barbaric mutilations that were still the punishment for crime, the cruelty of many native customs, the lack of imperial control over outlying provinces, the primitive state of national development – all tended to be forgotten in the wave of world sympathy evoked by the tactics of the Italian Government.' A. H. M. Jones and Elizabeth Monroe, *A History of Ethiopia* (Oxford University Press, 1966 edn), p. 246.
64 Baldwin Papers, Vol. 123, Hoare to Baldwin, 5th September, 1935; Iain Macleod, *Neville Chamberlain* (Muller, 1961), p. 186; Middlemas and Barnes, op. cit., quoting Baldwin to Davidson, 9th September, 1935.
65 Cab. 21/412, ff.271–6, Hoare's Cabinet memoranda on his discussions with Laval, 10th September, 1935 (also in F.O. 401/35, J 4768 and 4769/1/1); *Nine Troubled Years*, pp. 167–9, where the date of Hoare's Assembly speech is given, incorrectly, as 12th September.
66 It was only on 6th September that Hoare was asking his staff 'If there is a conference on Raw Materials what are the kind of proposals that will be made, what is the safest line for us to get it on to, and what advantages, if any, could we get out of it? Could I have a rough draft on these points before I go to Geneva.' F.O.800/295, f.212.
67 F.O.800/295, ff. 190, 199; *Nine Troubled Years*, p. 170.
68 *The Times*, 12th and 13th September, 1935, carried the full text. There are lengthy extracts in Henig, op. cit., pp. 126–8.
69 Inis Claude, *Swords into Plowshares* (University of London Press,

1965), pp. 258–9.

70 F.O.800/295, ff.219–24, Hoare to Wigram, 14th September, 1935.

71 *Nine Troubled Years*, p. 169.

72 F.O.800/295, ff.219–24, Hoare to Wigram, 14th September, 1935.

73 Cab. 21/412, ff. 269–70. Record of discussion between Hoare and Laval, 5.30 p.m. 11th September, 1935.

74 Henig, op. cit., pp. 119–20.

75 F.O.800/295, ff.219–24, Hoare to Wigram, 14th September, 1935.

76 Ibid., ff. 234–7, Hoare to Eden, 17th September, 1935.

77 Brian Bond (ed.), *Chief of Staff. The Diaries of Lieutenant-General Sir Henry Pownall*, Vol. 1: 1933–1940 (Leo Cooper, 1972), p. 81. As late as 4th December Pownall's diary was recording that 'Ministers are grumbling, especially Hoare and Eden, that the Services have done so little since September to put themselves right'. Ibid., p. 91.

78 F.O.371/19137, J 5179/1/1, Hoare to Drummond (telegram), 23rd September, 1935.

79 Parker, op. cit., p. 307.

80 F.O.371/19129, J 4233/1/1, Treasury memorandum of 30th August, 1935.

81 Cab. 23/82, 43 (35).

82 Ibid., 44 (35).

Chapter 6: The Hoare-Laval 'Pact'

1 Vansittart Papers, 1/16, Memorandum on Reform of the League of Nations prepared for the Cabinet Committee on Foreign Policy, 13th July, 1936.

2 The initial sanctions resolutions are in Ruth Henig (ed.), *The League of Nations* (Oliver & Boyd, 1973), pp. 129–34. A recent study of the working of international sanctions says of those imposed in 1935 that 'their economic impact was clearly much reduced by the non-co-operation of Austria and Hungary and the neutral policies of the United States, Germany and Switzerland'. Margaret P. Doxey, *Economic Sanctions and International Enforcement* (Oxford University Press, 1971), p. 54. The only raw material for which League powers were the dominant suppliers to Italy was wool: the United States, Germany and other non-sanctionists provided major amounts of Italy's other raw

material needs. Moreover, Italy's exports were well distributed in different markets, much reducing the country's vulnerability to a League embargo on imports from Italy.

3 Cab. 23/82, 45 (35).

4 Cab. 23/82, 47 (35).

5 The course of the exchanges between the two governments is well summarised in R. A. C. Parker, 'Great Britain, France and the Ethiopian Crisis 1935–36', in *English Historical Review*, Vol. LXXXIX, No. 351 (April, 1974), pp. 307–10.

6 Parker, op. cit., p. 309.

7 305 H.C.Deb., cols 17–33.

8 Geoffrey Warner, *Pierre Laval and the Downfall of France* (Eyre & Spottiswoode, 1968), p. 109.

9 Templewood, *Nine Troubled Years* (Collins, 1954), p. 174.

10 Warner, op. cit., p. 110; Parker, op. cit., pp. 310–11; James C. Robertson, 'The Hoare-Laval Plan' in *Journal of Contemporary History*, Vol. 10, No. 3 (July 1975), pp. 436–7.

11 Avon, *Facing the Dictators* (Cassell, 1962), pp. 286–7; Parker, op. cit., p. 311.

12 Parker, op. cit., p. 315. The Spanish representative had objected to the exclusion of iron and steel from the original list when iron ore was included since an embargo on Spanish ore exports to Italy would result in increased sales for those countries exporting finished iron and steel. In a move to meet the Spanish objection the Canadian delegate (who was later repudiated by his government) proposed the addition, in principle, of all the excluded items: he did not, in fact, expect that an oil embargo would be attempted on the assumption that lack of co-operation from non-member states would render it nugatory.

13 W. N. Medlicott, *British Foreign Policy since Versailles 1919–1963* Methuen, second edition 1968), p. 147; Robertson, op. cit., p. 456.

14 Avon, op. cit., p. 291; Robertson, op. cit., p. 438.

15 F.O.371/19163, J 8384/1/1, quoted in Parker, op. cit., pp. 320–21; Avon, op. cit., p. 292; Robertson, op. cit., pp. 438–9.

16 F.O.371/19164, J 8419/1/1, quoted in Parker, op. cit., pp. 314–15. Two days later Hankey, in a private conversation, gave Hoare very similar advice. Roskill, *Hankey*, Vol. III (Collins, 1974), p. 187.

17 Cab. 16/136; Parker, op. cit., pp. 315–16; Brian Bond (ed.), *Chief of Staff. The Diaries of Lieutenant-General Sir Henry Pownall*, Vol. 1: 1933–1940 (Leo Cooper, 1972), p. 89.

18 Parker, op. cit., pp. 316–17.

19 *Nine Troubled Years*, pp. 174–5; Sir Maurice Peterson, *Both Sides of the Curtain* (Constable, 1950), p. 118.

20 F.O.371/19165, J 8629/1/1; Parker, op. cit., p. 317; *Nine Troubled Years*, p. 175; Iain Macleod, *Neville Chamberlain* (Muller, 1961), p. 188.

21 Royal Archives GV K2506/1, Hoare to Wigram, 2nd December, 1935. Quoted in part in Keith Middlemas and John Barnes, *Baldwin* (Weidenfeld & Nicolson, 1969), p. 881 and Parker, op. cit., p. 317.

22 Cab. 24/257, ff.207–12, C.P.212 (35); F.O.371/19164, J 8418/1/1.

23 Cab. 24/257, ff. 295–6, C.P.225 (35), conversation between Vansittart and Garibaldi, 25th November, and between Hoare and Garibaldi, 28th November, 1935, circulated to the Cabinet, 29th November.

24 *Nine Troubled Years*, p. 178.

25 They are in Cab. 23/82, 50 (35). Substantial extracts are quoted in Corelli Barnett, *The Collapse of British Power* (Eyre Methuen, 1972), pp. 371–3 and Frank Hardie, *The Abyssinian Crisis* (Batsford, 1974), pp. 147–51.

26 Roskill, op. cit., p. 189.

27 As evidenced, for example, in Adm.116/3049, memorandum by the Admiralty Plans Division, 'Summary of Present Situation in Regard to Italo/Abyssinian Crisis' [11th December, 1935].

28 Zetland Papers, D609/6, f.135, Zetland to Willingdon, 6th December, 1935.

29 Cab. 21/420, Report of C.O.S. Committee on assurances to be obtained from other powers to safeguard the situation in the event of an aggression by Italy, 4th December, 1935. Although British forces and possessions in the Mediterranean and the Middle East were clearly at the greatest risk the Air Staff was at this time seriously considering the possibility of air raids on Britain itself. It was necessary to maintain absolute secrecy about this 'in order not to start a panic in the country'. Hodsoll Papers, 4/15, Hodsoll to Sir Russell Scott, 16th December, 1935 (Hodsoll was head of the Air Raids Precautions Department of the Home Office, Sir Russell Scott, its permanent under-secretary).

30 Bond, op. cit., pp. 84, 89.

31 Temp.Pap., XIX/6, 'December 1935 Crisis'.

32 307 H.C.Deb., cols 319–432. The Dalton quotation is at col. 328; those from Hoare at cols 343, 345 and 346; and from Austen Chamberlain at cols 351–3.

33 D.O.114/66, Record of meeting, 5th December, 1935, quoted in David Carlton, 'The Dominions and British Policy in the

Abyssinian Crisis' in *Journal of Commonwealth and Imperial History*, Vol. 1, No. 1, (1972), p. 76, note 8.

34　F.O.371/19166, J 8837/1/1.

35　F.O.371/19165, J 8569/1/1, quoted in Parker, op. cit., pp. 313–14.

36　F.O.371/19167, J 8997/1/1, minutes of 3rd, 4th and 5th December, 1935; Cab. 24/257, f.321, C.P.234 (35), Record of conversation between Vansittart and the French ambassador, 6th December, 1935.

37　Ibid. Beaverbrook may also have been informally involved in the effort to counter the anti-British press campaign. According to his unpublished retrospective account of the crisis he went to Paris on the same train as Vansittart and on the day the Hoare-Laval talks opened dined with the proprietor of *Paris Soir* and the commentator 'Pertinax'. A. J. P. Taylor, *Beaverbrook* (Hamish Hamilton, 1972), p. 358.

38　Hoare's own later recollection was that from the station he was 'taken at once to the Quai d'Orsay'. *Nine Troubled Years*, p. 179. The account in the text is based on an interview with Sir Paul Mason, 13th April, 1972.

39　Cab. 24/257, ff. 319–20, C.P.233 (35), Record of meeting held at the Quai d'Orsay on 7th December, 1935, also in F.O.371/19167, J 8993; Avon, op. cit., p. 299; *Nine Troubled Years*, pp. 179–80.

40　Cab. 24/257, ff. 322–4, C.P.235 (35), Hoare's note on his conversations, initialled in Paris, 8th December, 1935, with annexes as to procedure, draft telegram to Rome, and details of the territorial proposals (also in Temp.Pap., VII/1). The territorial proposals are reproduced in Henig, op. cit., pp. 139–41.

41　Avon, op. cit., p. 300.

42　Cab. 24/257, f. 324.

43　Interview with Sir Paul Mason, 13th April, 1972.

44　Cab. 23/82, 52 (35).

45　F.O.371/19168, J 9108/1/1.

46　Cab. 23/82, 53 (35); F.O.371/19168, J 9154/1/1.

47　Cab. 23/82, 54 (35).

48　Temp.Pap., XIX/6, 'December 1935 Crisis'.

49　Ibid.

50　*Nine Troubled Years*, p. 184; 307 H.C.Deb., col. 856.

51　Temp.Pap., VIII/1, Patrick to Hoare, 12th December, 1935.

52　Beaverbrook Papers, Templewood file 1. Beaverbrook to Hoare, 14th December, 1935, quoted in Taylor, op. cit., p. 359.

53　Cab. 23/82, 55 (35).

54 Cab. 23/82, meeting of ministers, 16th December, 1935; Ibid., 55 (35); Avon, op. cit., pp. 309–10.

55 Temp.Pap., XIX/6, 'December 1935 Crisis'; Avon, p. 309. The account in *Nine Troubled Years*, pp. 184–5, does not mention the joint visit from Baldwin, Chamberlain and Eden and gives the impression, almost certainly inaccurately, that Baldwin and Chamberlain came separately.

56 Cab. 21/412, f. 114, Vansittart to Hankey, 16th December, 1935, enclosing 'the draft of a conclusion for Sam on Thursday'; Beaverbrook Papers, Templewood file 1, 'Draft of the Speech that Sir Samuel Hoare intended to deliver if he had not resigned'; Taylor, op. cit., p. 359; *Nine Troubled Years*, p. 186; Neville Chamberlain Papers, 2/23A, diary entry for 18th December, 1935.

57 Temp.Pap., XIX/6, 'December 1935 Crisis'; R. R. James (ed.), *Chips: The Diaries of Sir Henry Channon* (Weidenfeld & Nicolson, 1967), pp. 45–6; Amery, op. cit., p. 184.

58 It was seen by Baldwin only, and was not included in the general Cabinet series until after 1946. The brief version is Cab. 23/82, 56 (35). The fuller account, which has been used here, is in Cab. 23/90B. There are extensive quotations from the latter in Hardie, op. cit., pp. 186–90.

59 99 H.L.Deb., col. 278.

60 *Nine Troubled Years*, p. 185; Neville Chamberlain Papers, 2/23A, diary entry for 18th December, 1935.

61 307 H.C.Deb., col. 2016.

62 Temp.Pap., XIX/6, 'December 1935 Crisis'.

63 Royal Archives, GV K2506/3, Hoare to Wigram, 18th December, 1935. One of Hoare's Foreign Office private secretaries, Frederick Hoyer-Millar (later Lord Inchyra), took the letter to Buckingham Palace on Hoare's instructions at about 8 p.m. But according to the etiquette for these occasions, Hoare's written resignation should have gone to the Prime Minister. Hoyer-Millar was hauled over the coals by the No. 10 staff for this lapse. Interview with Lord Inchyra, 15th December, 1971.

64 Taken from the draft in the Beaverbrook Papers.

65 See, for example, among critics, Harold Macmillan, *Winds of Change* (Macmillan, 1966), p. 449, and Harold Nicolson, *Diaries and Letters 1930–1939* (Collins, 1966), pp. 232–3; and, among friends, L. S. Amery, *My Political Life*, Vol. III (Hutchinson, 1955), p. 185, and James, *Chips*, pp. 47–8.

66 307 H.C.Deb. Hoare's speech is at cols 2007–17, the debate itself, at cols 2018–28. Much of Hoare's speech is reproduced in

Henig, op. cit., pp. 142–6.

67 This sentence, perhaps the most famous of the whole speech, was adapted from Vansittart's draft, which had suggested: 'No one else in Europe has moved a ship, a machine or a man'. Cab. 21/412, f. 116.

68 It was recalled, for example, in the *Daily Telegraph*, 22nd January, 1957, and Lord Templewood wrote to (Sir) Colin Coote to correct it. Temp.Pap., XVII/8, Templewood to Coote, 23rd January, 1957.

69 307 H.C.Deb. Attlee's speech is at cols 2018–30 (his accusation at col. 2029); Baldwin's at cols 2030–9; and Chamberlain's at cols 2039–42.

70 They are in Temp.Pap., VIII/5.

71 Lothian Papers, GD 14/17/310, ff.435–7, Linlithgow to Lothian, 21st December, 1935, Lothian to Linlithgow, 31st December, 1935.

72 Temp.Pap., VIII/5, Winterton to Hoare, 19th December, 1935, Chamberlain to Lady Maud Hoare, 19th December, 1935.

73 Taylor, op. cit., pp. 359–60.

74 Baldwin Papers, Vol. 123, f.250, Hoare to Baldwin, 22nd December, 1935.

75 Temp.Pap., VIII/5, Patrick to Lady Maud Hoare, [19th?] December, 1935; Austen Chamberlain Papers, 41/1/68, Memorandum on invitation to join Mr Baldwin's government, written by Chamberlain, 21st and 22nd December, 1935.

76 Brabourne Papers, Vol. 20, Butler to Brabourne, 19th December, 1935.

77 *Nine Troubled Years*, p. 178.

78 Ibid., p. 192.

79 Runciman Papers, R2/40/1–24, Vansittart to Runciman, 13th December, 1935; F.O.371, C 9652/1/1, Vansittart to Lindsay (British Ambassador in Washington), 21st December, 1935, quoted in Lowe and Marzari, op. cit., p. 289.

80 Runciman Papers, op. cit., Vansittart to Runciman, 13th December, 1935.

81 References in Warner, op. cit., p. 118; Robertson op. cit., pp. 439, 440.

82 When Vansittart came to write his memoirs his own view of his role in the Hoare-Laval talks became strangely diminished. He claimed that he was in Paris, on a 'busman's holiday' and participated in the talks, at Hoare's invitation, almost fortuitously; and that he did not know what Hoare's Cabinet instructions were, if any. Both assertions are impossible to square with

the evidence: as he told Wigram on 2nd December, Hoare had from the first determined that Vansittart would accompany him at the talks and, far from being ignorant of Cabinet decisions, Vansittart told Runciman on 13th December (in defence of the Hoare-Laval plan) that 'the Cabinet did actually decide that we had to get negotiations working before Thursday [12th December] otherwise they wouldn't postpone the oil sanction'. See Vansittart, *Lessons of My Life* (Hutchinson, 1943), pp. 53-4; Vansittart, *The Mist Procession* (Hutchinson, 1958), pp. 538-9.

83 *The Memoirs of Captain Liddell Hart* (Cassell, 1965), Vol. 1, p. 288.

84 Arnold J. Toynbee, *Acquaintances* (Oxford University Press, 1967), p. 288; Peterson, *Both Sides of the Curtain*, p. 301.

85 E. Wiskemann, *The Rome–Berlin Axis* (Oxford University Press, 1949 edn), p. 81.

86 See, for example, for a modern assessment, P. Raffo, *The League of Nations* (Historical Association, 1974).

Chapter 7 : Return to High Office

1 Beaverbrook Papers, Templewood file 1, Beaverbrook to Hoare, 15th January, 1936; A. J. P. Taylor, *Beaverbrook* (Hamish Hamilton, 1972), p. 361.

2 Temp.Pap., VIII/6, Hoare to Chamberlain, 8th February, 1936; Baldwin Papers, Vol. 170, ff. 301–2, Hoare to Baldwin, 8th February, 1936; *The Times*, 8th and 10th February, 1936.

3 Roskill, *Hankey*, Vol. III (Collins, 1974), pp. 201–13; Andrew Boyle, *Trenchard* (Collins, 1962), pp. 692–7; Prem 1/196; Cab. 21/424.

4 Prem 1/196, Ormsby-Gore to Baldwin, 11th February, 1936. On 1st March Chamberlain recorded in his diary that Baldwin knew his view that 'I still think Sam the best' choice for the new appointment. K. Feiling, *The Life of Neville Chamberlain* (Macmillan, 1946), p. 278.

5 Temp.Pap., VIII/6, Hoare to Chamberlain, 23rd February, 1936.

6 309 H.C.Deb., cols 1872–3.

7 Iain Macleod, *Neville Chamberlain* (Muller, 1961), p. 193; Brabourne Papers, Vol. 21, Butler to Brabourne, 11th March, 1936.

8 Baldwin to Chamberlain, 6th March, 1936, quoted in Macleod, op. cit., p. 193, footnote.

9 Temp.Pap., VIII/6, Baldwin to Hoare, 13th March, and 9th April, 1936; Baldwin Papers, Vol. 170, ff. 306–7, Hoare to

Baldwin, 13th March and 10th April, 1936 (the latter also in Temp.Pap., VIII/6.)

10 *Glasgow Herald* and *Manchester Guardian*, 6th June, 1936; *Observer*, 7th June, 1936. The *Manchester Guardian* was pursuing a conscious policy of strengthening Hoare's position *vis-à-vis* Chamberlain as the successor to Baldwin. W. P. Crozier, *Off the Record: Political Interviews, 1933–43* (Hutchinson, 1973), p. 59.

11 Cab. 23/84, 43 (36).

12 Cab. 27/606, quoted in Corelli Barnett, *Collapse of British Power* (Eyre Methuen, 1972), pp. 379–80.

13 Adm 167/94, Hoare memorandum to the Defence Policy and Requirements Committee, 22nd June, 1936; 314 H.C.Deb., col. 1039, 315 H.C.Deb., cols 194–5.

14 Lord Chatfield, *It Might Happen Again* (Heinemann, 1947), p. 98.

15 The developments can be traced in Prem 1/282 and the Weir Papers 19/14. See also Roskill, *Hankey*, Vol. III, pp. 291–3; Templewood, *Nine Troubled Years* (Collins, 1954), pp. 205–6; Chatfield, op. cit., pp. 102–10; Boyle, op. cit., pp. 697–703.

16 Chatfield, op. cit., p. 104.

17 Trenchard Papers, IV/54/103, Hoare to Trenchard, 26th July, 1937 (also in Boyle, op. cit., p. 703, where it is slightly misquoted).

18 *Nine Troubled Years*, p. 215. The Duke of Windsor wrote of Hoare that 'Although he had never been one of my intimates, our acquaintanceship went back to the First World War, and we had often been thrown in contact in the intervening years while Sam slowly but steadily progressed up the Conservative party ladder to posts of increasing importance.' *A King's Story* (Cassell, 1951), p. 339.

19 *A King's Story*, pp. 339–40. Lord Templewood confirmed that this passage represented the gist of their conversation by reproducing it in *Nine Troubled Years*, p. 220.

20 Beaverbrook Papers, Templewood file 1, Hoare to Beaverbrook, 10th December, 1936. Hoare's retrospective account of the crisis is in *Nine Troubled Years*, pp. 215–24, written on the basis of a series of rather cryptic and elliptical notes in Temp.Pap., IX/8.

21 *Nine Troubled Years*, p. 256; Avon, *Facing the Dictators* (Cassell, 1962), p. 383.

22 Cab. 27/622; Ian Colvin, *The Chamberlain Cabinet* (Gollancz, 1971), pp. 19–20; Barnett, op. cit., p. 444.

23 *Nine Troubled Years*, p. 255.

24 Avon, op. cit., pp. 435–6; Temp.Pap., IX/3, Notes on Admiralty and other matters, 1936–7.

25 Temp.Pap., IX/3, ibid.; *Nine Troubled Years*, pp. 208–9; *The Times*, 26th January (leader) and 27th January, 1937; 319 H.C.Deb., cols 36–8 and 785–906.

26 Temp.Pap., IX/3, ibid.

27 Lord Templewood, *Ambassador on Special Mission* (Collins, 1946), p. 10.

28 Temp.Pap., IX/2, Hoare's notes on various topics; Neville Chamberlain Papers, 2/23A, diary entry for 5th May, 1937.

29 See T. H. O'Brien, *Civil Defence* (Official History of the Second World War, H.M.S.O., 1955). The Hodsoll Papers (Hodsoll was the first head of the A.R.P. department and later Inspector-General of Civil Defence) contain much material on A.R.P.

30 Interview with Sir Arthur Hutchinson (who was principal private secretary to all three Home Secretaries), 21st September, 1971.

31 John Wheeler-Bennett, *John Anderson, Viscount Waverley* (Macmillan, 1962), pp. 199–205.

32 Charles Graves, *Women in Green* (Heinemann, 1948), pp. 1–9; interview with Sir Arthur Hutchinson, 21st September, 1971; H.O.186/105. The original idea was that W.V.S. would recruit women for A.R.P. services of local authorities but under Lady Reading's dynamic leadership it soon became an organisation quite separate from local authorities.

33 Temp.Pap., XVII/8, Lady Reading to Lord Templewood, 22nd April, 1947.

34 Macleod, op. cit., p. 260; Wheeler-Bennett, op. cit., pp. 212–14; Temp.Pap., X/4, Hoare to Chamberlain (undated, but almost certainly October 1938).

35 *Nine Troubled Years*, pp. 228–9; 324 H.C.Deb., cols 1315–21 (4th June, 1937).

36 Interview with Sir Arthur Hutchinson, 21st September, 1971; *Nine Troubled Years*, pp. 231–2.

37 Brabourne Papers, Vol. 22, Butler to Brabourne, 1st January [1938].

38 *Nine Troubled Years*, p. 232.

39 Ibid., p. 229. The original draft of the book, which Lord Templewood sent, among others, to Sir Edward Bridges, head of the Treasury, and Sir Norman Brook, Secretary of the Cabinet, had mentioned Fisher's opposition to Maxwell's appointment. Bridges expressed surprise at the revelation, as did Brook, who had himself been serving in the Home Office in 1938. Brook observed that 'Maxwell's great success as Permanent Secretary is so well known that this revelation will discredit Fisher, rather

than Maxwell. But I would be happier if it were not generally known that anyone had doubted his capacity to do the great service which he undoubtedly rendered as Head of the Home Office.' Lord Templewood deleted the reference. Temp.Pap., XIX/12, Bridges to Templewood, 6th January, 1954, Brook to Templewood, 15th January, 1954, Templewood to Brook, 18th January, 1954.

40 342 H.C.Deb., cols 267–377, 631–730.

41 The Lord Chancellor, introducing the second reading debate in the Lords, said that 'a large part of this Bill is due to the work and activities of the noble Viscount [Templewood]'. 155 H.L.Deb., col. 390 (27th April, 1948).

42 *Nine Troubled Years*, pp. 243–4.

43 For a comprehensive and authoritative recent account see A. J. Sherman, *Island Refuge: Britain and Refugees from the Third Reich 1933–1939* (Paul Elek, 1973).

44 *Nine Troubled Years*, p. 240.

45 Cab. 23/93, 14 (37), Cabinet meeting of 16th March, 1938, quoted in Sherman, op. cit., p. 88.

46 Sherman, op. cit., p. 267.

47 Ernest Jones, *The Life and Work of Sigmund Freud* (Pelican, 1964), pp. 638–9; Martin Gilbert, *Plough my own Furrow* (Longmans, 1965), pp. 397–8.

48 Temp.Pap., XVII/8, letter to Hoare, 6th December, 1951. A few years later another former German refugee was stimulated by reading a press review of *Nine Troubled Years* to write to Lord Templewood to tell him that 'his human, kind and clever treatment of Refugees from Nazi oppression' was not forgotten by those who had benefited from it. Ibid., XIX/13, E. Wallach to Templewood, 5th October, 1954.

49 See, for example, Brian Bond (ed.), *Chief of Staff. The Diaries of Lieutenant-General Sir Henry Pownall*, Vol. 1: 1933–1940 (Leo Cooper, 1972), pp. 166–7, 173–4.

50 Harold Macmillan, *Winds of Change* (Macmillan, 1966), p. 440.

51 L. S. Amery recorded in his (unpublished) diary for 21st February, 1938, after a breakfast conversation with Hoare, that Hoare 'was inclined to think that Eden's attitude had been influenced by personal vanity; generally speaking Sam thinks him vain, unstable and not really a heavyweight'. Hoare's own considered retrospective account of the circumstances of Eden's resignation is in *Nine Troubled Years*, pp. 255–80. When an agreement was signed with Italy in April Lord Tyrrell, the distinguished former Ambassador in Paris and permanent head of the Foreign Office,

wrote to Hoare to congratulate him on 'such a splendid vindication of the foresight, statesmanship and courage which you displayed in December 1935'. Temp.Pap., X/3, Tyrrell to Hoare, [26th] April, 1938.

52 L. S. Amery, unpublished diary, entry for 12th March, 1938.

53 See, for example, the Cabinet meeting of 12th September, 1938, Cab. 23/95 and Keith Middlemas, *Diplomacy of Illusion: The British Government and Germany 1937–39* (Weidenfeld & Nicolson, 1972), p. 246.

54 At a meeting of the Foreign Policy Committee on 18th March Hoare and Stanley (President of the Board of Trade) were alone in arguing that some support should be given to France, although they conceded that 'not a soul in this country could give any direct guarantee to Czechoslovakia itself'. Cab. 27/623.

55 *Nine Troubled Years*, pp. 288–9, 329. The development of the crisis is traced in pp. 285–326; various brief notes in Temp.Pap., X/5 and XIX/6, do not add materially to this account.

56 339 H.C.Deb., cols 153, 157–8, 161; *Nine Troubled Years*, p. 322.

57 Temp.Pap., X/3, Hoare to Chamberlain, 5th October, 1938 (also in *Nine Troubled Years*, p. 386); Beaverbrook Papers, Templewood file 11, Hoare to Beaverbrook, 10th October, 1938.

58 Temp.Pap., XIX/6, notes headed 'Munich-Prague'.

59 Temp.Pap., X/4, Hoare to Chamberlain, [October] 1938; 341 H.C.Deb., cols 1087–1214.

60 Temp.Pap., XIX/6, 'Munich-Prague'.

61 Ibid.

62 *Nine Troubled Years*, p. 328, which omits the name of Mussolini, included in the original speech.

63 Ibid., p. 329.

64 Ibid.

65 Beaverbrook to Dr Cox, 1st June, 1938, quoted in Taylor, *Beaverbrook*, p. 382; Peter Howard in *Sunday Express*, 1st January, 1939, and *Daily Express*, 13th August, 1939.

66 He had sold the family mansion at Sidestrand in 1936 and at the end of 1937 moved into the newly completed Palladian-style residence at Templewood, whose construction and landscape-gardening had been a major leisure interest for him over the previous 15 years or so.

67 In *Nine Troubled Years*, p. 200, the Midland Bank invitation is dated, seemingly in error, as early in 1936, soon after his resignation. The approach was made by the chairman of Midland Bank, Reginald McKenna, who in fact remained chairman until 1943.

68 Beaverbrook Papers, Templewood file 11, Lady Maud Hoare to Beaverbrook, 4th November, 1938. Part of the letter is quoted in Taylor, p. 386, where it is mis-dated 4th December.

69 Temp.Pap., X/3, Beaverbrook to Hoare, 22nd November, 1938, X/4, Beaverbrook to Hoare, 1st September, 1939, X/5, Beaverbrook to Hoare, 17th November, 1939; with copies in the Beaverbrook Papers, Templewood file 11. See also Taylor, op. cit., p. 386. Taylor gives no source for the actual amount of the payments, which is nowhere referred to in the correspondence.

70 Prem 1/388; *Nine Troubled Years*, pp. 420–21.

71 Temp.Pap., XI/1, Beaverbrook to Hoare, 30th October, 1939 (also in Beaverbrook Papers). Quoted in Taylor, op. cit., p. 399.

72 Temp.Pap., VIII/6, Hoare to Chamberlain, 17th March [1938].

73 An excellent study of this phase of British foreign policy, using new evidence (and incidentally giving full credit to Hoare's role), is Robert Manne, 'The British Decision for Alliance with Russia, May 1939' in *Journal of Contemporary History*, Vol. 9, No. 3 (July 1974), pp. 3–26. See also Sidney Aster, *1939: The Making of the Second World War* (Deutsch, 1973), pp. 157ff.

74 Cab. 23/98, Conference of Ministers, 8th April, 1939, quoted in Aster, op cit., p. 134. It was decided to give a guarantee to Greece, but not, at that time, to Turkey.

75 Cab. 27/624, Foreign Policy Committee meeting, 19th May, 1939, quoted in Aster, op. cit., p. 179.

76 Cab. 27/624, FP 36 (39).

77 Cab. 27/624, FP 43 (39). The resultant report from the Chiefs of Staff, considered by the Foreign Policy Committee on 25th April, was in fact somewhat equivocal about the usefulness of Soviet forces outside their own country and was interpreted by Chamberlain as giving support to his position. But the report did point out 'the very grave military dangers inherent in the possibility of any agreement between Germany and Russia'. Cab. 27/624, FP 44 (39). And by 16th May the Chiefs of Staff had come out quite unequivocally for a Russian alliance. Cab. 53/11.

78 Cab. 27/624, FP 48 (39). See also Cab. 27/624, FP 45 (39) and 47 (39) and Cab. 23/99, 27 (39).

79 David Dilks (ed.), *The Diaries of Sir Alexander Cadogan 1938–1945* (Cassell, 1971), p.182; F.O. 371/23066, C7469/3356/18.

80 Cab. 23/99, 30 (39).

81 Cab. 27/625, FP 58 (39); Cab. 23/100, 39 (39), Cabinet meeting of 26th July, 1939.

82 *Nine Troubled Years*, p.352.

83 Ibid., pp. 392–3; Temp.Pap., X/5, 'Notes on events 21st August – 3rd September, 1939'.
84 Cab. 23/100, 48 (39).
85 351 H.C.Deb., cols 280–5; Aster, op. cit., pp. 380–86.
86 Temp.Pap., X/5, 'Notes on events etc.'; *Nine Troubled Years*, p. 394.

Chapter 8: From War Cabinet to Madrid Embassy

1 Roskill, *Hankey*, Vol. III (Collins, 1974), pp. 413–14. Hankey had retired at the end of July 1938 after 22 years as Cabinet Secretary and was created a Baron in February 1939.
2 Templewood, *Nine Troubled Years* (Collins, 1954), p. 395.
3 Churchill, *The Gathering Storm* (Reprint Society edn, 1950), p. 330.
4 *Nine Troubled Years*, p. 396.
5 The committee's minutes are in Cab. 92/111.
6 *Nine Troubled Years*, pp. 398–9; Temp. Pap., XI/2, notes for Land Forces Committee; Churchill, op. cit., p. 365.
7 Temp.Pap., XI/2 and 3, holograph and typescript notes by Hoare on the period September 1939 to May 1940.
8 *Nine Troubled Years*, pp. 422–3.
9 Ibid., p. 423; 351 H.C.Deb., cols 683–92.
10 Temp.Pap., XI/2 and 3, Sept. 1939 – May 1940 notes.
11 352 H.C.Deb., cols 389–90 (11th October, 1939).
12 *Nine Troubled Years*, p. 397; H. Morrison, *Government and Parliament* (Oxford University Press, 1954), pp. 54–5; R.J. Hammond, *Food*, Vol.I (History of the Second World War, H.M.S.O., 1951), pp. 58–9. The committee's minutes are in Cab. 74.
13 *Nine Troubled Years*, p. 397; C. B. A. Behrens, *Merchant Shipping and the Demands of War* (History of the Second World War, H.M.S.O., 1955), pp. 54, 65–8, 86.
14 Temp.Pap., XI/2 and 3, Sept 1939 – May 1940 notes.
15 Ibid., XI/1, Hoare to Chamberlain, 21st February, 1940.
16 Ibid., XXIII/1, 'My Third Mission' (typescript of the Spanish section of unpublished book, *Three Missions*).
17 *Nine Troubled Years*, pp. 405–6; Temp.Pap., XI/5, Hoare to Lothian, 7th October, 1939.
18 A reading of Lloyd George's speech (351 H.C.Deb., cols 1870–4) does not fully support Hoare's charge. It is true that he said, in relation to a point about continuing to treat Italy and the Soviet Union as neutrals, 'We do not want to multiply our enemies. We have got quite as much as we can do to conquer

one without adding one or two more.' (col. 1872); but that could
be interpreted as realist rather than defeatist. The main burden
of Lloyd George's speech was to emphasise the need to examine
carefully any proposals for an honourable peace that might be
forthcoming. For saying this, and laying himself open to misrepresentation abroad, he was severely taken to task by, among
others, Duff Cooper (col. 1879), David Grenfell (col. 1880),
Henry Page Croft (col. 1883) and Vyvyan Adams (cols 1890–1)
– and by much of the press.

19 *Nine Troubled Years*, p. 413; Temp.Pap., XI/5, Hoare to
Lothian, 21st November, 1939.

20 Henry Pelling, *Britain and the Second World War* (Fontana, 1970),
pp. 62–3. Something like Churchill's plan was later adopted by
the Supreme War Council on 5th February, 1940. The allied
forces were now, however, to be 'volunteers', on the pattern of
German and Italian interventions in the Spanish Civil War. Sir
Llewellyn Woodward, *British Foreign Policy in the Second World War*,
Vol. I (H.M.S.O., 1970), pp. 79–80; J. R. M. Butler, *Grand
Strategy*, Vol. II (History of the Second World War, H.M.S.O.,
1957), p. 107.

21 Temp.Pap., XI/1, Hoare to Chamberlain, 26th December,
1939.

22 David Dilks (ed.), *The Diaries of Sir Alexander Cadogan 1938–1945*
(Cassell, 1971), pp. 245–7; Temp.Pap., XI/2 and 3, Sept. 1939–
May 1940 notes; Woodward, pp. 68–9.

23 *Nine Troubled Years*, pp. 404, 406; Temp.Pap., XI/5, Hoare to
Lothian, 25th September and 7th October, 1939.

24 F.O. 800/325, f.384, memorandum by Charles Peake (for Sir
Alexander Cadogan), 2nd December, 1939, on a conversation
with Herbert Morrison at dinner 'tête à tête ... the other night'.

25 Temp.Pap., XI/2 and 3, Sept. 1939 – May 1940 notes.

26 Ibid.; Avon, *The Reckoning* (Cassell, 1965), p. 84.

27 Temp.Pap., XI/2 and 3, Sept. 1939 – May 1940 notes; *Nine
Troubled Years*, p. 427; W. P. Crozier, *Off the Record: Political
Interviews, 1933–43*, (Hutchinson, 1973), pp. 158–61 (Crozier
interview with Hoare, 28th March, 1940).

28 The Hoares had given up 18 Cadogan Gardens when they
moved into Admiralty House on Hoare's appointment as First
Lord in the summer of 1936.

29 Temp.Pap., XI/2 and 3, Sept. 1939 – May 1940 notes. Hoare
gives the date for the dinner as 3rd April, but this is clearly in
error, as the minelaying did not take place until 8th April. In
fact all the dates mentioned in this section of Hoare's notes are

incorrect – one of several indications that they were not, as some have assumed, e.g., Pelling, *Britain and the Second World War*; Middlemas, *Diplomacy of Illusion: The British Government and Germany 1937–39* (Weidenfeld & Nicolson, 1972), a contemporary diary.

30 See T. K. Derry, *The Campaign in Norway* (History of the Second World War, H.M.S.O., 1952).

31 Temp.Pap., XI/2 and 3, Sept. 1939 – May 1940 notes. Chamberlain told his sister that Churchill 'changed his mind four times' over Trondheim. Neville Chamberlain Papers, 18/1/1153, Chamberlain to Hilda Chamberlain, 4th May, 1940.

32 Neville Chamberlain Papers, ibid. Hoare's version of his response to Chamberlain's appeal was: 'I said I would give it a try for a month. The P.M. could not face a crisis during the Norwegian trouble.' Temp.Pap., XI/2 and 3, Sept. 1939 – May 1940 notes. In the diary of Hoare's principal private secretary at the Air Ministry the episode was referred to (under 29th April) as 'Winston crisis'. Interview with Sir Folliott Sandford, 6th April, 1973. On the detailed arrangements for the change see Prem 1/404; also Derry, op. cit., p. 165.

33 Temp.Pap., XXIII/1, ch. 1 of 'My Third Mission'.

34 Hugh Dalton, *The Fateful Years* (Muller, 1957), pp. 300–301.

35 *Nine Troubled Years*, pp. 427–8.

36 Temp. Pap., XI/2 and 3, Sept. – May 1940 notes; interview with Sir Folliott Sandford, 6th April, 1973.

37 L. S. Amery, unpublished diary for 29th April, 1940; *Nine Troubled Years*, p. 430, where Amery's words are given as 'The Government must go'.

38 360 H.C.Deb., col. 1264.

39 Amery diary for 8th May, 1940; 360 H.C.Deb., cols 1266–77.

40 Temp.Pap., XI/2–3, Sept. 1939 – May 1940 notes.

41 *Nine Troubled Years*, p. 431.

42 Temp.Pap., XII/2, Winterton to Hoare, 9th May, 1940; Harold Nicolson, *Diaries and Letters 1939–1945* (Collins, 1967), p. 79; Amery diary for 8th May, 1940.

43 Butler, *The Art of the Possible* (Hamish Hamilton, 1971), p. 83; Dalton, op. cit., pp. 306–7.

44 A. J. P. Taylor, *Beaverbrook* (Hamish Hamilton, 1972), p. 409.

45 Temp.Pap., XI/2–3, Sept. 1939 – May 1940 notes; Cab. 65/7, 116 (40).

46 Temp.Pap., XI/2–3, Sept. 1939 – May 1940 notes; XII/4, Hoare to W. Astor, 15th May, 1940.

47 Ibid., XII/4, Hoare to Chamberlain, 14th May, 1940.

48 Taylor, op. cit., p. 411. Hoare dropped Hankey's letter on a visit to Beaverbrook and for some reason it was never returned to him. Also reproduced (without, however, the name of the sender) in David Farrar, *G – For God Almighty: A Personal Memoir of Lord Beaverbrook* (Weidenfeld & Nicolson, 1969), p. 37.

49 Temp.Pap., XII/4, Hore-Belisha to Hoare, 13th May, 1940.

50 Ibid., Moore-Brabazon to Hoare, 13th May, 1940. In his published memoirs Lord Brabazon wrote that 'Of all the people I have known I would as cheerfully serve Sam as anybody'. *The Brabazon Story* (Heinemann, 1956), pp. 181–2. And to Lord Templewood himself he wrote, soon after the book's publication, 'You were the kindest, most considerate boss I ever had in my life and never shall I forget it'. Temp.Pap., XVIII/9, Brabazon to Templewood, 10th October, 1956.

51 Temp.Pap., XII/4, Nicholson to Hoare, 17th May, 1940.

52 Ibid., Webb to Hoare, 15th May, 1940.

53 Ibid., Bracken to Hoare, 15th May, 1940.

54 Ibid., XI/2–3, Sept. 1939 – May 1940 notes.

55 F.O. 371/24519. Peterson had no inkling that he was going to be replaced until 12th May and was understandably annoyed. That his successor was to be the Foreign Secretary under whom he had worked during the Abyssinian crisis provided no consolation for hurt pride. Sir Maurice Peterson, *Both Sides of the Curtain* (Constable, 1950), pp. 228–32.

56 Cab. 65/7, f. 73 (War Cabinet meeting of 13th May), f. 89 (15th May), f. 124 (20th May), f. 147 (23rd May); F.O. 371/24527, ff. 174, 180; Templewood, *Ambassador on Special Mission* (Collins, 1946), p. 18.

57 *Cadogan Diaries*, p. 282. Cadogan's account (pp. 286–8), *inter alia*, described Hoare's agreement to take the Spanish appointment as 'The rats leaving the ship' and – astoundingly – nominated Hoare as the future 'Quisling of England'. There seems to be no rational explanation of Cadogan's attack, which has completely mystified those who knew both men. Despite his diary vitriol Cadogan recognised the value of Hoare's Spanish mission, expressing in a letter to him some three months after it had begun 'all our admiration and gratitude for the good work you have been doing in Spain'. Temp.Pap., XIII/17, Cadogan to Hoare, 13th September, 1940. After the war Templewood corresponded extensively with Cadogan when writing *Nine Troubled Years* and received a great deal of help from him (including extracts from his diaries!); on at least one

occasion Cadogan was his guest at the Wimbledon tennis championships which Templewood always attended as President of the Lawn Tennis Association.

58 *Ambassador on Special Mission*, pp. 15, 31; Temp.Pap., XI/2 and 3, Sept. 1939 – May 1940 notes.

59 *Ambassador on Special Mission*, pp. 15–16.

60 Temp.Pap., XIII/2, Hoare to Chatfield, 13th September, 1940; XIII/17, Hoare to Bracken, 6th June, 1940, Hoare to Beaverbrook, 29th August, 1940; XIII/20, Halifax to Hoare, 30th July, and 15th August, 1940, Hoare to Halifax, 8th, 10th and 30th August, 1940.

61 Beaverbrook Papers, Templewood file 11, Hoare to Beaverbrook, 29th May, 1940.

62 Temp.Pap., XIII/16, Churchill to Hoare, 23rd October, 1940; XIII/17, Beaverbrook to Hoare, 5th September, 1940; XIII/20, Halifax to Hoare, 30th July, 1940; F.O. 800/323, ff.152–3, Halifax to Churchill, 17th August, 1940.

63 Amery to Linlithgow (telegram), 10th June, 1943, quoted in N. Mansergh and E. W. R. Lumby (eds), *Constitutional Relations between Britain and India: The Transfer of Power 1942–7*, Vol. III (H.M.S.O., 1971), pp. 1051–2. See also ibid., pp. 330, 895–7, 949 and 1047 (Amery to Churchill, 8th June, 1943: 'I still feel, in spite of your misgivings, that Sam Hoare has not only the knowledge but also courage and, in his own way, personality'.)

64 Temp.Pap., XIII/19, Amery to Hoare, 10th June, 1943.

65 Ibid., XVII/8, Amery to Templewood, 24th February, 1954.

66 Sir Patrick Donner who, as the young secretary of the India Defence League, worked closely with Churchill in his campaign against the Government of India Bill, was never forgiven by him for voting in favour of the Munich agreement. Churchill did not speak to him for several years and even when he deigned to recognise him he always called him 'Donner', not the 'Patrick' he had always been in the India Bill days. Interview with Sir Patrick Donner, 21st March, 1973.

67 Michael Howard, *Grand Strategy*, Vol. IV (H.M.S.O., 1972), pp. 159–67; Temp.Pap., XIII/21, Eden to Hoare, 27th November, 1942; XXIII/1, ch. 8 of 'My Third Mission'; *Ambassador on Special Mission*, pp. 172–83.

68 Temp.Pap., XIII/16, Churchill to Hoare, 23rd October, 1940.

69 In Temp.Pap., XIII; there is additional correspondence with Halifax in F.O. 800/323.

70 See, for example, his secret memorandum of 7th July, 1942, on

the monarchist movement in Spain, in Temp.Pap., XIII/22; *Ambassador on Special Mission*, p. 298.

71 For the economic blockade in relation to Spain and a full recognition of Hoare's important part in it, see W. N. Medlicott, *The Economic Blockade*, Vol. I (History of the Second World War, H.M.S.O., 1952), pp. 529–48, Vol. II (H.M.S.O., 1959), pp. 282–313, 419–45, 547–81. See also Sir John Lomax, *The Diplomatic Smuggler* (Arthur Barker, 1965), pp. 68–121.

72 F.O. 800/323, Hoare's dispatch, enclosed with Hoare to Halifax, 26th July, 1940. There was a good deal of criticism in the left-wing press of any 'appeasement' of Spain which would not in any case, so it was maintained, prevent Spain from joining its fellow fascist regimes in war against Britain, e.g., *Tribune*, 5th July, 1940, *Daily Mirror*, 17th June and 13th August, 1940. For illustrations of Hoare's difficulties with Dalton and the Ministry of Economic Warfare see F.O. 800/323.

73 Temp.Pap., XIII/20, Hoare to Halifax, 1st October, 1940.

74 Ibid., Hoare to Halifax, 18th December, 1940. At Madrid Hoare was also the main diplomatic point of contact with Vichy France, mainly through the Vichy French ambassador in Madrid and the Canadian chargé d'affaires at Vichy. See Woodward, *British Foreign Policy*, Vol. 1, pp. 409–32; Temp. Pap., XXIII/1, ch. 4 of 'My Third Mission'.

75 Temp.Pap., XII/2, Hillgarth minute to Hoare, 2nd June, 1940.

76 Ibid., XXIII/1, ch. 1 of 'My Third Mission'.

77 *Ambassador on Special Mission*, p. 131. Lord Eccles who, as economic adviser to both the Madrid and Lisbon embassies, attended many of these meetings, has recorded that, under Hoare's 'superbly competent' chairmanship, they taught him 'many useful lessons about the definition of each man's job in the team, and how to ensure that everyone knew what the others were doing, so far as it would help them in their own work'. Letter to the author, 21st September, 1972.

78 *Ambassador on Special Mission*, pp. 131–2, 266–7.

79 Carlton J. H. Hayes, *Wartime Mission in Spain 1942–1945* (Macmillan, New York, 1945), p. 35. Hayes was American ambassador in Madrid.

80 Temp.Pap., XXIII/1, ch. 6 of 'My Third Mission'.

81 Ibid.; *Ambassador on Special Mission*, pp. 52–3.

82 *Ambassador on Special Mission*, pp. 115–16.

83 Lomax, *The Diplomatic Smuggler*, pp. 84–5 (quoted by permission of the author).

84 Ibid., pp. 85–6.
85 Ibid., pp. 87–8.
86 Ibid., p. 86.
87 Crozier Papers, interview with Hoare on 24th October, 1941 (when Hoare was on home leave); *Ambassador on Special Mission*, pp. 164–71.
88 Lomax, *The Diplomatic Smuggler*, p. 120.
89 Hayes, op. cit., pp. 35, 298, 303–9; Temp.Pap., XIII/27, R. J. Bowker to Templewood, 16th January, 1945, Templewood to Eden, 14th April, 1945; XIII/28, Templewood to Ernest Bevin, 1st January, 1946; George Hills, *Franco* (Robert Hale, 1967), p. 358; Medlicott, op. cit., Vol. II, p. 548, footnote.
90 *Ambassador on Special Mission*, pp. 23, 25, 45–8, 116, 173–4, 221–2, 249–56, 284.
91 Many of these are in F.O. 800/326, ff.180–215, from which, however, some items have been removed 'until 2016'.
92 Temp.Pap., XIII/16, Hoare to Churchill, 27th June, 1940.
93 F.O. 800/326, f. 202, Hoare telegram to Foreign Office, 1st July, 1940.
94 Temp.Pap., XXIII/1, ch. 2 of 'My Third Mission'.
95 The German-Spanish plot was revealed publicly for the first time in 1957, when volume X of *Documents on German Foreign Policy 1918–1945* was published (H.M.S.O., 1957). See *Daily Express*, 1st and 2nd August, 1957; *The Times*, 1st August, 1957.
96 *Ambassador on Special Mission*, pp. 212–16; Temp.Pap., XXIII/1, ch. 9 of 'My Third Mission'; Howard, *Grand Strategy*, pp. 522–34.
97 *Ambassador on Special Mission*, pp. 257–64; Temp.Pap., XXIII/1, ch. 11 of 'My Third Mission'; Medlicott, op. cit., Vol. II, pp. 557–76.
98 Temp.Pap., XIII/16, Hoare to Churchill, 17th April, 1944.
99 Beaverbrook Papers, Templewood file 11, Hoare to Beaverbrook, 10th May, 1944.
100 Temp.Pap., XIII/16, telegrams to Hoare, 27th June and 1st July, 1944.
101 Temp.Pap., XIII/8, Amery to Hoare, 3rd July, 1944.
102 Temp.Pap., XIII/7, Templewood's memorandum on 'The Allied Attitude towards the Franco Government', dated 16th October, 1944.
103 It is reproduced in *Ambassador on Special Mission*, pp. 300–304.
104 Temp.Pap., XIII/7, Templewood's draft of communication to be made to General Franco, 13th November, 1944.

105 Churchill's letter to Franco is reproduced in *Ambassador on Special Mission*, pp. 304–6.
106 134 H.L.Deb., cols 374–417 (19th December, 1944) and 430–60 (20th December, 1944) Templewood spoke at cols 374–85 and 458–60.
107 Temp.Pap., XIII/16, Churchill to Templewood, 23rd December, 1944.

Epilogue: The Last Years

1 Temp.Pap., XVII/16. On Templewood's return, Sir Edward Bridges, the head of the Treasury, wrote to congratulate him 'on the great success of your tour'. Ibid., Bridges to Templewood, 13th June, 1946.
2 *Advertiser's Weekly*, 15th January, 1953, where the overall increase of 441,026 in the number of copies sold by the *Sunday Dispatch* in 1946 was attributed to the Templewood serialisation. Templewood's notes and and correspondence on *Ambassador on Special Mission* (Collins, 1946), are in Temp.Pap., XVIII/6.
3 Temp.Pap., XVIII/7.
4 Ibid., XIX/1–14.
5 Ibid., XVIII/9.
6 Ibid., XX/9–XXII/2, XXIII/1–4.
7 Copies are in Temp.Pap., Pam. 1–3.
8 144 H.L.Deb., cols 415–25, 449–52 (26th November, 1946).
9 Ibid., col. 423.
10 James B. Christoph, *Capital Punishment and British Politics* (Allen & Unwin, 1962), p. 38.
11 155 H.L.Deb., col. 475 (26th April, 1948). See also 198 H.L.Deb., col. 570 (9th July, 1956); Templewood's memorandum to the *Royal Commission on Capital Punishment: Minutes of Evidence 28–29* (H.M.S.O., 1951); Temp.Pap., XVI/1–9.
12 156 H.L.Deb., cols 32–8, 175–8 (1st and 2nd June, 1948).
13 157 H.L.Deb., col. 1044 (20th July, 1948).
14 185 H.L.Deb., cols 137–88 (16th December, 1953); 198 H.L.Deb., cols 563–842 (9th and 10th July, 1956).
15 201 H.L.Deb., cols 1165–1242 (21st February, 1957).
16 Temp.Pap., XVII/8, Attlee to Templewood, 20th March, 1950, Churchill to Templewood, 25th October, 1954.
17 Ibid., XVII/7.
18 *Listener*, 29th January, 1959; Temp.Pap., XVII/5, Templewood to Julian Symons, 11th March, 1959.
19 215 H.L.Deb., cols 415–20.

20 Percival Spear, *The Oxford History of Modern India 1740–1947* (Oxford University Press, 1965), p. 365.

21 *The Times*, 9th May, 1959.

22 *Ambassador on Special Mission*, p. 11.

23 Ibid., p. 10.

Index